BY MATT TAIBBI

The Divide: American Injustice in the Age of the Wealth Gap

Griftopia: A Story of Bankers, Politicians, and the Most Audacious Power Grab in American History

The Great Derangement: A Terrifying True Story of War, Politics, and Religion

Smells Like Dead Elephants: Dispatches from a Rotting Empire

Spanking the Donkey: Dispatches from the Dumb Season

WITH MARK AMES

The Exile: Sex, Drugs, and Libel in the New Russia

THE

DIVIDE

THE

DIVIDE

AMERICAN INJUSTICE IN
THE AGE OF THE WEALTH GAP

MATT TAIBBI

ILLUSTRATIONS BY MOLLY CRABAPPLE

SPIEGEL & GRAU

NEW YORK

W

This is a work of nonfiction. Some names and identifying details have been changed.

Published in the United States by Spiegel & Grau, an imprint of
Random House, a division of Random House LLC,
a Penguin Random House Company, New York.

SPIEGEL & GRAU and the HOUSE colophon are registered
trademarks of Random House LLC.

Library of Congress Cataloging-in-Publication Data
Taibbi, Matt.
The divide : American injustice in the age of the wealth gap / Matt Taibbi.
pages cm
ISBN 978-0-8129-9342-4
eBook ISBN 978-0-679-64546-7
1. Social justice—United States. 2. Income distribution—United States. 3. Rich
people—United States. 4. Poor—United States. I. Title.
HM671.T35 2014
303.3'72—dc23
2013024907

Printed in the United States of America on acid-free paper

www.spiegelandgrau.com

4   6   8   9   7   5

Book design by Christopher M. Zucker

For Max

Fairness is what justice really is.

—Potter Stewart

CONTENTS

INTRODUCTION

Over the course of the last twenty years or so, America has been falling deeper and deeper into a bizarre statistical mystery.

Take in the following three pieces of information, and see if you can make them fit together.

First, violent crime has been dropping precipitously for nearly two decades. At its peak in 1991, according to FBI data, there were 758 violent crimes per 100,000 people. By 2010 that number had plunged to 425 crimes per 100,000, a drop of more than 44 percent.

The decrease covered all varieties of serious crime, from murder to assault to rape to armed robbery. The graphs depicting the decline show a long, steady downswing, one that doesn't jump from year to year but consistently slumps from year to year.

Second: although poverty rates largely declined during the 1990s, offering at least one possible explanation for the drop in violent crime, poverty rates rose sharply during the 2000s. At the start of that decade, poverty levels hovered just above 10 percent. By 2008 they were up to 13.2 percent. By 2009 the number was 14.3 percent. By 2010, 15.3 percent.

All this squares with what most people who lived in Middle America knew, and know, instinctively. Despite what we're being told about a post-2008 recovery, despite what the rising stock market seems to indicate, the economy is mostly worse, real incomes are mostly declining, and money is mostly scarcer.

But throughout all this time, violent crime has gone down. It continues to decline today. Counterintuitively, more poverty has not created more crime.

The third piece of information that makes no sense is that during this same period of time, the prison population in America has exploded. In 1991 there were about one million Americans behind bars. By 2012 the number was over 2.2 million, a more than 100 percent increase.

Our prison population, in fact, is now the biggest in the history of human civilization. There are more people in the United States either on parole or in jail today (around 6 million total) than there ever were at any time in Stalin's gulags. For what it's worth, there are also more black men in jail right now than there were in slavery at its peak.

See if this syllogism works, then.

> Poverty goes up;
> Crime goes down;
> Prison population doubles.

It doesn't fit, unless some sort of alternative explanation comes into play. Maybe all those new nonviolent prisoners fit into some new national policy imperative. Maybe they all broke some new set of unwritten societal rules. But what?

While on a visit to San Diego to do research for this book, I heard a crazy story.

The subject was the city's P100 program, under which anyone who applied for welfare could have his or her home searched preemptively by the state. Ostensibly, authorities were looking for evidence that the applicant had a secret job or a boyfriend who could pay bills, or was just generally lying about something in order to cheat the taxpayer out of that miserable few hundred bucks a month.

One Vietnamese woman, a refugee and a rape victim who had only recently come to America, applied for welfare in San Diego. An inspector came to her door, barged in, and began rifling through her belongings. At one point, he reached into her underwear drawer and began sifting around. Sneering, he used the tip of the pencil eraser to pull out a pair of sexy panties and looked at her accusingly. If she didn't have a boyfriend, what did she need these for?

That image, of a welfare inspector sneeringly holding up panties with a pencil end, expresses all sorts of things at once. The main thing is contempt. The implication is that someone broke enough to ask the taxpayer for a handout shouldn't have *sex,* much less sexy panties.

The other thing here is an idea that being that poor means you should naturally give up any ideas you might have about privacy or dignity. The welfare applicant is less of a person for being financially dependent (and a generally unwelcome immigrant from a poor country to boot), so she naturally has fewer rights.

No matter how offensive the image is, it has a weird logic that's irresistible to many if not most Americans. Even if we don't agree with it, we all get it.

And that's the interesting part, the part where we all get it. More and more often, we all make silent calculations about who is entitled to what rights, and who is not. It's not as simple as saying everyone is the same under the law anymore. We all know there's another layer to it now.

As a very young man, I studied the Russian language in Leningrad, in the waning days of the Soviet empire. One of the first things I noticed about that dysfunctional wreck of a lunatic country was that it had two sets of laws, one written and one unwritten. The written laws were meaningless, unless you violated one of the unwritten laws, at which point they became all-important.

So, for instance, possessing dollars or any kind of hard currency was technically forbidden, yet I never met a Soviet citizen who didn't have them. The state just happened to be very selective about enforcing its anticommerce laws. So the teenage *farsovshik* (black market trader) who sold rabbit hats in exchange for blue jeans outside my dorm could be arrested for having three dollars in his pocket, but a city official could openly walk down Nevsky Avenue with a brand-new Savile Row suit on his back, and nothing would happen.

Everyone understood this hypocrisy implicitly, almost at a cellular level, far beneath thought. For a Russian in Soviet times, navigating every moment of citizenship involved countless silent calculations of this type. But the instant people were permitted to think about all this and question the unwritten rules out loud, it was like the whole country woke up from a dream, and the system fell apart in a matter of months. That happened before my eyes in 1990 and 1991, and I never forgot it.

Now I feel like I'm living that process in reverse, watching my own country fall *into* a delusion in the same way the Soviets once woke up from one. People are beginning to become disturbingly comfortable with a kind of official hypocrisy. Bizarrely, for instance, we've become numb to the idea that rights aren't absolute but are enjoyed on a kind of sliding scale.

To be extreme about it, on the far end—like, say, in the villages of Pakistan or Afghanistan—we now view some people as having no rights at all. They can be assassinated or detained indefinitely outside any sort of legal framework, from the Geneva conventions on down.

Even here at home, that concept is growing. After the Boston marathon bombings, there was briefly a controversy where we wondered aloud whether the Chechen suspects would be read Miranda rights upon capture. No matter how angry you were about those bombings—and as a Boston native, I wanted whoever was responsible thrown in the deepest hole we have—it was a fascinating moment in our history. It was the first time when we actually weren't sure if an American criminal suspect would get full access to due process of law. Even on television, the blow-dried talking heads didn't know the answer. We had to think about it.

Of course, on the other end of the spectrum are the titans of business, the top executives at companies like Goldman and Chase and GlaxoSmithKline, men and women who essentially as a matter of policy now will never see the inside of a courtroom, almost no matter what crimes they may have committed in the course of their business. This is obviously an outrage, and the few Americans who paid close attention to news stories like the deferred prosecution of HSBC for laundering drug money, or the nonprosecution of the Swiss bank UBS for fixing interest rates, were beside themselves with anger over the unfairness of it all.

But the truly dark thing about those stories is that somewhere far beneath the intellect, on a gut level, those who were paying attention understood why those stories panned out the way they did. Just as we very quickly learned to accept the idea that America now tortures and assassinates certain foreigners (and perhaps the odd American or three) as a matter of routine, and have stopped marching on Washington to protest the fact that these things are done in our names, we've also learned to accept the implicit idea that some people have simply more rights than others. Some people go to jail, and others just don't. And we all get it.

I was originally attracted to this subject because, having spent years covering white-collar corruption for *Rolling Stone*, I was interested in the phenomenon of high-powered white-collar criminals completely avoiding individual punishment for what appeared to be very serious crimes. It's become a cliché by now, but since 2008, no high-ranking executive from any financial institution has gone to jail, not one, for any of the systemic crimes that wiped out 40 percent of the world's wealth. Even now, after JPMorgan Chase agreed to a settlement north of $13 billion for a variety of offenses and the financial press threw itself up in arms over the government's supposedly aggressive new approach to regulating Wall Street, the basic principle held true: Nobody went to jail. Not one person.

Why was that? I quickly realized that it was impossible to answer that question without simultaneously looking at the question of who *does* go to jail in this country, and why. This was especially true when the numbers were so stark, zero-to-a-few on one hand, millions on the other.

Finding the answer to some of this turns out to be easy, just simple math. Big companies have big lawyers, most street criminals do not, and prosecutors dread waging long wars against bottomless-pocketed megabanks when they can score win after easy win against common drug dealers, car thieves, and the like. After winning enough of these blowout victories, the justice bureaucracy starts drifting inexorably toward the no-sweat ten-second convictions and away from the expensive years-long battles of courtroom attrition.

Unquestionably, however, something else is at work, something that cuts deeper into the American psyche. We have a profound hatred of the weak and the poor, and a corresponding groveling terror before the rich and successful, and we're building a bureaucracy to match those feelings.

Buried in our hatred of the dependent, in Mitt Romney's lambasting of the 47 percent, in the water carrier's contempt for the water drinker, is a huge national psychological imperative. Many of our national controversies are on some level debates about just exactly how much we should put up with from the "nonproducing" citizenry. Even the George Zimmerman trial devolved into a kind of national discussion over whether Trayvon Martin was the kind of person who had the right to walk down the street unmolested, or whether he was a member of a nuisance class, a few pegs down on that sliding scale of rights, who should have submitted to . . . well, whatever it was that happened.

The weird thing is that the common justification for the discrepancy in prison statistics—the glaring percentage of incarcerated people who are either poor, nonwhite, or both—is that the ghetto denizens are the people who commit the crimes, that their neighborhoods are where the crime is at.

And the common justification for the failure to prosecute executives in corrupt corporations for any crimes that they might commit is that their offenses aren't really *crimes* per se but mere ethical violations, morally unfortunate acts not punishable by law. President Obama himself would hint at this in an infamous *60 Minutes* interview.

But in practice, as I would find out in a years-long journey through the American justice system, things turn out to be completely different.

Yes, there's a lot of violent crime in poor neighborhoods. And yes, that's where most of your gun violence happens.

But for most of the poor people who are being sent away, whether it's for a day or for ten years, their prison lives begin when they're jailed for the most minor offenses imaginable. Can you imagine spending a night in jail for possessing a pink Hi-Liter marker? For rolling a tobacco cigarette? How about for going to the corner store to buy ketchup without bringing an ID?

They are sent away because they do the same things rich people do at some time in their lives, usually as teenagers—get drunk and fall down, use drugs, take a leak in an alley, take a shortcut through someone's yard, fall asleep in a subway car, scream at a boyfriend or girlfriend, hop a fence. Only when they do these things, they're surrounded by a thousand police, watching their every move.

Meanwhile the supposedly minor violations that aren't worth throwing bankers in jail for—they turn out to be not so minor. When an employee at the aforementioned British banking giant HSBC—whose executives were ultimately handed a no-jail settlement for the biggest money-laundering case in the history of banking—started looking into how people on terrorist or criminal watch lists opened accounts at his company, he found something odd. In many cases, commas or periods were being surreptitiously added to names, so that they would elude the bank's computer screening systems.

"That's something that could only have been done on purpose, by a bank employee," he said.

What deserves a bigger punishment—someone with a college education who knowingly helps a gangster or a terrorist open a bank account? Or a high school dropout who falls asleep on the F train?

The new America says it's the latter. It's come around to that point of view at the end of a long evolutionary process, in which the rule of law has slowly been replaced by giant idiosyncratic bureaucracies that are designed to criminalize failure, poverty, and weakness on the one hand, and to immunize strength, wealth, and success on the other.

We still have real jury trials, honest judges, and free elections, all the superficial characteristics of a functional, free democracy. But underneath that surface is a florid and malevolent bureaucracy that mostly (not absolutely, but mostly) keeps the rich and the poor separate through thousands of tiny, scarcely visible inequities.

For instance, while the trials may be free and fair, unfair calculations are clearly involved in who gets indicted for crimes, and who does not. Or: Which defendant gets put in jail, and which one gets away with a fine? Which offender ends up with a criminal record, and which one gets to settle with the state without admitting wrongdoing? Which thief will pay restitution out of his own pocket, and which one will be allowed to have the company he works for pay the tab? Which neighborhoods have thousands of police roaming the streets, and which ones don't have any at all?

This is where the new despotism is hidden, in these thousands of arbitrary decisions that surround our otherwise transparent system of real jury trials and carefully enumerated suspects' rights. This vast extrademocratic mechanism, it turns out, is made up of injustices big and small, from sweeping national concepts like Eric Holder's Collateral Consequences plan, granting situational leniency to "systemically important" companies, to smaller, more localized outrages like New York City prosecutors subverting speedy trial rules in order to extract guilty pleas from poor defendants who can't make bail.

Most people understand this on some level, but they don't really know how bad it has gotten, because they live entirely on one side of the equation. If you grew up well off, you probably don't know how easy it is for poor people to end up in jail, often for the same dumb things you yourself did as a kid.

And if you're broke and have limited experience in the world, you probably have no idea of the sheer scale of the awesome criminal capers that the powerful and politically connected can get away with, right under the noses of the rich-people police.

This is a story that doesn't need to be argued. You just need to see it, and it speaks for itself. Only we've arranged things so that the problem is basically invisible to most people, unless you go looking for it.

I went looking for it.

THE DIVIDE

CHAPTER I

UNINTENDED
CONSEQUENCES

Tuesday, July 9, 2013, a blisteringly hot day in New York City. I'm in a cramped, twelfth-story closet of a courtroom, squeezed onto a wooden bench full of heavily perspiring lawyers and onlookers, watching something truly rare in the annals of modern American criminal justice—the prosecution of a bank.

The set for this curiosity is the city's 100 Centre Street courthouse, a beat-up old building located far downtown, just a stone's throw from the thicket of gleaming skyscrapers housing the great financial powers of Wall Street.

It's a pretrial hearing. The defendants—nineteen individuals plus the corporation itself—are here today to argue a motion to dismiss. There's no press here that I can see, despite the historic moment. And it *is* historic. This case, filed by New York County District Attorney Cyrus Vance Jr., represents the only prosecution of a bank to take place anywhere in America since the collapse of the world economy in 2008. (In fact, it's the first since the early 1990s.)

So who's the defendant? Is it Citigroup? Goldman Sachs? Wells

Fargo? JPMorgan Chase? Bank of America? After all, these companies had all been involved in countless scandals since the financial crisis of '08, a disaster caused by an epidemic of criminal fraud that wiped out some 40 percent of the world's wealth in less than a year, affecting nearly everyone in the industrialized world. If ever there was a wave of white-collar crime that cried out for a criminal trial, it was this period of fraud from the mid-2000s. And it would make sense that the defendants should come from one of these companies. In the years since the crash, all of them, and a half-dozen more too-big-to-fail megafirms just like them, had already paid hundreds of millions of dollars in civil settlements for virtually every kind of fraud and manipulation known to man.

Moreover, District Attorney Vance had once seemingly had all these Wall Street firms in his sights. He'd sent subpoenas out to Goldman and other companies the previous year. So surely one of these banks in those big skyscrapers a few blocks south of here must be the one on trial.

Nope. In the end, the one bank to get thrown on the dock was not a Wall Street firm but one housed in the opposite direction, a little to the north—a tiny family-owned community bank in Chinatown called Abacus Federal Savings Bank.

As a symbol of the government's ambitions in the area of cleaning up the financial sector, Abacus presents a striking picture. Instead of a fifty-story glass-and-steel monolith, Abacus is housed in a dull gray six-story building wedged between two noodle shops at the southern end of New York's legendary Bowery, once the capital of American poverty.

This is the bank in court today, dragged to the cross to take the blame for the many sins of the financial sector. It is a grimly comic scene. The judge, the Honorable Renee White, is a legendary city curmudgeon, a wraithlike woman with a long turtlish neck and orange hair who seems unhappy not only to be listening to a motion to dismiss but to be on planet Earth at all.

Before the hearing began, in fact, she'd barked at a young Chinese woman who'd had the audacity to dip her head near the floor to sneak a drink from a water bottle in her bag, trying to fight off the stultifying heat. "No refreshments!" the judge yelled. "You should have had your lunch before you came to this courtroom!"

The young woman meekly put her bottle back into a bag. Judge White craned her long neck and glared. A burly bailiff, acting as many bailiffs do—as the physical manifestation of his judge's whimsy—hovered angrily past to make sure the offending bottle was no longer visible.

"Is she always like this?" I whispered, to no one in particular.

"What are you talking about?" a lawyer in front of me answered. "She's in a *good* mood today."

Judge White frowned and then went about the dreary task of reseating the courtroom. She sent Cantonese-speaking defendants to her left, Mandarin-speaking defendants to the right, and had a single translator plopped into the middle of each bewildered group.

Some of the accused were low-level loan officers, immigrants mostly, who had been as young as twenty-one or as old as seventy at the time of arrest. None of them were what one would describe as wealthy persons. None were millionaire CEOs of the Jamie Dimon/ Lloyd Blankfein ilk. Instead, they were mostly Chinese immigrants in cheap blouses and worn suits, people who spoke little English or none at all, and who looked white with shame and confusion as they huddled around their respective translators.

Many of these criminal masterminds had been earning as little as $35,000 a year at the time they were hauled in for what the state described as a far-reaching scheme to falsify loan applications for home mortgages that their bank, Abacus, ultimately went on to sell to the government-sponsored mortgage dealer, Fannie Mae.

What were these nineteen people charged with? The case had been sold to the court and to the public—by Vance, mostly—as having something to do with the financial crisis, setting up the bank as a scapegoat for the 2008 blowup. Vance bragged that it was the first indictment in New York of a bank since the BCCI crisis in 1991, and he subtly compared Abacus to the aforementioned bailout all-stars like Citigroup and Bank of America, ostensibly the true villains of the financial crisis, by warning that Abacus's crimes might ultimately lead to the taxpayer footing the bill. "If we've learned anything from the recent mortgage crisis," he said, "it's that at some point, these schemes will unravel and taxpayers could be left holding the bag."

Vance made sure to play rough with the defendants, just to let them know how angry The People were about the financial crisis. In an extraordinary scene over a year before, on May 31, 2012, Vance had hauled all nineteen of the Abacus defendants into court to face indictment. For the benefit of the press, he had them chained not only at the hands and feet but to one another.

This otherworldly chain gang of bewildered immigrants had been led into the courtroom like a giant, slow-moving snake. It was like a scene out of Bagram or Guantánamo Bay—all that was missing were the hoods.

Incredibly, three of the nineteen people who were put in chains had already been arraigned by Vance and released on bail. Prosecutors had asked them to voluntarily report to court that day, and they came, having no idea what for. When they appeared, Vance had had them cuffed and chained all over again, then paraded into court to be rearraigned, purely for the benefit of the cameras.

"I'm no softie on crime," says Kevin Puvalowski, the attorney for Abacus and a former federal drug prosecutor. "But I've seen death penalty defendants treated with more dignity."

Again, on the same day as this bizarre photo op, Vance had stood up in a press conference and described the indictment of Abacus as a direct blow against the behavior that had caused the financial crisis. "The lessons of the financial crisis are still being learned," he said sternly.

And in its limited coverage of the case, the press mostly upheld the notion that the Abacus indictment was aimed at the heart of the financial crisis. "The indictment against the bank and its employees describes the sort of scheme that led to the financial crisis of 2008," wrote *The New York Times* in a typical account, "when the risk of mortgages to borrowers was disguised and passed on to investors."

As for Vance, he got what he wanted out of the presser: a trophy. In subsequent coverage in newspapers like *The Wall Street Journal*, he would henceforth be referred to as the DA who "indicted a bank for mortgage fraud."

But this case had nothing to do with the financial crisis. In fact, it was clear just from reading the indictment that the improprieties uncovered at Abacus were highly idiosyncratic and specific to Chinatown's immigrant population. Though tax evasion wasn't part of the case, it lurked in the background. Clearly, many mortgage applicants, who worked in cash businesses in the immigrant Chinese community, had not wanted to declare all their income.

After the Abacus indictment, in fact, I heard whispers from a police source with long experience in Chinatown that some of the bank's customers may have been involved in schemes like trademark counterfeiting—not exactly a surprise, since it's hard to visit Chinatown and not run into someone selling phony Prada bags or Rolex watches out of the back of a van somewhere.

Thus the underlying crime in this case seemed to be that Abacus's customers could afford to pay for a mortgage but didn't want to say how, exactly. They had been, in other words, not overreporting but underreporting their incomes.

There was also a bizarre racial component to the case. Buried in the charges was the thinly veiled assumption that Abacus senior management encouraged their borrowers to commit fraud in their applications because they knew they could rely upon the generally accepted cultural proposition that Chinese people, like the evil Lannisters in *Game of Thrones*, always pay their debts. Vance's indictment more or less says this out loud, claiming that Abacus management "falsely told employees that the exceptionally low default rate of Abacus-originated loans made the underlying accuracy of loan documents insignificant."

The description had been true—the Abacus mortgage holders had paid their debts. In fact, from the date of the first offense as defined by the prosecutors, the quasi-governmental Fannie Mae had made a profit of $220 million on Abacus-issued home loans. In all, Abacus had one of the lowest default rates in the entire country. It was about 0.5 percent, roughly ten times better than the average.

Thus this was a very different kind of case from the more common fraud of the financial crisis era, which mostly involved gigantic banks and mortgage lenders selling the toxic and ultimately worthless subprime mortgage loans of broke and underemployed middle Americans as AAA-rated investments to state pension funds, foreign trade unions, and other suckers. Abacus was almost certainly a case about hiding income; the financial crisis was caused by a snake-oil scheme to sell worthless loans as gold.

Everyone got what they wanted from the Abacus prosecution. The city got to say it was being tough on financial crime. The press got to run a thrilling picture of harsh justice. Vance got a line to add to his résumé. The only losers were the public, who had no idea that the real culprits for the financial crisis were being set free, while the bank on trial had nothing to do with the losses that had been suffered by almost every ordinary American in the crash. As one city investigator put it, Abacus was "the Lee Harvey Oswald of banks—a patsy."

In any case, this same collection of freaked-out immigrant patsies were back in court now, this time without their chains. Most of the defendants had their own lawyers, as did the bank itself, so the courtroom was fairly packed with defense counsel. Most of these defense lawyers had filed "Clayton motions," a New York state legal procedure in which a defendant can ask a judge to dismiss charges on the general grounds that doing so would be in furtherance of justice.

Among other things, a Clayton motion asks the judge to consider "the purpose and effect" of punishment and the "impact on the public interest" of a dismissal. They are motions, in other words, that ask a judge to consider the consequences of prosecution, balanced against the public interest.

One by one, defense counsel stood up to argue to the ostentatiously bored Judge White why their clients should be let go. Some argued their clients were too old or too young, or had been at the bank for only a few months, or had never in their whole lives been in trouble with the law. (They virtually all argued that.) Some said their clients had been new on the job and had simply filled out a few papers incorrectly according to the instructions of superiors. The list of reasons for leniency went on and on.

But finally one of the defense lawyers, a former city prosecutor named Sanford "Sam" Talkin, a man with a deep tan and a neatly shaven head, got to a larger and more dangerous point. Gently waving a hand in the direction of the Abacus defendants, Talkin confronted Judge White. "Your Honor," he said, "I want you to compare them to Citigroup. Just last week Citigroup settled for $968 million for either underperforming or defaulted home loans. . . .

"But this pales in comparison to Bank of America, which paid $6.8 *billion* dollars, with a *b*, for underperforming or defaulted home loans. Civil settlement, no criminal charges . . . Wells Fargo Bank, $3.3 billion, no criminal prosecution . . . Ally GMAC, $3.3 billion, civil settlement, no criminal charges. JPMorgan Chase . . . another $3.3 billion for the same purpose, civil settlement, no criminal charges."

Talkin's point was clear—all these other, far richer banks had been caught selling defective loans that had actually cost victims huge amounts of money, and nobody from those giant companies was being arrested. But in the Abacus case, unlike in cases involving too-big-to-fail banks, the state could not identify so much as a dollar of loss suffered by the state as a result of the loans.

The defense lawyer pleaded with the judge: How did this make sense?

The judge frowned. "Are you arguing selective prosecution?" she grumbled. "I don't know what the point is."

The room was silent for a moment. Talkin gamely went on and pleaded with the judge. Abacus was a family-owned, family-run bank. It had been founded by seventy-two-year-old immigrant Thomas Sung and was run by his two fiercely loyal, American-born daughters, Vera and Jill Sung, both of whom were lawyers and one of whom, Jill, had been a New York City prosecutor. Yet none of the Sungs had been indicted. The highest executive on trial, Talkin noted, was a midlevel salaried employee named Yuh Wah Wang, a man who made $90,000 a year and had never earned a bonus of higher than $1,500. He was here only to satisfy the legal requirement needed to indict a company, that a "high managerial officer" be involved.

And it was ridiculous, Talkin argued, to put this man in this position and equate him with the banking titans who ran those other mortgage fraud schemes. "They're putting him in that position where every other major bank in this country goes—"

Her Honor cut him off. "I don't want you to tell me about all the other banks in the world," she snapped.

Talkin paused, gathered himself, and shifted to make a political case. Clearly deferring to the judge's legendary temper, he tiptoed into a kind of Ghost of Christmas Future argument, trying to explain to her how bad this would all look someday, with all these other companies getting off, and here's this old immigrant making $90K a year being held up as the linchpin of the financial crisis. "People will look at how the courts operate," he pleaded. "And it will look at your honor's decision."

Judge White rolled her eyes and indicated that Talkin should move on. He did, eventually giving way to Puvalowski, attorney for the bank itself.

Puvalowski was the big gun among the defense attorneys. He was not only a former federal drug prosecutor, but more recently the deputy inspector general of the TARP program, having served as the right-hand man for well-known bailout critic Neil Barofsky, sometimes described as the Eliot Ness of the financial crisis. Together, the two men had publicly challenged the Obama administration, and particularly then–treasury secretary Timothy Geithner, for failing to properly supervise the hundreds of billions of bailout dollars rushing out of the public piggy bank to prop up those too-big-to-fail banking giants in the skyscrapers to the south.

The career turn had made Puvalowski something of a pariah among the big banks downtown, but it had also made him the perfect choice to defend this little immigrant community bank that was being set up as the fall guy for the financial crisis.

But Puvalowski was having a bad day. The big, burly, red-haired Polish American had for days been suffering from an unstoppable nosebleed, and it had continued right through the proceeding. Earlier in the day he'd begun his presentation but then had had to excuse himself, literally to try to stop the bleeding. The bank defendants were fairly chewing their fingernails in panic, watching the big lawyer shove tissues up his nose, and when he finally exited to an adjoining room to lie down, there was a hush in the courtroom, a *Down goes Frazier!* vibe.

When Talkin finished his presentation, however, Puvalowski returned. The bleeding having stopped, he plowed through a powerful defense of the company. His primary point was that it was impossible to charge the bank with larceny when nobody had lost any money. Vance had shamelessly told the press that the Abacus case had involved "thousands of loans" in which borrowers were instructed to inflate their assets, and yet the final indictment pointed to only thirty-one loans, and none of them had lost a dime. "You cannot turn a $220 million profit into a theft no matter how you do back flips in the indictment," he said.

He moved on to argue that the state had erroneously availed itself of New York's powerful securities law weapon, the Martin Act, for the obvious reason that the mortgages that Abacus had sold were not securities. He cited a Supreme Court case that specifically held that residential mortgages were not securities.

Recovering himself, he spoke more and more loudly, getting on a roll, attacking the indictment count by count. Even Judge White seemed to snap awake, peppering Puvalowski with questions about the Martin Act arguments, almost seeming genuinely interested.

And then at the very end, Puvalowski returned to the same themes as Talkin. "The district attorney has repeatedly suggested that this is somehow a financial crisis case. That's frankly a farce. If every bank had done as good a job writing loans for Fannie Mae, we wouldn't have had a financial crisis."

Puvalowski pointed in the direction of Wall Street. "You can't throw a rock without hitting a bank that cost Fannie Mae billions of dollars in loss, but you know it's not in this courtroom."

Briefly awakened, Judge White soured at this argument and snapped, "I don't want to get into extraneous matters. I'm tired."

She retreated, turtlelike, leaning back into her great chair.

And that was that. There would be no more of this gratuitous comparing of the Abacus chain gang to Citigroup or Bank of America fat cats in Judge White's courtroom. The hearing ran its course, and Judge White retired to consider the arguments, though few present really expected her to fully dismiss the charges. This was not the kind of case where judges typically spent a lot of time considering the "consequences" of criminal prosecution.

What Judge White was calling "extraneous matters" was the nebulous concept of context: Why did some people go to jail, while others committed the same crime and walked? Judge White wasn't much interested in the question—and legally, maybe, she was right not to be—but I was.

By the time of the Abacus hearing, in fact, I'd spent years crisscrossing America in search of answers to that question of why some criminals went free, while others committing the same crimes felt the full weight of the state's power.

To say that the rich go free while the poor go to jail turns out to be a gross oversimplification. It's far more complicated than that, and in a way more horrible.

We're creating a dystopia, where the mania of the state isn't secrecy or censorship but unfairness. Obsessed with success and wealth and despising failure and poverty, our society is systematically dividing the population into winners and losers, using institutions like the courts to speed the process. Winners get rich and get off. Losers go broke and go to jail. It isn't just that some clever crook on Wall Street can steal a billion dollars and never see the inside of a courtroom; it's that, *plus* the fact that some black teenager a few miles away can go to jail just for standing on a street corner, that makes the whole picture complete.

The great nonprosecutions of Wall Street in the years since 2008, I would learn, were just symbols of this dystopian sorting process to which we'd already begun committing ourselves. The cleaving of the country into two completely different states—one a small archipelago of hyperacquisitive untouchables, the other a vast ghetto of expendables with only theoretical rights—has been in the works a long time.

The Divide is a terrible story, and a crazy one. And it goes back a long, long way.

On June 16, 1999, a little-known official from Bill Clinton's White House named Eric Holder published a memorandum entitled "Bringing Criminal Charges Against Corporations."

Few people in America knew who Eric Holder was back then. At the time, the young African-American lawyer was a former U.S. attorney best known for prosecuting the lurid corruption case of Congressman Dan Rostenkowski. The esteemed congressman had been charged, among other things, with using congressional funds to buy ashtrays for friends and for trading in officially purchased stamps for cash at the House post office.

Like most revolutionary manifestos, the Holder memo, as it's now known, was barely read at all when first published. Back in 1999, there seemed to be little need for a drastic change in American policy with regard to the prosecution of white-collar crime. Though the Department of Justice at the time was still woefully underpowered to take on certain types of crime—health care fraud went on almost completely unchecked in the 1980s and 1990s—Holder's memo was nonetheless written in the wake of years of fairly vigorous prosecutions of companies that had committed crimes like theft, fraud, and market manipulation.

From the Drexel Burnham Lambert insider trading case in 1988 (which led to the demise of one of the biggest houses on Wall Street) to the Daiwa Bank case in 1996 (in which the Japanese powerhouse was caught hiding billions of losses and was ultimately fined a record $340 million by Janet Reno's Justice Department) to the infamous Bankers Trust case in 1999 (in which the bank was caught diverting unclaimed customer funds in order to boost its profits), federal prosecutors for more than a decade had put together a not-entirely-unimpressive record of busting high-level white-collar offenders.

Ivan Boesky, Michael Milken, and Charles Keating were sixteen-point bucks on the Justice Department wall, and there was quantity as well as quality in the prosecutorial record, with more than a thousand defendants put in the dock and more than eight hundred actually sent to jail for crimes that had led to the country's last serious financial crisis, the savings and loan disaster.

At first blush, the Holder memo actually appeared to be a get-tough-on-white-collar-crime memo. In fact, during the Bush era, it would be spoken of derisively as an antibusiness document. It reads that way a little bit, too, opening with a sort of approving legalistic coda, sung in praise of the whole idea of criminal prosecution of the white-collar criminal.

"Corporations should not be treated leniently because of their artificial nature," Holder wrote. ". . . Vigorous enforcement of the criminal laws against corporate wrongdoers, where appropriate, results in great benefits for law enforcement and the public, particularly in the area of white collar crime."

Then the young attorney laid out a whole series of "factors" that the state might consider when deciding whether to charge a company. Among them were two entries that would prove extremely controversial:

One factor the prosecutor may weigh in assessing the adequacy of a corporation's cooperation is the completeness of its disclosure including, if necessary, a waiver of the attorney-client and work product protections. . . .

Another factor to be weighed by the prosecutor is whether the corporation appears to be protecting its culpable employees and agents. Thus, while cases will differ depending on the circumstances, a corporation's promise of support to culpable employees and agents, . . . through the advancing of attorneys fees . . . may be considered by the prosecutor in weighing the extent and value of a corporation's cooperation.

Translated into English, what this meant was that a company could push the Justice Department into a charge-filing mood just by refusing to waive attorney-client privilege or by paying its employees' legal fees. This concept would give prosecutors powerful weapons in their negotiations with companies, essentially forcing them to lay down their shields even before the battle started.

As is often the case with Holder, these passages represented an incoherent mix of inspired book-smart innovation and grossly impractical real-world cluelessness. The idea of going after companies that hid behind attorney-client privilege was an aggressive, solid concept. Law enforcement officials had long complained about companies that hid behind their lawyers. If, say, a company had suffered a loss thanks to a rogue employee, it might come to the state begging for an embezzlement investigation, and in such a case the company seldom had any problem opening its entire kimono for the state, waiving privilege immediately if it had any chance of getting its money back.

But if the company itself was in trouble, and the state came sniffing around, a firm's leaders would typically pull a kind of damsel-in-distress routine. They would say they *wanted* to cooperate, absolutely, but simply couldn't show the state everything, because so much of its internal communications were privileged.

Holder's memo called BS on that. Essentially, it told companies: if you want us to really be convinced you're cooperating, that you're committed enough to fixing your problems that we don't have to throw all of you in jail, you should waive privilege and show us everything.

This was a bold stroke, real on-the-edge lawyering, the kind of thing every white-collar prosecutor had to love. It was like giving cops bigger guns or faster cars. More weapons to fight bad guys is what every law enforcement officer wants. And this weapon was a powerful one.

But the next idea—dinging companies for paying the legal fees of its employees—that was something else. That would prove to be a design error on the order of the flammable fuel tank in 1970s-era Ford Pinto hatchbacks. Years later it would blow up in the face of the federal government in spectacular fashion (more on that later).

At the time, however, the Holder memo seemed like a powerful get-tough weapon to shove in the federal investigator's holster. Thus the idea that it would someday be seen as the genesis of a revolutionary leniency policy crafted on behalf of America's rich would have seemed preposterous to anyone reading the document at the time. Holder himself probably would have been stunned. (In fact, he would later be stunned by interpretations of many different parts of his memo.)

"It's funny, looking back now, the way the Holder memo was originally thought of as this very aggressive thing," says one former federal prosecutor. "The talk was that he'd gone too far in the other direction."

But that's only because people were focusing on the wrong part of the memo. Farther down, under the heading "Charging the Corporation: Collateral Consequences," Holder began to trace the first outlines of what would become his accidental revolution. Again, he was writing about factors the government might consider in deciding whether to file charges:

"Prosecutors," he wrote, "may consider the collateral consequences of a corporate criminal conviction in determining whether to charge the corporation with a criminal offense."

Collateral consequences.

What did that mean? Holder went on to explain:

> One of the factors in determining whether to charge a natural person or a corporation is whether the likely punishment is appropriate given the nature and seriousness of the crime. In the corporate context, prosecutors may take into account the possibly substantial consequences to a corporation's officers, directors, employees, and shareholders, many of whom may, depending on the size and nature (e.g., publicly vs. closely held) of the corporation and their role in its operations, have played no role in the criminal conduct, have been completely unaware of it, or have been wholly unable to prevent it.

This was a dully written but entirely reasonable-sounding proposition. All Holder was saying was that when prosecutors were looking at a big company that might be guilty of criminal conduct, it was okay for them to look at the innocents as well. The shareholders who would lose their shirts when a stock plummeted, the innocent line employees who would lose their jobs, the lawyers and executives whose careers would wrongly be tainted—all these people, Holder said, should figure into the prosecutor's calculations.

To charge or not to charge? For any prosecutor, federal or state, that had always been the eternal question. It had always been difficult to justify not filing criminal charges, when crimes had been committed, even if many people would be harmed in the process.

But Holder's memo proposed a new out. Consider the collateral consequences, it said, and if the math isn't there, hold the charges. Seek other forms of justice instead. Fines. Civil sanctions. Cease and desist orders. Deferred prosecutions. There are other ways, Holder wrote, to get the job done.

Like a scientific paper on fractal theory or gene mapping, the Holder memo was an insider's take on a cutting-edge problem. Dealing with corporate crime in the new century would require a new set of prosecutorial and regulatory tools. Increasingly, companies were growing, in size, beyond the old regulatory parameters.

One reason was globalization, in which advances in communications technology and production efficiency incentivized big companies to become essentially stateless entities, with operations spread all over the world. Where once you had a Boeing or a Hershey's keep its factories and headquarters snuggled decade after decade in the same state or company town, you now had huge multinational firms peppering China and India with factories, and banking havens like Antigua and Jersey with corporate offices, as they raced around the earth in search of tax, labor, and other advantages. The whole world with its myriad sets of laws and rules presented endless opportunities for regulatory arbitrage. It would be harder for the cop on the beat to chase an offender that simultaneously existed everywhere and nowhere.

Moreover, even within the United States there had been intentional, lobbied-for changes in corporate structure: the repeal of the Glass-Steagall Act, which had prevented the mergers of commercial banks, investment banks, and insurance companies (this repeal led to the creation of megafirms like Citigroup), and Supreme Court decisions rolling back bans on interstate banking (which led to a string of mergers, resulting in the formation of giant national banks like Wachovia and Bank of America). In the finance sector at least, these changes allowed companies to be more enormous and difficult to regulate than they ever had been before.

Maybe Holder foresaw what was coming, or maybe it was just an incredible coincidence, but by the time he returned to the Justice Department under Barack Obama eight-plus years later, the business world would be dominated by companies whose potential collapse would not merely cost a few jobs here and there but would threaten the stability of the entire world economy. Holder couldn't have known it at the time, but through his 1999 Collateral Consequences memo, he had designed a get-out-of-jail-free policy for a kind of company that hadn't existed yet: the too-big-to-fail mega-firm that simply couldn't be reined in with conventional criminal laws.

But all that was in the future. For a time, after Holder left the Clinton White House, it looked as if none of this would ever matter at all.

After Bill Clinton and Janet Reno stepped down and George Bush and John Ashcroft took their places, it seemed for a while like Collateral Consequences was destined to become a historical footnote. The first few years of Bush's presidency were marked by a series of high-handed white-collar criminal prosecutions of executives at companies like WorldCom, Enron, Rite-Aid, and Tyco, and those investigations were notable for the state's relative indifference to their collateral consequences.

The Bush administration and the Republican Party would definitely earn a reputation for being in the pocket of big business, and not only through legislation like the Medicare Modernization Act (a grotesque and shameless handout to the pharmaceutical industry), the Bankruptcy Abuse Act (a similarly shameless handout to the consumer credit industry), and the Clear Skies Act (a huge, and hugely Orwellian, handout to the energy industry). There were also horrific regulatory surrenders like the Securities and Exchange Commission's 2004 decision to lower capital reserve standards for the top five investment banks, a move that eventually helped three of those banks (Merrill Lynch, Bear Stearns, and Lehman Brothers) to borrow themselves out of existence.

And the accounting scandals of the 2000s did involve a lot of current and former Bush cronies, to the extent that a number of key regulators (including Ashcroft himself) faced calls to recuse themselves from investigations.

But the Bush Justice Department without a doubt also aggressively pursued a handful of symbolically important criminal investigations of big companies, apparently motivated by more than just the desire to score points on an issue that, thanks to Bush and Cheney's relationships to some of the defendants, threatened that White House politically. The scandals seemed genuinely to take the state by surprise, and emotions like anger and a sense of betrayal could be detected as the Bush Justice Department in some cases went all *Walking Tall* on some of the corporate targets.

The most shocking moment in the counteroffensive came on July 24, 2002, when federal agents stormed the Manhattan town-house of seventy-eight-year-old Adelphia cable CEO John Rigas—who along with his sons had used his company as a personal piggy bank for years, embezzling billions—and dragged him out on the street to be perp-walked before the cameras. The same day Adelphia itself was charged with fraud by the SEC. The company, meanwhile, had been pushed into bankruptcy a month before the arrest. Nobody shed much of a tear for any of these firms. A historical note that gives lie to later suggestions that the markets would panic in the face of criminal investigations of Wall Street: when Rigas was busted, the stock market actually rallied to its second-biggest one-day gain ever, thanks to the widespread perception that the state was taking out corporate America's garbage.

Stories like these made the Collateral Consequences idea seem irrelevant, a minor notion floated by a minor Clinton lawyer, now gathering dust in the Bush White House.

Then came Arthur Andersen.

The venerable accounting firm was swept up in the Enron scandal and charged criminally by the Bush Justice Department for destroying files and perhaps collaborating in Enron's accounting schemes. The government offered the company a deferred prosecution agreement, one that would have required an admission of wrongdoing.

Arthur Andersen wanted no part of that. It essentially told the government to blow itself. In a scathing letter sent to prosecutors in March 2002, the accounting firm's lawyers blasted the government for what it claimed were high-handed tactics.

"The department proposes an action that could destroy the firm, taking the livelihoods of thousands of innocent Andersen employees and retirees," the letter read. The letter further argued that in an industry where trust and a reputation for honesty were essential, asking Arthur Andersen to admit to its guilt was tantamount, in the business world, to a criminal conviction.

This letter spoke directly to the Collateral Consequences memo. Here was a major company, an employer of thousands, using its innocent employees as a kind of human shield in a desperate last-ditch attempt to stave off a criminal prosecution. It was a high-stakes stare-down in which Andersen's lawyers all but dared the government to pull a My Lai and machine-gun its innocent employees into a ditch.

But instead of blinking, the Bush Justice Department doubled down. It charged the firm, criminally, on a single felony count. A jury convicted. Almost immediately afterward, the firm collapsed. And 28,000 jobs were lost.

Instead of blaming the lost jobs on the leadership of a ninety-year-old accounting firm that had been too stupid to realize that its only salable product in the financial marketplace was honesty, government officials over the next few years quietly began to recoil from their own decision to press forward with charges against a clearly guilty company.

The first sign of change came with a Supreme Court decision in early 2005. The high court, led by infamous blowhard William Rehnquist, overturned the Arthur Andersen conviction, ruling that the jury instructions had been so broad that the firm could have been found guilty even if high officials in the company had not intended to break the law.

Rehnquist insisted that the state needed to offer a higher burden of proof: that the mere fact that Andersen had shredded two tons of documents in the Enron case was not enough, and that prosecutors had to show "consciousness of wrongdoing" as well. (What did they think they were doing with all that shredding? Cleaning?)

Six months after that court ruling, the Justice Department heaved a big sigh of regret and made a great show of dropping the case. "The government has determined that it is in the interests of justice not to re-prosecute Andersen," federal prosecutors wrote in November 2005.

This would be one of the first of a series of decisions not to retry high-profile corruption cases. Whereas before the state had kept coming and coming, Jason Voorhees–like, after corrupt companies, after Arthur Andersen it started to lose its appetite for battle.

Subsequently, in both the financial and the mainstream press, it became gospel that the experience of Arthur Andersen proved that such prosecutions of otherwise functioning companies are inappropriate. "There was an initial outbreak of moral condemnation after Enron and the bubble burst," Larry E. Ribstein, a corporate law professor at the University of Illinois, told *The Washington Post*. "That was a time for people to take a deep breath. Instead, a lot of these things were rushed into prosecution, and now we're seeing the fallout."

Academics piled on, writing paper after paper about the misguidedness and impropriety of the Andersen prosecution. There were critics in Congress, critics in the media, critics from the big law firms in New York and Washington. No 28,000 jobs lost were ever mourned as much as the 28,000 jobs lost in the Andersen case.

Thereafter, the government began to think differently about prosecuting big companies. No matter how big the crime, the new thing was to think about the possible endgame first. And the worst possible endgame became the starting point for all future "to charge or not to charge" discussions. "From that point forward," says Eliot Spitzer, "every time one of these things came up, someone always brought up Arthur Andersen."

During this whole time, at the end of the Bush years, Eric Holder was in private practice at Covington & Burling, a major corporate defense firm based in Washington, D.C. The firm's clients at the time included four of the biggest banks in the world: JPMorgan

Chase, Bank of America, Citigroup, and Wells Fargo, in addition to Freddie Mac and a little-known mortgage-registration company called MERS.

In the cozy confines of C&B, Holder seemed to experience, if not a change in heart exactly, a change in perspective. His 1999 memo, though ignored by the Bush administration on the Collateral Consequences score, had survived and become unintentionally important policy (the way a joke becomes unintentionally funny) in other arenas.

In particular, his 1999 memo was used as the basis for a 2003 memo written by a Bush administration official, deputy attorney general Larry Thompson. Thompson was something of a hero to young prosecutors in the Justice Department, an old-school law-and-order type who backed his troops in battle. "He had our backs" is how one former federal prosecutor put it. His new "Thompson memo" repeated the Holder guidelines under which companies could get (or lose) credit for cooperation, depending upon whether they waived attorney-client privilege.

The Thompson version was more explicit and aggressive, but the root concept was the same as Holder's. Unfortunately, some of Holder's bad ideas survived in the memo along with the good ones.

This would have a major impact on one of the biggest corruption cases of the early 2000s, the KPMG tax-shelter case. KPMG, a Netherlands-based firm that even today is one of the "big four" global auditing companies, along with such titans as Ernst & Young and PricewaterhouseCoopers, was accused of serially selling bogus tax shelters to extremely wealthy clients, depriving the IRS, and by extension other regular, cough-it-up-every-April taxpayers, of at least $2.5 billion.

The government had KPMG dead to rights in the case. Before the state had even made a decision on whether to indict it, the company preemptively surrendered a little, like an octopus releasing ink, issuing a statement saying that it took responsibility for the "unlawful conduct by former KPMG partners."

As in the case of Arthur Andersen, there was a bit of a human-shield defense going on here, as the government was implored to consider the consequences of indicting the firm and wiping out 18,000 jobs.

The Washington Post even came out with a house editorial entitled "Don't Destroy KPMG," in which it begged the Bush Justice Department to spare the thousands of jobs. "It's hard to see the good that could come of indicting KPMG as a firm," the paper wrote, adding, "KPMG has forced out the partners responsible for the problem and is apparently prepared to cooperate in prosecutions of individuals—which would have far greater deterrent value than a corporate indictment."

That made sense to just about everyone, and so unlike Arthur Andersen, KPMG was not criminally indicted and instead got a deferred prosecution deal, to go with $456 million in penalties. And as is not common practice today, authorities in 2005 launched those criminal indictments of KPMG's individuals, hauling in nineteen former executives on broad-ranging tax fraud conspiracy charges, including several former partners.

But there was a crazy catch with the case. As one exasperated investigator explains it, many of the KPMG executives had clauses in their employment contracts guaranteeing that in the event of a problem, the firm would pay their legal fees. But KPMG, in order to get credit for fully cooperating, had to stiff its former execs on the legal fee question. It turned out that at a meeting back in February 2004, the federal prosecutor in the case, Justin Weddle, had told KPMG executives that if the company planned on paying its employees' legal fees, the state would "look at that under a microscope."

KPMG promptly responded by sending letters out to its employees, explaining that it had "no obligation" to pay fees but would do so provided the employees cooperated with the government. Even in that case, they would cap fees at $400,000.

Years later a high-ranking Justice Department official would cringe to recall that episode. "We *want* everyone to have good lawyers. So why do that?" the official said. "That was just fucking stupid. The whole idea is stupid. It put everything at risk."

It sure did. Shortly after the Feds strong-armed KPMG on the legal fee issue, a district judge named Lewis Kaplan tossed the indictments of thirteen of the individuals on Sixth Amendment grounds, that is, that the defendants had essentially been denied counsel. Kaplan raged in particular against the Thompson memo, blasting the Justice Department for way overstepping its prosecutorial bounds.

Noting with undisguised anguish that the indictment "charges serious crimes" that "should have been decided on the merits," Kaplan ripped Thompson & Co. for going too far. He didn't mention Holder and didn't seem even to be aware of him. In fact, in his ruling, Kaplan cited a key section of what he thought was Thompson's memo, which read as follows—the emphasis here is Kaplan's:

> Thus, while cases will differ depending on the circumstances, a corporation's promise of support to culpable employees and agents, *either through the advancing of attorneys fees* . . . or through providing information to the employees about the government's investigation . . . may be considered by the prosecutor in weighing the extent and value of a corporation's cooperation.

This was exactly Holder's language, but Judge Kaplan laid it all at Thompson's feet. "The Court well understands," he wrote, "that prosecutors can and should be aggressive in pursuit of the public interest." But in this case, the Department of Justice

> deliberately or callously prevented many of these defendants from obtaining funds for their defense as they lawfully would have absent the government's interference. . . . This is intolerable in a society that holds itself out to the world as a paragon of justice.

A Second Circuit court later somberly upheld ~~an's savage~~ ruling. This left the Justice Department—still c~~ed in the nine-~~

egg omelet that was the Supreme Court's self-righteous flipping of the Andersen case—facing another barrage of incoming egg.

Having gone after two of the world's biggest accounting firms, both of which were clearly guilty of major systemic infractions, the Justice Department ended up completely overturned in one case and partially overturned and torn a new one by an angry judge in another.

Furiously, the attorney general's office quickly got to work tearing up the relevant portions of the Holder and Thompson memos, replacing them with new memos. The first one was written in 2006 by a deputy AG (or DAG) named Paul McNulty, and the second one in 2008 by another DAG, Mark Filip. The new rules more clearly defined what companies could get "cooperation credit" for and tossed out the whole concept of giving credit for anything but disclosing information.

And here's the punch line in all this: when the Thompson memo was overturned, an enterprising reporter from *The Wall Street Journal* named Peter Lattman traced the Thompson memo back to Holder and found the now-privately-practicing attorney at his new cozy home at Covington & Burling.

Asked about all the hoopla, Holder expressed two things. The first was a chuckling appreciation that his name had miraculously been left out of it all, that all that judicial ire that could have been directed toward his memo had instead been lobbed at Thompson's. "And I'm sure Larry [Thompson is] glad today that there's now a McNulty memo and he doesn't have to be reading about the Thompson memo all the time," Holder quipped.

Lattman, who now writes for *The New York Times*, remembers that Holder wasn't troubled at all by his call. "It was a jocular conversation," he recalls.

The second thing Holder expressed to Lattman was a kind of new appreciation for the point of view of the big company facing federal investigation. He told the reporter that his memo had been misinterpreted, that it had never been intended to force companies to waive privilege, that it had been intended only as a positive thing—

you know, *if* a company waived, that was something you could consider as a plus.

Being on the business end of those policies now, defending such companies, he saw how tough they could be. "Today, it's maddening," he complained. "You'll go into a prosecutor's office . . . and fifteen minutes into our first meeting they say, 'Are you going to waive?'"

Holder, in other words, had gone from helping the State Department secure cooperation from corporate defendants using the white-collar equivalent of thumbscrews all the way to the other side of the argument as a highly paid corporate flack, whining that *his own ideas* were unsustainable intrusions upon commercial privacy.

Such flip-flops are so common among this type of lawyer that most finance-sector observers scarcely even raise an eyebrow at them. "You'll have a guy who as a prosecutor was tossing everyone in jail," laughs one Wall Street reporter, "and six months later he's a partner at some firm, and it's almost like he thinks insider trading should be legal."

Holder was and is exactly that kind of character. But when he would return to government years later, the flip-flops would stop. Even as attorney general, he would remain a corporate lawyer at heart.

In his capacity as a private defense lawyer, however, Holder was not yet in position to push the doctrine of Collateral Consequences in the federal Justice Department. All the same, it seemed like someone in power was reading his memo.

In 2004, before the Supreme Court killed the Andersen case, the federal government had made sparing use of such tools as deferred prosecution agreements and nonprosecution agreements, deals that allowed companies to stay in business without taking a criminal charge.

There were only five such deals in 2004. In 2005, after Andersen, the number jumped to twenty. By 2006 the number of DPAs and

NPAs combined jumped to twenty-one. By 2007, as the next great era of corporate scandal in American history—the great mortgage-backed securities scam of the 2000s—was beginning to spill into public view, the number of DPA/NPA deals jumped to an incredible forty-one.

It's important to explain that the government has always had many tools at its disposal for dealing with corporate crime. In every case, the issue was always how far the state wanted to push things. One method was to gather a ton of evidence against an entire industry, gather all the major players into a room, and simply demand widespread structural changes. This was how then–New York attorney general Spitzer had done it in his so-called Global Settlement, in which virtually the entire investment banking industry was very publicly hauled behind the woodshed and forced not only to pay fines but to make significant structural changes in the way it handled IPOs and produced financial analyses.

A key feature of the Spitzer settlement was the way the evidence was laid out openly so that the public could see the companies' internal communications. At Lehman Brothers, for example, analysts admitted to giving cushy ratings to companies in exchange for more investment banking business, not caring if ordinary investors who were not in on the game got screwed. In another example, an analyst joked about giving an overenthusiastic rating to a company called Razorfish. "Well, ratings and price targets are fairly meaningless anyway," he wrote. "But yes, the 'little guy' who isn't smart about the nuances may get misled, such is the nature of my business."

Dumping all this out in public not only had a definite shaming angle, it also provided fodder for private litigators, who were now ivy to industry behavior. Federal prosecutors would sometimes ac ve the same end by filing a complaint as soon as they had evidence nstead of rushing into an agreement with the target firm, essentiall elling a story to the public that had a kind of jurisprudential value ll its own—it put the truth out.

In another a roach, if the state wanted to fully clean house, it could work corpor e crime cases just like narcotics or racketeering cases, starting by charging small players and working their way up the chain. This had been the government's approach in the savings and loan crisis, when the state started with the littlest of fish and worked its way up to criminally charging whales like Charles Keating of Lincoln Savings and David Paul of CenTrust Savings Bank. "That's how they did it back then," says a New York City police investigator who has worked on major bank cases. "In the S&L thing, they started at the branch manager level and just rolled their way up."

Deferred prosecution agreements and nonprosecution agreements represent a third course. Companies pay fines and enter into nominally restrictive agreements, but they also frequently are allowed to settle without admitting wrongdoing, which essentially shields them from private litigation. If the Spitzer approach was aimed at changing the behavior and the S&L approach was aimed at sending a powerful political message, the NPA/DPA route represents a more collegial process in which the state and the targeted company work together to disgorge its criminal liability in a way that typically keeps everybody out of jail and also helps keep the target firm out of civil court. In many of these agreements, the evidence is kept mostly secret. These agreements sometimes have a less adversarial feel than the cops-and-robbers approaches of Spitzer, Robert Morgenthau, and the S&L prosecutors. They often read like agreements hashed out in friendly meetings by like-minded legal colleagues from similar cultural backgrounds, which is often exactly what they are.

It's important to note that this isn't always the case. The deferred prosecution agreement is sometimes a harsher strategy than, say, extracting a plea deal from a company. In a plea, the courts are in charge of monitoring compliance with the deal. In a DPA, it's the prosecutor—the person who really cared enough to go after the dirty company to begin with—who gets to be the watchdog of the deal.

But even the DPA began to fall out of favor, sort of, just as a fresh-faced politician from Illinois named Barack Obama was taking the national political scene by storm. After his election, state and federal prosecutors took their next great evolutionary step in the dispensation of white-collar justice. From abandoning criminal prosecutions in favor of deferred prosecutions and nonprosecution agreements, the state now began to emphasize fines as a new means of settling with white-collar criminals.

In 2008, when the state handed out twenty-five NPA/DPA deals, a grand total of $289 million in fines was collected. Over the course of the next three years, the number of nonprosecution agreements held mostly steady, but the amount of fines collected increased more than tenfold. In 2009 the state collected $5.312 billion in settlements. In 2010 it was $4.682 billion. In 2011 it was $3.013 billion.

By then, two things had happened. One is that America had exploded in the biggest white-collar crime wave in its history. The other is that Eric Holder had rejoined the Justice Department, this time as Barack Obama's attorney general.

Holder was in office for four long years before anyone at Justice said anything out loud about Collateral Consequences.

But even before the phrase hit the public's ears, a close observer of the situation could tell that the new regime was vigorously employing some kind of new policy—he or she may not have known it had anything to do with a memo written in 1999, but it was clear enough that something very different was going on.

As the biggest Wall Street companies screamed their way through one criminal scandal after another without facing corporate indictments or even criminal indictments against individuals, it was obvious that the nation's law enforcement officials had undergone some kind of radical transformation. Crime after heinous crime was being committed, and nobody was getting arrested.

There had to be a plan here, a conscious strategy. But what?

That plan ended up being Collateral Consequences. But it wasn't as though it was a conspiracy all along, a secret plan to give get-out-of-jail-free passes to the nation's biggest corporate offenders.

No, it was more like the Holder Justice Department got there by accident, through sheer incompetence, timorousness, and oversensitivity to bad press. It arrived, organically as it were, at a policy of utter regulatory surrender.

A key reason had to do with personnel. A crucial consequence of disasters like the Arthur Andersen and KPMG cases from the Bush years is that politicians more and more became sensitive to the idea that high-level corporate prosecutions can result in serious vote-losing public relations consequences, if they're bungled in spectacular enough fashion. Thus as the years passed, politicians more and more often appointed people who were essentially other politicians to jobs traditionally occupied by hard-core career-prosecutor types.

The transformation would be similar to the one that had gone on in the media in the 1990s and 2000s, when the press went from being the home of middle-class ascetic cranks who hated everyone and dressed like overcaffeinated Jesuits (always with food stains on their ties) to being a destination profession for young Ivy Leaguers who saw a journalism career as a gateway to high society.

The same process was now about to transform the federal law enforcement system, thanks in large part to new president Obama, who ushered in a herd of Ivy Leaguers and high-powered corporate defense lawyers to be his top crime-fighting officials. This new crowd of bookish lawyers was headlined by the Columbia University/Covington & Burling duo of Holder as attorney general and Lanny Breuer as head of Justice's Criminal Division, essentially the top crime-fighting job in the country.

This new crew, derided as "tourists" by two different ex–DOJ officials I spoke with, attacked their posts with the attitudes of corporate lawyers, stressing risk avoidance above all and insisting that senior-level officials have their fingers in the smallest of pies. Reports began to surface of senior DOJ officials micromanaging the cases of regional prosecutors from afar and instilling a general terror of screwing up among the ranks, leading to a general unwillingness to bring cases that had any chance of losing.

A few early episodes set the tone for the new administration. One involved a horrible tragedy that scarred the department for years.

The episode grew out of the trial of former Alaska senator Ted Stevens, who was accused of accepting more than $250,000 in gifts. Essentially Stevens, like every bent government official in every third-world country that ever existed, had induced private interests to build him a boffo house, getting the Alaska-based pipeline company, the VECO corporation, to build him a "splendid" retirement "chalet." Federal prosecutors went after Stevens and eventually convicted him on seven felony corruption counts in what was perceived as a big win-win inside the Obama White House, being as it was a victory in a major corruption case *and* a crushing blow to a long-loathed Republican Party stooge who for years had been an exacting gatekeeper to federal contracting largesse—Stevens had chaired the Senate Appropriations Committee for more than half a decade.

But even as the Stevens case was all but finished, it went sideways, and Obama administration officials had to wake up to the garish spectacle of the gnomish Stevens grinning and waving to the cameras, a free man, arms around his wife and children, and celebrating the new administration's incompetence in the pages of *The New York Times.*

Here's what happened. In the early 2000s, Senator Stevens had reportedly sent the CEO of VECO, Bill Allen, a formal letter asking for a bill for any goods and services his company had provided to Stevens in the construction and remodeling of the "chalet."

But in court, Allen—the state's chief cooperating witness—had testified that after receiving the letter, he had had a conversation with an emissary of Stevens named Bob Persons, who told him to ignore the senator's letter, because Stevens was just "covering his ass" in asking for the bills. This key testimony had been among the reasons Stevens got convicted.

But it later came out that there existed a series of FBI agents' notes, called 302 forms, showing that agents at one point had talked to Allen, and Allen had reportedly said he didn't remember that conversation with Persons.

This is pretty much the definition of exculpatory material. Had

Stevens's lawyers known about these notes, they would have been able to argue in court that the "covering his ass" conversation never happened. Whether the jury would have bought that story is another question, but the defense would have been able to argue it.

Six Justice officials, who became known as the Stevens Six, would eventually become subjects of an investigation for prosecutorial misconduct. On April 7, 2009, just months into the Obama presidency, the judge in the case, one Emmet Sullivan, wrathfully dismissed the charges against Stevens in what the *Times* described as a "lacerating" fourteen-minute speech. The judge, furious about a "troubling tendency" of prosecutors to stretch the boundaries of ethics in pursuit of a conviction, appointed a Washington lawyer named Henry F. Schuelke III to investigate the case.

The so-called Schuelke report would not come out for three more years, but when it did surface, it contained a startling tale. Obama's new appointees had inserted a young prosecutor named Brenda Morris as lead prosecutor in the Stevens case days before trial, infuriating the rank-and-file prosecutors in Alaska who had run the case since its inception.

Morris, Schuelke said, had reportedly provided the new administration with direct access to the case, developing a "direct reporting relationship" with then–acting attorney general Matt Friedrich and his senior deputy Rita Glavin, who was brought in by President Obama to run the Criminal Division during the transition period of his administration. Glavin, a career Justice official, was a favorite of the new administration and moved up after Obama's election until Holder's Covington & Burling buddy Breuer could secure the job full time.

In any case, Morris reportedly developed a relationship with Glavin and Friedrich during the Stevens case that cut a few links out of the usual chain of command, allowing the new administration to bypass line prosecutors and officials like Bill Welch, who ran the Public Integrity Section nominally in charge of the case. The Schuelke report ultimately pointed the finger squarely at the higher-ups and concluded that in their zeal to convict the Republican stooge Stevens, the new crew had botched the case. As Schuelke wrote:

> During a meeting with Mr. Friedrich, Ms. Glavin and Mr. Welch, Ms. Morris recommended, without prior consultation with Mr. Welch, that FBI 302s of witness interviews not be disclosed as Jencks Act (18 U.S.C. § 3500) material, a position contrary to Mr. Welch's preferred practice. Mr. Friedrich and Ms. Glavin endorsed Ms. Morris's recommendation and 302s were not disclosed to the defense until a week before trial. . . . In other words, the specially picked lead attorney who had been airlifted into the Stevens trial days before it began proposed not turning over the exculpatory notes, and the acting Attorney General and Acting Head of the Criminal Division agreed with the decision.

But Friedrich, Glavin, and Morris were not the officials who ultimately incurred the wrath of the Obama administration. Instead, not long after he arrived on the job, an enraged Lanny Breuer, furious about the bad press, went after other members of the Stevens Six like Ed Sullivan and Nicholas Marsh, both of whom were transferred to outback jobs in the Office of International Affairs.

"Siberia" is how one DOJ official put it.

Then in September 2010, in an incident that rocked the Justice Department, Marsh committed suicide ahead of the release of the Schuelke report. Marsh's attorney Robert Luskin, who insisted his client would have been exonerated, said Marsh had been grieving because he believed the report would prevent him from continuing to work as a prosecutor.

Curiously, Lanny Breuer issued the public statement on behalf of the department. "Our deepest sympathies go out to Nick and his family," he said.

In a fateful irony, the Schuelke report ultimately came to no con-clusion about Marsh, putting most of the weight on two lower-level Justice employees, despite concluding that senior officials had en-dorsed the plan not to turn over the 302s.

This episode would cast a pall over the entire Justice Department for years to come. Career Justice officials came away from the inci-dent not only worried that the higher-ups would meddle in the day-to-day prosecution of cases, but terrified that their bosses would not support them in the trenches. Things got so bad after this inci-dent, and the similarly dispiriting decision not to retry Senator Ste-vens, that Holder himself, in a move that one former DOJ official described as going over "like a fart in church," made a tour of all the bigwigs in the Justice Department and personally promised that he would have their backs in the future.

In any case, shortly after the Stevens case went sideways, Breuer announced a plan to revamp the Justice Department's Criminal Di-vision's Fraud Section, whose chief failing seems to have been that it had been created during the Bush administration. In fact, the Fraud Section had been productive during the Bush years, expanding its footprint in several areas that had been overlooked, from securities fraud to violations of the Foreign Corrupt Practices Act to corpo-rate accounting cases from the Enron era. Health care fraud prose-cutions had gone from basically nil—fraudsters stole from Medicare wantonly in the 1990s—to thriving, reportedly saving more than $7 billion.

But Breuer didn't want the program to continue in its current form. He told reporters in August 2009 that he was looking for a "superstar" or a "rock star" lawyer to lead "cases of extraordinary importance" in the Fraud Section.

Meanwhile, most of the players who had actually pushed white-collar cases to trial in the pre-Obama years were quietly phased out. Kirk Ogrosky, who had run the health care fraud division, left in April 2010. Deputy Chief Mark Mendelsohn, who had run Foreign Corrupt Practices Act cases, left that same year. Another deputy chief, Paul Pelletier, called the "heart and soul" of the Fraud Section by reporters at the DOJ watchdog site *Main Justice,* left in 2011. Fraud chief Steve Tyrrell left in early 2011 as well.

The "rock star" Breuer eventually hired to run the Fraud Section was Denis McInerney of the white-shoe defense firm Davis Polk, whose main claim to fame was—get this—defending Arthur Andersen in its obstruction-of-justice case. McInerney hadn't prosecuted a case in over fifteen years at the time of his hire. His headline experience as a prosecutor had been a racketeering trial against the head of an eye-care products company.

Eventually, the Criminal Division's Fraud Section would be entirely deemphasized in favor of a shiny new Obama-created institution called the Financial Fraud Enforcement Task Force, which was created around the same time that McInerney was hired.

Morale at the Justice Department plummeted after that, thanks to a series of strange decisions. For one thing, Holder decided not to retry Stevens, continuing a pattern of backing off big cases after setbacks. In another key case, Angelo Mozilo, the erstwhile head of Countrywide Financial and the living, spray-tanned symbol of corruption in the subprime markets, was quietly informed by the DOJ that he was not a target for criminal prosecution just four months after he settled with the SEC in a civil case for the relatively paltry sum of $67.5 million, much of which was paid by an insurance policy. Mozilo had earned nearly half a billion dollars pumping America full of fraudulent mortgages. The SEC had already released emails from Mozilo in which he denigrated his own subprime snake oil. "In all my years in the business, I have never seen a more toxic product," he wrote in one message. Mozilo was the perfect symbol of the mortgage scandal, and it was a bizarre decision to say the least for the government to let him know he was off the hook before the statute of limitations expired on his possible crimes.

The government similarly decided not to press forward with cases against a number of other prominent financial fraud targets. In early 2010 the DOJ decided to end the investigation of AIG Financial Products chief Joe Cassano, the patient zero of the financial crisis, whose half-trillion-dollar portfolio of unsecured credit default swaps imploded in 2008, forcing the government to bail out AIG and sending the world economy into a tailspin. Cases involving Ponzi scheme artists Bernie Madoff and Allen Stanford were restricted to a few defendants apiece, while banks and other institutions that aided their frauds got off clean. It would be years before the Obama administration would begin again to look at the role played in the Madoff scandal by JPMorgan Chase, Madoff's banker.

Meanwhile, after the first trial of baseball great Roger Clemens ended in a mistrial, the government pushed forward, keeping dozens of agents and lawyers on the case and deciding ultimately to retry the arch-villain, accused of lying about taking steroids. Ironically, Clemens had originally been represented by, of all people, Breuer, and some speculated that Lanny had decided to take a second whack at Clemens so as to avoid accusations of favoritism. Incredibly, the DOJ still ultimately lost the Clemens case, and it was the way they lost it that was most distressing. "There were two pieces of evidence in that case, the needle and the trainer, and it still took them ten weeks to put on the trial," groans one former federal prosecutor. "*And* they lost. That's the kind of thing that makes you hesitate before you try a credit-default-swaps case."

The key thing, the one thing that almost every current and former federal prosecutor who lived through this period talks about, is that in the early years of the Obama administration, a huge premium was placed on not losing. Breuer and Holder acted like the corporate stewards they were and gravitated toward a bottom-line strategy of prosecution. They became attracted to a cost-benefit-analysis vision of law enforcement, where the key questions weren't *Who did what?* and *What the hell should we do about it?* but *Will we win?* and *How badly will the press screw us if we lose?*

That, in turn, led to more and more resolutions arrived at under the Collateral Consequences theory, where not only did guilty companies not have to suffer the collateral risks of prosecution, but the Department of Justice itself avoided its own form of collateral damage in the form of bad press and political fallout.

Accepting high fines and/or deferred prosecutions with limited admissions of wrongdoing up front, instead of risking long battles with high-priced lawyers who could deal the department black eyes, seemed like a win-win.

The only problem was that the Justice officials who were employing this new doctrine, like a lot of overeducated people, were all just narrow-minded enough and just lacking enough in self-awareness to not quite see the consequences of the new math they were employing.

They thought they were employing an economy-saving doctrine of situational leniency, but they somehow failed to understand that by coming up with a calculus to determine who was big enough and important enough to command jurisprudential mercy, they were simultaneously making a calculation about who was small enough and unimportant enough *not* to qualify.

So it wasn't just about avoiding prosecutions of firms whose collapse could disrupt the world economy or cost lots of jobs and votes. It was also about avoiding prosecutions that could be politically embarrassing, costly in manpower and resources, or just plain difficult.

"Prosecutors have to be fighters," explains one former DOJ official. "You're gonna lose sometimes. But they never wanted to lose, ever."

The problem was, this failure of prosecutorial backbone took place during an epic crime wave. On the street, the incidence of crime had been falling almost everywhere. But in America's boardrooms, it was a different story. It was a very bad time for prosecutors to suddenly become afraid of the courtroom.

By Barack Obama's second term, it was clear to most rational observers of the financial sector that the crash of four years before hadn't been some kind of accidental market screw-up—not a "thousand-year flood," as some pundits first called it. Instead, it had been a widespread crisis of institutional policy. And a core part of this policy, it turned out, was crime.

Not mere technical violations, mind you, not just a thumb on a scale here and there, but crime, real crime, the kind of thing people once went to jail for. Specifically, this was a massive criminal fraud scheme, something akin to a giant counterfeiting operation, in which banks mass-produced extremely risky, low-quality subprime mortgages and with lightning-quick efficiency sold them off to institutional sucker-investors as highly rated AAA bonds. The hot potato game targeted unions, pension funds, and government-backed mortgage companies like Fannie Mae on the secondary market.

It was a modern take on the Rumpelstiltskin fairy tale. Big banks took great masses of straw (i.e., the risky home loans of the poor, undocumented, and unemployed) and spun it, factory style, into gold (i.e., AAA-rated securities). They used a technique called securitization that allowed banks and mortgage lenders to take vast pools of home loans belonging to underemployed janitors and immigrants and magically convert them into investments that were ostensibly as safe as Microsoft corporate bonds or the sovereign debt of Luxembourg, but more lucrative than either.

The sudden introduction of these magic mortgage bonds into the marketplace pushed most every major institutional investor in the world to suddenly become consumed with the desire to lend money to American home borrowers, even if they didn't know to whom exactly they were lending or how exactly these borrowers were qualifying for their home loans.

As a result of this lunatic process, houses in middle- and lower-income neighborhoods from Fresno to the Jersey Shore became jammed full of new home borrowers, millions and millions of them, who in many cases were not equal to the task of making their monthly payments. The situation was tenable so long as housing prices kept rising and these teeming new populations of home borrowers could keep their heads above water, selling or refinancing their way out of trouble if need be. But the instant the arrow began tilting downward, this rapidly expanding death-balloon of phony real estate value inevitably had to—and did—explode.

In other words, it was a Ponzi scheme, no different than the Bernie Madoff caper, only executed on an exponentially huger scale. The scheme depended upon the ability of a nexus of large financial companies to factory-produce and sell these magic home loans fast enough, and in big enough numbers, to continually keep more money coming in than going out.

Once the bubble burst, lawsuits were filed everywhere and whistle-blowers emerged by the dozen, showing, in graphic documentary detail, how nearly every major financial company in America had chosen to participate in this enormous fraud. It was the very definition of systemic corruption, but curiously, despite what looked like mountains of evidence, almost nobody with any connection to the crisis was even threatened with criminal prosecution.

For instance, court filings showed that Bank of America—a Covington & Burling client, remember—had teamed up with the unscrupulous, now-defunct mortgage lender Countrywide to sell more than a billion dollars' worth of questionable loans to Fannie and Freddie. They had done so through a special mortgage loan program that, unbelievably, was named "Hustle" in internal bank documents. Under "Hustle," Bank of America intentionally removed underwriters and compliance officers from the loan origination process, explicitly aiming to make sure that loans "moved forward, never backward."

Then there was Washington Mutual, which became part of JPMorgan Chase—another Covington & Burling client—after a taxpayer-subsidized shotgun merger in 2009. Once the sixth-largest bank in America, WaMu was selling $29 billion worth of subprime loans every year during the height of the crisis. After its collapse, investigators from the Senate's Permanent Subcommittee on Investigations uncovered evidence that the bank had conducted its own internal investigations into the mortgage markets as early as the mid-2000s, and had found fraud in as many as 83 percent of the loans produced by some of its own regional offices. Yet the bank did not alert regulators, did nothing to stop the fraud, and continued to sell billions in subprime for years.

Then there was Wells Fargo, yet another Covington & Burling client, which between 2002 and 2010 certified at least 6,320 home loans for federal backing, despite the fact that the bank itself, in its own internal assessments, had found that these loans were "seriously deficient."

Citigroup, another client of Holder's old firm, had done essentially the same thing, having "defrauded, falsified information or misled federal government entities" by falsely certifying thousands of loans for federal backing during the crisis years. It eventually paid $158 million in civil fines for this behavior, but nobody was ever charged or indicted for the crime.

Between 2005 and 2007, Goldman Sachs underwrote more than $11 billion of mortgages backed by the federal government and sold billions more in mortgage-backed products. When the bank's senior managers saw, in late 2007, that the great masses of mortgage products they were producing were toxic and destined to blow up to catastrophic effect, the bank not only didn't alert regulators but accelerated its efforts to sell off its dangerous products to hedge funds, other banks, and other unsuspecting customers as quickly as possible. "Let's be aggressive distributing things," said CFO David Viniar. "Are we doing enough to sell off cats and dogs?" countered CEO Lloyd Blankfein, referring to the loser mortgages on the bank's books.

Not just banks but everybody in the entire factory process was involved. When a longtime financial executive named Michael Winston joined Countrywide in the mid-2000s, he was startled one day to see a license plate belonging to one of the booming mortgage company's top executives that read "FUND 'EM." When Winston asked the executive what the plate meant, he was told that Countrywide's policy was to give loans to everyone.

"But what if the person has no job?" Winston asked.

"Fund 'em," the Countrywide executive laughed.

At the ratings agencies like Moody's and Fitch and Standard & Poor's, which performed the critical-to-the-fraud function of over-rating the toxic mortgage securities, high-ranking executives openly discussed in emails the corrupt corporate strategy of giving phony ratings in exchange for cash from the big banks. "Lord help our fucking scam," wrote one executive from Standard & Poor's. In an-other, one of the company's top analysts complained that the firm's model for rating mortgages was no more accurate than "flipping a coin."

The basic scheme—mass-producing and mismarking mortgages—was exacerbated by other major industrywide ethical failures. Many of these same firms, in their desperation to cut every conceivable cost en route to the creation of mortgages, knowingly engaged in mass perjury by creating whole departments of entry-level cubicle slaves devoted to "robo-signing"—read: inventing—chains of title and other key documents. In other cases, they hired outside compa-nies to do the dirty work for them.

In just one single locale, the clerk's office in Essex County, Mas-sachusetts, thirteen hundred different mortgage documents, in-cluding chains of title, were discovered to have been signed by a "Linda Green," although the signatures were written in twenty-two different styles. "Linda Green" worked for a company called DocX, which at the height of the boom was processing about half of all the foreclosure documents in the United States.

Similar piles of documents signed by corporate phantoms with names like "Crystal Moore" and "Bryan Bly" and "Jeffrey Stephan" were found by the hundreds and thousands in virtually every county courthouse in America.

Many of the same banks also engaged in mass tax evasion by unilaterally bypassing untold millions in local county registration fees, using instead a private electronic registry system called MERS that had been created by Wall Street—Countrywide founder Mozilo was the "inspiration" for the system's creation—specifically as a means to avoid paying legally mandated fees to local county clerks' offices for paper registrations. ("SAVE MONEY. REDUCE PAPER-

WORK," read a MERS brochure.) In the late 1990s, companies like Chase, Bank of America, Fannie, and Freddie had gone searching around for a legal opinion that would justify the creation of this electronic registry system.

The firm that ended up writing that opinion was, you guessed it, Covington & Burling. In 2004 the same firm reaffirmed the supposed legality of this tax-evasion-enabling registry system in yet another opinion letter, again on behalf of the great banks and mortgage companies that benefited directly from the shortcuts this system provided.

At the height of the crisis, this bank-created MERS system was in charge of maintaining the records for 67 million mortgages—and the entire company was staffed by just forty-five people.

Years later, as Holder and Breuer manned the two top jobs at Justice, and twenty-two other attorneys from the firm sat in key positions at the department, the nation experienced an unprecedented paperwork crisis in its court system, as literally millions of foreclosures were pushed into court by banks brandishing perjured and/or fraudulent paperwork. Many of the phony docs were MERS mortgages. The register of deeds in just one city, Salem, Massachusetts, sent Holder the paperwork for 31,897 fraudulent foreclosure documents and asked for a criminal investigation, because of the "pattern of fraud" they demonstrated.

Holder passed.

Most all of the companies involved with the mortgage fraud had one last thing in common: none of them reported any of their bad behavior to the government. "Wall Street's entire argument before the crisis had been that if crime happens, if fraud happens, we'll report it, that the markets would want to report it, purely out of self-preservation," says Spitzer. "But that's exactly what they didn't do."

Junk mortgages pushed through the courts using phony documents and sold off onto the markets using phony ratings, all as a matter of policy: almost every major player on Wall Street was involved, and many of these companies had left behind mountains of documentary records detailing their offenses. State and federal prosecutors all over the country, as well as federal investigators from Senate committees and special task forces like the Financial Crisis Inquiry Commission, found themselves awash in evidence.

Evidence of what, though? Lawyers on all sides of the issue to this day debate just exactly what kinds of criminal charges might have been filed against either companies or individuals for the offenses that caused the mortgage crisis. One can make arguments for charges of simple fraud ("A million cases a year" is how former banking regulator William Black famously estimated the level of criminal fraud during the bubble years), larceny, falsifying records, accounting fraud, embezzlement, tax evasion, and a number of other crimes. One former prosecutor I spoke to joked that he could have rolled any of a hundred different robo-signers all the way up to the CEO level. Others insist that the mortgage scandal was precisely the kind of difficult-to-prosecute, highly organized scam that the Racketeer Influenced and Corrupt Organizations (or RICO) laws were designed for.

In fact, there was one mortgage fraud case in which federal prosecutors did employ the RICO laws—but in an awesomely telling detail, the main target was a black street gangster named Darnell "D-Bell" Bell, who later pleaded guilty to ripping off banks and mortgage lenders by buying homes with no money down using straw buyers.

So the only time RICO was used to fight mortgage fraud was when the criminal was a black gang member and the victims were banks. (Ironically, nobody thought to wonder how it was possible for a Lincoln Park gang member to buy 222 houses with no money down. Heading into that particular rabbit hole would have led to the larger crime, but nobody did.)

At the national level, at the systemic level, government response was virtually nonexistent. The federal government pushed exactly one single criminal prosecution against individuals at a major bank for crimes related to the financial crisis, a fraud case involving two testosterone-jacked Bear Stearns hedge funders who had told investors in their subprime-laden fund that they were "comfortable with where they are" just days after one of them privately confided to his wife that "the subprime market is toast." That fund later imploded, helping cause the collapse of Bear Stearns, which in turn helped trigger the financial crisis. Despite a seeming abundance of damning emails and text messages, a jury acquitted, and the Justice Department never stepped to the plate again.

Why? From time to time, secondhand accounts leaked out that suggested that the absence of such prosecutions was part of a conscious strategy not just in the Justice Department but throughout the Obama administration. A book by Ron Suskind called *Confidence Men,* published two years into Obama's presidency, quoted then–treasury secretary Tim Geithner as saying that exposing the fraud would create financial panics. "The confidence in the system is so fragile still," he reportedly said. ". . . A disclosure of a fraud . . . could result in a run, just like Lehman."

A year or so later *The New York Times*'s star finance writer, Gretchen Morgenson, ran a piece suggesting that Geithner had in 2008 warned off then–New York attorney general Andrew Cuomo from pursuing "hard-charging" prosecutions. "[Geithner's] worry," according to Morgenson's sources, "sprang from a desire to calm markets, a goal that could be complicated by a hard-charging attorney general."

But as the years passed and the markets settled, the notion that the economy was too fragile to handle a prosecution began to seem increasingly absurd. Surely there was someone, some company or other that had helped cause the crisis, that could be targeted to send a message.

The question was, which one would you start with? Which offending megabank, lender, or ratings agency offered the best chance to score a high-profile symbolic prosecution? Who would be first on the dock?

The federal government never really stepped up to the plate. The job was left to the states, and even they could come up with only one target.

That target, it turned out, was Abacus Federal Savings Bank. There were a million ironies in the choice of this particular institution, but one of the most striking was that the case grew out of an incident that the bank itself had reported to the authorities. On December 11, 2009, Vera Sung, the forty-four-year-old daughter of the bank's founder and a former New York City prosecutor, was on the sixth floor of the Abacus offices. The tall, angular, attractive Chinese-American woman was out of the prosecuting game now and in private practice. On that day, she was representing her family business—Abacus—in a simple real estate closing. The deal involved a Chinese woman who had taken out a loan to buy a house in Brooklyn.

This Brooklyn deal had seemed routine, but at the end of the process, during the filling out of the so-called HUD-1 form summarizing all the closing charges, the borrower's lawyer hit her with an unusual question.

"The lawyer started telling me that the client was asking about the extra checks she'd written," Vera recalls.

The "extra checks" turned out to have been written at the behest of the loan officer in charge, Qibin "Ken" Yu, and seemed to be some kind of payment for fudging the income verification portion of the loan application. Mortified, Vera huddled up with her sister, Jill Sung, the general counsel for the bank. Both women realized right away that the "extra checks" were problematic, and they shut down the closing.

After the incident, the two women say they played everything by the book. Abacus hired a pair of fraud consultants, including a former prosecutor named Ann Vitale and a company called the Mercadien Group, to conduct external investigations of the firm. They also in short order contacted two key federal agencies, the Office of Thrift Supervision (a primary banking regulator that has since been wrapped into the Office of the Comptroller of the Currency) and Fannie Mae. Abacus had to tell Fannie Mae because the giant government-sponsored mortgage company was a primary purchaser of the mortgage loans Abacus created.

Both agencies investigated, and about a year after Vera first discovered the "extra checks" problem, in February 2011 to be exact, the OTS issued a lengthy order demanding that the bank overhaul its loan practices. Among other things, the regulator demanded that some other employees, who appeared to have been involved with Yu-like activities, be fired. A few others left on their own. Some of these individual employees, like Yu, became embroiled in local criminal investigations, which seemed entirely appropriate, even to the Sungs.

But as far as the company itself went, the OTS didn't recommend a fine. And though the federal regulator had the power to force the Sung family to sell the business, or demand wholesale changes to the executive management of Abacus Federal Savings, it did neither. The system seemed to work the way Wall Street and the financial community is always telling us things can work: companies self-report their ethical issues, then work together with regulators to correct problems while preserving viable, job-creating businesses going forward.

But it didn't work out that way. While the Sungs were trying to clean up their mess with the OTS and Fannie Mae, the original loan applicant, furious that she had not gotten her financing for the Brooklyn home and had lost her deposit, had reported the whole incident to the local police precinct in Chinatown.

That simple local police report became the genesis of Vance's investigation into Abacus. Thus despite the existence of a nationwide epidemic of fraud and white-collar crime that could have and should have been investigated by powerful federal regulators like the OCC, the OTS, the Federal Reserve, the SEC, the CFTC, and other bodies, the first and only prosecution of a bank to take place in America came out of a simple report filed in a common city police station.

Why Abacus? Why not, say, JPMorgan Chase? Jamie Dimon's megabank was caught up in dozens of scandals during the same period covered by the Abacus investigation—everything from money laundering to energy price manipulation to mismanaging customer funds to robo-signing to antitrust violations to charging excess overdraft fees to hiding billions of dollars of losses in the infamous "London Whale" episode, in which the bank hid the fact that one of its lunatic traders in Europe had nearly destroyed the firm by doubling and tripling down on exotic bets on corporate credit.

All told, in just the three years since Vera Sung stumbled into Ken Yu's real estate closing, Chase—again, a Covington & Burling client—had paid out more than $16 billion in regulatory settlements. The $16 billion represented an incredible 12 percent of its net revenue during that time period. This was before a $13 billion settlement in the fall of 2013, a deal that ate up about half of the bank's net for that year.

Yet throughout all this time, neither the bank nor any of its high-ranking employees were ever once criminally indicted. No Chase employee in any of those cases ever felt handcuffs on his wrists. In fact, Chase was not even forced to admit wrongdoing in most of these settlements.

This seemed to be Collateral Consequences in action, but no one could say for sure.

It was easier to be sure once Abacus was indicted. Two seemingly small details in the case are what seem to confirm the thesis.

First, Abacus was never offered a deferred prosecution agreement by the state. Vance's office took a hard line, apparently not willing to accept anything less than a plea to actual criminal charges. The reader is asked to remember this detail as he or she goes forward through the numerous tales of nonprosecution or deferred prosecution agreements that are yet to come in this book.

The second fact is that at the very moment Vance was marching his defendants into court on the day of the indictment, the FDIC and the OCC were in the Abacus offices, preparing to take action if the negative publicity resulted in a run on the bank.

"They were worried about a run," says Thomas Sung. "They knew something could happen."

This is significant because it says something about the government's willingness to conduct a prosecution that it knew might result in a bank failure, job losses, and/or other "collateral" damage.

Both state *and* federal authorities apparently had no problem taking that risk with little, politically unconnected Abacus.

A defender of the Justice Department in this instance will naturally protest that the Abacus case had nothing to do with Eric Holder, because Abacus was not prosecuted federally. But upon closer examination, Collateral Consequences showed loudly in this case.

Mainly, it showed in those "extraneous matters"—in the non-prosecution of every other bank in America that really was guilty of responsibility for the financial crisis. Those noncases certainly can be laid at the institutional feet of Holder's Justice Department.

And if Eric Holder's voice wasn't the direct inspiration, the spirit of Collateral Consequences certainly moved Cyrus Vance, who sent subpoenas to many Wall Street firms but chose to indict only a small, globally nonconsequential Chinatown bank.

Abacus isn't just the only bank in the entire country to face indictment since the financial crisis. It's also the first company that we know of that was officially deemed small enough to destroy. Too-big-to-fail, meet small-enough-to-jail.

The case of Abacus Federal Savings showed everyone the outlines of the now obvious, but still unofficial, selective-leniency doctrine. The absurdity of its application in the world of white-collar crime was clear enough. We were letting major systemic offenders walk, bypassing the opportunity for important symbolic prosecutions, and instead committing the limited resources of the nation's financial police to putting the smallest of small fry on the rack for negligible offenses.

But there was another major flaw in the new approach that nobody in charge had likely even bothered to consider.

It may have been unknown to the Ivy Leaguers like Holder and Tim Geithner who were crafting the new policy, or maybe they simply didn't care, but the Collateral Consequences idea had been dreamed up at a time when local police departments all over the country were instituting new statistics-based street policing strategies that functioned according to logic that was exactly opposite that of the Holder memo.

These were programs like the infamous CompStat system and other lesser-known outgrowths of the celebrated "broken windows" urban policing strategies, programs whose effectiveness depended upon massive numbers of low-level arrests for minor violations.

All over America, indigents or the merely poor were being hauled in in ridiculous numbers, often detained even if just for a short time, given tickets, and searched. These cast-a-wide-net street-policing strategies were ostensibly designed to snag illegal guns or serious criminals with outstanding warrants, but they didn't always work out that way. At exactly the time Holder was penning his famous memo in the late 1990s, the abjectly purposeless arrest was becoming more and more common, even as, perversely, the numbers of actual violent crimes committed had begun to drop precipitously.

And as every individual who's ever been charged with a crime knows, anyone facing criminal arrest can expect collateral consequences. A single drug charge can ruin a person's chances for obtaining a student loan or a government job. It can nix his or her chances of getting housing aid or a whole range of services—even innocent members of your family may lose access to government benefits. You can lose your right to vote and your access to financial aid. You can even have your children taken away.

But no police anywhere were officially asked to weigh the collateral consequences of arrests for prostitution, stealing cars, assault, selling weed, jumping turnstiles, even the simple offense of being homeless. There's no memo in the Justice Department that wonders aloud what happens to the families of those sorts of arrestees. Instead, the new trend in policing is and has been to aggressively no longer care about any of it.

Indeed, it looked very much like someone was trying to implement Collateral Consequences in a vacuum. Well-heeled lawyers seemed to be working to make the traumatic consequences of arrest obsolete for the clients of other well-heeled lawyers, all the while pretending, or maybe asserting, that this could be done without considering the rapidly expanding role of the police and the criminal court system in the lives of ordinary people.

Whether they knew about it or cared about it, that's what the new policy was turning out to be: For the small subset of offenders who are guilty of truly systemic, transformative, organized crime, for offenders to whom losing a big case could be politically embarrassing, let's carefully consider the collateral consequences of criminal prosecution. But for everybody else, let's ignore them more than ever before.

The architects of Collateral Consequences seemingly didn't realize they were starting a revolution. They were accelerating a government-sponsored sorting of the entire population into arrestable and nonarrestable classes.

CHAPTER 2

FRISK AND STOP

Sometime just after midnight on August 9, 2012, Tory Marone staggered across the West Side Highway in Manhattan toward the Hudson River. Smallish, white, with scruffy red hair and a red goatee, the twenty-six-year-old jammed his hands in the pockets of his sweatshirt and headed toward a pier, looking for a place to sleep it off.

Tory was drunk and high, which wasn't unusual. What was unusual was not having a place to sleep. Tory was usually halfway homeless. When he didn't have his own place or when his mother out in Long Island wasn't letting him in, he'd move from here to there, crashing at one friend's house for a few days, then moving on to another friend's house, then maybe staying with his dad, a career drug dealer. Or he'd sell enough drugs himself to get a hotel room for a few days. Officially he lived nowhere, but he always had a roof over his head. That's what it meant to be halfway homeless, and he'd been living that way for as long as he could remember.

But now it was 2012 and both his parents were dead. His mother was dead—he said it was of cancer. Her being sick was why the state had taken his two little sisters away back when he was eighteen and put them in foster homes. He hadn't seen or heard from either of them since. That was eight years ago.

What Tory remembered about his father was that he mostly sold weed, but he'd hustle whatever he could get his hands on. Tory's dad got sent upstate for four years on a dope-dealing charge when Tory was four years old, and then went back upstate for two years when Tory was ten. For later busts he did time in the city, at Rikers Island for instance, but those were shorter sentences, a year or less. According to Tory, he had died under mysterious circumstances—Tory hinted that he had been murdered—about a year before.

So in the summer of 2012 Tory was suddenly no longer halfway homeless, he was for-real homeless. So far it wasn't so bad, except when it rained. One of the first things he learned about being for-real homeless is that if you get wet, you stay wet. And sometimes it was hard to find a place where you could sleep without being kicked, spat on, hassled. That was one of the things on his mind right now. He was wasted, and he had a really bad headache that just wouldn't go away. He needed to just lie down in peace somewhere.

One of the places he'd discovered where he could sleep without too much trouble was a little grassed-over park across from Twenty-Fourth Street—right near Chelsea Piers, where during the day the yuppies hit golf balls toward New Jersey at an outdoor range and played pickup basketball on fancy indoor courts. During the night it's quiet and green and there are a few benches near some trees. He crossed the highway and collapsed onto one of them. There was no one else around. He rubbed his head, then folded his arms and went to sleep.

Knock knock knock!

It was a few hours later. He woke up with a start.

"Come on, asshole, get up," he heard a voice saying, and there was a flashlight in his face. "Let's go, get up!"

Only one thing in the world sounds like that: police.

He was still out of it, but he got up, as quickly as he could. He couldn't tell what time it was, except that it was still dark. The policeman's paperwork would later say it was 4:49 a.m.

Tory hadn't been homeless for long, but he already knew the deal. The sign at the edge of the pier said PARK CLOSES AT 1 A.M., and Tory knew he couldn't be there, but he also knew how to act when he got rousted. Why would he argue with a police? What's he going to do—win? He knew what he was supposed to do here.

"Okay," said Tory, rubbing his eyes. "I'm getting up. Just let me walk out of the park. I'm going, I know."

The police didn't say anything to him. There were two of them, he could see, one big and one not so big—apart from that, he was still too messed up to distinguish much.

Tory asked again, "Can I go? I'll walk out of the park. I'm not arguing, I'll go right now."

"Just shut up," he was told.

That's when he saw that one of the two officers was writing in a pad.

Tory sobered up immediately. He wasn't educated, but he knew this math cold: a cop writing something meant he was about to be handed a summons, which in turn meant a court appearance and then jail if he couldn't pay the two-hundred-dollar fine or whatever it was, which he probably couldn't. Or, more likely—he knew himself—he'd skip the court appearance, then it'd be a bench warrant, turning him into a fugitive.

He thought, *Why all this hassle? I'm offering to walk out of the park. Why write me a ticket you know I can't pay? I'm offering to leave.*

Tory lost his cool.

"You're writing me a ticket?" he protested. "What the fuck?"

One of the police reached over to grab Tory. "Come on," the officer said. "Let's go."

"Go fuck yourself!" Tory shouted. He still couldn't believe they were writing him up. Even as a corrupt way to make money, it made no sense. Tory didn't have any money. If anything, they were losing on the deal—they'd end up having to feed him in jail. Plus, all the paperwork, and he knew how police hated paperwork. The street math of it didn't work out for Tory. The not understanding started to make him panic.

Both officers grabbed Tory, who started to struggle. He screamed and swore as they dragged him off to a squad car. On the way into the car, he kicked a tire. In the three-count misdemeanor affidavit written up later on—Tory got charged with resisting, disorderly conduct, and loitering in city parks—Officer Marcus Rollins filed the following report:

> Deponent further states that when he was placing the defendant under arrest for the offense described above, defendant refused to hold his arms out and repeatedly pulled away from deponent in an attempt to prevent deponent from placing handcuffs on deponent's wrists, and shouted in substance: I HATE COPS. YOU'RE ALL PIGS. I HATE ALL OF YOU. YOU FAT MOTHERFUCKER.

They drove Tory away, threw him in jail for the night, then released him on his own recognizance, giving him a court date for a month or so later to answer the misdemeanor charges.

A month later Tory missed the court date.

The city issued a bench warrant.

Four months passed. Tory, now officially a fugitive, got better at being homeless, although the cold weather was starting to be a problem. He hung out mostly in Brooklyn and Lower Manhattan, although occasionally he would make his way out to Long Island. From time to time he saw his younger brother, his only real family, who had a job just south of Twenty-Third Street in Manhattan. One night in December, after seeing his brother at work, Tory was walking the streets. He was high again, maybe a little drunk, too. He crossed Eighth Avenue at around Twenty-First Street and once again got stopped by the police.

This time he hadn't even had a chance to commit a crime yet; this time he was just walking around looking homeless and stoned. They stopped him, asked him for ID, searched him, no probable cause other than that he looked dirty and high. Classic use of New York's stop-and-frisk program, with Tory being white the only thing weird about it.

In his pockets the police found half a joint, and there's a funny thing about that. Way back in 1977, New York City decriminalized the possession of small amounts of marijuana, the law being that if you had less than 25 grams on you and smoked your weed in private, the police weren't supposed to arrest you.

But then in the 1990s the city began implementing this stop-and-frisk program, where police could stop and search just about anyone for any reason. And stop-and-frisk provided the city police with a magic spell they could use to circumvent the lax marijuana law.

In 2011, the year before Tory got arrested, another year when exactly nobody on Wall Street was arrested for crimes connected to the financial crisis, New York City police stopped and searched a record 684,724 people. Out of those, 88 percent were black or Hispanic. The ostensible justification for the program is looking for guns, but they find guns in less than 0.02 percent of stops. More often, they make people empty their pockets and find nothing at all. Or sometimes, like in Tory's case, you get your pockets emptied and suddenly you're standing there on the corner of Eighth Avenue and Twenty-First Street with half a joint sitting in your open hand.

Now that's not "private use" anymore. Now you're "knowingly or unlawfully possessing marijuana and such is burning or open in public view." Now you've got a chargeable offense and your arresting officer gets to make his summons pad one sheet thinner. Patrol cops in most precincts had to empty one pad a month, it turns out, part of their precinct-ordered "productivity goals," or at least so say some sources.

The point is, Tory Marone went from privately having a joint in his pocket to publicly waving it around on Twenty-First Street with the help of one of New York's finest, and he went off to jail once again.

A few days later he was being arraigned in the borough's misdemeanor court, not far from the same sprawling Manhattan courthouse where TV-world actor Sam Waterston had expertly played a tough-talking prosecutor-with-a-heart-of-gold on *Law & Order*. The judge set bail at $1,500 on the resisting and $1,000 on the marijuana, but he might as well have said a million—Tory didn't have a dollar.

The bail was probably that high because Tory had nineteen prior misdemeanor arrests, most all of them of similar character, although there were no felonies on his sheet.

A few days later the judge made it official and whacked his gavel, sentencing him to do his bid on Rikers Island, one of the most vicious and dangerous places in America. Once home to a thousand slashings and stabbings a year in the 1980s, there are still dozens of inmate-on-inmate crimes a month. Rumors of guard-sponsored "fight clubs" pitting inmates against each other have plagued the place for years.

I would meet Tory there a few days later. Officially, his sentence was for waving a joint around on Twenty-First Street and missing a court appearance. Unofficially, the explanation was a little bit different.

"Basically, he mouthed off to a cop," explains a city public defender.

That, and he was a repeat offender. But then, not all repeat offenders are created equal.

At more or less exactly the same time that Tory Marone was being offered his deal to spend forty days at Rikers for half a joint that was all-the-way hidden in his pocket, the U.S. Department of Justice, in the person of still–assistant attorney general Lanny Breuer—Holder's right-hand man, the head of the department's Criminal Division, and ostensibly still the top crime-fighting official in the country—was making a historic announcement. The announcement took place just a stone's throw from where Tory was waiting in jail, just across the East River, in Brooklyn.

Along with the head of the Justice Department's Eastern District of New York office, Loretta Lynch, Breuer called a press conference to formally announce that the United States had decided to levy a record fine against the Hong Kong and Shanghai Banking Corporation, better known as HSBC, a pillar of British finance and the largest bank in Europe. The bank, which had a major U.S. subsidiary called HBUS, had been charged with committing an astonishing list of crimes—a laundry list that included pretty much every kind of crime a bank can possibly be charged with.

The bank admitted to laundering billions of dollars for drug cartels in Mexico and Colombia, washing money for terrorist-connected organizations in the Middle East, allowing rogue states under formal sanctions by the U.S. government to move money freely by the tens of billions through its American subsidiary, letting Russian mobsters wash money on a grand scale using a see-no-evil traveler's checks program, and helping tax cheats and other crooks from Miami to Los Angeles to Peru hide hundreds of millions of dollars in nearly anonymous "bearer share" accounts.

Essentially, HSBC, as perhaps the biggest and most accessible "reputable" bank in Asia, Africa, Central America, and the Middle East, had enthusiastically opened its vaults, including its American vaults, for most every kind of antisocial and/or criminal organization on the planet, allowing mass murderers, human traffickers, and embezzlers unfettered access to the safety and comfort of U.S. dollars.

"You go down the list, they violated every goddamn law in the book," says former Senate investigator Jack Blum, whose pursuit of Lockheed in a bribery case led to the passage of the Foreign Corrupt Practices Act. "They took in every imaginable form of illegal and illicit business."

So what was the penalty for laundering up to $7 billion for Central American drug cartels? For allowing Russian "used car dealers" to deposit $500,000 a day for years in U.S. banks using traveler's checks? For supplying the Al Rajhi Bank of Saudi Arabia, whose founder was revealed after 9/11 to have been one of the original twenty benefactors to al-Qaeda, with more than 1 billion U.S.

dollars—a bank HSBC's own compliance officers recommended abandoning after it was caught supplying Chechen extremists with traveler's checks in 2005, but which it continued to do business with through 2010? For allowing 25,000 U.S. banking transactions totaling $19.4 billion with the sanctioned state of Iran over a six-year period, and allowing similar transactions from prohibited locales like North Korea and the Sudan?

Breuer couldn't wait to tell the world the answer to that question. He flashed a prideful smile as the press settled to hear the announcement.

As a partner at Covington & Burling, Breuer had become well known in the legal community for representing rich, high-profile targets of congressional investigations—his clients ranged from Halliburton to Yahoo! to the aforementioned Roger Clemens.

Congressional aides to this day joke about Breuer, who was often the liaison between targets of congressional investigations and the young House and Senate aides who were crawling up his clients' backsides. "The guy would call you up late at night and leave messages, and he'd talk in this really slow, whiny voice," says one former House aide. "He'd be like, 'Hi, this is *Len-n-n-ny*, we've, uh, got that document you were asking for.'"

The aide nicknamed Breuer "Jon Lovitz" because of his voice and "the overall impression that the guy was a pussy," as he put it. When Breuer was appointed in Obama's first term to head the Department of Justice's Criminal Division, staffers on the Hill were shocked.

"This is a corporate flack who was such a zero, you had twenty-five-year-olds in Congress who wouldn't return his phone calls," recalls one. "And suddenly we all look up, and he's head of the Criminal Division of the Justice Department. We're all like, 'How did that happen?'"

So Breuer was now on the other side of the aisle, no longer defending a recent target of a Senate inquiry, but prosecuting one. HSBC earlier that summer had been raked over the coals by the notoriously uncompromising Permanent Subcommittee on Investigations, led by irascible Michigan Democrat Carl Levin.

Incidentally, Levin's committee, which had no prosecutorial power, had on multiple occasions since the financial crisis tried to jump-start criminal indictments or regulatory actions by undertaking long investigations that agencies like the SEC, the OCC, and the Justice Department seemed reluctant to do themselves.

When the FBI was out chasing Roger Clemens for perjury, Levin's crew was making a case in a lengthy report that Lloyd Blankfein and other Goldman officials had lied to Congress. When the SEC and the OCC and the CFTC were slow to go after the banks, derivative dealers, and home lenders responsible for the sweeping fraud in the mortgage crisis, Levin's committee gathered evidence against firms like Washington Mutual, Deutsche Bank, and others.

But the Senate had no power to actually do anything other than shine a light. It had done so again in the HSBC case, and now, apparently, the Justice Department was actually going to follow up for once. But how?

Breuer paused before beginning his remarks. He opened with a few niceties and introductions, then got right to the point.

"HSBC is being held accountable for stunning failures of oversight—and worse—that led the bank to permit narcotics traffickers and others to launder hundreds of millions of dollars through HSBC subsidiaries," Breuer told the waiting press. "The record of dysfunction that prevailed at HSBC for many years was astonishing. Today, HSBC is paying a heavy price for its conduct, and, under the terms of today's agreement, if the bank fails to comply with the agreement in any way, we . . ."

Reporters looked at each other. We *what*?

"We reserve the right to fully prosecute it," Breuer went on.

Stunned silence fell over the room. Did they just hear him right? What exactly was the penalty he was announcing?

Nothing. In terms of jail time, anyway, the penalty was nothing. No individual would be charged with anything or have to pay a dollar in fines. No person in any of HSBC's banks anywhere in the world had to have so much as a ticket on his record.

The only penalty was a settlement. It was a big fine: $1.9 billion, at the time the biggest such fine in history—which sounds impressive until you realize the sum equaled about five weeks of revenue for a bank that earned somewhere north of $22 billion a year. Oh, and HSBC had to partially—not fully but partially—defer some of its bonus payments to top executives.

And it had to apologize, which it did. "We are profoundly sorry," said CEO Stuart Gulliver.

The cops had let HSBC walk out of the park.

In accepting the HSBC settlement terms, Lanny Breuer was still thinking like a defense lawyer. The sheer size of the sum he'd just extracted from the giant Euro bank clearly impressed him in a positive way, in his new role as assistant attorney general, in the same way a number that same size would likely have negatively impressed him all the way to an aneurysm, had it been dropped on him in a defense capacity.

But it was just money. It was a big number, but it didn't mean anything to any actual human beings. It didn't come out of any individual's pocket at the bank. In terms of individual punishment, it was still actually a smaller sentence than Tory Marone's forty days at Rikers.

Nonetheless, at the press conference that day, you could see it on his face: *One point nine billion dollars—I negotiated a hell of a deal!*

And when the questions started shooting his way from the press, he seemed to be saying: What do you want from me? This is probably as much money as we were going to get.

"I don't think the banks got off easy," he said, adding, "We've held them very much accountable. I'm not sure you can find a more robust resolution."

But Breuer was standing less than a mile from a homeless drifter who at that very minute was getting a "more robust solution" for having half a joint in his pocket.

For aiding and abetting drug cartels suspected in more than twenty thousand murders, groups famous for creating the world's most gruesome torture videos—the Sinaloa Cartel in particular, with its style of high-volume reprisal killings and public chainsaw-ings and disembowelings, makes al-Qaeda look like the Peace Corps—HSBC got a walk. Tory Marone, for smoking their product and passing out on a park bench, got sent to jail.

This meant the very lowest kind of offender in the illegal drug business, the retail consumer at the very bottom of the drug food chain, had received a far stiffer sentence than officials at HSBC who were hundreds of millions of dollars deep into the illegal drug busi-ness, not for any excusable reason but just to seek profits to pile on top of profits.

With a few exceptions, the press had mostly been quiet in the years of nonprosecutions that followed the 2008 crash. But the HSBC settlement was met with almost universal outrage, with a dash of genuine wonder mixed in. "What's a bank got to do to get into some real trouble around here?" wrote *Forbes* magazine, add-ing, "The 'I'll never do it again' defense has probably never worked in a courtroom, but it was a good-enough promise for U.S. regula-tors in the case of HSBC's money laundering activity . . . let's just call the world's biggest, most systemically important financial firms what they are: Immune."

"It is a dark day for the rule of law," wrote *The New York Times*, in an unusually pointed editorial. ". . . Clearly, the government has bought into the notion that too big to fail is too big to jail."

Even high-ranking former prosecutors were appalled. "The mes-sage this is sending is if you want to engage in money laundering, make sure you're doing it within the context of your employment at a bank," former assistant attorney general Jimmy Gurulé said. "And don't go small. Do it on a very large scale, and you won't get prose-cuted."

"It's essentially telling the executives in these institutions crime pays," said Neil Barofsky.

But for all the criticism, and despite Breuer's odd performance at the HSBC presser, the actual policy that had guided the decision was still semidisguised. It would not be formally unveiled until a week later, at the next outrageous settlement, this one involving the Swiss banking giant UBS for its part in a worldwide price-fixing scandal known as the LIBOR affair.

The presser announcing this extraordinary nonprosecution came just five days before Christmas 2012, and it hit an amazing new low in the annals of public groveling before a rich and powerful company.

Involving thousands of transactions, hundreds of individuals, and somewhere between nine and sixteen of the world's biggest banks, the LIBOR affair at the heart of the UBS settlement was, numerically speaking, probably the biggest financial scandal ever. At the time, it was both the biggest antitrust case and the biggest price-fixing case ever to surface (some serious competitors have since reared their heads). By working together to rig global interest rates through their manipulation of the London Interbank Offered Rate—a projection of the rate at which banks charge one another to borrow and lend money—banks like UBS, Barclays, the Royal Bank of Scotland, and perhaps as many as six other companies (according to British regulators) impacted the price of hundreds of trillions of dollars of financial products, everything from mortgages to credit cards to municipal bonds to swaps and even currencies.

British and American regulators had UBS officers cold. They had them, in writing, baldly offering bribes to rig rates. "I will fucking do one humongous deal with you," begged one trader who wanted a UBS buddy to fix the rate. "I'll pay, you know, $50,000 dollars, $100,000 dollars."

The anger and resentment of federal investigators toward greedy corporate criminals who inexplicably stole money when they were already rich—the anger that bled through in scenes like the Adelphia perp walk in the early Bush years—that was a thing of the past.

The new attitude toward the white-collar criminal was perfectly exemplified by Breuer at the December 20 press conference in New York announcing the UBS deal. The head of the enforcement division bowed and scraped before UBS at the presser, all but apologizing for bringing any action at all against the Swiss company.

In fact, there seemed almost to be a concern that Breuer would not be able to handle the public groveling job all by himself. The Justice Department therefore brought extra firepower to the announcement, as Eric Holder himself was in attendance. Breuer had the floor to start, but before long, Holder would have to step in.

The HSBC settlement had been a deferred prosecution agreement, putting the bank under a kind of probation for five years. UBS was even worse—a nonprosecution agreement. British and American officials identified forty individuals, including eleven managers, who participated in the historic rate rigging and at least seven more senior executives who knew what was going on. They also found that "certain UBS managers and senior managers" in the bank's Group Treasury, which oversees finances for the entire company worldwide, had repeatedly told subordinates to "err on the low side" in setting interest rates, a practice that caused the market's view of UBS's health to be systematically overinflated.

For this incredibly serious crime, which had consequences for nearly every person in the world who has money or buys or sells anything, and which makes the shenanigans at Abacus Federal Savings Bank seem like kindergarteners whispering during naptime, the UBS parent company completely escaped prosecution. Its Japanese subsidiary was allowed to plead to a single felony count, while two former UBS employees were charged with crimes. But the parent company was affirmatively nonprosecuted and let off with a $1.5 billion fine. The bank didn't have to admit to anything in the deal, except the need to pay the government money to go away.

After the travesty of the HSBC settlement, reporters at the UBS presser were actually hostile from the start. They were all over Breuer the instant he opened the floor for questions. The first thing he was asked was why there was no indictment. Breuer sighed at the question.

"There are many factors," Breuer said. ". . . Looking at the severity of the conduct, looking at the collateral consequences, we think we arrived at a very robust, very real, and very appropriate resolution."

There was that word "robust" again. Another reporter wanted to know why UBS got off scot-free, given that it was a repeat offender that only a few years ago had been whacked in a major tax evasion case.

"This bank was previously—I mean, you had brought a case with regard to their behavior on tax evasion in 2009," the reporter asked. "This is a bank that has broken the law before. So why not be tougher?"

Breuer shrugged and delivered the first of many extraordinary quotes that would come out of his mouth that day.

"I don't know what tougher means," he said.

Reporters kept pressing him: Why couldn't he be tougher?

"Our goal here," he said finally, "is not to destroy a major financial institution."

How would a criminal plea do that?

"I'm not saying that," Breuer said.

Well, then, what are you saying?

"In deciding how you're going to pursue an institution," Breuer said, "you have to at least evaluate whether or not innocent people might lose jobs or there might be some sort of a collateral event."

What collateral event? What the hell are you talking about?

"It's not so much that we were worried about any one thing," Breuer went on. "We're trying to figure out what was the appropriate resolution."

The crowd of reporters was getting restless by now—Breuer was losing control. At this point, Holder tagged Breuer out of the ring, smoothed his tie, and stepped to the lectern.

Thirteen years after authoring his Collateral Consequences memo, Holder was finally going to explain it, out in the open, to the entire world.

"I'm not talking about just this case, but in others that we have resolved, the impact on the stability of the financial markets around the world is something that we take into consideration," Holder began.

The room was suddenly very quiet.

"We reach out to experts outside of the Justice Department to talk about what are the consequences of actions that we might take," Holder explained, "[and] what would be the impact of those actions if we wanted to make a particular prosecutive [*sic*] decision or determination with regard to a particular institution."

The crowd of reporters listened in stunned silence to this speech.

"So that," Holder concluded, "factors into the kinds of decisions that we make."

The attorney general of the United States had just admitted, in front of a room full of reporters, that he asks Wall Street for advice before he prosecutes Wall Street.

Holder then went on and, finally, pointed all the way back to 1999.

"It started back when I was the deputy attorney general. It was called the Holder memo then. It's gone through a number of iterations since then. . . . I think we have to understand, though, what has happened today is that UBS—UBS has been charged criminally. Now, we can parse that if we want to."

But UBS itself had not been charged criminally. Only UBS Japan had been. Apparently that was what he meant by "parsing."

Moreover, Breuer's and Holder's comments together suggested a significant expansion of the ideas in the original Holder memo. While the 1999 paper was restricted to a discussion of when it might be appropriate to avoid filing criminal charges against a systemically important company, the policy now seemed to have expanded to include individuals at those companies.

This was a radical departure. In a way, the original Holder memo had some sense to it. Unless a company was corrupt through and through, it did seem reasonable to try to avoid destroying it and to protect the jobs of innocent employees if possible. This was certainly an appropriate area to think about using prosecutorial discretion.

But what Breuer and Holder were saying at the UBS presser made no sense at all. How would arresting executives for serious crimes affect "innocent victims"? It wasn't as though hauling away a few dozen rate fixers at UBS, or a few especially guilty money launderers at HSBC, would lead to the destruction of those firms.

These were massive companies, massively capitalized, and they had regulators in a dozen countries ready to help them through any transition that would be necessary.

Collateral Consequences was out of the bag. After years and years of mysterious nonprosecutions and expertly negotiated cost-of-doing-business fines, we finally had the policy it all led to.

And once it was out, it seemed that the Justice Department was anxious to make sure that the public understood that it was no slip of the tongue. After HSBC and UBS, both Breuer and Holder took Collateral Consequences on a kind of public relations tour, beginning with an episode of PBS's *Frontline* that aired a few weeks after the UBS settlement, in January 2013.

In that show, Breuer gave a detailed interview on the subject. "In any given case, I think I and prosecutors around the country, being responsible, should speak to regulators, should speak to experts," he said. "Because if I bring a case against institution A, and as a result of bringing that case there's some huge economic effect . . . if it creates a ripple effect so that suddenly counterparties and other financial institutions or other companies that had nothing to do with this are affected badly, it's a factor we need to know and understand."

Breuer was here repeating Holder's mantra that before moving against an industry target, the Justice Department essentially had to ask industry experts for advice. He was also now expanding the possible collateral consequences to include a "ripple effect" that would impact the whole economy, including innocent victims not just within the target firm, but perhaps also in other firms as well. *If we press charges,* in other words, *we just don't know what might happen—to everybody!* We were now officially in the realm of an Edward Lorenz "butterfly effect" theory of crime fighting: a single indictment might be felt all the way around the world, and forever.

This interview startled even the most hardened observers of politics in Washington. Two U.S. senators, Republican Chuck Grassley of Iowa and Ohio Democrat Sherrod Brown, were so appalled that they sent Holder a letter demanding an explanation for Breuer's *Frontline* interview.

It didn't take long for them to get their answer. In early March 2013, Holder appeared before the U.S. Senate and trotted out Collateral Consequences formally, adding that the sheer size of the companies in this postcrisis, too-big-to-fail environment essentially tied his hands.

Grassley told Holder he couldn't recall any high-profile prosecutions that led to "any high-profile financial criminal convictions in either companies or individuals," and he asked Holder to explain.

Notably, Holder pulled out Collateral Consequences as an answer to this question about not just companies but individuals. "I am concerned that the size of some of these institutions becomes so large," he said, "that it does become difficult for us to prosecute them."

Holder during this Senate hearing did not mention that he had come up with this idea fourteen years earlier, long before too-big-to-fail was even imaginable.

He went on. The problem comes, he said, "when we are hit with indications that if you do prosecute, if you do bring a criminal charge, it will have a negative impact on the national economy, perhaps even the world economy."

This was a variation on Breuer's "butterfly effect" interview. We just don't know what will happen if we press charges, so . . . let's not. It was a stunning series of admissions. Even *Barron's* was appalled. "The nation's chief law-enforcement official admitted the decision to prosecute depends not on the law, but the impact on the financial markets," wrote columnist Randall Forsyth.

Breuer, meanwhile, was in the process of moving back to private practice. That same month, he returned to Covington & Burling, which in an extraordinary coincidence was already representing Citigroup in a major class-action lawsuit filed over LIBOR rigging. His firm was one of a group of defense firms that argued that the suit should be dismissed on the grounds that the setting of rates was not really a competitive process, and that while municipalities and states and pension funds and other entities that lost money when LIBOR rates were artificially depressed may have been *defrauded,* they weren't victims of antitrust violations. "The plaintiffs, I believe, are confusing a claim of being perhaps deceived," a defense lawyer from another firm argued, "with a claim for harm to competition."

The judge in the case bought this bold and ballsy argument, and the main civil LIBOR suit was dismissed, meaning that while British and American regulators had taken in upward of $4 billion in fines, the actual victims of the manipulation would likely get nothing.

But Holder's testimony had at least ended the mystery. It was obvious now that the once-modest selective-leniency idea that he had cooked up in 1999 had grown exponentially and was now loosed from its cage, running wild in American society like a strung-out lab animal, wrecking things and mutating by the minute. It had gone from a simple tool to save a few jobs to a magical thing that was enabling the transformation of the world's biggest banks into bona fide organized crime operations, companies that had now gone far beyond shredding a few documents and were engaged in everything from rigging energy prices to manipulating interest rates to drug trafficking.

Privately, there was a furious debate in Washington and on Wall Street about the efficacy of the new policy. Many people made the very sensible argument that it would indeed be economic suicide to indict and perhaps destroy such systemically important companies as UBS and HSBC, and that such actions would devastate the world economy in ways that indicting, say, Abacus Federal Savings Bank had not.

But this argument didn't make sense with regard to individuals, and if you thought about it, it didn't make sense with regard to companies, either. "You can't just say, 'We can't indict because they're too big' and then just throw up your hands," says Barofsky. "If a bank's size is the only thing preventing you from indicting, making the bank smaller should be a condition of the settlement, so it doesn't happen again. If you've got them by the short hairs, you've got to make them break up."

This, ultimately, is the obvious flaw in the "systemic importance" argument. The Justice Department could rationally make that argument exactly once. If it let an HSBC or UBS skate on systemic importance grounds, but then allowed that same company to retain its dangerously outsize systemic importance, it would simply be inviting more violations. Minus any effort to make the companies safer for prosecution, Collateral Consequences appeared far more likely to be what some line prosecutors believed it to be—an excuse that allowed incompetent and lazy officials with a defense-lawyer mindset to avoid difficult contested trials and simply take cash up front and declare victory for the cameras.

None of the settlements proposed anything like breaking up the companies, or even hinted at a thwarted desire to bring white-collar offenders to trial. Instead, the new public relations strategy seemed to be to try to pass off these financial settlements as the best-case scenario for justice in a complex new world.

The attorney general of the United States was saying that the economy had grown so complicated that his own office was now and henceforth helpless to decide on its own when it was okay to prosecute, that before it moved against any high-powered target, it needed to ask the "experts" on Wall Street if the economy would survive such an action.

Of course, it wasn't like that on the streets anymore. On the streets, more than ever, they arrested first, asked questions later.

On December 14, 2011—almost exactly one year before the HSBC settlement was announced—two black men in their forties, lifetime friends named Michael McMichael and Anthony Odom, made the mistake of driving a nice-looking white Range Rover in the South Bronx.

The two guys were ex-cons who had been in the game decades ago, in their youth in Brooklyn, but had now gone straight. "You get tired," says Anthony, a seventies-cool dude in pitch-black shades and a Walt Frazier cap. He had just taken a test to work in the MTA.

His buddy Michael sported a shaved head, gold-rimmed glasses, careful grooming, and a single long chain with a cross around his neck. He looked like a city preacher, the kind of retired tough guy who could conduct a Scared Straight seminar.

The two men were driving from a Dunkin' Donuts on 163rd Street to a BP gas station on 161st Street and Washington when they stopped at a red light. Suddenly a pair of policemen appeared at each door. The police promptly pulled the two men out of their car and tossed them into a van that had driven up behind them, appearing out of nowhere.

Before they even had a chance to breathe, Michael and Anthony had their hands behind their backs, cuffed to the walls of the van, headed for God knows where, for who knew what reason. "What the hell . . . ?" they asked each other.

Did the police say anything about why they'd been picked up? Did they ask them questions, tell them what they were being charged with?

"You clearly don't know the New York City police," says Anthony. "They don't be asking you anything."

The van screamed all over the Bronx, and the two men, who hadn't been in a police car in ages, worried quietly as they listened to the chatter on the radio. They worked out the method: an undercover policeman on the ground somewhere would stand on a street corner, wander over to a group of people, then walk off and whisper into his jacket, "These four."

They later found out the undercover cop is called a "ghost." When the ghost says the word, backup arrives, and whoever the ghost points to gets chucked into the van. After an hour or so, the van was starting to fill up. The cops and their ghosts were scooping up dope fiends and tossing them into the back of the truck. Other times, the ghost picked out suspects on the street, and the police in the backup crew snatched the wrong people—for instance, they grabbed a woman, when the ghost had been directing them toward a group of men.

"They weren't even getting the right people," says Anthony. "They were just getting bodies."

Nor were they bothering to search their detainees before they raced off to the next body snatching. In the second or third hour, Anthony, his hands starting to ache badly, looked down and saw something amazing. One of the fiends the cops had grabbed was wriggling his hands around in his cuffs, trying to pull his works out of a secret pocket in his jeans. The dude was trying to *shoot heroin* in the back of a police van, with his hands cuffed!

Anthony wriggled sideways, but he had nowhere to go. "I'm like, what if this guy sticks me? What do I do?"

Michael was watching that scene in horror but also still listening to the radio. When there were about four or five bodies in the van, he heard the ghost's voice come over the radio. "He's like, 'We need three more.'"

Michael cocked his head and thought: *They've got a quota?*

As Michael told his story, something clicked in my head. A few weeks before I met Michael, a public defender had told me, with a smile, to go take a ride on the M35 bus from East Harlem to Ward's Island. Didn't completely explain what it was about, just told me to take a ride.

So I took the ride, which began on East 125th Street, across the street from a Jamaican chicken place. I hopped on, stuck in my MetroCard, then rode to the last stop, where I found myself in a dismal expanse of institutional buildings, one of which was a drug rehab clinic, another a mental hospital, the third a homeless shelter. I wandered over to the rehab center and talked to two guys in the program named Domingo Soto and Frankie Rivera who were doing chores, taking the trash out.

"Yeah, man, the UCs hit the bus about twice a week, looking for fare beaters," said Soto. "The rule is, every cop has to bring home a body."

"A body?" I asked.

"Yeah," he said. "If you got four cops, they gotta bring home four bodies. There's a van hiding somewhere. If they only get two fare beaters, they stick 'em in the van, handcuff 'em, then go out searching for the other two."

"They send undercover police out to bust homeless fare jumpers?" I asked. "To bust homeless fare jumpers on their way to a homeless shelter?"

I thought the whole point was to get them to the shelter.

"Uh-huh," Rivera said. "Twice a week, they sweeping that bus. It's a shame, too, because you be losing that bed in the shelter when they take you in."

So I told this story to Michael, the man who got arrested for being black and driving a Range Rover in the South Bronx. He wiped his bald head and thought. "Yeah, come to think of it," he said, "there were about eight people involved in that operation. And they got eight of us."

He went on. After riding in the van all day, the two men were dragged back to the Forty-Second Precinct in the Bronx and sent to the precinct cells. Arms free, the dope fiends started shooting up for real now.

"I couldn't believe it," said Michael. "I was actually embarrassed for the cops, for their professionalism. Right there in the cells, they were shooting *her-on*."

At the precinct they found out, finally, that they were being charged with suspicion of possession of marijuana. That's the way it would show up in their complaint, that an officer smelled the drug somehow from a distance.

"It's winter," Michael explained. "We got the windows rolled up, and they're smelling marijuana from outside the car somewhere. From across the street, I guess."

They soon got released on their own recognizance, but with a case still on their heads. For the next year, they kept asking the police to produce the supposed marijuana. They offered to pay for a DNA test if any kind of drug was recovered. The police never did produce the elusive joint, but as time went on, the DA started offering the two men deals.

"They're like, 'Just plead and pay a twenty-five-dollar fine,'" says Michael.

"Then it was community service," says Anthony. "They're like, 'Just take two hours of community service.' Then, when we said no, they were like, 'Why won't you take it? It's just two hours.'"

Michael and Anthony, like Tory Marone, had been caught up in a new kind of law enforcement technique. The basic principle in both cases is volume arresting. It's fishing for crime with dynamite. In bad neighborhoods, in immigrant neighborhoods, in parks and alleys, you arrest first, ask questions later.

In Michael and Anthony's case, the police undertook their own kind of cost-benefit analysis. If you toss a nice-looking truck with two black men in it, you have a good chance of catching a gun, drugs, or a fugitive on a warrant. Bring 'em all in, shake the net, see what wriggles.

"They're fishing with a big net," says Michael. "And they were catching some people, too," he added, referring to the dope dealers and users.

Of course, if you police neighborhoods that way, you're going to get some innocent people, too. But the system doesn't work in reverse. It doesn't admit error; that would look bad. So what it does is it moves cases forward anyway, even when there's nothing there.

It took a full year for the city to drop the charges against both men, and that was only after the state begged, practically on its knees, for both men to accept some kind of guilty plea. Only when they refused for the umpteenth time, and the city finally admitted that it had no case, was the matter dropped.

In the course of that year, Anthony lost out on the MTA job. The drug arrest had rendered him ineligible. It was a classic instance of a collateral consequence, but this was the acceptable kind. Some black guy from the Bronx losing a job, what's that compared to the principle of keeping a serially offending British money launderer and admitted ally of the world's most vicious drug cartel in business?

"Who cares about me?" says Anthony. "They don't care. Obviously."

After the New Year in January 2013, I took the F train across Manhattan to Queens, hopped on the Q100 bus at Queensbridge, and rode to Rikers Island. When you get to Rikers, there's a long line of people, almost all of them black or Hispanic, most of them young, most female. They're bringing packages of socks and underwear, money for the commissary, things for their sons and grandsons and boyfriends.

At the front gate you take all your valuables and put them in a locker, then you go through the metal detectors and get to a parody of an airport terminal—a bunch of beat-to-hell waiting gates covered in pen scratches and graffiti, where visitors are gathered to wait for the buses that will take them to the dorms. On this side of the Divide, everything takes forever, and long lines are part of everyday life.

After I found the gate I was looking for, and got two left-hand fingerprints scanned while I registered for a visit, a young black woman saw me checking a clock and laughed.

"It's gonna be four hours, honey," she said.

"Four hours total, or four hours from now?" I asked. It had already taken an hour and a half to get inside the building.

"Four hours from now," she said. "Maybe three."

I shrugged and waited. She was wrong, fortunately—the shuttle came pretty quick, a blue-and-white-painted school bus into which the driver hustled us, telling us that the Eric M. Taylor Center, or EMTC, was the second stop. We got out there, walked to a grim one-story building entrance that looked like an abandoned ice station in Alaska, or maybe a Soviet drunk tank. At the door a corrections officer stopped us and trained our attention on a wall full of Polaroid photos of young and mostly Hispanic men with their heads and necks split open. In one picture I could swear you could see a sliver of larynx. The idea was to impress upon us what happens when you bring in contraband and inmates fight over it.

The officer barked at us, "You bring contraband in here, you're not going home. You bring in money past that line"—he pointed to a doorway two feet in front of me—"or any kind of ID, it's a felony. One to three years. You're not going home today, you got that?"

I emptied my pockets into another locker, took off my hat and sweatshirt and belt, walked inside, then went through a half strip search conducted by a female officer who made me pull my pants halfway down, a search seemingly intended to be humiliating without being terribly effective. Then it was lots of time in a waiting room watching a too-loud broadcast of an asinine show called *Judge Alex* that you couldn't turn off, in which a no-necked, steroidal TV judge referees idiotic family disputes between mostly black and mostly obese defendants, dressing them down with big words and high volume when they get out of line. The room full of black women watched the program carefully, almost spitefully—there was nothing else to do.

Eventually they brought us into the visiting room. It's a gymnasium, a basketball court, only with a series of cheap little round tables laid out in rows, each one with two beat-up plastic patio chairs facing each other. Wordlessly, the guards began bringing in the inmates. A long line of young black and Hispanic men in gray jumpsuits filed in, each one taking a place opposite his girl or mom or kids. I was the only male visitor in the place.

Finally they brought in Tory. His jumpsuit was a different color—lime green. He started my way, and they made him stop and hand over a rosary necklace first. He walked with his shoulders hunched over, his face expressionless. As a journalist, I was searching for some kind of story from him about how scary it was inside, but he'd been practicing the I'm-not-scared look his whole life. He wasn't bad at it.

I asked him about the green jumpsuit.

"Got caught with contraband," he said. "They found money on me. This marks me as having fucked up."

They gave him seven more days for that, bringing the total to forty-seven. He shrugged: no big deal. One thing he did complain about was the food. "If you don't get food from the commissary, it's not enough," he said. "You get hungry." Apart from that, it wasn't so bad. He wasn't going to be there long enough to get a job, so all he could do was wait out the days, watch TV, walk in the yard.

He didn't even ask me what I was doing there, why I was visiting him, who I was. So I had to bring it up myself. Not expecting him to care, I told him that I'd found him at random, by looking for someone in New York who'd been sentenced to jail time for a stupid drug charge at exactly the moment the government was announcing, in New York, that it wasn't going to seek jail sentences for anyone in the biggest drug-money-laundering case in history.

He nodded. "Okay. So they arrest someone like me instead, is that it? That's what your book is about?"

"Basically," I said.

He nodded again and instantly forgot what we were talking about. "I'm never coming back here, though, I promise you that," he said, apparently thinking he had to lay the same line on me all prisoners reflexively lay on authority figures. "I'm getting a job when I get out. I've got it set up."

"Okay," I said.

We moved on to some other stuff, then a few minutes later he came back to the topic of his arrest. "I'll tell you one thing I do know," he said. "It's not about what you do. It's about who you are. Like I know, if I'm in Manhattan, I go to the Upper East Side, I go to Eighty-First Street, I'm getting arrested."

Tory Marone is one of the few white people you'll see in New York who looks like an obvious candidate for stop-and-frisk. He looks rough enough that someone might call the police if, say, he walked into a Hugo Boss store. As I would later find out, though, the definition of "appropriate target for police harassment" is expanding.

Anyway, Tory scratched his head, looking confused. "It's just— I don't know, I'm like a magnet for cops."

———

Why do we put people in jail? We understand the concept instinc-tively, generally, but most people don't know the actual legal justifi-cation. I didn't know it.

"Why do we put people in jail?" asked Neil Barofsky, the former prosecutor and TARP inspector. "That's the question?"

"Right," I said. "What do they teach in law school?"

"Well," he said, "there's general deterrence, individual deterrence, and justice for victims."

General deterrence is all about sending a message to the whole community of possible offenders. Individual deterrence is to send a message to the individual caught. And justice for victims speaks for itself.

Financial crimes of the HSBC-UBS type cry out for jail terms on all three counts. Both deterrence angles are very compelling, be-cause it's a community of offenders that would likely be powerfully deterred by jail, if they thought it was a real possibility.

And when you're talking about crimes that affect so many peo-ple, the justice-for-victims aspect screams for jail, as few of these settlements came close to fully compensating victims for their losses. (In some of them, like the LIBOR settlements, there was no compensation at all for victims.)

But these no-jail financial settlements, in which the money doesn't come out of any individuals' pockets, while they may do a lot for enforcement budgets, are virtually the only solution the state could come up with that doesn't provide any real deterrent to indi-viduals at all. Take, for instance, the Goldman Sachs Abacus settle-ment (as opposed to Chinatown's Abacus Bank, a different case), in which the bank paid $550 million. A lot of money, but far less than the bank's annual profits. Goldman even after that settlement could just think of itself as having received a $16.5 billion bailout from the state, instead of the $17 billion it actually got just through the AIG rescue.

In a case like that, where the fine is insignificant compared to the company's revenue, the settlement is almost an antideterrent. It just helps set the price for getting caught, and it makes the cost-benefit analysis for criminal behavior simpler.

Even if you think the settlements are rational, they ignore the flip side. The flip side is where the excuses that prosecutors almost always give about the sweetheart settlements with banks like HSBC (that they're the best deals the state can get, that evidence is hard to gather, that they may very well have lost had they prosecuted, etc.) fall apart.

The problem isn't just that prosecutors make these deals. More to the point, it's that they're not ashamed of them. And they don't act like they need to be.

The street criminal is hated, despised. It's understood that sending him anywhere but to jail is grounds for public outrage. You'll never see a local prosecutor call a press conference and pat himself on the back for letting a car thief or a mugger of old ladies off with a fine. Any local DA who made a deal like that for any reason, even a good one, would generally have enough sense to stay indoors and cancel the presser.

But that's not what we're seeing with these white-collar cases. The government has not only made soft-touch, no-jail deals with criminal offenders repeatedly, but its officers have then tried to argue with straight faces that they're good deals. There's no attempt to explain or apologize for an enforcement failure. Nobody ever publicly complains about the difficulty of gathering evidence.

In the HSBC case, for instance, the Department of Justice boasted about what a "robust" settlement it had achieved. It gushed in its press release about the unprecedented amount of money seized. Nowhere did it indicate any regret or apology to the public that no individual would have to face any penalty for what prosecutors themselves were describing as an "astonishing" record of dysfunction and "stunning" failures of oversight. Indeed, everybody seemed pleased as punch with the result.

But even though nobody from the government ever says anything out loud about a lack of evidence being the real reason nobody from these companies goes to jail, we're all—including reporters who cover this stuff—still supposed to accept that as the *real* explanation. It's a particular feature of modern American government officials, particularly Democratic Party types, that they often expect the press and the public to give them credit for their unspoken excuses. They'll vote yea on the Iraq war and the Patriot Act and nay for a public option or an end to torture or a bill to break up the banks. Then they'll cozy up to you privately and whisper that of course they're with you in spirit on those issues, but politically it just wasn't possible to vote that way. And then they start giving you their reasons.

And let's be fair, on this issue, there are plenty of reasons. It's true, regulators don't have the resources to fight armies of high-priced lawyers who get paid by the minute to gum things up and beat cases back by attrition. And when your little team of government lawyers tries to beat back all the furious foot-high motions flowing from the Davis Polks and Covington & Burlings of the world, you often find yourself arguing before judges appointed by politicians who were elected with big-business money, jurists who in the best-case scenario will play it right down the line but even then will make you earn every yard on your way to the end zone. And then at trial, you might find out that some reputable firm like Ernst & Young or even, perhaps, an actual federal regulator knew about and okayed your target's conduct all along and did so on paper. This is something you don't often have to worry about with a Lincoln Park gangster— a permission slip to deal coke from the local precinct captain.

The law isn't supposed to be about unspoken excuses and behind-the-scenes calculations. The beauty of the system is that judges and juries are allowed to consider only what is seen and heard in open court. In between the white lines of this arena, it's all supposed to make sense. This is where we all get to be equal again. In the defendant's chair, rich and poor ride the same roller coaster, face the same music. Case has to match case. Sentence should match sentence.

But they don't match anymore. They probably never did, and probably it was never even close. But at least there was the illusion of it. What's happened now, in this new era of settlements and nonprosecutions, is that the state has formally surrendered to its own excuses. It has decided just to punt from the start and take the money, which doesn't become really wrong until it turns around the next day and decides to double down on the less-defended, flooring it all the way to trial against a welfare mom or some joker who sold a brick of dope in the projects. Repeat the same process a few million times, and that's how the jails in America get the population they have. Even if every single person they sent to jail were guilty, the system would still be an epic fail—it's the jurisprudential version of *Pravda*, where the facts in the paper might have all been true on any given day, but the lie was all in what was not said.

That's what nobody gets, that the two approaches to justice may individually make a kind of sense, but side by side they're a dystopia, where common city courts become factories for turning poor people into prisoners, while federal prosecutors on the white-collar beat turn into overpriced garbage men, who behind closed doors quietly dispose of the sins of the rich for a fee. And it's evolved this way over time and for a thousand reasons, so that almost nobody is aware of the whole picture, the two worlds so separate that they're barely visible to each other. The usual political descriptors like "unfairness" and "injustice" don't really apply. It's more like a breakdown into madness.

CHAPTER 3

THE MAN WHO COULDN'T STAND UP

He laughs about it now, but when Andrew Brown was a little kid growing up in the projects of Brooklyn's Bedford-Stuyvesant neighborhood—one of the roughest neighborhoods in America—he wanted to be a cop.

"I'm serious, I wanted to be police," he says. "I used to watch police shows on TV, and I thought it was real cool."

Asked what shows he watched, he smiles. "I used to watch *CHiPs,*" he says. "And *Kojak.* All of that."

It didn't turn out that way. It went another way entirely. The thing is, Andrew has a past. He doesn't deny it, he owns it. It's part of what makes his story as crazy as it is. He started off on the wrong side of the law, then spent most of his adult life clawing his way back to the right side of it, just to get to the point where he could walk down the street with his head up.

And then, as soon as he got there . . . but better to let him tell the story.

"I was born in 1977, Long Island College Hospital, Brooklyn,

New York," he says. "My mother was Arsenia Brown, 'Arsenia' like Arsenio Hall, but with an 'a.' I have five sisters, three on my mother's side, then two from my father."

What about his father?

"I've been avoiding that question for a long time," he says. "My birth certificate didn't have my father's name on it. A lot of fathers do that, because they don't want to be on the child support."

Still, now thirty-five, a little shorter in stature but with the powerful build of an NFL fullback, Andrew still speaks fondly of his father. His dad was around in the Bed-Stuy projects when Andrew was growing up, and he still plays a role in Andrew's life. But he never lived with Andrew and his mother.

Andrew's first home was in the Tompkins projects. "Four eighty-six Willoughby Avenue, that was our first place," he says. It's a grim little stretch of brick buildings built in the shadow of the elevated M subway line, dead in the center of Brooklyn, far from any museums or amusement parks or any other place white New York might visit. The absolute last place on your list of New York tourist destinations, perhaps, but one of the most heavily policed areas in the country. "A red zone" is how Andrew puts it.

Thirty-five years later Andrew lives two avenues over from Willoughby, in an apartment on Myrtle Avenue. Except for the years he would spend in jail, he's spent his whole life in this small stretch of project buildings. In thirty-five years, he traveled three blocks, but that trip was longer than it sounds.

Two families lived in that Willoughby apartment, one belonging to his mother, and the other to her sister, Andrew's aunt. "It was me, my two sisters, my cousin, his little brother, my aunt, and her son's father," Andrew says. "Oh, and my grandfather, Theodore Brown."

Andrew never got along with his aunt, a strict Jehovah's Witness who wasn't shy about disciplining her wild nephew. His grandfather was another story—Andrew loved his grandfather. He remembers one time his aunt was chasing after him to let him have it and he ran into his grandfather's room and hid under the bed. "He let me hide there," he remembers. "He was cool."

By 1986 Andrew's aunt and her kids had moved out and gotten their own place. Andrew's mother, Arsenia, was beginning to have problems. Just nine years old, Andrew would come home and see his mother sitting on a couch, nodding out, trying to stay awake. He didn't understand anything about drugs at the time and didn't know what was going on. One day his cousin—that would be his aunt's son—came over and told Andrew to bring his sisters over to his aunt's house around the block.

"I thought it would just be for the afternoon," he says. "It was for three years." His aunt took custody of him and his sisters while his mother struggled to get clean.

This was in 1986. New York in the 1980s was one of the angriest, most racially divided places in the world. This was the time of subway shooter Bernie Goetz, the Howard Beach massacre, and the Central Park jogger case. It was a time when blacks protesting the beating of four teenagers by a mob of young whites in the Brooklyn neighborhood of Bensonhurst could be met by a crowd that, unfazed by TV cameras, waved watermelons at them and chanted, "Niggers go home!" The city was a war zone, a tinderbox of race hatred ready to blow at any time.

Andrew wasn't aware of any of that at the time. When he first had to move out of his mother's house, he was just a regular nine-year-old kid—the kids in the neighborhood called him "Cookie Ears" because he liked to eat chocolate chip cookies and he had little ears. He went to school and spent a lot of his time home listening to records like Kurtis Blow's *America* on his cousin's record player. "If I Ruled the World" was his favorite track. He listened to the dreamy rap-fantasy classic over and over again, closing his eyes, imagining being other places. *If I ruled the world, was king on the throne / I'd make peace in every culture, build the homeless a home.* He remembers his cousin used to get angry because he'd ruin the needles on the record player, trying to scratch like the MCs.

In 1989 Andrew's mother got clean, and he was able to go home. But things weren't the same. After years of friction with his aunt, who Andrew suspected only wanted custody because it boosted the size of her welfare check, Andrew was turning angry. He started to get in fights and have other problems. Then in 1991 old Theodore Brown had a stroke and died right there in the apartment, in his bed. Andrew remembers he was given his grandfather's room, the first time he'd ever gotten his own room, but the old man dying messed him up. "I didn't even want the room," he says.

It was after that when he started getting into real trouble. Police caught him and some friends smashing an abandoned car in a parking lot, picked him up, and brought him back to his mother's door. "They still did that back then," he says now, wistfully. "I mean they'd just bring you home to your mother, instead of processing you."

Another time police saw him with a cap gun, mistook it for a real gun, and drew their own guns on him, telling him to drop the weapon. He dropped the weapon. Again, they brought him back to his mother, who was beside herself, as she was every time he got into trouble.

She'd call Andrew's father, who'd come over and straighten him out, but he always ended up back in trouble again. "I was starting to be in the streets," he says, selling drugs, stealing. An older guy in the neighborhood taught him about stealing jewelry, taught him how to set people up, take their chains and rings. You could take the jewelry to a pawnshop, but sometimes it wasn't even about the money. "Sometimes you just wore it," he says.

Nobody was calling him Cookie Ears anymore. Some of his friends caught him messing around one day with a pair of glasses, aiming them like they were a gun. The glasses were Liz Claiborne glasses, had a big "LC" logo on them. So people started to call him "LC." He started to play around with the name, like it meant different things: "Loose Cannon" maybe, or "LoCo." Or sometimes he'd be "Little Cookies."

By 1992 Arsenia was beginning to deal with serious health issues. She was a diabetic and had a bad heart, and she was going crazy over Andrew's problems. It all came to a head early that year, during a school vacation. Arsenia was literally trying to keep Andrew from going outside; she didn't want him in the streets and hanging out with the wrong people.

Too sick to handle the growing boy herself, she asked Andrew's sister Tanja to keep him in the apartment one night. Andrew made a scene and forced his way outside. His mother warned him that if he left, she'd lock him out. Andrew said fine, you do that. Out of spite, he stayed out all night.

The next morning he came home and found his mother had been taken away to the hospital. She had literally been sick with worry. Andrew was devastated. He cried, made up with her. "I promised I would never get in trouble again," he says now, adding that he really believes he meant it when he said it. But it didn't last long. He got arrested one more time that fall, a robbery case that went to family court and got dismissed. Then, in May 1992, Andrew was arrested in a more serious case, an assault that grew out of an incident in which he and a bunch of neighborhood kids were joyriding in the elevator of a local high-rise project and got into an altercation with one of the residents.

Andrew ultimately pleaded to a lesser offense in that case and got out with time served, but before he did, he spent the whole summer of 1992 in Spofford Juvenile Detention Center in the Bronx, a jail for minors that would eventually be condemned and shut down by the city in 2011 after generations of complaints about its filth and brutality. In July 1992 he learned in a telephone call that his mother had been hospitalized again. She was, he was told, very seriously ill. Andrew to this day wonders if his arrest that summer played a role in her final illness.

A few months later, in December 1992, Arsenia died. Andrew was actually selling crack when he heard the news. "There was a scrap metal yard near where I lived, and all the workers there were addicts," he says. "I was standing there when my stepfather came and found me."

It took most of the next ten years for Andrew to get over that series of events—his guilt over what happened, the feeling that he'd put his mother in the hospital, the memory of being on the streets selling drugs when she died. But also the anger about the juvenile charge he took in the elevator assault case, an incident he guessed would end his life before it even began.

After his mother died, Andrew went off the grid. He stopped going to his probation meetings, stopped going to school. The housing police came to take him away from his mother's apartment, took him and his sisters to a youth home in the Bronx.

Andrew walked out of the waiting room of the youth home and never came back. The next six to seven years of his life were a blur of guns, arrests, jail time, pointless violence.

Andrew spent most of the early 1990s on a tour of the correctional facilities of New York State, everywhere from youth prisons like Spofford and Harlem Valley Secure Center to Rikers Island, to the Ulster Correctional Facility, to prisons in Catskill and Coxsackie. At each stop, he fought constantly. Ask him about Rikers, his first adult jail, and he'll tell you he got bashed over the head with a scrub brush practically the moment he entered the facility and then had to fight fifteen or twenty times before he found a way to do his time. "It was at least that many before I got relaxed and I was just waiting to go home," he says. He got out of Rikers in 1996 and was free for exactly thirty-four days before he got busted again on a weapons charge and went back inside. He fought so much at his next jail, in Ulster County, that they moved him to Greene County, where he got involved in a stabbing and got moved to Coxsackie, where at one point he served 365 consecutive days in the hole, supposedly for a verbal threat.

When Andrew talks now about his mentality in those days, he shakes his head. "I was in a no-caring zone," he says. "I had so much guilt over everything, my mother. . . . I was just waiting for someone to put me out of my misery."

When he finally got out of jail on that charge, he didn't know what to do with himself. His father sat him down and tried to talk him out of the life.

"He said, 'What if it was me who got robbed in the streets? How would you feel?'" Andrew took that talk hard, and he says he never robbed anyone again. But what else was there? He'd tried a few times to get a job, but it never felt real. One time he remembers working at a sporting goods store in his teens. "I think I cleaned a bathroom," he says. "And a guy gave me a pair of sneakers."

The idea of getting a job still wasn't serious to him. Plus, Andrew by now had a master's degree in the streets. He'd been fighting pretty much constantly for almost a decade. It was a hard thing to turn off. And he still had ties to the neighborhood. When he got out of jail, his old mentor was still there, only now he was older, and heavier, and Andrew didn't think he was so tough anymore. There was a public showdown, and Andrew told off his old mentor in front of the whole projects. The way Andrew tells it, the man was so shocked at being pushed around by his former followers that he ran off and holed up to get drunk somewhere, apparently to get his courage up. Then he came back to the spot on the street where Andrew was selling drugs, pulled out a gun, and fired.

The bullet went through Andrew's right arm. Andrew fell down, then staggered to a friend's house, where his friend's mother called an ambulance. When Andrew woke up in a hospital bed, *he* was under arrest, ostensibly for having a gun—the friend's mother would later testify that police pressured her to say Andrew had hidden a gun in her house, threatening to arrest her and take her kids away. Andrew was acquitted of the charge.

The man who shot him wasn't so lucky. "I think he's got like two hundred fifty years now," says Andrew, shaking his head sadly. A lot of the people he grew up with have long sentences now, seven years, fifteen years, twenty. He knows that could have been him. He also knows he could have ended up dead or, worse, killed somebody else during this time in his life. "I consider myself lucky, that I got it straightened out in time," he says.

Looking back, Andrew doesn't even remember there ever being anything real at stake in any of that violence and craziness. "There was all this testosterone, that's all it was ever about," he says. "You'd be getting in fights, people would be getting shot over nothing, and the crazy thing is, it was never about no money. Like you'd look at someone the wrong way, or someone would bump into someone, and people would be getting shot over that."

When his arm healed, and he made it through the gun case without being convicted, Andrew began to look at the world differently. He realized he had to change his life. He was twenty-three years old.

Right around the time Andrew was shot, just as he was starting on the road back to a normal life, the city of New York was itself making a profound change in course, radically altering its policing policies. It was more than a minor strategic change, it was a revolutionary turnaround. But the amazing thing is, nobody noticed, at least not at first.

Years later a City University of New York professor named Harry Levine would be poring through New York City arrest statistics for drug offenses when he would notice something fascinating. Interested in seeing what the impact had been since the city decriminalized the possession of small amounts of marijuana in 1977, Levine was shocked when he looked at the numbers for simple possession arrests.

"From 1978 to 1988, about three thousand possession arrests a year," he said. "From 1988 to 1998, about three thousand possession arrests a year. But then, from 1998 to 2008, it jumps to thirty thousand possession arrests per year."

What happened in 1997 and 1998? What changed?

Levine pauses. "Howard Safir," he says.

Who?

"Exactly," he says, laughing. "You haven't heard of him. I call him the colorless, odorless, tasteless Howard Safir. He was Rudy Giuliani's second police commissioner. The first was Bill Bratton—Mr. Broken Windows."

Rolled out in 1994 by Bratton and the newly elected Mayor Giuliani, who had made "zero tolerance" the platform of his crime strategy, the much-celebrated broken windows policing strategy purported to control serious crime by getting police to focus on minor crimes like fare beating, jaywalking, littering, and loitering.

The theory, and it's not completely illogical, is that increased contact with the police leads to criminals deciding more and more often to leave their guns at home, lest they be swept up for jumping a turnstile or tossing a cigarette butt on the street.

Marijuana arrests went up under Bratton, but they didn't skyrocket. That didn't happen until Bratton made the fatal mistake of becoming more of a national celebrity than the notoriously attention-hungry Rudy Giuliani. "Bratton made the cover of *Time*," laughs Levine, referring to the January 15, 1996, issue that came with the headline "Finally, We're Winning the War Against Crime." Bratton, smiling a little, posed for the cover dressed with flair in a Bogartesque trench coat while standing on a dark, misty, conspicuously empty New York City street.

"He didn't sneer and snarl, and he wasn't a complete and total unbelievable asshole, and everyone could see that," says Levine, referring to Bratton. "So naturally, Rudy got rid of him."

The *Time* cover came in January; by April 1996, Giuliani had replaced Bratton with Safir, a nondescript, non-trench-coat-wearing, mostly unknown law enforcement bigwig who'd met Giuliani when the latter was a U.S. attorney during the Reagan years. Safir for most of his early career had been a narc. He made it as high as assistant director of the DEA in 1977. But the middle part of his career was spent with the U.S. Marshals Service, where he was the associate director of operations from 1984 to 1990.

The Marshals Service, when it isn't chasing Dr. Richard Kimble or cracking meth-dealer heads in Harlan County, Kentucky, is primarily involved with the dreary business of transporting felons. Levine believes that Safir learned an important lesson in his time with the marshals.

"I think Safir saw that violent crime was dropping," he says. "That there were fewer felonies."

And with that, he thinks, Safir decided to make a radical change in the way police did business, one that piggybacked nicely on top of Bratton's broken windows strategy. "Policing in America from the very beginning was always about responding to reported crime," says Levine. "You know, it's 'Help, I've been shot, I've been stabbed, I've been raped, somebody stole my car.'" There was enough of that to keep policemen everywhere employed for most of the twentieth century.

But then in the early 1990s, for reasons that are still a mystery to cops and academics alike, crime started dropping. Some say it was the advent of computer databases and advanced policing methods. Others say it was because of changes in the drug trade. Still others say it was cultural or had to do with the behavioral tendencies of a new influx of immigrants. Curiously, for instance, the drop in violent crime is most pronounced in cities with high immigrant populations.

Anyway, nobody really knows why crime dropped in the early 1990s, just that it did. In New York and in other cities where the policy was copied, the broken windows strategy may have had some impact, though plenty of academics dispute this. Undeniably, though, a few things happened. For one thing, the city early in Bratton's tenure instituted a system called CompStat, which forces police precincts to take a quantitative approach to crime: each precinct has to submit weekly statistical reports to central command. Not only precincts but individual officers were now measured against one another not by the quality but by the quantity of arrests they made. Moreover, the computerized system allowed police to turn the simple act of writing a summons for peeing on a sidewalk or jumping a turnstile into part of a massive intelligence-gathering operation. Every contact between a police officer and some kid walking down the street went into the big machine and made it a faster, more muscular weapon for finding and tracking subject populations.

You add CompStat to stop-and-frisk—the policy instituted in the early 1990s that allowed police to stop and search virtually anyone at any time, even inside the hallways of a privately owned apartment building—and what you ended up with was a kind of automated policing system that incentivized officers to fan out into neighborhoods like commercial fishermen, throwing nets over whole city blocks and making as many arrests as they could. "It was a machine," Levine says, "for writing tickets, making arrests, and collecting data."

Before long, police departments all over the country were using a form of CompStat. Los Angeles, Washington, Philadelphia, and San Francisco were major early converts. The city of Baltimore switched to a similar system called CitiStat in 1999, and this became the inspiration for the notorious ComStat system memorialized in the TV series *The Wire*.

But the steep drop in violent crime presented police with a problem. If making arrests is the only way to advance in your career, but crime is dropping, what do you do? Furthermore, what to do if the only way to make a living wage is to rack up as much overtime as possible? In the Safir era, NYPD starting salaries were on the low end for professional police forces in America, beginning at about forty thousand dollars. How do you add hours in an era when crime is dropping?

The answer turned out to be, you simply create arrests. By multiplying marijuana arrests by a factor of ten in the space of a few years, Safir's police force drastically increased its workload. "One million police man-hours per year" is Levine's calculation just for marijuana possession arrests in the years since Safir took over the NYPD.

And that was just weed. By the mid-to-late 2000s, police stops had multiplied all across the board for a range of seemingly minor offenses. The numbers by 2012 would be 600,000 summonses a year, more than three times the levels from the late 1990s. Of those, "only" 50,000 were for simple marijuana possession. Another 140,000 would be open-container violations for carrying alcohol in public. An additional 80,000 summonses per year would be written for "disorderly conduct." And an incredible 20,000 summonses per year would be given out for riding bicycles on sidewalks.

Meanwhile, during the mid-2000s, a state arbitrator forced the NYPD to slash starting *yearly* salaries for new officers to a preposterous $25,100. The reduced pay forced some 4,500 officers to quit in a period of a few years in the middle of the decade. The ones who stayed on the job had to really scramble to make a living wage. They did so by inventing an entirely new way of doing the job. It would be a revolution in what Levine calls "sub-misdemeanor policing."

If, like me, you lived in New York throughout some or all of this time and didn't notice, you're not alone. The change took place almost completely outside the field of view of white, professional New York. The big change was in poorer neighborhoods. In places like Bedford-Stuyvesant, the change was profound.

November 2003, a little after midnight. Andrew Brown was standing on a mostly deserted stretch of Bed-Stuy, at the intersection of Broadway and Lewis Avenue, selling weed. To his left, in the direction of Broadway, you could see the elevated subway tracks where the M and J trains would pass by from time to time. Directly in front of him, at 4 Lewis Avenue, was the project apartment building where he was then living with a girlfriend, someone he'd been seeing for years.

Andrew was still in the life, but he was getting tired. He wasn't a soldier anymore, just a salesman, trying to get by. He was worn down and thinking all the time of ways to get out. There had to be something better. He had little nieces and nephews and liked to spend time with them; that made him happy. In the back of his mind, he started thinking about wanting a family of his own. It didn't seem all that possible, given where he was in life—how could he support kids?—but it was something to think about. His girlfriend at the time, though, didn't even want to discuss it. Before Andrew, she had been with someone else, and that guy got locked up, sent away for many years. Andrew sensed that maybe she was waiting for him.

Anyway, on that November night in 2003, the streets were mostly empty, business was slow. Someone approached Andrew, there was a quick discussion, and Andrew handed the man a five-dollar bill. He didn't know that right at that moment an off-duty detective was driving by, and he got on his radio and called in a bunch of uniforms. "They came all the way from the Fort Greene projects, sirens blaring, running lights the whole way," says Andrew. Fort Greene was just about fifteen or twenty blocks away on a map, but it seemed like a long distance to come and a lot of theatrics just to get a dude on the street who *maybe* had just sold a little weed.

By the time the uniforms arrived, Andrew was standing alone on the street. He heard the sirens coming and instinctively started walking, not running, across the street, to the parking lot next to the 4 Lewis Avenue project building. A van screamed into the lot and a tall white officer jumped out.

"Make me run!" the policeman screamed.

Andrew frowned. "What?" he said.

"Go ahead, run! Make me chase you!" the officer repeated, putting his hand on his gun.

Andrew sighed. He'd noticed that there was a new type of policeman appearing on the streets lately, a kind who liked to act like he was in the movies. Those were always trouble. He slowed down.

"I ain't running," he said calmly.

It's not like Andrew was looking forward to this encounter, but he wasn't all that worried about it, either. He didn't have any drugs on him, wasn't carrying a gun. And even if they brought him in, he'd deal with it. It's not like he'd never been arrested before. The way he saw it, he had a job, selling drugs, and they had a job, trying to bust him. He understood how this worked.

But now the taller officer was lunging at him and grabbing him, hard, by the throat. He shouted at Andrew to get down, then used some kind of crazy karate move to sweep Andrew's leg out from under him. Andrew fell to the ground, his face on the pavement, and felt himself being cuffed. Another officer jumped out of the van. Andrew felt the tall cop put a knee in his back. Andrew was lifting his face to try to get it off the asphalt when he heard one of them talk to the other.

"Get the mace!" he heard.

Andrew thought, *Oh shit.* Next thing he knew, he was having a can of mace emptied in his eyes. It was about 1:20 a.m. He howled. "I probably woke up the whole projects," he says now.

They took him away to the precinct, where he got charged with an "observation sale," which is a kind of drug charge that's a step down from a hand-to-hand or criminal possession. Nobody finds any drugs on anybody, but a policeman says he saw something happen. The case never went anywhere.

In the summer of the next year, Andrew was in that same spot, the 4 Lewis Avenue project building, coming downstairs from his girlfriend's place, when he saw some police milling around in the first-floor hallway. Not good. Andrew's rule of thumb is, if you can avoid it, don't be in an enclosed place with the police where nobody can see you, because you never know what might happen. He didn't want to turn around and go back upstairs and attract attention that way, so he tried to just walk quickly to get out the front door.

He didn't quite make it. The police stopped him and tried to search him right there in the hallway. Andrew struggled a little and made it out the front door, but one hand was already cuffed by then. Outside the building, the gang of uniformed police cuffed him and searched him with half the projects watching. Andrew was wearing just a tank top and shorts. "They practically stripped me buck naked right there on the street," he says. Then they pushed him forward toward a van that was parked out in front of the building and searched him again before throwing him into the back.

The van took off, and Andrew went on a little tour of Brooklyn, speeding east up Jefferson Avenue, then north up Malcolm X Boulevard. Every now and then, the police would stop the van, and somebody like Andrew would get tossed inside. "Once they full the van up, they bring you back to the precinct," he explains.

Back at the precinct, the police tried to tell Andrew that they'd found drugs on his seat in the van.

Andrew protested: *But you searched me twice before I even got in the van, pulled my pants down in front of all of Lewis Avenue!*

That case didn't go anywhere either.

There was a third incident right around that time, at exactly the same spot, 4 Lewis Avenue, right next to the elevated subway tracks on Broadway. Andrew, on the phone at the time, sees the police searching his friend's car. He walks over. A policeman intercepts him, grabs his phone, and throws it on the ground, breaking it.

Andrew frowns and points at the ground.

"Man, that isn't even my phone!" he complains. He'd borrowed it from a friend.

Before he can say anything else, police have him cuffed and toss him onto the ground. He cranes his neck to try to see the plate number of the unmarked police car, but the plate is bent in at the corners, and he can't quite read the number.

"It's a trick they use, so you can't read the plate," he says. When the police finish tossing his friend's car, they uncuff him. Andrew looks at the bits of phone on the ground and says, "Aren't you gonna pick me up?"

"What?" the detective snaps.

"Man, I didn't get down here by myself," Andrew says. "You ought to at least help me up."

The policeman rolls his eyes and drives away.

All the same, things started turning around for Andrew at that time. His mind was unfreezing, waking up to new possibilities. He broke up with the girl and settled down with someone new, a petite, pretty girl named Shanette he'd known for years, who lived down the street closer to Myrtle Avenue. Shanette was different; she wanted to settle down with Andrew. Andrew hadn't had too many good things in his life and committed to her immediately.

By the mid-2000s, they were married, and it wasn't long before Andrew accelerated what he would later call his "transformation." He worked to become less angry, stay focused on the good things in life. There was a milestone when Shanette had their first child, a son they named Andrew Jr., or A.J. He remembers the pride he felt signing his name on A.J.'s birth certificate.

They had two more kids, Amir and Amare (the "three A's," he jokes), plus Shanette already had a daughter of her own. The six of them moved together into a little three-room apartment at

921 Myrtle Avenue, which was just three blocks from his first home on Willoughby, but there was that long journey in between.

He started to go to classes to get his CDL, a commercial driver's license, with the idea that he would get a job driving a bus. Shanette, she was going to work for the housing authority. Everything was trending in the right direction—except for one thing.

He was out of the life, but the police never got the memo. If anything, he was getting stopped by the police even more.

The random nature of his situation started to sink in. In crime, out of crime, it didn't matter. What was constant was that the police had a buffet of options they could use to arrest any young man on the street in his neighborhood, and they used all those options, seemingly without regard to whether there was any cause to or not.

Like they could pick you up, arrest you, at any time, for "disorderly conduct," which could mean just about anything. Their crime-fighting methods could best be described as accidental. They mostly just swept up every fish in the pond and threw back the ones they couldn't stick with a charge.

The crazy thing was, anyone could be police. Black, white, Hispanic, in uniform, out of uniform, marked cars, unmarked. That old cliché about cops you could spot a mile away in "unmarked" blue Plymouths didn't work in twenty-first-century Brooklyn, where the police could be driving anything: Lexuses, tricked-out SUVs, sports cars, beaters, the whole gamut. There was a special "crime squad" with a mandate to get guns by any means necessary that had a rep for driving really nice cars, and their officers were known for wearing sharp clothes. You could just be walking down the street and someone could grab you, which happened to Andrew more than once.

After the macing incident, Andrew had seen a lawyer who specialized in police abuse cases. He learned about what was legal and illegal, what his rights were, and how to file a complaint with the Civilian Complaint Review Board, an independent review group with subpoena power that had been created in 1950 to investigate police misconduct. The CCRB's power had grown slightly over the years after incidents like the Tompkins Square Park beatings in 1988 and the Abner Louima incident—that was the one where police sodomized a Haitian man with a plunger after he was arrested outside a Brooklyn nightclub in 1997—and there was at least a place to go to complain if you got beaten up or harassed.

Andrew didn't blame the police for the way his early life had turned out. He knew he had to answer to himself for most of the wrongs of his past, especially the last year of his mother's life. There were plenty of other negative influences as well. But as he increasingly began to realize, the police were a definite negative presence in this landscape. Even as a little kid, even when his mother was still alive, he'd been roughed up by police, and he vividly remembered police threatening to arrest his mother for negligence when she tried to intervene in one of his arrests. For most of his life, he hadn't really thought about the police one way or another—they were just there, like the weather, a thing to be dealt with: he and his friends were on one side, and they were on the other side. But now that he was trying to get out of crime, he wanted to get away from them, too, so he tried to learn how to do it, what the rules were.

One day he was on his way home from his commercial driver's license class, walking less than fifty yards from his apartment entrance, when someone just grabbed him from behind. "What is it? I didn't do anything!" he shouted, and before he knew it, two plainclothes detectives, one on each side of him, were pushing him up against some scaffolding.

One of the police was a huge black guy; he doesn't remember the other so well, but what he does remember is that they both used handcuffs on him, so that he eventually had two sets of handcuffs digging into his wrists.

"What'd I do?" Andrew asked.

"You fit the description," one of the police answered.

Andrew knew it was pointless to ask *what* description. "Everybody in my neighborhood fits the description," Andrew explains.

The big black officer then flipped Andrew around and threw him onto the ground, pushing his face into the wet sidewalk—it was a wet night, too—before driving his knee into Andrew's back.

Next thing he knew, he was again being loaded into a van, taken for another ride, and this time they stopped at a nearby fire station, where there was an even *bigger* van waiting, this one half full of more cuffed people. At the fire station, the police asked Andrew: Do you want to go home, or do you want to go to the precinct?

Here again you get into the weird nature of this new policing system. The police in this case actually *wanted* to send Andrew home. Their strategy is to roust up everybody, search them for guns or drugs, run their names for warrants. If you get a hit, great. Finding guns, making arrests, and writing summonses is what turns line patrolmen into sergeants and lieutenants. But if you don't find anything, well then, you've just brutalized some guy walking home, for no reason at all, and the last thing you want is a paper trail. So better just to let the guy go, hope the situation goes away.

But Andrew had been through the CCRB process. He didn't want it to just go away.

"No way. You're not going to throw me on the ground like that and then just let me go," he said. "You might as well take me to the station now."

So they took him to the station, processed him, strip-searched him, then gave him a summons for disorderly conduct. New York Penal Law 240.20, subsection 5: "Obstructing pedestrian traffic."

In other words, he was arrested for standing on the sidewalk.

Andrew knew all about the disorderly conduct statute. It reads: "A person is guilty of disorderly conduct when . . ."

Then there's a whole list of stuff you can't do, like make noise, make an obscene gesture, refuse a lawful order to disperse, or "obstruct vehicular or pedestrian traffic."

"Last time I read that law," one public defender would joke to me later, "I thought to myself, 'Shit, I violated that one five times just today.'"

The obstructing traffic section is meant to apply to people who are willfully blocking cars or people on the sidewalk, or to be used as a tool for crowd control at things like protests, but in practice it's code for being black on a Tuesday night.

Andrew had actually taken that charge before, around the corner from the "fit the description" incident, on Throop Avenue. He had been standing with a group of people alongside a building when the police rolled up in numbers and gave about a dozen people tickets for disorderly conduct. Andrew got littering on top of disorderly conduct, for flicking a cigarette butt onto the street from the sidewalk. What Andrew thought he had learned from that incident was that the police don't like it when you stand up against a building.

So the next time he came that way, he was taking a stroll with his dog Roxy, smoking a cigarette, and ran into a couple of friends. This time he made it a point to move *away* from the building. He leaned over and told his friend: "Let's move to the corner."

So they moved to the corner. Next thing he knew, two vans tore down the street and slammed their brakes at the corner of Throop and Myrtle. Police jumped out.

"You've gotta move off the corner!" they shouted.

Andrew frowned. "Y'all just got finished telling me last time to stay away from the building," he said. "So now I'm off the building, and you say I can't be here? I'm walking my *dog*."

The police didn't answer. They took him to a station, strip-searched him—there's almost always a strip search—processed him, then sent him on his way with another summons: disorderly conduct, obstructing pedestrian traffic.

Not long after, he went to the grocery store on Throop Avenue, just around the corner from his Myrtle Avenue place. About ten yards from the store, he saw that the store door was closed and there were two uniformed cops inside, talking to the owner. Not only was the store closed, but there were police inside it: Andrew turned around. He made it as far as a fire hydrant on the corner of Throop and Myrtle before the two cops caught up to him. "Hey, you," one shouted. "Stop."

Andrew kept walking.

"Hey," said one of the two police, and he took Andrew's arm.

Andrew, not in the right mood for this, tried to pull away. Next thing he knew, his face was up against an iron grate, and the two police were pushing his arm up to the point where it felt like it was going to break. Andrew yelled out: "What is it this time?"

"You fit the description!"

They kept slamming him against the grate; he could feel his shoulder joint giving. Freaking out, he calmed down just enough to try some logic with the two officers.

"Hey, hey, listen!" he shouted. "If I fit the description, let me hear it over the walkie-talkie. If I really do fit the description, we'll talk, okay?"

The cops didn't go for the idea. Instead, they dragged him to a squad car. Andrew, struggling, didn't want to get into the car. One of the two police threw open the door; the other went around the car, opened the back door on the other side, and jumped into the backseat, getting ready to drag Andrew in from the other side.

The absurd tag-team operation in place, the first officer pushed Andrew's head against the roof of the car, knocking his brand-new black leather Yankee cap to the ground. *Hey, that cost me fifty dollars,* Andrew thought. Next thing he knew, he felt himself being pulled into the back of the car by his legs, sideways. He was looking at his cap on the ground as the squad car door slammed shut.

The usual routine: a trip to the precinct, a strip search, and a summons for disorderly conduct. It would later come out that the "description" was of a black male in an eight-ball jacket, carrying *five* guns. Andrew was dressed in all black and the Yankee hat. When asked later in a deposition how Andrew fit the description, the arresting officer couldn't say.

More time passes. It's November 2012. Andrew has a real job now, wears a tie to work. He's thirty-five years old. He drives a shuttle bus for the new Resorts casino near the Aqueduct Racetrack in Queens, ferrying people to and from the subway station.

It's a good job. He doesn't make a ton of money, but he pays the bills, takes care of his kids. He leaves every afternoon in a black tie and white-collared shirt, comes home after midnight most every weeknight. He sleeps until seven or eight in the morning, then helps Shanette get her eleven-year-old daughter and little A.J., now three, ready for school. Amir and Amare are too young for school yet and spend the day ping-ponging around the apartment while Andrew wishes he could be catching up on his sleep.

The family has a big L-shaped couch upholstered with water-damaged black leather, a wide-screen TV, a video-game console, their Rottweiler mix Roxy, who's friendly most of the time, and a few pieces of furniture. The only thing hanging on the apartment's faintly discolored walls is a framed series of studio-made photographs of Andrew with his arms around Shanette back when she was pregnant with their first baby, her bare belly exposed to the camera, Andrew smiling, his forearm wrapped around her, his hand resting on her navel.

His usual schedule is he gets off from work around 11:30, and his father comes to pick him up at the company's bus depot, then drives him back to Myrtle. That's what happened on November 14, a Wednesday night. His father dropped Andrew off right at 921 Myrtle, directly in front of his building. Andrew climbed out of the car, still dressed in his black tie and collared shirt, a plastic work ID hanging around his neck, obviously a working man coming home after a long day, his fullback's build and short mini-dreads the only hints of his tough past still visible.

He got out of the car, spotted a friend from his building, and together they decided to walk across the street to an all-night store to get something to eat. On the way there, Andrew pulled out his phone and handed his friend some headphones, so he could listen to a song Andrew had written for Shanette:

> *I been sitting here thinkin what the hell is going on*
> *I been sitting here thinkin 'bout the things that I done*
>   *wrong*
> *And I just wanna be in your life in your life forever*
> *Can we just leave, leave the past, leave the past, move on*

Andrew and his friend walked back across the street and stopped in front of their building to listen to the end of the song. While they were listening, Andrew spotted two uniformed police coming around from behind the building. He didn't want to go back into the building, didn't want to run, didn't want to make any false moves at all. They were housing police, and he knew they were looking for tickets to write. He braced himself for the situation.

One of the two officers walked around Andrew and his friend and stood between them and the doorway of 921 Myrtle. This was their own building, remember, where they actually lived. The policeman said:

"You're blocking pedestrian traffic."

It was nearly one in the morning. There was nobody on the street, let alone the walkway outside a project apartment building.

Andrew sagged his shoulders.

"Come on, man," he said. "Look at me. I'm in a tie. I got my work ID around my neck. I'm coming home from work. Are you serious?"

The police demanded to see IDs. Andrew refused, knowing that once he did, they would just write him another summons for blocking pedestrian traffic. Before long, there were police all over him, and there was that mysterious van again, screeching into the parking lot in front of his house. They cuffed him, pushed him toward the vehicle, and Andrew got prepared for yet another night in a precinct, another strip search.

Just before they put him in the van, a sergeant finally did appear.

"It's too late," Andrew said. "If you'd just talked to me first, we could have done this differently. But you got aggressive with me, cuffed me, put me in the van already. Now that it's gone this far, you might as well take me in."

The sergeant complied. They took him away in the van. Another strip search, another summons. Under "offense," it reads: "Obstructing pedestrian traffic."

He made it home in the middle of the morning, got a little sleep, and went off to work again the next day.

I met Andrew by chance in a lawyer's office months later. He had the summons in his pocket, all crumpled up. I unfurled the paper, squinted at it. Sure enough, it read, "Obstructing pedestrian traffic." Like most white people, I had no idea you could be arrested for such a thing.

As with a lot of the young New Yorkers I'd talked to about this subject, the number-one emotion that came through when Andrew told me this whole story was exhaustion.

"The thing is, you get a twenty-two-, twenty-three-year-old police stopping you, and you're thirty-five, forty years old, and he still talks to you like you're a child," he says.

February 21, 2013. Andrew has to appear in court to answer his summons for obstructing pedestrian traffic. He's actually got two summonses, one for standing in front of his building, the other for smoking indoors. In the latter case, he was standing outside, smoking, when his son A.J. ran into a convenience store. Andrew chased him inside, and a policeman spotted him and wrote him up.

Andrew had originally pleaded not guilty to the smoking violation—though he was technically smoking indoors, it was only briefly, and he felt the policeman was just jumping on a chance to dump a ticket on him—but now that he was actually in court, he was ready to just plead that one out. He had, after all, been smoking indoors. On the other one, however, the summons for standing in front of his own home, he wasn't pleading, no matter what they offered him. He was actually hoping that the officer who'd stopped him would show up in court, because he was genuinely curious to hear how he'd defend the summons.

The building at 346 Broadway in Lower Manhattan is, I imagine, the grimmest kind of courthouse you can find anywhere in New York State. It's a filthy, half-crumbling building full of beat-up, yellowed hearing rooms packed with rows of skewed pine benches covered with everything from cigarette wrappers to Oreo crumbs. Andrew's case was in a urine-colored hall called Part 3, a miserable place manned by about a half-dozen impatient-to-the-bone civil servants, including two grumpy bailiffs who spent all their time barking at people for using cell phones or talking, a couple of mute court clerks, half shielded by a partition, who never looked up from their desks, and two very elderly and barely lucid old white men who were the court-appointed defenders taking turns defending the virtually all-black crowd of summons defendants.

Lastly there was His Honor, a Judge John J. Delury, a white-haired old fellow who seemed terminally exhausted and concerned almost entirely with getting the case in front of him over with and moving on to the next one, and on to the next one from there, and then on and on as fast as possible, probably to the end of his life, another thing I imagined he maybe wanted to get over with as soon as he could—who knew?

Andrew waited for his case to be called. The action was monotonous and depressing. A court clerk would call out a name and an offense ("Jamel Williams, open container of alcohol"), and inevitably a black male somewhere between the ages of puberty and infirmity, probably dressed in a ski parka and low-hung jeans, would amble to the front of the court. There he would be greeted by one of the two court-appointed attorneys.

The lawyers were not the young, sharp, idealistic types sent to man felony and misdemeanor courts by organizations like Legal Aid. They were both elderly private lawyers working on contract with the state, dealing out mountains of public-urination or loitering cases for a few nickels a day, the legal equivalent of digging graves or cleaning public toilets, desperate work.

The young black defendant would whisper a story in one or the other lawyer's ear, then the lawyer would bargain with the judge. Or was it the old defense lawyers and the judge bargaining with the defendants? More often than not, it seems like the judge and the lawyer are cooperating in their efforts to get people to settle.

"This place is fucked up," whispered Andrew. "You see people coming in here drunk, and they're answering summonses for being drunk. Like you can smell it four rows away sometimes."

"Mohammed A—I want to say Adil," called out the harried clerk. "Public urination."

This time the defendant wasn't black. It was an older bald Middle Eastern man who looked terribly ashamed to be there. He walked up, whispered to one of the two old lawyers, who were a human version of Statler and Waldorf of *Muppet Show* fame, with one taller and liver spotted, the other shorter and with a pig's face.

"Do you have a medical condition?" Statler asked. The man shook his head, then leaned over and whispered. "Oh," said Statler. "Oh, I see. Hmm."

The lawyer turned to the judge. "Your Honor, this story is so incredible, it has to be true. This gentleman is a taxi driver, and he has a special bottle he carries so that he can go to the bathroom. And he was driving, and it was raining, and . . ."

He leaned over to his client again for more details, and suddenly Statler reared back. "Wait, were you inside the cab or outside of it?" he said. Next thing you know, the defense lawyer is turned toward his "client" and interrogating him in front of the microphone. "It doesn't matter that you stopped your cab, you got out of the cab, you understand? You're exposing yourself outside the cab, on a public street!"

As if to make his point more clear to his foreign client, he gestured, pretending to unzip and whip it out before the court.

"Counsel, some of your gestures are a little too graphic," the judge admonished.

"I'm sorry, Your Honor," Statler said. "It's just—"

"But I had a bottle . . . ," the taxi driver repeated, in heavily accented English.

"It doesn't matter that you had a bottle," his lawyer chided. "You can't pull that thing out on a street! Children could see!"

It was amazing. This poor sap of a defendant had received a simple public urination summons, and his own lawyer was now about to talk him into a child molestation charge in court. It was like a punch line in a *Truly Tasteless Jokes* collection.

After some more tragicomical wrangling, the devastated taxi driver pleaded on the peeing charge and took a fine. We watched some more justice administered, almost all of it penny-ante stuff: open-container violations, a stolen bike, a few traffic cases.

Soon the arresting officers from both of Andrew's cases arrived. There was a tall black guy on the smoking charge, and a buzz-cut, hulking white dude on the obstructing pedestrian traffic case. So we'd have a trial after all.

Andrew decided to step into the hallway to make a call. On his way out, he held the courtroom door open and gestured to the bailiff.

"I'm going to be right outside, I just need to make a call," he said.

"Close the door, or you'll get another summons!"

About ten minutes later the clerk called out his name.

"Andrew Brown?" she said.

"He's outside," the bailiff responded, jerking his thumb toward the door.

Statler followed the bailiff's thumb. *Uh-oh. Well, let Andrew explain the story to the man; hopefully he'll get it.* I figured it would take five minutes to explain.

Five minutes passed. Then it was ten. I started to wonder what was going on, then I heard a commotion in the hallway. I got up, and just as I made it to the door, the lawyer burst in and looked mournfully at the bailiff. "That guy won't shut the fuck up!" he yelled.

I went outside. Andrew was pacing in obvious consternation.

"What happened?"

"I was trying to tell the guy I just wanted to pay the fine on the first one and contest the second, and he wouldn't let me talk," Andrew said. "He comes out here, says something about how the judge will probably let me off with a fifty-dollar fine for both of them. Like a two for one. He's like doing that maneuvering thing. And I'm trying to tell him no, I want to fight the second one, and he got all pissed at me and ran inside."

A court officer had to intervene and get Andrew the other lawyer. After some minutes, the other lawyer came out. Again, this was a very old man who looked too tired for this work. He stood there examining Andrew's papers for a moment. Despite the fact that he must have been doing this for years, it was clear that the papers told him nothing, that they were an absolute mystery to him.

"Look, I'll pay the fine on the first one, okay?" Andrew said.

"This public smoking one?" the lawyer asked.

"Yes," Andrew said. "Just forget about that. I'll pay it, it's okay. But this other one, I want to fight it."

The lawyer looked at the summons. He looked and he looked. A spider crawled halfway up the wall next to him. Still he looked at it. Finally, after many minutes, he turned to Andrew.

"It says here you were obstructing pedestrian traffic," he said.

"That's what it says," Andrew said. "But I was standing in front of my own house at one in the morning."

"But what are you arguing?" he said. "I don't understand."

I made the mistake at this point of trying to talk to the lawyer myself, trying to point out the absurdity of a man being arrested for standing in front of his own apartment. Oddly, just the mere fact of me trying to talk Andrew's lawyer into fighting for his client attracted police attention. An officer in the hallway who had been listening to this conversation stepped in and pointed at me.

"Sir, I have to advise you," he said. "Conversations between an attorney and his client are private. Confidential, like. So you're going to have to back off."

This wasn't true, but it wasn't worth arguing. I left it alone. The lawyer returned to reading the summons, frowning, still clearly struggling with why Andrew was contesting it.

"Well," he said to Andrew, "were you being a wise guy or something?"

Andrew explained that he was not. "No, no, I was coming home from work," he said. "I was wearing a *tie!*"

The lawyer looked up. "You have a job?" he asked with undisguised, obnoxious surprise.

"Yeah," said Andrew. "I drive a shuttle bus."

"Huh," the lawyer said. "Well, the judge will probably give you fifty dollars for both of them," he said at last.

Andrew buried his face in his hands. "I just explained to you," he said. "I'm not pleading to anything on that second one. Do you understand?"

The man nodded. "Oh, I see. Well," he said finally, "what about twenty-five for both? Would you take that?"

Andrew's eyes opened to the size of tea saucers. I thought he was going to scream. Instead, he bit his lip and said, "No, I won't take anything. I want you to ask the officer in there what pedestrian traffic he is referring to in that summons. It was one in the morning. The street was empty. This is in front of a residential building, my own building."

"You want me to ask him what traffic he's talking about?" the lawyer said.

"Yes, exactly."

"And you won't take twenty-five?"

"I won't take anything," Andrew repeated.

The man shrugged, as if to say, *It's your funeral.*

They went inside.

Andrew stood before His Honor. The summons charges from both cases were read out. The lawyer instructed the court that Andrew was willing to plead to the first case. At this, the judge dismissed the first police witness, the young black officer who had written Andrew up for smoking. That left only the other officer, the one who'd hit Andrew up with the obstructing charge and who'd signed his name on the summons.

Andrew, Waldorf, and this officer stood before the judge in a line. The judge asked what the heck was going on.

"Your Honor," the lawyer said with a pronounced tone of apology, "I've been instructed by my client not to plead on this offense." It was as though the lawyer didn't personally want to touch Andrew's "not guilty" plea.

"And why not?" the judge asked.

"I didn't do nothing," Andrew said.

The judge frowned and looked at the paperwork. He went through the same routine as Andrew's lawyer, only he processed the information a lot faster. It was clear, in fact, that this was the princi-pal difference between these two men.

"It says here you were blocking pedestrian traffic," the judge said.

"There wasn't no traffic," Andrew said. "It was one in the morn-ing, in front of my own house."

The judge nodded, then instantly looked at the lawyer. "Will he take fifty for both of them?"

This comedy was now moving to Zucker Brothers territory.

"No, Your Honor, like I said, he's not pleading," cried the lawyer in anguish.

"Hm," the judge said. He turned back to Andrew. "So you say the street was empty, huh?"

"Yes, sir," Andrew said.

"Okay, then," he said. He turned to the officer, made him raise his hand and swear in as a witness.

"Why did you give this man a summons?" the judge said.

"Your Honor," the officer said, "the defendant and his friend were completely blocking the entranceway to the building."

"Were there any other people on the street?"

"Your Honor, the point is, they were standing in a way so that nobody could pass—"

"But were there any other people on the street?"

The policeman took a moment to gather himself, then sighed. "I didn't see any, Your Honor."

"Okay, then," the judge said. "Not guilty. Next!"

Out in the hall, Andrew was shaking his head. "You see how many times they tried to get me to take a deal?" he said. "Even my own lawyer?"

He went down the hall to pay his fine on the smoking case.

After Andrew left, I went back into the courtroom. At a lull in the action, I asked the lawyer out into the hall to speak. He rolled his eyes, then finally came out.

I tried to start over with him, gave him my card, offered to shake his hand. Looking angry at first, he said he was sick and didn't want to touch anyone. Then he softened up suddenly and introduced himself. He gave his name and said he was working on contract for the state. He didn't always do this stuff, he said—he sometimes did arraignments and other duties.

He fingered my business card, stared at it. "What exactly are you doing here again?"

"I'm writing a book," I said. "It's about the criminal justice system. Among other things, about cases like this."

"But what about a case like this could possibly be the subject of a book?" he asked.

"Well," I said, "we just watched, in court, a policeman admitting to falsely arresting someone. You don't find that interesting?"

He shrugged.

"Also," I said, "have you ever heard of a white person being arrested for obstructing pedestrian traffic?"

"Well, white people don't live in those neighborhoods," he said.

"But white people live somewhere," I said. "And nobody arrests them for obstructing pedestrian traffic."

"That's because that's not where the crime is. The crime is out there."

He jerked a thumb in the direction of Brooklyn.

"Low-class people," he said, "do low-class things."

December 2012, just after ten a.m., a first-floor courtroom in Brooklyn. A fifty-four-year-old Latina prostitute with frizzy, matted hair and ripped jeans is trying to stand up before the judge, but she's whacked out, nodding and leaning to one side. She tried to keep her eyes open when they first brought her up from the pens, but now they're almost totally closed.

"The people's offer is time served and a misdemeanor," a voice, presumably the prosecutor's, mumbles into a microphone.

The accused does not react. Her eyes are still closed.

"Correction, the revised offer is a violation," the same voice grumbles.

This time the woman opens one eye, just barely. She's surprised. This wasn't in the script.

The defendant's court-appointed attorney is an attractive, idealistic young white woman with shoulder-length brown hair and a long skirt who looks like she should be an academic, a sociologist maybe. The public defenders in these higher courts are almost all workaholic do-gooders, passionate and almost unreasonably committed to their jobs. On the macro level, they can't do much about the convictions factory. They're like partisans trying to slow an invasion by throwing their bodies under tank treads. But on the day-to-day, case-to-case level, they don't miss much.

In this case, the PD is flipping through her client's file and then stops. She's spotted it. The whatever-it-is that's made the no-longer-young, tired-looking Hispanic man pulling arraignment duty for the DA's office that day reduce his offer, she sees it.

"Your Honor," she says. "The allegation here is that the defendant was approached by an undercover officer." She pauses, flips through her papers again. "But the supporting document is made out by a different officer, a Sergeant . . ."

I'm in the gallery, and a lawyer next to me first chuckles, then leans over and whispers.

"Under law, the judge can dismiss if it's not a legally sufficient document," the lawyer says. "And there's something fucked with this arrest—both sides know it. Otherwise the arresting officer would have made out the affidavit."

The complaint says an undercover officer—a UC—offered the woman twenty dollars for a sexual act outside a park somewhere north of three in the morning, and the defendant accepted. Why we're paying detectives to offer people twenty bucks for sexual acts in parks after three in the morning is a question nobody's much interested in answering at that moment. More interesting to those present is the fact that both the police and the DA's office seem to know the arrest was screwed up somehow. Maybe the undercover officer crossed some kind of entrapment line, maybe he woke the defendant up to offer her the twenty bucks, who knows. But they're going on with the case anyway.

"Yeah, there's no way she's getting off," the lawyer next to me whispers. "She's got thirty-five priors."

The woman's record is all misdemeanors, mostly for prostitution-type offenses, lots of loitering. But thirty-five priors nonetheless. Nobody with thirty-five priors gets a complete walk in this court-room.

I crane my neck to try to see what's going on, and all I can see is defense, prosecution, and judge leaning toward one another, nego-tiating. Somebody mutters into a microphone: "Her supervisor will accept time served and the violation." Then there's nodding all around, and suddenly, like a football team breaking a huddle, all parties retreat to their own stations. A gavel is rapped, and the de-fendant, nodding but eyes still closed, is led away. She's agreed to the violation.

If you just walked in off the street and watched that scene, you wouldn't think much of it. But to people who do this for a living, the decision by a haggard and probably homeless streetwalker to pay a fine for a bad arrest comes down to an elaborate series of mathe-matical calculations, most of which the public has no conception of.

In a vacuum, that prostitute's case probably would have been tossed out. There was something wrong with the arrest, and if it were somehow to go all the way to trial, the state would probably lose, a fact seemingly recognized by all sides in their brief, ten-second deliberation.

But the state doesn't have to win at trial, a truth captured in an-other common expression in this courtroom: "The punishment is the process."

The state could charge a misdemeanor anyway and demand high bail and almost certainly get it. After her arrest, the fifty-four-year-old woman had been interviewed at the precinct house by a (prob-ably bored and sleep-deprived) bureaucrat from the nonprofit Criminal Justice Agency, who asked her questions about her ad-dress, her criminal history, whether she would have family coming to the court this morning (she would not), and whether she'd ever missed a court appearance.

The answers were all bad ones. Tons of convictions, tons of arrests, a history of missed appearances, it all added up to one thing: If the state asks for bail, she's not getting it.

Bail. In criminal cases big and small, it's the whole thing. Everything comes down to bail.

Lawyers in this courthouse have yet another saying: "If you go in, you stay in. If you get out, you stay out." If you get arrested for a B misdemeanor in New York City—let's say it's prostitution—you might face a punishment of fifteen to ninety days. But if you don't make bail, you'll almost automatically spend at least that long in jail waiting for trial.

The state knows this, so essentially, charging a person who can't make bail with a B misdemeanor is the same as convicting that person. You file the charge, the judge sets high bail, you go back inside, and then you eventually plead to time served, because, well, why not? You've already done the time.

The only difference is, you've got a conviction now, which means the next time you get arrested, the denial of bail—or a punishingly high bail—will be even more automatic. Additionally, every misdemeanor conviction in New York carries a two-hundred-dollar surcharge, plus you have to have a DNA sample taken if it's your first. And that's true for a violation of every single penal law in New York State, excepting traffic violations. So your DNA is on file forever, and giving the sample costs fifty dollars, a testing procedure that, of course, you pay for yourself.

So if you're a prostitute with no fixed address and a long criminal history hauled in during the wee hours of a Tuesday morning for accepting some undercover cop's sting offer of twenty bucks for a sex act outside a park, you're pretty much automatically looking at two weeks to three months in jail, plus a two-hundred-dollar fine ("That's like ten blowjobs," comments one public defender righteously) from the moment the city decides to file the charge. And even in the relatively rare instance where God smiles upon you and sends an undercover officer your way who doesn't know how to make a legal arrest, you will still plead guilty and pay the violation for loitering.

You're paying the fine not for what you did, mind you, but simply out of recognition that you'd be paying a lot more if the state decided to be difficult and proceed with its messed-up case.

This is the essence of Justice by Attrition. It's like a poker game where after arrest, the accused sits down at the table with one chip. But the other player, the state, has a stack of chips fifty feet high. Will you play, or will you fold?

Most everybody folds.

Well, so what, right? If you commit a crime, why shouldn't it be easy for the state to get a conviction? We can't waste the public's money on trials for every back-alley sex act in New York. That would cripple the city budget in half a week.

That's true, but what starts to happen is, the authorities get mission creep. Convictions are so easy, the police eventually stop waiting for the actual crime to be committed. Instead of waiting to watch a sex act for pay actually take place, the police, even better, will simply arrest a woman for "loitering for the purpose of engaging in a prostitution offense."

"Loosely translated," one attorney put it to me, "that means standing on the street in hot pants."

Police will bring in a streetwalker for "engaging in conversation" or "attempting to stop" a man on the street. One Manhattan lawyer says 70 percent of her prostitution cases are technically loitering charges. But out of a hundred such cases she had in one year, only four defendants decided to fight the charges.

"It's a resources game," says Roy Wasserman, a Brooklyn-based public defender. "If they have the money to bail out, they fight it. If they don't, they plead. It all comes down to that."

Making "standing on the street and looking hookerish" against the law leads to all sorts of absurdities, especially when you're relying upon (usually young) policemen to make that distinction. A good example is a 2009 case in Portland, Oregon, when a thirty-six-year-old writing teacher named Ann Marie Selby missed a bus and got arrested for suspicion of being a prostitute when she decided to walk home. Just as in New York, where "making eye contact" with drivers is often considered an element of the "loitering" crime, police claimed they saw Selby looking into the windows of passing SUVs, which led them to be suspicious.

When they stopped her and asked her what she was doing, she kept walking. They then physically got in front of her, at which point she explained that she had been to a spa and even pulled out a receipt to prove it.

When police took the receipt away, Selby, realizing it was her only evidence, lunged for it, knocking a police notebook into the street. That got her a harassment charge ("offensive physical contact" being the specific kind of harassment) in addition to the suspicion of being a hooker charge.

We hear about cases like that and they make news when the people arrested are innocent (and white). The problem is, nobody much cares about the people who are guilty.

"People make such a big deal about innocent people being thrown into jail," says David Mills, a professor at Stanford who helped lead the charge to reform California's infamous three-strikes program. "I don't know anyone, intellectually, who's in favor of innocent people being arrested and jailed. What's much more interesting is how we treat the guilty."

And that's the problem with Justice by Attrition. It's not just that it catches up innocent people in its massive dragnet. It's also that it applies disproportionate punishment to the guilty. How many upscale New Yorkers have ever been arrested for public drunkenness, for carrying a joint or a bottle of pain pills, for having a knife or a box cutter in a car?

Police, if they wanted, could throw a net over the exit of any nightclub in Lower Manhattan on a weekend night and score a couple of dozen drug cases. Or they could crack down on the Wall

Street guys in suits who sneak into doorways for late-night rub-and-tugs or park their Lexuses near the Battery for after-work blow-jobs.

But they don't. The thing is, that sort of "quality of life" crime isn't really focused on much. In fact, the rise in broken windows arrests has paralleled a drop in arrests for these other kinds of offenders.

For instance, the disparity in arrests of prostitutes versus johns is growing all over the country. In Lansing, Michigan, police in the 1990s arrested prostitutes and johns in equal numbers. By the early 2000s, it was 3 prostitutes for every john. It was about 7 to 1 in Chicago, about 9 to 1 in Seattle, and in Boston the ratio was 11 to 1.

Meanwhile, misdemeanor arrests have skyrocketed everywhere. In one three-year period in New York between 1998 and 2001, they went up 37 percent. And you can see this in the courts. Almost everyone you talk to in criminal courts complains that they spend far too much of their time dealing with "bullshit" cases: car stops, weed arrests, loitering, disorderly conduct. A huge number of those misdemeanor cases are simply tossed out, or they're effectively ended when judges release the defendant on his own recognizance. But of the defendants who don't get released with no bail, an extremely high percentage are not able to make the bail. This suggests that when judges set bail in these nuisance cases, they're carefully picking numbers just high enough to keep people in jail.

A study by Human Rights Watch from 2008 bore this out. They looked at 117,064 nonfelony cases in New York that year and found that more than three-fourths of the defendants were released on their own recognizance. But 19,137 of the defendants were given bail of $1,000 or less, and an incredible 87 percent of those still couldn't post bail. Those people who couldn't make bail spent an average of fifteen days in jail awaiting trial.

Think about that. That's more than 16,500 people a year who did an average of two weeks in jail for misdemeanors. If you went to college, were any of those friends of yours? Nobody you knew passed out on a subway car, took X at a club, smoked a joint after work, paid for sex, or drank beer on the street?

No, almost all these people come from nonwhite or poor New York, and they're all people who don't have eight hundred dollars in cash in a bank account. Lawyers at the courts on Schermerhorn Street, where many of Brooklyn's cases play out, have a word for bail set just high enough so that people can't pay, but low enough so that bail bondsmen won't take the business.

"They call it 'nuisance bail,'" says Jane Fox, a public defender.

The courts didn't spend most of their time on this kind of stuff twenty or thirty years ago. The number of so-called quality of life arrests skyrocketed in the early 1990s, with the implementation of broken windows. And when studies started to surface showing massive racial disparities in the number of quality of life arrests—blacks and Hispanics made up 91 percent of all QOL arrests according to one study done in 1999, while whites, who made up 43 percent of the city's population, made up just 11 percent of all stops in the stop-and-frisk program—the city had a ready answer.

It claimed that it made no sense to look at QOL numbers alone, and that an 89 percent or 90 percent QOL rate was consistent with the fact that 85 percent of serious crimes were committed by blacks and Hispanics. In other words, their argument was that they arrested more people for bullshit crimes because they also arrested more people for serious crimes. They relied upon academic studies that told them that, generally speaking, the same people who committed serious crimes also committed minor crimes. A study by famed criminologists Michael Gottfredson and Travis Hirschi, for instance, opined that people who demonstrate low self-control in "a wide variety of criminal and analogous behaviors"—people who have issues with drinking or drugs, or have problems with school, interpersonal relationships, and keeping a job—"will not specialize in some [crimes] to the exclusion of others."

In other words:

Low-class people do low-class things.

This same thought process is buried in the way the initial Criminal Justice Agency interviews are evaluated. People who have jobs, family, a working telephone, a consistent address, no record of missed appearances, they're given good scores and consequently have a much better shot at bail. People with poor "self-control" scores, on the other hand, are given bad scores, and they tend to stay in.

Hirschi was convinced that people who were usefully busy didn't commit crimes. "The child playing ping-pong, swimming in the community pool, or doing his homework," he said, "is not committing delinquent acts." Hirschi didn't spend a whole lot of time looking at people who had good jobs and became criminals anyway, completely ignoring in this way a whole class of crime. White-collar crime by its very nature involves a high degree of self-control and planning. It's committed almost overwhelmingly by people who had enough self-mastery to make it through high school and college and hold down good jobs.

The policing policies that sprang up around these and other theories, and that were based upon the idea that crime is encouraged by poor family structure and neighborhood disorder, were all about creating an atmosphere that would check the unconscious impulse toward crime. Let's make people actually *think* before they jump a turnstile, and that impulse to think about consequences will be nurtured and grow with each arrest, and over time you'll create a law-abiding citizen.

It actually sounds good in theory. But there are two big problems with it.

One, it completely ignores the possibility that there are people who commit crime consciously, as a lifestyle choice—like, say, your banker at HSBC who opens an account for Sinaloa Cartel members. That guy is not jumping a turnstile. He might very well have a coke problem, or wander around drunk in public, or visit prostitutes, but the likelihood that he'll be arrested for any of these things is extremely low.

Second, what happens if those broken windows arrests are not legitimate arrests? What impulse do you inspire over time in your repeatedly arrested but often innocent defendant in that case?

Mostly what you're doing is creating a lot of really angry people.

Justice by Attrition turns courthouses like this giant complex on Schermerhorn Street into huge fun houses of unreasonableness and mindless punishment, where you can peek into just about any room and find someone absolutely beside himself with disbelief over what is happening to him.

Upstairs from the prostitute's case, I meet a public defender named Josh Saunders talking with his client, a young Hispanic man who's been charged with a domestic violence offense. The state is offering a B misdemeanor plus entrance into a counseling program, a year and a half of school for which the defendant will have to pay fifty dollars every time he goes to class.

"It's an enormous amount of money," Josh tells his client. "You have zero incentive to take that."

The client is out—free because the judge waived bail, so that's good news for him. But he's also got a job and the court appearances are no joke. Judges are not terribly understanding about defendants who try to reschedule hearings because they have jobs, or children, or other problems. And to fight a misdemeanor charge, even a *violation,* even if you're out on bail, usually means four or five trips to court at minimum. Every motion to suppress evidence or challenge the complaint means more time, more excuses to bosses, more babysitters you have to hire.

In February 2013 I was in a courthouse clerk's office when I overheard a man pleading with the woman behind the counter. I had seen the man in court before but couldn't place what the case was.

"But this is the *second time,*" he said. "I keep coming back to court, and the police keep not showing up."

"Well," the clerk said, "the police are very busy. Sometimes they just can't make it."

"It says here my new trial date is March twentieth," he said. "What if they don't show up then? How many times do I have to do this?"

"Sir, I don't know," she said.

The man's name turned out to be Andre Finley. Like Andrew

Brown, he lived in Bed-Stuy, although he was a newcomer. He had just moved from Harlem. He had a clean record, but he was one of twenty thousand New Yorkers in 2012 who were given a summons for riding a bicycle on the sidewalk. The actual Bed-Stuy sidewalk was empty, but that wasn't Andre's problem. He wasn't even contesting the case. The problem was the fine, which was a hundred dollars.

"The thing is, I'm on HRA," he said. That's what they call welfare in New York—HRA, the city's Human Resources Agency, provides temporary cash assistance. "I get like three hundred dollars a month. If they fine me, they're just paying money to themselves. I'm willing to do community service. I'm even willing to sit in jail for fifteen days if it comes to that, you understand? I get it, I rode a bike on a sidewalk, I'm not even disputing that. But I don't have a hundred dollars."

I asked him what happened on his case.

"So I was riding home at night," he said. "And I was riding on the sidewalk, I was. Suddenly out of nowhere, these two police come up to me and grab me. I could tell they were excited, they were like, 'We got one.' Next thing I know there's like five more police there, and they're patting me down, asking me if I have any warrants. I say, no, I don't have any warrants. And they're like, 'Are you sure?' Like they're surprised.

"So I say, 'Am I sure? I would know, wouldn't I?' So they run my name, and there are no warrants, and they let me go with this summons."

Finley had already had to come to court three times for that ticket. The first time, he'd pleaded not guilty just to get the chance to argue for a different kind of sentence, since he couldn't afford the fine. So they set a trial date for him in January 2013, and at that date, the arresting officers didn't show, so the state couldn't proceed. A month later, in February, the same thing happened, and they put his date back another month.

March rolled around and Finley came back to court on the ap-

pointed date. I showed up to see if he would succeed in talking his
way into jail this time. The judge was about an hour late. A hundred
people who had been told to appear at nine had to wait an hour just
to hear His Honor, a walrusy-looking old man with a shiny bald
head and a long handlebar mustache, give a speech that he clearly
thought was funny about the proceedings ahead.

"Get your wallets ready!" he cracked. "We take Visa and Master-
Card here, but no American Express!"

The fun began when a South Asian man was called up to the
front for peeing on a sidewalk somewhere in Brooklyn. He started
to explain himself in heavily accented English when the judge, irri-
tated already in his first few minutes at work, cut him off.

"Whatever you did, don't do it again," he said, banging a gavel.
"ACD. Next!" ("ACD" means "adjournment in contemplation of
dismissal," a prelude to having your case dismissed.)

The next few defendants weren't so lucky. Fifty dollars, a hundred, twenty-five. Minute after mindless minute, fine after fine.

"Just like a lemon," said Finley. "They just keep squeezing and
squeezing."

An hour or so later Andre got summoned to the front. The judge
took one three-second look at his summons and instantly recognized that there was an error on the ticket, that Andre shouldn't
have even had to go to court in the first place. (The officer had written him up for the wrong kind of bicycle-riding violation.) Case
dismissed. Good news, but it had taken nearly a year and almost
fifteen hours in court to clear it up.

This was a man who was literally trying to go to jail instead of
paying a hundred-dollar fine, and he couldn't do it without multiple
court dates and nearly a dozen hours of waiting and court time. It's
impossible to overestimate the impact, in terms of time and sheer
frustration, that all these mindless arrests and summonses have on
the people targeted.

"The really crazy thing is, you come to court and you'll sit there
all day waiting for your name to be called," Finley says, referring to

his trial dates. "I've probably sat ten hours in the three times I've come to court. That's my community service right there, when you think about it."

It shouldn't be like this, at least not for the more serious cases. New York State has a speedy trial law, which mandates that the state must bring a misdemeanor case to trial within ninety days of arraignment. But in practice, the process gets stretched out almost indefinitely, thanks to an incredibly devious perversion of the system that the state has long used to bully misdemeanor defendants into pleas.

The public defender Josh Saunders is a young, trim, well-dressed, fair-haired lawyer who went to a good law school and had a chance to go the highly paid corporate route, but he just couldn't stomach it. Like a lot of public defenders, the payoff for his job is that he likes working with clients who are actual human beings instead of bloodless companies, and he also likes the fact that he can sleep at night with a clear conscience. But Saunders is frustrated by the system. He's got a client who is a perfect example of the type of person victimized by the state's "speedy trial" trick.

Arrested on a domestic violence charge, Josh's client came to court only to find out that the prosecution was "not ready" to proceed with its case. Usually this means they don't have a witness lined up, or there's some other problem.

So the DA asked the judge for fifteen days. The judge granted the fifteen days, then looked down at his calendar and found that he had no availability to actually hear the case fifteen business days later. So instead, he scheduled the defendant's hearing for more than a month later.

But here's the catch. Days after the DA won his delay, he filed a "certificate of readiness," stating that the prosecutor's office was, indeed, now ready for trial. But the trial had by now already been adjourned for more than a month. (Commonly, it can be two or three months.)

Nonetheless, because the prosecutor had declared himself

"ready" two days after trial, the court only "charged" the state two days toward the ninety.

A month or so later the whole scenario could be repeated. In this fashion a case that is supposed to go to trial within ninety days can take a year, a year and a half, two years to be heard. For someone out on bail, like Josh's client, this is merely incredibly stressful and a major inconvenience.

But for someone in jail awaiting trial, it's a preposterously excessive punishment. It's especially harsh since most misdemeanor cases don't even threaten the defendant with that much jail time even in the case of conviction.

Thus the speedy trial concept, what some lawyers call the crown jewel of the Anglo-American legal system, is easily reduced to a complete joke.

Prosecutors won't say so openly, but privately, they will admit that when their cases are weak, they drive their cases through this Lincoln Tunnel of a procedural loophole, dragging things out as long as possible to force a plea. It usually works.

As with everything on this side of the Divide, the process is made to be humiliating and pointlessly time-consuming for everyone involved, lawyers included.

When I ask one lawyer how much time he's spent in courtrooms over his career, he snaps.

"You mean useful time?" he growls. "Because ninety-nine percent of everything we all do here is just totally fucking stupid."

If you're charged with a crime, and you get notice of a court appearance, you have to show up to a packed room at an appointed time that in reality is only an approximate time. If it says 10:30 a.m. on the notice, you may end up waiting three, four hours for your case to come before the judge.

During that time you are permitted to do exactly one thing: sit in court and watch the action. There is no talking, sleeping, eating, or *reading* in any of the courtrooms like the one on Schermerhorn Street. You must pay attention to the judge at all times.

Some of the judges are insanely touchy about these rules, too. Judge Charles Troia, a glowering dark-haired man who runs a courtroom on the eighth floor, has a particular mania for talkers and readers. He has his court officer bark out instructions on the matter repeatedly throughout the morning.

"In case you missed the sign," the officer yells out, "there's no reading, eating, or sleeping. Listen up! It's going to be a long night."

The ban on reading is particularly odd, given that some of the judges have literary ambitions. Judge John Wilson, who by the time this book is published will have moved from the Brooklyn courts to the Bronx, is notorious in this courtroom for having authored a children's book called *Hot House Flowers*.

The book is a leaden allegorical parable about immigration, in which a beautiful greenhouse full of well-nourished roses and other gorgeous flowers comes under attack by dandelion "weeds" from the uncivilized world outside, who sneak in as seeds through the hothouse roof. The weeds suck all the healthy flowers dry, but the flowers eventually summon the strength to boot the weeds back out into the desert.

"And in a little while," he writes, "the flowers of the hot house were standing tall and healthy, and their petals were beautiful once again."

After being ejected from the hothouse the weeds finally get the message.

Seeing the fate of her seeds, the dandelion stopped trying to send more into the hothouse.

Instead, the flowers who lived outside the hothouse tried to make their own world a better place.

And the flowers of the hothouse lived in peace.

"The moral of the story," chuckles one lawyer, "is that if you're a greenhouse flower that's great. But if you're not, stay the fuck out of the greenhouse."

A side note on Wilson—a gray-faced, mild-looking man who actually has a decent rep with defense lawyers, although low-income defendants who've either appeared before him or have friends who have are less crazy about him—his book is so infamous, protesters at one time planned to make dandelion T-shirts for defendants to wear in his courtroom. Wilson was briefly the judge in a case with direct relevance to Andrew Brown's situation and to the whole concept of QOL arrests in general.

In November 2011, there was a protest against stop-and-frisk in Brooklyn. A group of agitators, including actor Gbenga Akinnagbe (who played the frightening assassin Chris Partlow in *The Wire*), arrived at the city's Seventy-Third Precinct, where they stood chanting and waving signs. Suddenly the whole lot of protesters was arrested, originally for "obstructing government administration," the ostensible reason being that a police captain saw one of his officers leave the precinct and go back inside after seeing the crowd. In other words, a police officer was so frightened by the sight of a bunch of lefty protesters that he was "obstructed" from his duty to leave his precinct and go out policing.

When a videotape surfaced showing that the sidewalks were completely clear that day (the protest was not large), the charge was reduced to disorderly conduct. This time, however, it wasn't "obstructing pedestrian traffic" but "refusing a lawful order to disperse." Apparently, the police captain had ordered the crowd to leave, and they had not. The only problem was, the protesters weren't breaking any laws, a situation the state itself had admitted to when it dropped the charge of "obstructing government administration."

On the surface, this sounds like an annoying and trivial case involving the peculiar sort of mental masturbation one sees only from politically left-leaning protesters who have a tendency to go out into the world looking for ways to get arrested.

But look a little deeper, and the state's refusal to drop the stop-and-frisk protest cases over the course of nearly two years is highly symbolic, because there's a key legal issue buried in the case.

"The question is," says Daniella Korotzer, who represents some of the protesters, "do the police have a right to just tell you to move no matter what? And can you be arrested if you refuse?"

There are two important concepts here that work hand in hand. One, there's the idea that failure to follow a police order, no matter how stupid or unreasonable, is cause for an arrest or a summons. The second idea is that the prosecutor can essentially turn any misdemeanor case against almost anyone into a de facto conviction, simply by filing charges and following through long enough with pretrial pressure to wrest a plea out of the accused.

These two concepts operating together have resulted in a new policing method, one that relies upon thousands of arrests for trivial offenses, real and imagined.

Police spill out into neighborhoods and troll for arrestable subjects using methods that, again, are closer to commercial fishing than old-school surveillance and investigative policing. (There is even a roving factory boat you bring your catch to, i.e., the van cruising through the neighborhood.) You round people up, search them, and if they don't bend into exactly the shape you order them to bend to, you pull them in and slap them with a summons.

This is going on all over the country. In Baltimore, a former police officer named Peter Moskos wrote a book called *Cop in the Hood* that described how police routinely would order people to move off a spot—exactly what Andrew goes through once a month or so—and then arrest them if they're too slow or give an attitude or for any reason at all. They search people, look for drugs or guns, and then throw them back in the ocean, but not before arresting them for loitering. In one typical year, in 2005, more than 22,000 people in New York City were arrested for loitering. The vast majority of those arrests were dismissed, but the original crime in nearly all those cases—refusing to obey an order to move—was and is a legal absurdity, creating what one city councilman called an "epidemic of false arrest."

If you think Andrew's story of being repeatedly arrested for "obstructing pedestrian traffic" is fanciful or not representative, walk the streets of New York and ask any young male resident in the outer boroughs how many times he's been stopped, searched, and written up for failing to obey an order.

"How often? I'd say about sixty times before I turned nineteen," says Tyquan Brehon, a young man from the Bushwick area of Brooklyn.

Unlike Andrew, who looks like a tough guy from a distance, Brehon, now in his early twenties, looks like a musician or a stand-up comic. He's a slight young man with a big smile and a sarcastic sense of humor. He was working as a clerk at a Manhattan department store when I met him and was also trying to get into John Jay College. Like Andrew, he grew up watching cop shows, but he was more into the law side. "I watched a lot of *Law & Order*," he says. "I thought about being a lawyer, still do."

Tyquan never had any kind of real criminal history, but what he does have is something far worse: a mouth. Every time he gets stopped and frisked, he has something to say about it, and he ends up being dragged to jail. His most absurd story came when he was visiting his cousin across the street from Bushwick Community High (where he was going to school at the time), at the corner of Wilson and Palmetto. He and a bunch of his friends were getting ready to go play basketball when a pair of police rolled up.

"They put us all up against the wall," he says. "And I was like, 'What's this for?' And the guy says, 'Oh, a smartass, huh?'"

Not pleased with Tyquan's mouth, he rifled through Tyquan's pockets and found a pink Hi-Liter marker.

He looked up and down at the foyer of the apartment building where they were standing and noticed the walls were all marked up. "So," he said, "you're the one who's been doing all this graffiti."

Tyquan shook his head. "I turned and said to him, 'Man, what's wrong with you? How can you make black graffiti with a *pink* Hi-Liter?'"

The other kids laughed. That was enough for the burly Latino officer who was searching Tyquan. They dragged him to a squad car, kept him in a precinct for eight hours, then pushed him out a back door at four in the morning with a summons.

"What you have to realize, it stinks in those jails," he says. "You're in there with all these crazy people. For nothing."

It's cases like this that take up vast amounts of time in the Brooklyn courts. If it's not disorderly conduct by Hi-Liter, it's selling more than ten toys on the street without a license, or beating a fare, or occupying two seats on a subway car. "Deponent states that deponent observed the defendant at the above-listed location," reads one complaint in a case I watched in late 2012, "to wit the entrance of a McDonald's, and observed the defendant opening the door for a number of individuals."

The cases are almost all nuisance cases, yet they're charged with extraordinary precision. One of the more common violations—140,000 cases a year, remember—is the age-old drinking from an open container. In the summer of 2012, a judge named Noach Dear, rotating into Brooklyn for part-time duty, infuriated the city when he challenged the public drinking summons of a Latino man named Julio Figueroa.

"As hard as I try, I cannot recall ever arraigning a white defendant for such a violation," he told *The New York Times*. He later had his staff check and found that only 4 percent of all public drinking summonses were issued to whites, while 85 percent went to blacks and Latinos.

Ultimately this all comes down to discretion. If they want, the police can arrest you for just about anything.

In the courts you hear story after story: The carpenter on the way home from work gets a car stop and gets busted for having a box cutter in his truck. The undercovers who crowd into the Bushwick Avenue subway station when school gets out so they can bust teenagers jumping subway fares.

"I've had judges *set bail* on fare beats," sighs one lawyer at Schermerhorn. "It's literally shit like this all day long."

And once you take one plea, you might lose all kinds of things. Financial aid for schooling is out if you have a joint-in-your-pocket case. Welfare payments, beds at homeless shelters, Section 8 housing—it all might go up in smoke the instant you look at a police officer the wrong way.

This constant police pressure is more than a high-volume, high-cost tactical strategy to catch people up in more serious crimes, like holding guns or fleeing outstanding warrants. It's heavy-duty politics. It puts an entire segment of the population constantly on the defensive, gives it a criminal record essentially in advance, puts everyone in the dragnet up front, so that one false move leads to real time.

It's a system that's also set up to make consequences for nuisance arrests almost impossible, which emboldens police to ever-stupider behavior, which in turn leads to less respect for the law—an endless cycle of idiocy.

I first met Andrew in December 2012. I was at Stoll, Glickman & Bellina, a law office in Brooklyn that deals with police abuse cases, toward what I thought was the end of a months-long tour of the New York City criminal court system. I'd originally called Andrew's lawyer, Leo Glickman, regarding an unrelated story I kept hearing about in Brooklyn courtrooms, involving a rogue police precinct where the same small group of officers was routinely busting into homes, turning them upside down in search of drugs or guns, then threatening the occupants with arrest if they didn't sign consent forms after the fact.

There'd apparently been numerous lawsuits and settlements already involving these particular cops, and none of them had been dismissed from the job. More amazingly, it'd come out that at least a few of them had lied in court, and/or to grand juries, and yet they were still out there making arrests, and judges were still arraigning people based on their affidavits.

The thing is, there's generally no consequence for bad police behavior, even repeated or serially bad behavior. Even if individual officers are successfully sued, the only thing that happens is that the city's corporation counsel pays out some cash, and life just goes on as before. An officer's record of complaints or settlements isn't listed publicly. A defense lawyer who wants to find out if the officer who arrested his client has ever, say, bounced an old lady's head off a sidewalk or lied to a judge about witnessing a drug sale has to meet an extraordinary legal standard to get access to that info.

In order to look at an officer's record, you have to file what's called a "Gissendanner motion," the term referring to a 1979 case, *People v. Gissendanner.* In that case, a woman in the Rochester suburb of Irondequoit was busted in a sting cocaine sale by a pair of under-cover police. The court in that case held that the defendant isn't entitled to subpoena the records of arresting officers willy-nilly, but that you needed a "factual predicate" to look for records of, say, ex-cessive force or entrapment. In other words, you already need to know what you're looking for before you find it.

What this all boils down to is, if you really feel like it, you can definitely sue the New York City Police Department. Since so much of what they do happens on the street, in front of witnesses, you might very well even win. But even if you win, there's not necessar-ily any consequence. The corporation counsel's office doesn't call up senior police officials after lawsuits and say, "Hey, you've got to get rid of these three meatheads in the Seventy-Eighth Precinct we keep paying out settlements for." In fact, when there are successful lawsuits, individual officers typically aren't even informed of it.

What makes this so luridly fascinating is that this system is the exact inverse of the no-jail, all-settlement system of justice that gov-erns too-big-to-fail companies like HSBC. Big banks get caught committing crimes, at worst they pay a big fine. Instead of going to jail, a check gets written, and it comes out of the pockets of share-holders, not the individuals responsible.

Here it's the same thing. Police make bad arrests, a settlement comes out of the taxpayer's pocket, but the officer himself never even hears about it. He doesn't have to pay a dime. And life goes on as before.

Thus if you're a Tyquan Brehon or Andrew Brown, your sole option is to sue and squeeze some money out of the city. You can't secure an officer's dismissal, can't get a policy change, and can't get anyone brought up on charges.

"All they can do is get you a little money," says Andrew. "But I don't want money. I want to stop getting arrested."

Of course, it's not like that on the other side of the tracks. Just the opposite, in fact.

I was hanging out in misdemeanor court in Brooklyn one afternoon, chatting with a public defender, watching one street defendant after another get whacked with high bail. The lawyer sighed.

"The problem is, all the judges live in Connecticut," he said. "They don't live in these neighborhoods. They don't see these defendants as members of their communities. So sentencing and bail recommendations, all that shit becomes like a paint-by-numbers deal. They look at the chart, see what the guidelines say, and just spit out a number. Like in ten seconds. They could be selling livestock."

A few months later I was talking to a former federal prosecutor at an upscale café far from New York. The subject turned to sentencing. I told him the story about being in the grimy court in Brooklyn, listening to the public defender complaining about the judges all living in Connecticut.

"Oh, Jesus, tell me about it," he said. Then he told a story about a famous federal case that went sideways for exactly the opposite reason. The judge was from Connecticut, sure, but so was the defendant. Well, his billion-dollar company was, anyway.

Way back in the fourth quarter of 2000 and the first quarter of 2001, the insurance giant AIG was looking at having to release poor financial results, which surely would have sent its stock into a tailspin. To cover up the mess, it engaged in some Enronesque accounting, reaching out to another company, General Reinsurance, a firm owned by Warren Buffett's Berkshire Hathaway corporation. The two companies struck a pair of fraudulent reinsurance deals that hid losses on AIG's books. The scheme cost AIG shareholders more than $600 million.*

The case broke in the middle of the accounting-scandal era ushered in by Enron and WorldCom, and thanks to officials in the Bush Justice Department and New York state prosecutors like Eliot Spitzer, both AIG and Gen Re became major prosecutorial targets. The biggest fish of all in the case was Maurice "Hank" Greenberg, CEO of AIG. A judge eventually ruled that Greenberg had originated the scheme with a phone call to Gen Re CEO Ronald Ferguson on October 31, 2000.

Greenberg, probably best known for his driving animosity toward Spitzer and for his hilarious postretirement effort to sue the U.S. government for giving AIG an insufficiently generous bailout, was one of the most powerful men on Wall Street in the 2000s. A felony conviction of him at any time, but particularly after the financial crisis, would have sent a powerful message to Wall Street that no one is above the law.

Though four Gen Re executives and one AIG executive were ultimately indicted and convicted in the celebrated case, neither Spitzer nor the Justice Department could ever make a criminal case against Greenberg. One of the main reasons was that the lesser players in the case were given softball sentences, which left prosecutors with no leverage to roll any of the smaller fry into the really big fish.

One particularly garish example involved Chris Garand, a senior vice president of the Stamford, Connecticut–based Gen Re. Garand was convicted on three counts of securities fraud, three counts of

---

* How big a crime is a $600 million fraud? If one goes by FBI statistics, the Gen Re defendants' fraud cost AIG shareholders more in damages than was stolen by all auto thieves in the entire American Northeast in the year 2009, the year after the Gen Re defendants' convictions. Stealing a car in New York is grand larceny in the fourth degree and typically carries a sentence of up to four years. If the car is worth more, you might get grand larceny in the third degree, which takes it up to seven years. A luxury car worth more than $50,000 might get you as much as fifteen. At the very least, it's safe to say that a lot of car thieves drew a lot more time than the Gen Re defendants. As one public defender explained it, "Car thefts, they do those by the book."

mail fraud, three counts of making false statements to the SEC, and one count of conspiracy to violate federal securities laws and commit mail fraud.

Garand had lied to government investigators and helped concoct the scheme that helped AIG cover up its losses. Because of the sheer magnitude of the crime, federal sentencing guidelines actually permitted the judge—a Hartford, Connecticut, native named Christopher Droney—to fine Garand more than $29 million and give him, no joke, life in jail. (Well, technically it allowed Judge Droney to impose a sentence up to 160 years. But for all intents and purposes, Garand was facing life.)

The Feds didn't need Droney to go that far, but they wanted and needed Garand to get a stiff sentence, in order to secure his cooperation. Assistant U.S. attorney Ray Patricco said he sought a "substantial" prison term. Garand's lawyers at the firm Proskauer Rose said the state was looking for six or seven years.

But in March 2009, when it came time for Garand's sentencing hearing, nearly eighty people showed up in the federal courtroom in Hartford, including Garand's wife, Barbara (who reporters noted was a school board official in their suburban hometown of Saddle River, New Jersey), and his two daughters, aged fifteen and twenty-six. Garand's friends and relatives reportedly cried audibly throughout the two-and-a-half-hour hearing, pleading with the judge, telling him that Garand was a man of charity, well respected, and that putting him in jail wouldn't serve any purpose.

Garand himself told the judge he was "profoundly sorry" (in the course of researching this book I would hear this term a lot; executives from HSBC would use exactly the same language four years after the Gen Re fiasco), while his wife, Barbara, pleaded for his freedom. "These past few years have caused a great deal of pain to our family," she said. "Please don't take him from us. Our lives are in your hands."

Many of the Gen Re and AIG defendants made similar appeals. Gen Re CEO Ronald Ferguson, after being caught up in the scandal, went the Chuck Colson route and started studying to become a minister, telling the judge that a light sentence would help him fulfill a "mission from God." He said he wanted to "make a difference in the lives and comfort of others, the widows and the orphans, the lost and the least, and the left out."

As befits a higher corporate officer, Ferguson drew about five times as many supporters to his sentencing hearing as Garand (four hundred people, roughly), and he was portrayed in testimony as a "God-fearing family man who refuses even to swear, drink, or jaywalk." Steal $600 million, sure, but not jaywalk.

In the end, Droney was moved by the appeals for mercy and gave Garand a sentence of one year and one day. Ferguson, the alleged co-originator of the scheme, got two years. Even better, though, Droney allowed all five defendants to remain out of jail pending appeal, thereby removing any leverage the state might have to pressure them to cooperate.

Perhaps inevitably, all five of the Gen Re/AIG defendants had their sentences vacated two years later on a series of absurd technicalities. In 2011 a federal judge, Dennis Jacobs, suggested that the government had prejudiced jurors against the defendants by talking at trial about stock losses at AIG during the time when AIG was blowing up and causing a financial crisis. This, said Judge Jacobs, "prejudicially cast the defendants as causing an economic downturn that has affected every family in America."

This was a ridiculous reason to let five people get away with a $600 million fraud, even if it were true. But it wasn't. Judge Jacobs had his dates screwed up. The Gen Re defendants were convicted in February 2008, a good seven months before AIG became the national poster child for the imploding economy. Jacobs's entire theory about "prejudicial" evidence was off by more than half a year.

The moral of the story? Judges do listen to appeals for leniency, but only in selected cases. Sentencing guidelines in the Gen Re case gave a judge the power to help the state deliver convictions in one of the biggest criminal cases in the history of Wall Street. Instead, the prosecutors not only didn't get the main target, they lost all the little fish, too. The whole thing ended in a big fat goose egg.

"I mean, those guys could have gotten life. *Life*," says the former federal prosecutor. "That would have been a little much, of course. But nothing? Seriously?"

It's impossible to say that the judge in the Gen Re case was wrong to be moved to leniency. Those defendants, who knows, might not have been flight risks, and they might very well not even have been risks to jaywalk. The system gives judges the power to make those determinations. But the reality is that in the squalid halls of courts like Schermerhorn, impossibly high bail is routinely dumped on less-well-off defendants and is just as routinely used (in conjunction with tricks like the "certificate of readiness" gambit) to pressure those defendants into guilty pleas and other forms of cooperation. In the Gen Re case, prosecutors needed the judge to do what judges do a million times a day in inner-city courts: stick to the draconian book. Instead, he treated the defendants like people deserving of mercy. It's not that either way, in a vacuum, is wrong necessarily. It's more that the two approaches don't match, and there's no way that can ever be right.

CHAPTER 4

THE GREATEST BANK ROBBERY YOU NEVER HEARD OF

When one of the biggest bank heists ever took place right in the middle of the 2008 financial crisis, few people knew about it. Even to the victims, it was a secret for years. It was the perfect twenty-first-century crime—so broad in scale that it was practically invisible to the naked eye.

For years after the 2008 crash, a lot of time and effort was spent debating the question of whether Wall Street was guilty of actual crimes, or whether its executives were merely greedy and irresponsible. Barack Obama himself clumsily staked out a heavily parsed, lawyerly position on the question on *60 Minutes*.* But the question, as posed, mostly missed the point. The real issue wasn't *legal or illegal?* but *seen or unseen?* While some of the most dangerous behaviors in American big business were indeed against the law, they

---

* "Some of the most damaging behavior on Wall Street, in some cases, some of the least ethical behavior on Wall Street, wasn't illegal." Reporters took the quote to mean that what Wall Street professionals had done wasn't illegal, but that's not quite what Obama said. Like an Escher painting, the statement has more meanings the more you look at it.

were often, more importantly, outside the law, executed in an undefined legal space, in darkness.

In high finance, a few arenas are subject to some light and transparency—regulated stock exchanges like the NYSE and the NASDAQ, for example, places fit for day traders and suburban retirees and other such PG-rated softies. But for the most part, high finance is a night game where anything goes. This is the legacy of a generation of brilliant lawyers who've turned Wall Street into a perfect black box, the industry surrounded by the legal equivalent of tinted windows.

In the crash era, one story towers above the rest as a perfect example. The collapse of the Lehman Brothers investment bank and its subsequent lightning-speed, past-midnight-hour sale to the British banking giant Barclays was a sweeping two-act crime drama that overwhelmed the imagination of American law enforcement. Regulators simply couldn't see through those tinted windows to make out the monstrous frauds, robberies, and conspiracies that were raging out of control within both companies. And afterward the courts were too overwhelmed by the scale of it to do anything but acknowledge what had taken place.

This story began with simple, dumb greed and irresponsibility, progressed to frank illegality, and ended with a brilliant corporate mutiny and late-night merger that one former Lehman lawyer calls "the greatest bank robbery in history." The two firms involved, Lehman and Barclays, were at the centers of both the 2008 crash and the worldwide LIBOR interest-rate-rigging scandal that exploded into public view four years later, making this the ultimate cautionary tale. If regulators at any point had stopped to take a really close look at either company, multiple disasters might have been averted.

But nobody looked into either of those black boxes, at least not until it was too late. Lehman's collapse ruined thousands of institutions and individual investors around the world. A too-late lawsuit failed to recoup the lost money, meaning the only thing left in the end was a long, twisting tale of testosterone-fueled catastrophe buried in a mountain of paper—case No. 12-2322, U.S. Court of Appeals for the Second Circuit, *In re: Lehman Brothers Holdings, Inc.*

If you want to understand not only why Wall Street isn't policed but why many believe it can't be policed, you need only look carefully at this case. You can't police what you can't see, and you can't see in the dark.

THE BACKGROUND

Imagine an ordinary low-level swindle. A con man comes to a town and opens a store. He then buys lavishly from all the local merchants, on credit, to stock his shelves. For a few weeks he does a booming business, selling his swag for cash. But suddenly, before his bills come due, he flees town with the cash, stiffing the local hayseeds who've been gullible enough to give him credit. The huckster shopkeeper who bilked his creditors by "fraudulent conveyance" was a common enough character in small-town American crime that some states had to adopt felony laws against that sort of thing.

The Lehman story is exactly the same story, only the "town" here is the planet Earth, and the flight was an absurdly complex escape mechanism, a getaway so convoluted that some of the best lawyers in the world had trouble following it.

First, Lehman executives ran up a $700 *billion* tab engaging in almost indescribably reckless and antisocial behaviors, borrowing on a grand scale to create and sell products so dangerous that they very nearly collapsed the world economy in 2008. But before the bank itself went bankrupt that same year, the hucksters who ran the shop quietly sucked the cash out of the company, leaving tens of thousands of people and institutions to which Lehman owed money—from foreign orphanages to the city of Long Beach, California—high and dry.

The hucksters took the money out of the company in two ways. First, some of the principals who had helped ruin the company simply paid themselves hefty bonuses on the way out the door. Then, some of them came up with an even more inspired mechanism: they sold themselves to another big bank, the British firm Barclays. In this second part of the deal, key parts of which were executed literally in the middle of the night, billions of dollars were quietly moved into the coffers of Barclays and out of the reach of Lehman's creditors. Simultaneously, the insiders from Lehman who had come up with the idea took lucrative jobs at Barclays, taking hundreds of millions in future bonus payments to do so.

This is a hard story to follow. But if you keep that one image in mind, of a shopkeeper fleeing town in the middle of the night with borrowed profits, the collapse of Lehman Brothers—one of the great unpunished swindles of all time—starts to make sense.

Lehman Brothers succumbed to fraud, bad decisions, and book-cooking, dying not of any one specific thing but more generally of corruption itself, in the manner of elderly mobsters or Soviet rulers.

The company was founded by a pair of Bavarian-born immigrants to the American South, Henry and Emmanuel Lehman, who in 1850 set up a cotton-trading business based in Montgomery, Alabama. The pair moved north to New York less than a decade later and quickly expanded their business to include dealing in railroad bonds and investment banking. For the next century and a half, they and their descendants helped build America, helping finance or take public a long succession of foundational American corporations: F. W. Woolworth, Macy's, RCA, Digital, B. F. Goodrich, Studebaker, even Halliburton.

In the late 1970s and early 1980s, the company fell on hard times, as internal power struggles forced the ouster of some of its most talented executives, including former CEO Pete Peterson, and former M&A chief Stephen Schwarzman, who would later become two of the richest individuals in the world. The company briefly merged with American Express in the 1980s and was spun off again as an investment bank in the early 1990s. And then . . .

And then it headed into the late 2000s led by one of the most unlikable characters in American business, a man whose very name sounds like a thesaurus entry for "grasping, narcissistic creep": Dick Fuld. Nicknamed "the Gorilla," Fuld is a tall, cavern-eyed, hollow-cheeked bully who was famous for his quick-twitch meanness, his screaming intransigence, and his apparently congenital inability to blame himself for any problem. Fuld is the kind of person who would fall drunk down a spiral staircase and then sue the architect for building blurry steps.

Later on, after his firm collapsed, Fuld would never once publicly puzzle over his own mistakes. Instead, he said he would wonder "until they put me in the ground" why the government hadn't bailed him out. His seemingly terminal lack of self-awareness left him desperately hated by the firm's rank and file. In fact, in the weeks after he stepped down, Fuld would literally be punched out in the Lehman Brothers gym by one of his former minions, belted off a treadmill while wearing a heart monitor.

In the years leading up to the crash, Fuld and his right-hand man, a goonish henchman named Joe Gregory, acquired dictatorial powers within the firm. You've heard of the good-cop/bad-cop routine: Fuld and Gregory were bad-cop/worse-cop. Fuld was the notorious self-obsessed attention hog, while Gregory was the guy who stalked the halls dressing down and/or firing people to strengthen Fuld's grip on power. (Author and former Lehman executive Lawrence McDonald uses the word "shot" to describe Gregory's firings, as in "He shot two equities guys.")

Throughout the 2000s, the two men used the Stalinist technique of gradually filling the administrative ranks of Lehman with patsies and neophytes who would be forced to lean on them for key decisions. Twice they put nonaccountants—Erin Callan and Ian Lowitt—into the CFO job, overseeing the firm's accounting. Then they took one of their most talented financial strategists, Bart McDade—"our best risk taker," explains McDonald—and put him in a relatively inconsequential job fixing the equities department.

Fuld and Gregory wanted complete control over the company for a simple reason. They wanted to transform the bank's entire financial strategy into a vehicle for maximizing their personal compensation. The more risk the bank took on, the more money they made in the short term, and that was what it was all about. It wasn't enough to be the fiftieth- or sixtieth-richest guy on Wall Street. They wanted to personally be billionaires many times over, like the partners at Goldman or celebrated private equity chiefs like their departed betters, Steve Schwarzman and Pete Peterson.

"In 1998 the balance sheet* was $38 billion. In 2005 it was like $400 billion. And in 2007 it was like $700 billion," laughs McDonald. "This was all a plan to try to catch Goldman, to try to catch Peterson, to try to catch Schwarzman. It was just two guys, Dick and Joe, who wanted so bad to catch those guys."

Expanding Lehman was easy during that decade's exploding financial bubble. By the mid-2000s, the financial services industry had pushed all-in on a nuclear-powered poker game built around an irrationally escalating home housing market. Trillions of dollars were being gambled, and the pots kept getting bigger and bigger every day. But entering late 2006 and early 2007, some of the players at the table, already sitting on big stacks of winnings, began to think about cutting their losses and running. Reports had started trickling up from the ground about a potential disaster in the market for subprime residential mortgages, around which the whole game had been built, and the smarter players started planning their escapes.

For instance, at a meeting in December 2006, some of Goldman Sachs's most powerful executives concluded that they had too much exposure to subprime mortgages and had to start unloading the stuff, fast. Goldman needed to get "closer to home," as its CFO David Viniar put it, and unload its "cats and dogs," as CEO Lloyd Blankfein described the bank's subprime holdings.

So Goldman started unloading subprime in massive amounts,

---

* Like any business, an investment bank is just a pile of assets and liabilities, whose collective profile is commonly summarized by the term "balance sheet." This is a statement of a company's net worth, with all the stuff the bank counts as equity (like cash) in a financial win column on one side, and liabilities (all the money it owes) on the other. An investment bank that, say, suddenly went on a massive borrowing-and-gambling spree, betting heavily on subprime, would be "expanding its balance sheet."

famously dumping as much of its toxic cargo as it could on unsuspecting clients.

It was more or less exactly at this moment that Lehman decided to double down on subprime. "Right when Goldman and all those guys were having those meetings to get rid of this stuff, Dick and Joe were making the opposite decision," says McDonald.

One executive, Michael Gelband, a managing director and head of global fixed income, stood on the table and begged Fuld to reconsider. As far back as 2005, Gelband had given a presentation warning of the dangers of subprime and had been mostly ignored. By late 2006, at exactly the moment Viniar was persuading Goldman to reverse course, Gelband pleaded with Fuld to do the same. "The world is changing. We have to rethink our business model," he told Fuld.

Fuld blew him off. "You're too conservative," he said.

Soon afterward, at a March 2007 meeting, the board decided that the seeming collapse of subprime was not a problem but rather an opportunity to jump back in, and jump in huge. "The current distressed environment," concluded the board, "provides substantial opportunities."

Eventually, Fuld would be persuaded to dial back on the subprime strategy, but by then it was far too late, and the rollback strategies he employed were far too meager. More important, the bank by then had begun its descent into a muck of crooked borrowing schemes, all designed to whitewash the firm's already catastrophic financial condition.

Hiding the truth became harder when the famed Bear Stearns investment bank went bust in March 2008. After Bear's collapse, due to a fatally overenthusiastic miscalculation about subprime, regulators scanned the landscape and wondered what other Wall Street investment banking titans might be hiding toxic inventories from the markets. Their eyes settled on Lehman, and teams of investigators from the New York Fed (run at the time by an ambitious bureaucrat named Timothy Geithner) and the SEC set up shop at

Lehman to monitor the company's cash-flow situation, ostensibly to prevent another Bear from happening.

But Lehman kept protesting that it was in fine shape, and regulators somehow kept buying its explanation. In truth, the bank was already near the end of a long slide into a habit of desperately borrowing just to keep its doors open. It had started with borrowing cash in three-month loans, then it was one-month notes, and then the cycle got even tighter and crazier. By the end of 2007, Lehman was sometimes borrowing $100 billion or even $200 billion a day or more just to stay afloat. The life-saving cash injections came from overnight "repo" loans from banks like Fidelity that Lehman took out at the end of every single business day. And the first thing in the morning, it was paying off those loans by taking out matching amounts of "intraday" loans from banks like JPMorgan Chase. Then it was rinse, repeat: continue the cycle by rolling the loans later that night.

Chase's was a junkie's banking strategy, shooting speed in the morning and spending all day foraging for the cash to dope down at night, an endless quest to chase the debt dragon.

One banker who was part of a team that later conducted a forensic examination of the Lehman bankruptcy talked about this insane financing strategy. He recounts talking to a Lehman employee who was responsible for arranging the overnight loans. "Between six in the morning when you get in or seven in the morning, you're contacting trading desks, and by the end of the day, you have to find lenders for $200 billion," he said. "I mean, it's crazy. . . . I didn't know that's how these people functioned. Nobody did."

How do you get someone to lend you $200 billion overnight? The simplified answer is that you pledge collateral for cash. Lehman would go to a company like Chase or Fidelity carrying armfuls of corporate loans and commercial mortgages and whatever else it had in the cupboard, and dump them on that bank's doorstep, asking for billions of cash in return. Normally it could simply roll the same loans over and over again, but as its cash needs grew, it began to get more and more desperate, pushing ethical boundaries left and right.

First it lied about the quality of its collateral, and then it came to the ultimate counterfeit collateral scheme. In the wake of the collapse of Bear Stearns, Lehman's leaders decided to try a sort of financial publicity stunt called a "liquidity pool": they would show the world they weren't as broke as Bear Stearns by announcing the existence of a giant pile of liquid assets that they could call on in an emergency to pay their bills.

In June 2008 their CFO, Ian Lowitt, announced in a conference call that Lehman had a big stack of $45 billion in assets, a reserve fund that was "never stronger."

But most of what made up that $45 billion liquidity pool would turn out to be stuff that Lehman had already hocked once or twice to other banks and institutions in exchange for cash. Chase, for instance, accepted a $5 billion chunk of collateral that had been pledged to this liquidity pool. In another case, Lehman pledged nearly $3 billion of notes that its own employees derided as "goat poo" as collateral to Chase and to the liquidity pool, making the deal a triple-whammy: it overrated the notes and then pledged the overrated notes for collateral to two different places at once. (The deal, known as the Fenway or Hudson Castle deal, was actually a regulatory quadruple-whammy, as it also involved a complex Enronesque self-dealing scheme of questionable legality.)

Investigators later concluded that of the $30 billion in assets that was supposed to be in the pool in the bank's last days, perhaps only $1 billion or $2 billion was actually available to the bank. The rest had long ago been put up for cash to help the bank pay for its subprime addiction.

The bank had taken an even more decisive step in the direction of fraud when it invented a devious and desperate accounting trick called Repo 105 to Botox its balance sheet.

To simplify: Lehman was borrowing huge sums of money at the end of every quarter—as much as $50 billion—and booking those loans as sales. This is a little like taking out a cash advance on your credit card and telling your wife you earned the money pulling extra overtime shifts selling Amway products door to door.

Things got so bad that in mid-June 2008 the ranks finally mutinied. Fifteen of the company's managing directors stood up to Fuld and demanded radical changes. It was roughly this same group of senior employees who would later resurface in another mutiny, during the firm's collapse. But for now the group tried to save the firm by urging Fuld to change course.

Outflanked, Fuld had no choice but to comply. He fired Gregory and began moving from department to department, asking traders to chop down the bloated balance sheet, get rid of a billion in risk here, a billion in risk there.

But it wasn't enough. Lehman was in debt significantly beyond its eyeballs. It was still borrowing huge amounts every day and was exquisitely vulnerable to the slightest change in public perception about its soundness.

As investigator Anton Valukas later explained in his report on the firm's bankruptcy, even the slightest slowing in sales of things like subprime collateralized debt obligations (CDOs) would make Lehman's lenders nervous about the hundreds of billions in cash loans they were forking over every day—and the instant those lenders lost confidence, the end would come, exploding-death-star style.

"Confidence was critical," Valukas wrote. "The moment that repo counterparties were to lose confidence in Lehman and decline to roll over its daily funding, Lehman would be unable to fund itself and continue to operate."

Crucially, authorities by then had already been contacted about illegalities and improprieties within the bank. One of its lawyers, Oliver Budde, had gone to the SEC in April 2008 with evidence that a number of Lehman executives, including Fuld, had been systematically underreporting their income to the IRS through their misuse of a kind of stock award called restricted stock units. Fuld's misstatements alone represented hundreds of millions of dollars in underreported income.

But the SEC blew Budde off. "If we had a properly functioning SEC and regulatory structure," he says, "my information would have raised gigantic red flags at the SEC, who then should/would have notified all the related regulators. . . . It should have had monumental impact."

Meanwhile, another whistle-blower, a senior accountant named Matthew Lee, had alerted not only senior executives at Lehman but Lehman's auditor, Ernst & Young, to serious improprieties at the firm. Among other things, Lee told Ernst & Young all about the Repo 105 scheme in June 2008, months before the firm collapsed.

None of this, however, came out in time to prevent investors from buying stock in Lehman in the months before its collapse.

How many people would have invested in Lehman if such information had been known? But it wasn't, making it a classic disclosure offense. One former high-ranking SEC official said he was shocked that no enforcement action was ever brought. Valukas, too, identified numerous areas where "colorable" claims could be made, like Repo 105 and the liquidity pool.

Budde insists that all sorts of charges could have been filed against Lehman executives. "I say bust them," he says, citing Repo 105, the stock award problems he uncovered, and the Hudson Castle deal, which, he says, "is Enron-type bullshit. If it was punishable then, why not now? No relevant laws were changed in the meantime."

But nobody was ever charged, a fact that is all the more incredible when one considers that the bank practically had regulators living in its backside from the moment Bear Stearns collapsed through the end.

One incredible moment in the precollapse history of Lehman underscores the two-faced approach the government took toward policing this bank. Among the banks that Lehman was borrowing its massive amounts of cash from in its last years was JPMorgan Chase. In the kinds of repo loans Lehman was taking out, the borrower is usually forced to post a slightly larger amount of collateral than it gets back in cash. If you want $100 billion in cash, for instance, you normally have to post $105 billion in collateral. That extra 5 percent, called a haircut, is standard in almost every loan of this type.

But Chase was not asking for a haircut from Lehman prior to 2008. It was engaged in "100 percent collateral intraday lending," which just means it was giving out massive bundles of cash in exchange for exactly equivalent amounts of collateral. Insiders and investigators who later examined these deals now say that Chase had simply been lazy. "They weren't paying attention" is how one source puts it.

This was so irresponsible that in January 2008, the Federal Reserve—doing its job as the primary banking regulator—went to Chase, tapped the firm's leaders on the shoulder, and suggested that they start paying more attention to their relationship with Lehman. "They were like, 'You guys have to manage your risk better,'" one investigator said.

Chase followed the Fed's advice and in early 2008 went back to Lehman and asked the bank for more collateral. Lehman, incredibly, told Chase it couldn't afford it—at least not yet. It begged Chase to allow it to start paying more collateral by degrees, 1 percent at a time, until it could get to the point where it was paying that 5 percent haircut.

What's amazing about this is that the Fed saw fit as early as January 2008 to warn Chase about Lehman's instability. But nobody ever warned the public. Nobody stepped in after the bank cooked its books in Repo 105, or misreported taxes, or made fake disclosures, or lied outright to investors. Nothing was done. The government merely sat back and watched the catastrophe unfold, allowing new victims to pour money into the walking-dead bank right up until its collapse.

THE SHIP BEGINS TO SINK

By the end of the summer of 2008, Fuld realized that the bank could not continue to stay afloat on its own. He needed a savior, someone to whom he could sell, and sell quickly, his rapidly disintegrating empire of "goat poo."

Fuld would sell to anyone, public or private, it made no difference. A federal rescue was possible. Bear Stearns had gotten one— Geithner and the Fed had helped JPMorgan Chase buy the company. But when Lehman posted a $2.8 billion loss in the second quarter, Treasury Secretary Hank Paulson, a former head of Goldman Sachs, Lehman's bitter historical rival, had told Fuld that if he didn't find a buyer, Lehman would go the way of the mammoths. One more losing quarter, he implied, and Lehman would be kaput.

Freaked out, Fuld tried to save Lehman in August 2008 by selling the firm to the Korea Development Bank. On August 22 the firm seemed poised to survive on the strength of that merger, as shares in the firm actually rose 5 percent that day on the rumors. But the state-owned Korean bank soon backed out, and on September 9, Lehman shares plummeted 45 percent to $7.79 a share. The next day the company announced a $3.9 billion third-quarter loss. The markets panicked and began unloading Lehman stock like it was tainted with plague.

It was Wednesday, September 10. A week before, Sarah Palin had reenergized the Republican Party with a dazzling speech on the floor of the Republican National Convention in St. Paul, Minnesota. The troubles of Wall Street barely rated a blip at that convention, but the truth was that the first big domino in the 2008 crash was about to fall. Lehman Brothers was dying. Without a buyer, it would be dead within a week, or sooner.

Fuld himself was already toast, but he didn't know it yet. By the time the seventh anniversary of September 11 arrived, a Thursday, the once-feared Gorilla's desperation to throw himself into the arms of Bank of America, Barclays, the taxpayer, or really anyone who would even consider saving his firm had reached levels of both the darkest tragedy and the blackest comedy.

He tried Morgan Stanley's John Mack on Thursday, September 11, only to be told by Mack that there was "too much overlap" between the firms.

Next he tried Bank of America's Ken Lewis, who he was convinced would be there for him in a pinch. He called Lewis repeatedly throughout the next day, Friday the twelfth.

Strangely, however, Lewis didn't call him back, not even once. Fuld, characteristically, saw no significance in this fact. Probably, he thought, Lewis wasn't checking his messages. No way he wouldn't answer the calls of *Dick Fuld*!

Humorously, Fuld would keep calling Lewis for days, until finally—and this isn't a joke—Lewis got his *wife* to answer his phone for him.

Moments like this are the backstory to the 2008 crisis: Ken Lewis's wife had to break the news to Dick Fuld that Bank of America would not be rescuing Lehman Brothers.

In fact, Lewis decided he wasn't going to buy Lehman Brothers unless the government got the taxpayer to buy all its toxic stuff, leaving only the edible, profitable parts for Bank of America. This was something that the federal government had already done in the Bear Stearns deal, and would do again in the Wachovia and Washington Mutual deals, and would even do that very week for Lewis himself in the Merrill Lynch deal.

But it wouldn't do it for Lehman Brothers. Hank Paulson was Rick Blaine in *Casablanca,* not willing to sell the transit papers to Victor Laszlo, not for any amount of money—there was apparently no price he would consider to save Dick Fuld.

Unable to sell himself to any bank in America or Asia, Fuld now called Bob Diamond, the CEO of the British giant Barclays, and asked if they could meet. This set in motion a chain of events that would lead to Lehman's last crooked trade.

Diamond agreed to meet Fuld. On that Friday, September 12, the

Barclays chief made a stealth visit to the Lehman offices downtown, coming in through the service entrance ("The garage, I guess, the back way," he would testify later) and then taking a long service-elevator ride with Fuld, just the two of them, up to Fuld's thirty-first-floor offices.

In that ride up the service elevator, Diamond ripped out what was left of what passed for Fuld's heart.

A lipless, pale-faced Irish Catholic from Concord, Massachusetts, who wears Coke-bottle glasses and appears in public wearing the pinched, joyless manner of a constipated nun, Diamond, who came up through the banking ranks at Morgan Stanley and First Boston, was one of the great ambassadors of American financial culture. Among other things, he helped export the cherished practice of unnecessarily massive executive salaries to the English business world, once even attracting criticism from British officials for his lack of "humility" and "modesty" when it was reported that he had paid himself the hilarious sum of £63 million in a single year.

Diamond was himself only four years away from being washed down the drain of history in his own lurid corruption scandal— more on that later. But on that Friday, September 12, he would find himself in the fantastically satisfying position of being able to push one of the great assholes of our times, Dick Fuld, to the brink of unemployment and total humiliation. In the elevator, Diamond cavalierly told Fuld that he wasn't interested in buying Lehman Brothers unless Fuld was willing to sell the firm basically for free. "It would have to be a rescue situation," he told him coldly. "Meaning if this is a very, very distressed price."

Diamond's elevator dissing left Fuld devastated. Of course, upon hearing that Barclays would buy Lehman only if Fuld gave it away, Fuld—again, according to court testimony—promptly did the predictable thing. He turned around and told the Lehman board that the deal was very much alive, that Barclays had only just started its due diligence process, that it had nothing to worry about. It was now late Friday evening, and Lehman's share price had closed at $3.65. The firm was in its final death throes.

Meanwhile, as the weekend of September 13–14, 2008, began, a series of meetings kicked off across town, at the offices of the New York Fed, that would dramatically reshape not just the American economy but the economy of the entire world. Hundreds of bankers and lawyers from most every bank and major Wall Street law firm in the city gathered at the regal, marble-floored building to hammer out a rescue of the insurance giant AIG, which like Lehman was also spiraling toward collapse and ruin.

The rescue of AIG that those men and women cooked up, in which the government assumed AIG's debts in full, had the consequence of saving AIG customers like Goldman and Deutsche Bank from billions of dollars that they would otherwise have lost. Moreover, the Fed and the U.S. Treasury, in the persons of Timothy Geithner and Hank Paulson, would shortly thereafter allow both Goldman and Morgan Stanley to convert themselves into commercial bank holding companies, thereby gaining access to billions of dollars of emergency financing from the Federal Reserve.

The deals the government and Wall Street worked out that weekend to save the likes of AIG, Goldman, Deutsche Bank, Morgan Stanley, and Merrill Lynch were unprecedented in their reach and political consequence, transforming America into a permanent oligarchical bailout state. This was, essentially, a formal merger of Wall Street and the U.S. government.

Only one actor was left out of the party: Lehman Brothers. When Fuld proposed that the government let Lehman make the same move to become a commercial bank, giving it the same life-giving access to the Fed's billions, Paulson told him to stuff it.

By Sunday morning, Fuld was ready to do Diamond's humiliating "sell yourself for free" deal. But when he tried to crawl from his knees into Diamond's lap, he found out even that deal was now impossible.

It turned out that an obscure British regulatory provision prevented Barclays from taking over Lehman's trading obligations without a shareholder vote, nixing any immediate mano-a-mano Barclays deal. When the British financial regulator, the Financial Services Authority (FSA), refused that weekend to provide a waiver for that requirement, the original Barclays fire-sale buyout proposal—which came to be known as "Barclays One"—was basically dead.

Beyond desperate now, Fuld called Paulson that Sunday and begged him to call British prime minister Gordon Brown to intervene. Paulson said he was busy. Fuld then begged Paulson to ask George Bush to call Brown. Same thing—no dice. Fuld even thought about reaching out to Jeb Bush to induce George to call Gordon Brown, but that idea, too, somehow collapsed.

Wearily, Fuld then ended where he'd begun, trying to sell himself to John Mack at Morgan Stanley one last time. Mack told Fuld he had enough problems of his own.

By the next morning, Fuld was out, stepping down when the last hope of avoiding bankruptcy vanished. A new group, led by the aforementioned "best risk taker," Bart McDade—a Lehman official with a reputation for integrity, a man who had once publicly questioned Fuld's subprime strategy—and a few dozen executives loyal to him, stepped in to take over. This new group faced the same devastating financial reality that Fuld had, but they had one thing going for them: the absence of Fuld. Without having to worry about propping up Lehman long enough to save Fuld's reputation, they were free to make one final, brilliantly ice-cold deal to save themselves. What would they do?

THE MUTINY

Sunday night, September 14, 2008. The world was changing. AIG was being nationalized. Goldman and Morgan were on their way to their own cushy rescues. Merrill Lynch was being shotgun-wedded to Bank of America. Wachovia was on its way to being swallowed up by Wells Fargo. All those companies were being saved, but Lehman was left without enough money to open for business the next morning. If it didn't declare bankruptcy by morning, the bank would implode, and its leveraged-to-the-hilt, $700 billion nuke-bomb of a balance sheet would detonate, perhaps igniting a global chain reaction of losses.

That last Sunday evening, some of the remaining executives and board members were still unconvinced that the government would actually risk such a scenario by letting Lehman fail. According to testimony, in fact, Henry Kaufman, one of Lehman's directors, argued that Sunday for "calling the government's bluff," and just going ahead and opening for business the next morning, essentially daring the government not to bail Lehman out.

But the Fed and the SEC kept calling the Lehman board that Sunday and assuring the company: We're not joking, you clowns. There's no bailout. Declare bankruptcy now—it's your only option.

When the grim reality that no bailout was coming finally sank in, the company shifted gears. With Fuld gone and the fiction of a last-minute, company-saving deal finally gone with him, these seasoned veterans of high-risk, daredevil finance decided to make one last inspired trade. They decided to rob their own bank.

"Traders have no loyalty to anybody," one former high-ranking Lehman executive explained to me, describing the moment. "The writing is on the wall: Lehman is dead. So one nanosecond later they're looking for the next trade: How can we make money? And the way we can make money is by marking everything down and getting Barclays to give us big bonuses."

That Sunday evening McDade placed a phone call to Bob Diamond, over at Barclays, and asked if he was still interested in doing the humiliating fire-sale transaction. Diamond said yes, and told McDade to set up a meeting for seven the next morning.

The next morning all the principals from both sides gathered—minus Fuld, of course—at Lehman's offices on 745 Seventh Avenue. And they started working on a deal. Well, two deals actually.

On the morning of September 15, 2008, the surviving principals at Lehman huddled and began working on two merger-like deals—a real one, which was a straight-up pillaging heavily tilted in Barclays's favor, and, unknown to most all the people working on it, a fake one, more seemingly equitable, full of careful math and dressy contractual bells and whistles about obligations to Lehman employees.

A veritable army set to work on the fake deal, early that Monday morning. Ad hoc workstations were set up on the thirty-second floor of the Lehman building, with rows of computers, phones, and work spaces put together on the fly. Hundreds of bankers, accountants, and lawyers from both the Lehman and Barclays sides ran back and forth, preparing to crunch numbers for a massive sale.

All this would turn out to be for show, although the people in those workstations didn't know it.

Ostensibly, the huge teams of Lehman and Barclays employees were trying to arrive at a real-world price for the stuff Barclays was planning to buy. The transaction was not going to be an outright merger with Lehman Brothers; it was going to be an asset purchase agreement, which was much better from Barclays's point of view, since it meant it got to just buy the stuff it wanted and let the rest of Lehman go down the toilet of the bankruptcy bureaucracy.

In order to do that, Barclays had to settle on a price for all the stuff in Lehman's financial warehouse, which was why all those bankers were crunching numbers at full speed, trying to price Lehman's books. And at the end of that Monday, all those hundreds of people in those thirty-second-floor workstations did in fact come up with the rough outlines of a deal. They came up with what is called a "book value" for Lehman's inventory—a value that matched what Lehman's Treasury bills and mortgage-backed securities and currencies and other stuff, all mashed together, might have fetched on the street.

What they did was, they found $70 billion worth of stuff that was actually worth something (assets) and then matched it to $70 billion worth of bills Lehman still had to pay (liabilities). What Barclays was supposedly getting, therefore, was a matched set of good stuff and bad stuff that had a net total value of zero. It would then pay the fire-sale price of $250 million for the Lehman name and business.

This was the deal that would be presented both to the Lehman board and to Judge James Peck's bankruptcy court. This deal was designed "for posterity": for the eyes of the Lehman board, the judge, and the outside world. It was, outwardly, a pretty good deal for both sides under the circumstances. Barclays would take on a matched set of billions in assets versus billions in liabilities, and for its trouble would get to take over one of the oldest broker-dealer businesses in America for a few hundred million bucks.

The value for the public was that the economy wouldn't be further destabilized by an outright collapse (which, who knew, might necessitate further bailouts), while there was considerable value to many Lehman employees and executives in being able to continue working, see deals to fruition, rescue careers.

But what almost none of those hundreds of bankers and lawyers knew was that late into that first Monday evening and into the wee hours of the next morning of Tuesday, September 16, Diamond and a small team of his most trusted advisers had pulled a small group of carefully placed Lehman insiders aside and set to work cutting the real deal with them.

We'll never know what might have happened had this second deal, which would be weighted far more severely in Barclays's favor, been presented to the board. Who knows? It might have been accepted. It's not like there was a parade of other buyers for the hulk of Lehman Brothers. But what's crucial to understand is precisely that—that we'll never know. The other players—Lehman's creditors, the company board, the rest of the market—never got a chance to step up to the plate.

This second deal was done in the ether, in an extralegal dimension where so much of Wall Street business is increasingly transacted. It was the legal equivalent of "dark liquidity" or "dark pools," places where huge blocks of stock trades are executed between major institutional buyers and sellers without passing information on to the hayseed public, which knows only how to buy and sell stocks on regulated stock exchanges. A dark pool trade is conducted between two huge players who don't want to deign to let the NYSE or any other stock exchange know their business. What went down between Barclays and the Lehman insiders was something very similar: a dark pool merger, executed outside the dreary confines of courts and board meetings.

The second deal was struck very much in the manner of a political coup d'état. It was done with cinematic élan, before dawn. Bob Diamond secured the revolt by agreeing to pay a small crew of key insiders bonuses of millions of dollars apiece to do a secret job.

There were about a dozen of these insiders. They included McDade, who replaced Fuld as president, plus head of investment banking Hugh "Skip" McGee, equities chief Jerry Donini, CFO Ian Lowitt, Lowitt's deputy (and the highest-ranking actual accountant at Lehman) Martin Kelly, the treasurer Paolo Tonucci, the fixed-income chief Eric Felder, the restructuring head Mark Shapiro, and a managing director named Alex Kirk.

Collectively, just the nine men listed above would be offered an astonishing $302.9 million that week. Technically, much of that compensation was supposed to cover other work done in 2008 and 2009 and beyond. But in reality, most of that $303 million was paying for their service in one deal.

The nine Lehman insiders, to put things in perspective, were offered about three times the compensation of the nine highest-paid New York Yankees that year. And they were essentially getting paid to play one game.

Just three of the principal negotiators—McDade, McGee, and Donini—managed to strike deals for an incredible $112,360,000 in future compensation among them. Many of the deals were struck at blinding speed and at very curious hours. Many of the insiders later testified that they got their windfall offers for future compensation as Barclays employees in the predawn hours of Tuesday, September 16, which by an extraordinary coincidence happened to be just in time to have their futures sorted out before they all went to a scheduled six a.m. emergency meeting of the Lehman board, where the Barclays deal was to be discussed and, ostensibly, approved.

Take Ian Lowitt, Lehman's chief financial officer. A South African with a British boarding school education who had come to Lehman in the early 1990s by way of the McKinsey consulting firm, Lowitt had a crucial role in the company, and his cooperation was needed. Sometime before dawn on that Tuesday—before 5:10 a.m., according to his testimony—Lowitt received a call from Rich Ricci, one of Diamond's chief negotiators.

Ricci told Lowitt that Barclays wanted to hire him, and that his compensation package would be worth about $6 million. Included in that package, Ricci told him, was a 2008 cash bonus of $4.56 million. That wasn't pay for the work he'd already done that year at Lehman. It was pay for just three months of future work that year at Barclays.

When later asked for the reasoning behind that $4.5 million cash bonus for three months' work, Lowitt testified that he was just that cool of a guy. He said he was "a valuable person for them to have as part of Barclays."

Other Lehman executives got similar calls that morning. All would later profess to be confused by questions about what they had done to earn the money. Paolo Tonucci, who worked under Lowitt and would play an important role in completing the deal over the course of the rest of the week, was offered a cash bonus of $1.85 million and a "special cash award" of $700,000. When later asked what the money was for, he repeated Lowitt's "value" line. "I assumed," he said, "that it was going to a group of senior employees that Barclays felt would be of future value to the organization."

Alex Kirk was offered $15 million. When later asked what he had done to earn the money, he had a hilarious answer.

Q: And what were your bonus arrangements or agreements with Barclays?

KIRK: About the end of October . . . they informed me that they would pay me $15 million in two separate installments.

Q: Did you receive either of those payments?

KIRK: Both. . . .

Q: Why did you get payments in the amounts that you did from Barclays having worked there for such a short period of time?

KIRK: I don't know.

Martin Kelly, one of the senior bean counters in the company, and a man whose sloppy email habits would later play a key role in the case, received a package similar to Tonucci's that included another "special cash bonus" of $700,000, and totaled about $1.7 million. When asked later in court if he knew what the bonus was for, Kelly looked in bankruptcy judge James Peck's face and said he'd never asked.

Most all of these monster compensation deals were completed before dawn that Tuesday morning, just before that scheduled meeting of the Lehman board at six. Lowitt, Kelly, Tonucci, Kirk, McDade, and the rest of the insiders went to that meeting bursting with enthusiasm, suddenly ready to collectively give a big thumbs-up to the "asset purchase agreement."

What they didn't mention to the board was that they'd all just finished accepting multimillion-dollar bonus offers. Although the board was told that eight Lehman executives, including McDade, would continue to work at Barclays as a condition of the deal (these would later be referred to in the press and elsewhere as the "elite eight"), the board, again according to court testimony, was not told about other Lehman execs who had already cut future employment deals, like Kelly, Tonucci, and Kirk. The board wasn't told about the predawn negotiations that very morning, and never had a clue that many of the people who would be working on the fine print of the pseudomerger were already, in effect, working for Barclays. When asked at trial a year and a half later why they had neglected to mention that information, many of these insiders offered parodies of nonanswers.

This is from Lowitt's testimony. The questioning attorney here is Bob Gaffey of Jones Day, representing the Lehman estate.

GAFFEY: So I take it then, sir, you don't have a recollection of speaking up at the board meeting and saying, I have some views about whether we should do this deal but I've just been approached by Barclays and they've offered me six million dollars. You don't recall that? Having that thought process?

LOWITT: I don't recall going to that board meeting.

This answer threw Gaffey. Almost any other story would have been swallowable, but here was the former CFO trying to say, with a straight face, that he didn't remember, at all, the single most important meeting in the history of Lehman Brothers, which was incidentally the backdrop for the biggest bankruptcy ever.

GAFFEY: You would agree with me, sir, that a board meeting of an iconic huge corporation—it's just filed for bankruptcy, considering a transaction to sell substantially all of its assets—is a fairly big event in the life of a chief financial officer, do you not?

LOWITT: I wasn't involved in negotiating the transaction. And I wasn't involved in drafting the transaction. And so, I think that was probably components of why I don't recall that board meeting. I was also, obviously, quite tired.

The insiders not only went through this board meeting without fully explaining their giant side deals, they boldly and enthusiastically presented the asset purchase agreement for the board's approval, describing the deal as a "wash."

Nobody seems to remember who used the term first, but multiple board members remember hearing it. Barclays, in other words, wasn't making money on the deal. It was buying, from Lehman, a package that was equal parts good stuff and crap.

Board member Michael Ainslie, for instance, specifically recalls that concept because he and other board members had already been briefed on their new responsibilities—that they were now beholden to the creditors of Lehman's estate and were charged with representing them at board meetings. "We had been briefed already that we were now working for the creditors," he said. Hearing that the deal was a wash, he said, was a relief. "This deal structure seemed to eliminate the possibility of a loss to Lehman, or claims that would more than offset the value of the assets being transferred."

Satisfied that nobody was getting shafted in the deal, the board approved it at that meeting on Tuesday, September 16.

The next day Harvey Miller of Weil, Gotshal & Manges, the lead lawyer for Lehman, went to federal bankruptcy court and presented the deal to Judge Peck for preliminary approval. Most people close to the case seem to believe that the Weil, Gotshal lawyers were genuinely in the dark about the secret deal, at least through the end of that week. And what Miller presented to the judge that Wednesday was the same deal: the wash of equal parts assets and debts.

Judge Peck saw the deal and approved it twice that week: once on Wednesday, and once on Friday afternoon. Between Wednesday and Friday, the structure of the deal was changed fundamentally—instead of a straightforward dump of assets and liabilities, the deal was now going to be centered on a complex three-way trade.

During the bankruptcy, the Fed had lent Lehman $45 billion to keep its doors open, and in exchange for that cash, Lehman delivered $50 billion in collateral to the Fed. Again, the mismatched numbers are normal in this sort of loan: the idea here was that if Lehman screwed up and couldn't pay the cash back, the Fed would just swallow all that collateral, taking a little extra for its trouble, which also happened to be insurance in case of a poor valuation.

In the new deal between Lehman and Barclays, Barclays would take over the Fed's repo, which dramatically complicated the deal.

Still, even though the structure of the deal was totally different, the same concept of a wash was presented to Judge Peck. And sometime between one and two a.m. in the wee hours of Saturday, September 20, Peck signed a sale order that ended with a simple conclusion.

> The consideration constitutes reasonably equivalent value or fair consideration.

This was legalese for "It's a square deal." It was also, for all intents and purposes, a done deal. The sale would be formally completed the following Monday morning, but that was just t-crossing and i-dotting. All the important stuff had already been disclosed to the court.

One small thing was left undone. One of Lehman's lawyers, a woman named Lori Fife, stood up that afternoon of Friday, September 19, and told Judge Peck that there was some "confusion" about which of Lehman's subsidiaries would end up being sold. It was nothing big, nothing to worry about, just some stuff that had to be worked out. And it would be, over the weekend. When they were finished working it out, Fife promised, the judge would hear all about it, in writing.

The changes, Fife told the judge, "we've clarified in a clarification letter which we're hoping to finalize and actually present to Your Honor whenever it comes down here."

During the two feverish weekend days to come, September 20–21, this minor side point was worked out. The clarification letter was nothing, just a little addendum to the deal, barely worth talking about, except that it changed the math in Barclays's favor by a minimum of $5 billion. Ultimately, perhaps much more.

THE LOST WEEKEND

Sunday, September 21. Time was running out for Saul Burian. He was supposed to play a key role in one of the biggest transactions in the history of investment banking, a deal the whole world was watching, and yet he couldn't get anyone on either side of the deal to talk to him or to anyone else on his team. It was late on a Sunday night, and the deal was closing before the start of business on a Monday. It was like manning center field, with a World Series–ending fly ball screaming right at you, but nobody's given you a glove.

"You're standing there, and you're the least informed people in the room," he says. "And this is a deal that has enormous importance not just for thousands of employees, but for people around the world. I'd say it was unsettling, yes."

Burian was the managing director of the restructuring division of Houlihan Lokey Howard & Zukin Capital, the investment bank that the Lehman Brothers creditors' committee had hired to oversee the firm's bankruptcy. In lay terms, Burian and his small team of Houlihan bankers were the financial advisers to everyone around the world who was owed money by the dying megafirm.

That was a lot of people.

Burian represented, as another lawyer put it to me, the "great unwashed" of Lehman's unsecured creditors. And on the weekend of September 20–21, 2008, it was his job to oversee the historic, last-minute sale of what was left of Lehman to the British banking giant Barclays, which had emerged the week before as Lehman's would-be savior, gallantly (in true British fashion, one might say) stepping in to buy the cratering investment bank. In the process, Barclays was also, perhaps, preventing a global financial tsunami, by keeping the first in a series of great corporate dominoes from falling over completely.

Burian and some other Houlihan employees, as well as lawyers from Milbank, Tweed, the law firm hired by Lehman's creditors' committee, had been invited into the skyscraper offices of Weil,

Gotshal & Manges, the powerful international firm that represented Lehman Brothers—not the bank's creditors, but the actual bank—to participate in the negotiations.

But for now the creditors were still being treated like a third wheel, literally on the outside. The Houlihan/Milbank teams that weekend were left to sit in separate conference rooms, away from the action, twiddling thumbs, while the real meetings went on all around them in other rooms, other floors. "We were at best an annoyance," Burian said later.

What was going down in that skyscraper that weekend was a momentous, unprecedented transfer of wealth and property. Essentially Barclays was staging the ultimate episode of *Storage Wars*, trying to both price and buy the cargo of one of the world's largest banking institutions in just a few frenzied meetings, with time playing a key role—it all had to be done before the start of business on Monday, September 22, 2008.

As one of the world's leading investment banks, Lehman Brothers was more than just a few thousand hotshots throwing big tips at strippers in Lower Manhattan. The bank was also a major cog in the world's financial infrastructure, a middleman for deals in practically every territory of every country on earth. It was the banker to unions and pensions, to great nations and to little towns, to boutique hotels and to giant hedge funds, to charities and to Arab princes.

More than 76,000 institutions and individuals would subsequently surface, claiming losses when Lehman collapsed. I would call dozens of the names on that list, speaking to Australian Boys' Clubs, missionaries in Africa, a hotel developer in Washington State, a lawyer representing a wine workers' union that lost $180,000 in pension money, and a string of officials in towns in the American Northwest. Even Bill Maher, the HBO star comedian, got no special status as a celebrity—he was somewhere down the list in the enormous line of Lehman losers.

The saddest story of all came from Robert Shannon, the city attorney for Long Beach, California. "Our town invested almost twenty million dollars with Lehman two weeks before its collapse," he said, laughing darkly. "Two weeks."

Shannon hadn't had anything to do with that deal, so when he saw the news on TV that September announcing that Lehman had collapsed, he was mostly just curious. "I thought it was just an interesting story," he said. A few hours later his phone rang, and someone from the city's finance department was on the other line. In about a minute, Shannon was white with panic. "That was when I realized how serious this was."

When the bad news hit that crucial September weekend, all those creditors—the wine workers' unions and Long Beaches of the world—had everything riding on companies like Houlihan and Milbank, and on Burian in particular. After all, the best (and perhaps only) hope to save any value at all for the Lehman creditors was to safely move the cargo off the Lehman-*Titanic* and onto the sturdy balance sheet of Barclays, a storied European bank whose very name carried the soothing implication of soundness, honesty, and old-world stability.

But there was a catch: if the deal to sell the Lehman cargo were put together in a way that was lopsided in Barclays's favor, then all those Long Beach firemen and African missionaries and Australian Boys' Clubs, and even the sheikhs running the Abu Dhabi Investment Authority—whose exposure to Lehman was somewhat greater than the mean, an incredible $609 million—would all lose out, as there would be less left over for those thousands of creditors to split up.

Unfortunately, from the start, the Lehman-Barclays deal was an awesomely complicated fix.

Again, in the days before its purchase of Lehman's assets, Barclays had quietly hired on all the key Lehman personnel who were involved with evaluating those assets. In exchange, Lehman deal makers jiggered the numbers of the deal in Barclays's favor to the tune of billions of dollars.

Those insiders had spent much of the chaotic week leading up to that weekend in the skyscraper negotiating the details of the secret discount. The insiders had smartly already presented the deal to a bankruptcy court without the discount figured in, and got the court's approval that Friday afternoon, just as Judge James Peck was about to take off for the weekend. The only hint of what was to come was Lori Fife's offhand comment about a "clarification letter."

The game then moved to the Central Park skyscraper offices of Weil, Gotshal, where the insiders would spend that fateful weekend "clarifying" the approved deal to move billions of extra dollars to the Lehman-Barclays insiders.

This was the arrangement being hammered out in the rooms from which Burian and the Milbank lawyers were excluded. None of the creditors' representatives had any clue as to what was going on, and their panic increased all weekend. Most of the team arrived mid-Saturday (Burian, who is Sabbath-observant, arrived after sundown) and failed repeatedly to get an audience with anyone involved with the deal. Houlihan and Milbank personnel even camped out strategically in different parts of the building, hoping for a chance to pull someone aside.

"Every once in a while," Burian said, "I'd catch someone in the hallway, in the bathroom, you know, getting coffee, you know, what's going on?"

All weekend long, phones rang and men and women rushed in and out of conference rooms. Big groups broke into little groups, while little groups scratched out side deals and rushed to rejoin big groups. The main action took place in a huge square-shaped conference room on the twenty-fifth floor. From outside that room, Burian said, he could occasionally hear spirited discussions going on, while officials from the Fed and the Treasury chimed in from a ceiling-mounted speaker system that applied an almost mystical aura to the proceedings. "You could hear, you know, like the voice of God," he said, "people on conference calls, coming through the ceiling."

But all day Saturday and then most of Sunday passed without the creditors' reps getting anything like a complete answer to a pair of very simple questions: What exactly was Lehman selling to Barclays, and for how much?

The lack of information coming the creditors' way from the Lehman-Barclays negotiators presented two distinct possibilities to Burian, both of them dire and deeply concerning. "Either they genuinely didn't have answers," he says, "or else they were refusing to show us stuff, and that got us pretty nervous."

A conference call between the Houlihan and Milbank folks and creditors all around the world had been scheduled for noon that Sunday, but that call was bumped to two p.m., then four, then six. Then it was eight o'clock, and then ten. And then finally a call actually happened at 11:30 p.m., a call in which Burian had to explain to exasperated creditors in places as far away as Japan that the committee, despite its frantic efforts at calculating the value of the deal, still basically had no idea what the hell was going on, what was in the deal and what wasn't. "It wasn't a pretty call," Burian later said.

It was after that call, after more "stomping around" and more stalking of coffee machines, that Burian finally lost it. He approached Harvey Miller, one of the Weil, Gotshal lawyers, who was standing outside a conference room where the deal was being negotiated. He told Miller the delay was ridiculous and that it was inconceivable that the largest transaction ever was about to be closed and nobody had time to inform the creditors' committee.

Miller sighed, told Burian to wait a minute, and then walked five or six feet to another executive named Michael Klein, who happened to be standing nearby.

None of the people on the creditors' committee knew that Michael Klein, as recently as a few weeks before, did not work for either Lehman Brothers or Barclays, or even have an inkling that he might ever do so. In fact, he had been at Citigroup for more than twenty years, from 1985 through July 2008, where he held the title chairman of international clients. Barclays CEO Bob Diamond had hired him just over a week before, and he would ultimately be paid the incredible sum of $10 million, essentially for his work on this one deal. "He was a mercenary" is how one lawyer described him to me later.

Klein was worth every penny. On the Saturday before the sale was completed, Klein personally sent an email to Diamond, bragging that he'd found more money to take from creditors and move to the Barclays side of the deal. "Great day," Klein said, of that Saturday. "We clawed back three billion dollars more."

So it was this Michael Klein who, in the wee hours of Monday, September 22, felt a tug in the skyscraper hallway. Lehman lawyer Harvey Miller had tapped his shoulder, whispered in his ear, and pointed to Burian. At the sight of Burian, Klein sagged like he was taking a bullet but, seeming resigned, motioned to Burian to follow him into a conference room.

It was inside that conference room that the $10-million-man Klein treated Burian, and by extension every firefighter, wine worker, African missionary, and Australian Boys' Club creditor on earth, to a demonstration of sheer chutzpah.

Klein understood that he was being asked to explain the contours of this gigantic transfer of wealth not to anyone with real juice on Wall Street, but to the representative of people whose only leverage was that they held a huge stack of paper claims against Lehman.

So Klein, showing what was apparently all due respect, scanned the room looking for a sheet of paper to write on. His eyes settled on "a credenza or somewhere on the table" where there happened to sit a stack of manila folders. He paused, took one of those folders, and for a few minutes, scribbled on it.

When he was finished, he showed Burian the following picture:

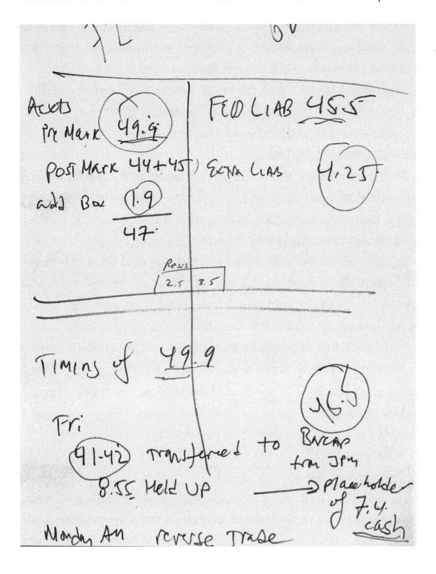

Burian stood back in amazement. Michael Klein had essentially diagrammed the biggest asset purchase in the history of finance on a manila folder. It was like submitting a design for a nuclear bomb to the Pentagon via a ballpoint drawing on the back of a napkin.

Burian stared at Klein's scribblings. He would testify later that he was awestruck by the moment, overwhelmed by the fact that he was participating in something so historically important. He was also relieved. Unlike almost everyone else in the world, he understood what Klein's picture meant. The manila folder contained a crude list of assets and liabilities, and a small set of calculations, but more than anything, it contained, at the very least—after all those days and hours of waiting—an answer, an explanation.

The manila folder asked the entire universe of Lehman creditors to accept on faith that the deal that had been reported to the court had changed, but only because the assets being transferred had since lost value in the market.

"We were relieved that there was an agreement," Burian said. As for what that agreement was, he told the negotiators that he believed them, of course, but that he would have to check it all out later. "It was trust but verify," he says.

Still, the absolute certainty with which the deal was explained to him acted like a balm on his nerves. They all seemed so *sure*. "I turned to all of them and said, 'If this is what's happening, then so be it,'" he said.

In truth, Klein in handing that manila folder over had acted as the getaway driver, the man responsible for delivering the Big Lie to Lehman's creditors. The lie was couched in a pair of those feverishly etched lines:

Pre Mark <u>49.9</u>
Post Mark 44–45.

In essence, Klein was telling Burian—whom he professed later not to even remember, testifying only that there was a "guy with glasses" at the meeting, where he had "grabbed a manila thing" and had a "recollection of drawing boxes"—that the Lehman assets had dropped from $49.9 billion in value when the deal was struck to "44–45" in current value, just due to market forces.

The "44–45" notation was a piece of great showmanship. Like a car salesman who throws in a new set of radials to close the deal, Klein was telling Burian that Barclays was actually rounding things up about a billion dollars in Lehman's favor—that the assets were actually probably only worth $44 billion now, but Barclays was going to give them credit for $45 billion. For good measure, you know, as a show of good faith. "They were going to cut us a break," Burian testified later.

Something didn't feel quite right to the lawyers for the creditors, the whole weekend didn't feel quite right, but there was no time to do anything about it. Houlihan and Milbank had no choice but to take Klein's word about the deal. The sale closing was hours away. There was no conceivable way to do due diligence (or to "diligence it," to use the verb form favored on Wall Street) in the hours remaining, and leverage-wise, there was no move left to make. If Lehman's creditors balked, the Barclays sale might collapse, and Lehman itself might be worth pennies in a matter of hours. There was nothing to do but take Klein's word on the math.

Burian quietly scooped up the manila folder, shoved it into a briefcase, and went home. He had no idea he had just witnessed the misappropriation of at least $5 billion.

And billions more were about to disappear in the final sale, through a variety of mechanisms so ingeniously conceived that it would take several years, dozens of lawyers, and hundreds of depositions to sort it all out.

The creditors ultimately did not object to the sale that next morning. They didn't support it, either. It was, they felt, the only move they could make under the circumstances.

"The reason we're not objecting is really based on the lack of a viable alternative," said Luc Despins, one of the Milbank counsel, that Monday afternoon of September 22, the day of the sale. "We did not support the transaction because there had not been enough time to properly review it."

In the months and years to come, the representatives of Lehman's creditors would unearth stunning details about just exactly what had gone on behind all those closed doors. The first part of that process of discovery would unfold like a classic detective story, in which clues slowly revealed themselves until the truth gradually came into focus. There would come a time when the Lehman creditors would be able to see the contours of the whole heist. They would have documents, emails, admissions even. But almost precisely at that moment of evidentiary victory, they were politically and legally checkmated. The creditors were thrust face-first into the immovable principle that underlies everything modern that Wall Street does: if a crime is complicated enough, and sanctified by enough "reputable" attorneys and accountants, then American law enforcement will inevitably be too slow or too weak to stop it.

THE INVESTIGATION

The Lehman bankruptcy swindle was singular because of its sheer size, and also because of the extraordinary circumstances surrounding that chaotic September week when the deal took place. ("The whole world is melting down out there" is how one Lehman executive described the week of the sale in court.)

But in another sense, it was a thoroughly common occurrence. Every day on Wall Street, money is stolen, embezzled, burgled, and robbed. But the mechanisms of these thefts are often so arcane and idiosyncratic that they don't fit neatly into the criminal code, which is written for the dumb crimes committed by common stick-up artists and pickpockets.

Wall Street crime, in part, is a confidence game in which the criminal justice system itself is the mark. Much like common street grifters, who bank on the victim's feelings of shame and guilt preventing him from going to the police, Wall Street criminals bank on the terminal intellectual insecurity of their regulators. They dare prosecutors to call what they've done crimes, knowing they'll be hesitant to disagree with the hotshot defense lawyers from New York and Washington who make forty or fifty times what they do.

So a foreign bank steals billions of dollars from dozens of American towns like Long Beach, but when the bank's lawyers call the transaction not theft but "clarification," American law enforcement is mesmerized by the semantics. It then declares the issue a civil matter and kicks the problem to the civil courts, where the best hope for the victims now is not for justice but mere remuneration.

From there it's just math. The civil battle almost always devolves into a war of resources, and here, inevitably, the richer party wins.

In December 2008, a few months after the sale, Luc Despins, the lead Milbank counsel representing one group of Lehman creditors, decided to leave Milbank, Tweed for a job at a new firm, Paul Hastings. On the way out the door, he called up Susheel Kirpalani at Quinn Emanuel, who represented the other major group of Lehman creditors. He told Kirpalani that even though the Lehman case was no longer going to be his problem, he wanted someone to follow through with it.

"He told me, basically, we never got all the documents," says Kirpalani. "And we think there's a five-billion-dollar hole there."

Kirpalani had already come to the conclusion that something was wrong with the Lehman sale. He was troubled by some language in a JPMorgan-Barclays dispute that he was asked to take a look at that referred back to the Barclays-Lehman deal. So he started asking questions.

Parallel to Kirpalani's inquiry, the other main firm representing the Lehman estate, Alvarez & Marsal, began asking its own questions on behalf of the Lehman creditors. "Issues started to bubble up," said the firm's CEO, Bryan Marsal. As A&M was crunching the numbers on the estate, Marshal said, they couldn't see "how the assets equaled the liabilities," and "questions were coming up" about "whether the transaction was really a wash."

So in January 2009 A&M formed a team to look into the transaction. They had just started work when they, and the rest of Wall Street, were hit with a bombshell. Tucked into Barclays's SEC filing for the fourth quarter of 2008 was the following sentence regarding the purchase of the Lehman assets:

> The excess of the fair value of net assets acquired over consideration paid [to Lehman] resulted in £2,262 m of gains on acquisition.

Two billion, two hundred sixty-two million pounds was about $4.2 billion at that time. Barclays was announcing to the world that it made more than $4 billion "on acquisition" of Lehman.

Remember, just a few months before, the bank had represented to the world, and to the court, that it was buying a matched set of assets and liabilities—a wash. In the week of the sale, nobody on the Barclays side said anything to anybody about making $4.2 billion on the deal. Now, a few months later, Barclays was quietly announcing it had made this massive, year-saving windfall on the Lehman deal.

"We were like, 'What the fuck?'" says one lawyer involved with the case.

"The [earnings statement], that was like that Robert Conrad ad where he's daring you to knock the battery off his shoulder," laughs another creditor attorney. "I mean, they come out five months after the sale, and they're like, 'Oh, by the way, we made four billion dollars on the deal.' And we're like 'Oh yeah? *How?*' It was the red flag of red flags."

Furious, the creditor attorneys pounded down the door of the Barclays-Lehman attorneys, demanding answers. How did you make $4 billion on the deal? Where had the gain come from? But they got bubkes. The Barclays attorneys refused to give them any information about the sale. Bryan Marsal, the partner at A&M, personally reached out to Barclays general counsel Jonathan Hughes and suggested some kind of mistake had been made. He got no answer, at least not a satisfactory one.

Even Lehman's own lawyers were telling them not to bother. When a lawyer for Milbank, Tweed reached out to Lori Fife of Weil, Gotshal—this is the same Fife who helped write the clarification letter, the same lawyer who told Judge Peck about that letter—Fife, like one of those Bay City cops who's always telling Philip Marlowe to get off a case, told the Milbank people to just lay off, why dontcha?

"I really am at a loss to figure out why you and the other committee professionals are spending so much time on the Barclays sale," she wrote in an email. "What could you or anyone for that matter do even if it turned out that the assets turned out to be greater? As you know, the sale has been consummated which effectively moots out any relief you might be seeking."

In other words, why do you care if the sale was dirty? What's done is done. Let's not be crying over spilled legal milk, shall we?

This is Lehman's *own lawyer* telling creditors they shouldn't care if Lehman got ripped off.

Shortly after that, unsurprisingly, the creditors decided they needed different lawyers. Weil, Gotshal, they realized, was hopelessly conflicted because of its role in the sale. So Weil, Gotshal, Fife, et al. were replaced by a firm called Jones Day.

The new firm soon filed a motion to the court requesting discovery under Rule 2004 of bankruptcy law. In short, the Jones Day lawyers wanted the right to investigate the sale—to issue subpoenas and depose the men and women who had put together the deal behind closed doors.

The Jones Day motion was filed on May 18. Judge Peck, somewhat surprisingly, approved the motion on June 25.

Now, the only remedy available to the creditor lawyers was something called a Rule 60 motion, a catchall phrase that describes a legal reopening of a court-approved transaction. The Jones Day lawyers planned to file a Rule 60 motion and ask the judge to exhume the Barclays-Lehman deal, perform an autopsy on the transaction, and perhaps grant some financial relief to Lehman's creditors.

The only problem was, a Rule 60 motion has to be filed within one calendar year of the transaction. So the Jones Day lawyers and their partners at Quinn Emanuel had roughly two and a half months to go through about 200,000 pages of documents and conduct dozens of depositions, to say nothing of preparing the actual brief.

An all-out hunt for information commenced. Lawyers at the firm worked as corporate lawyers sometimes do, unhealthily and around the clock, sorting through emails and taking depositions. They got little hints here and there that pointed to a secret, separately negotiated deal, but nothing like a smoking gun.

Then one day one of the Jones Day lawyers stumbled upon an email from Martin Kelly, Lehman's chief financial controller. The email was dated Tuesday, September 16, and had been sent at 5:10 a.m. from Kelly to the CFO, Ian Lowitt, with Paolo Tonucci cc'd. The email read:

> Well it took all night and lots of back and forth but the deal is done and ready for the Board. Final price did not change meaningfully—approx a $5b all in economic loss versus our marks and $3.6b of resi assets left behind.

Bob Gaffey, the top lawyer on the case for Jones Day, described the discovery of this email as the turning point in the case. "It was the gong-in-*Rocky* moment," he says.

Translated into English, the Kelly email said that Lehman and Barclays had negotiated a discount for Barclays—that Barclays was going to get its package of inventory for $5 billion less than "our marks"—where Lehman had actually valued the stuff.

The lawyers for the screwed creditors now knew that Barclays had managed to get a secret windfall baked into its takeover. Kelly had written that predawn email at the precise moment when men like Lowitt were getting their multimillion-dollar bonus offers; Lowitt said he had just gotten off the phone with Barclays exec Rich Ricci when he received this email from blabbermouth Kelly.

The attorneys kept at it. They were still taking depositions on September 12, 2009, three days before the one-year deadline. Their last deposition before filing was one of the most important, and it involved Michael Klein, the author of the manila folder.

Working right up to the wire, the Jones Day lawyers filed their motion on September 15. This original document outlined the parameters for almost the entire con for the judge, an investigative feat in itself. Many important details would surface in the trial that followed in the next year, but for the most part, it was all there in the original eighty-seven-page motion.

Among other things, the motion explained to the judge that virtually all the key negotiators on the Lehman side had accepted insanely lucrative employment offers as they were "negotiating" with Barclays.

The motion also laid out a variety of facts not disclosed to the court in the original sale, and it presented five possible legal reasons why Judge Peck might consider reopening the sale and granting relief to creditors in places like Long Beach and Vancouver and Milton, Australia.

Barclays, acting with appropriate alarm, brought in America's most preeminent corporate lawyer to defend itself in that proceeding, David Boies of Boies, Schiller. You probably remember Boies as the guy who represented Al Gore in *Bush v. Gore*.

Some of the lawyers on the other side were jazzed by the idea that they were up against such storied legal talent. "It was the highlight of my career," said one lawyer, "going up against David Boies."

Most of the rest of the world, however, had no idea that in a mostly empty courtroom in Lower Manhattan, a great legal battle was about to be played out, pitting the world's biggest name in courtroom litigation—Boies—against the aggrieved Lehman creditors, including firemen in Long Beach, wine workers in Napa, and orphans in Australia.

Beginning in April 2010 and continuing through the summer, the courtroom was treated to a parade of remarkably candid witnesses, who explained seemingly without much shame or fear of reprisal just what exactly *had* gone on behind closed doors during the week of the sale. The testimony of these deal makers from both Lehman and Barclays gradually brought into relief the contours of an audacious asset grab.

The secret deal, it turned out, actually had two key phases. The first was that Barclays always intended to secure a massive first-day gain on the deal. That was the $5 billion "loss" that Kelly referred to in that infamous 5:10 a.m. email, and that part of it was essentially wrapped up early that Tuesday morning, on September 16.

At trial and in depositions, one Barclays executive after another confirmed that the deal was intended to be heavily tilted in Barclays's favor from the start. There needed to be a "delta between asset valuation and liability valuation," said John Varley, the second-in-command at Barclays, adding that it was a "condition precedent" for the deal. Jonathan Hughes, Barclays's general counsel, said that a huge first-day gain was "a pre-condition for Barclays" and "of huge importance."

And the top man himself, CEO Bob Diamond, would explain it this way, using language that makes Alan Greenspan seem like Robert Frost or Richard Pryor:

> So when I say capital accretive, accretive to the capital ratios, which means that the asset liability mismatch had to have a mismatch in favor of a positive capital accretion or we weren't authorized to do a deal.

When I asked one of the lawyers in the case what "capital accretive" meant, he laughed. "The man has a way with words," he said.

Saying that Barclays had to have "a mismatch in favor of a positive capital accretion" was just another way of saying that it had to make money on the deal.

How much money? A nice round number, to start with—$5 billion. This was confirmed not only by the Kelly email but by testimony from a number of sources, like Tonucci for instance:

Q: You understood the $5 billion all in economic loss versus our marks to be a reference to a discount off the marks, correct?
TONUCCI: Yes.

So right from the start, from the wee hours of Tuesday morning before the deal was announced to the Lehman board, Barclays had already made $5 billion.

But it wasn't enough, as the second part of the deal showed.

In this second phase, which mostly took place that Friday, the Barclays executives decided that they weren't satisfied with a $5 billion discount—they wanted more. So they directed their newly bought-off stooges from the Lehman side to scour the Lehman books looking for more stuff to take. They ended up grabbing so much that it actually freaked out some of the Barclays executives, who worried they were getting too greedy.

Remember, these are people who had already absconded with $5 billion, so you can imagine the kind of excess that would prompt them to worry that they'd crossed a line. After working all Friday to lift everything that wasn't nailed down on the Lehman balance sheet, Rich Ricci, one of the key Barclays negotiators, told Lehman executive Alex Kirk—he of the mystery $15 million bonus—that "we won't be pigs, fine, you know, let's get on with it."

Kirk then quickly emailed McDade, telling him they could all stop looting the company for now, because Ricci had "told me he won't blow up this trade by being a pig."

Before they decided to stop being pigs, however, Ricci, Diamond, Klein, and the rest of the Barclays pirates succeeded in sucking somewhere between $5 billion and $7 billion, perhaps more, out of the estate.

Numerous other twists were buried in the Lehman deal. But the most ingenious revolved around the mechanism used to deliver the original $5 billion discount: the repo.

Here's why Barclays, at the last minute, restructured its purchase deal around Lehman's repo loan from the Fed—which it would "take over" on behalf of the Fed. In Lehman's last-gasp repo deal with the Fed, Lehman posted $50 billion in collateral in exchange for $45 billion in cash. Barclays then took over the loan with an agreement already in place with Lehman that Lehman would later terminate the repo, allowing Barclays to keep the $50 billion in assets in exchange for $45 billion in cash—a $5 billion gain for Barclays.

Transactions of this type, used to move billion-dollar hunks of money around, are couched in language that is essentially foreign to the layperson, as foreign as Swahili or Esperanto are to most Americans. It is a difficult, frustrating, atonal, counterintuitive, and thoroughly unattractive language. This place is a foreign nation all to itself, as unique and proud of its peculiar culture as, say, France. Because of the language problem, the only people competent to prosecute the crimes committed within its borders are other French people.

Only the problem is, to stretch this strained metaphor just a little further, if you spend enough time in France, you start thinking like a French person.

If you follow enough of these Wall Street cases, you start to see this phenomenon all over the place. You go into court the first day, and everyone in the room, right down to the judge and even the plaintiffs' attorneys, looks like Marcel Marceau. And they talk in blasé tones about acts of perversion that would shock a normal person to the point of screams.

The taking of the $5 billion by way of terminating the repo is a perfect example. The idea seems to have come from senior Lehman finance executive Gerry Reilly, who wrote to Lowitt and Tonucci and others that "defaulting on repo could be the best as discount could be taken from haircut," he said, meaning that Barclays could get paid by wolfing down the excess collateral (the "haircut"—the difference between the $45 billion loan and the $50 billion in collateral).

Kelly later said that "I understand that that was the mechanism, defaulting on the repo was the mechanism." Tonucci said the same: "The actual transfer of securities and cash was through the repo agreements, and essentially the termination of those repo agreements."

So by the middle of the week, by Thursday, September 18, Barclays had "stepped into the shoes of the Fed" and taken over the repo. It was ready to make this ingenious move.

But it had one final, extremely difficult obstacle to get over.

On September 19, the same Friday when Lori Fife mentioned the clarification letter, Lehman officially filed for bankruptcy. Under bankruptcy law, any bankruptcy calls for an automatic freezing of all open contracts. This is designed to protect creditors from money owed to them flying out of the dying company.

There is a specific exemption for repos. *But,* and this is an important *but,* if a repo is terminated, the creditor can liquidate the collateral to get repaid. But any excess collateral has to go to the estate.

In other words: if Barclays wanted to terminate that repo, it would have the right to liquidate Lehman's collateral—but it could claim only the $45 billion principal of the loan, not the haircut. The excess $5 billion would have to stay in the now-bankrupt Lehman, which means it would've gone to pay other claimants: Long Beach, the wine workers, and the other 75,998 creditors. By law, there was no way that Barclays could terminate the repo and get all $50 billion. It was entitled to only $45 billion. The excess $5 billion should have gone to the Lehman estate.

But it didn't.

Instead, Barclays and its lawyers huddled and came up with an ingenious gambit.

The first thing they did is they sent Lori Fife, the Weil, Gotshal lawyer, to Judge Peck's courtroom the Friday afternoon to tell His Honor that the deal was basically done, except they were going to clarify a point or two.

This was the aforementioned "clarification letter" announcement. Her actual words:

> we've clarified in a clarification letter which we're hoping
> to finalize and actually present to Your Honor whenever
> it comes down here.

The use of the past tense was particularly ingenious since the letter had not actually been written yet. It was written, however, the following day. The key part of the letter was actually drafted by a different firm that Barclays hired, Sullivan & Cromwell, which added the following in paragraph 13 of the "clarification letter":

> 13. Barclays Repurchase Agreement. Effective at Closing,
> (i) all securities and other assets held by Purchaser under
> the September 18, 2008 repurchase arrangement among

Purchaser and/or its Affiliates and LBI and/or its Affiliates
and Bank of New York as collateral agent (the "Barclays
Repurchase Agreement") shall be deemed to constitute
part of the Purchased Assets in accordance with Paragraph 1(a)(ii) above, (ii) Seller and Purchaser shall be
deemed to have no further obligations to each other
under the Barclays Repurchase Agreement (including,
without limitation, any payment or delivery obligations),
and (iii) the Barclays Repurchase Agreement shall terminate. Additionally, the Notice of Termination relating to
the Barclays Repurchase Agreement dated September 19,
2008 is hereby deemed rescinded and void ab initio in all
respects.

Despite its extreme camouflaging dullness, this paragraph is the
legal equivalent of a David Blaine act. What it says is that when we
terminated the repo yesterday, well, that didn't actually happen. But
we *are* terminating the repo now, and we get to keep all the excess
money.

Essentially, paragraph 13 unterminated the terminated repo,
then reterminated it on Barclays's own terms. Ingeniously lunatic
mind-loops like this are why one pays certain lawyers a thousand
dollars an hour.

The complicated maneuver allowed Barclays to avoid disclosing
to the court ahead of the deal that the repo had been terminated
and that it had kept the $5 billion. Even more amazingly, it did so
without asking Judge Peck's permission. When the judge had discharged them on the Friday night before, he had specifically instructed the lawyers on both sides that he was available to be reached
all weekend, should something important come up.

But this decision to unilaterally unterminate the repo and secretly pocket $5 billion apparently didn't rise to the level of some-
thing worth calling the judge over.

Former Lehman lawyer Oliver Budde, who had blown the whistle on Fuld's tax-reporting issues to the SEC and been forced out of the firm long before this moment, put it to me this way: "Once it was in the clarification letter all lawyers involved had to know what a big deal it was to terminate a $50b repo contract, thereby gifting $5b to Barclays that the court would have expected to go to the Lehman estate. So the decision to not go back to the judge for approval seems to me to have been a *very* ballsy decision."

With paragraph 13, Barclays and its lawyers had their $5 billion. The only remaining problem was how to explain the missing money to the creditors.

What to do there? Easy—just say that the markets moved, and that the stuff Barclays had "bought" from Lehman turned out to be worth $5 billion less than it had been worth the week before.

The reality, the $5 billion negotiated discount, was in paragraph 13 of the clarification letter. The cover story, that the markets had just moved $5 billion in the wrong direction, was in the drawing that Michael Klein had sketched on that manila folder for Saul Burian in the early hours of that last Monday morning.

A few hours after that manila folder incident, members of all sides went to court, and the sale was finalized. The creditors neither approved the sale nor disapproved it. That same Monday morning, the Barclays lawyers filed the "clarification letter" with the court, where, like Spielberg's Lost Ark disappearing into a reverse-zoom panorama of a vast federal government warehouse, it became one of twelve thousand documents filed in the docket to the Lehman case.

The quiet filing of that letter, with its inscrutable paragraph 13 buried in thousands of words of even more inscrutable legalese, was how Judge Peck was "informed" of the Barclays decision to keep the $5 billion from the repo.

In later court hearings in the action filed by Lehman's creditors, the principals essentially admitted to the entire scheme, in which one of the world's biggest and most respected financial institutions snookered a long-serving federal judge into putting his name on an exquisitely polished fake takeover deal designed to cover up a secret robbery of billions. Perhaps no judge in the history of Wall Street had ever had his underwear pulled so completely over his head, in such an important case.

But now, after the trial, this same judge would have a second chance to consider the same case. How would His Honor respond?

The defense had everything going its way. No court had ever accepted a Rule 60 motion to reopen such a massive deal. Judge Peck was no boat rocker, either. He was a well-known Wall Street bankruptcy lawyer who had been a partner at the high-priced New York firm of Schulte Roth & Zabel when he was appointed to the bench. He even went to the same law school as Barclays's famous defense lawyer, David Boies—NYU. Provided the judge adhered to convention, establishment opinion, and his own legal decision, Barclays was in the clear.

The Barclays lawyers didn't spend a whole lot of time contesting the basic facts of the case. They didn't disagree about the size and timing of the bonuses, or the meaning of paragraph 13, and so on.

What they mostly argued was that it was legally inappropriate to reopen the matter. The genie was out of the bottle, they told the judge. Finality is important in such transactions; Your Honor's hands are tied. And then they listed about nine thousand excellent reasons—not for nothing does Boies have that great reputation—why Judge Peck should not go back in time and do something about the unseemly secret withdrawal.

Then they added one more argument. This would be the sour grapes defense, the "our critics are just jealous and attacking us because we have assloads of money" argument. If you wait long enough, this line of defense emerges in almost every single Wall Street case that involves an aggrieved victim of a back-alley mugging asking for its money back.

In this case, Boies whipped the jealousy argument out in his closing. What he said was that the creditor lawyers had known about the clarification letter from the get-go and then had sat on it, waiting to see if Barclays would prosper after the deal, at which point they would pounce and try to sue Barclays for the crime of being successful:

> I guarantee you, Your Honor, that if the markets are crashed, if this transaction had been a failure, if Barclays had lost billions of dollars, they wouldn't be coming back in here and saying "let's redo the transaction."
>
> Their argument is that if they see something that they think was not adequately disclosed to the Court, they can put it in their pocket, wait until they see whether this turns out to be a good deal or a bad deal . . . and if it turns out that the enormous risk that Barclays took turns out to be successful, they can come in and take it out of their pocket and say this is a basis for undoing that Sale Order and taking another, they say today, $13 billion from Barclays.

The whole of Boies's argument was based upon the idea that the clarification letter had, in fact, been adequately disclosed, not just to the creditors' lawyers but to Peck himself. "There was no dispute about the existence of the Clarification Letter or the terms or that this Court had approved it," Boies said breezily at the start of his closing, at which point Peck suddenly and uncharacteristically balked.

"Let me be clear about something, Mr. Boies," Peck said. "I never approved the Clarification Letter."

Boies, taken aback, tried to retreat. "Okay, Your Honor," he said. "I would never—"

"It was filed in the docket of this case," Peck went on, to Boies's dismay. "There are now well over twelve thousand docket entries. I do not know everything that is contained in every docket entry." He frowned, then added: "No proceedings took place before this Court to approve the Clarification Letter per se."

Boies, unbelievably, refused to give up the subject. "Your Honor,

I won't address that part of it anymore if the Court wishes me not to," he said. Then summoning his world-renowned stones, he added a "but."

"*But*," he began, "I think that—"

"I'm just letting you know that that's an aspect of your argument that I reject," said Peck sharply.

The creditor lawyers glanced at one another. Was there hope? The judge had dropped hints throughout the case that he understood that there were major disclosure issues with the sale. The Jones Day lawyers, incidentally, had made an important strategic decision at the outset, not calling the transaction an outright fraud, but simply one beset with mistakes, some of them innocent. And in truth, the vast majority of the people who worked on the deal, particularly on the Lehman side, had no idea of what was going on in secret. The creditor attorneys argued, somewhat plausibly, that they were victims just like the others, kept from important details, in particular the secret discount.

The creditors therefore asked for relief due to "mistake, inadvertence or excusable neglect" or due to "misrepresentation (either innocent or intentional)."

This left Judge Peck with an out. He wouldn't have to accuse Barclays and its lawyers of fraud in order to give money back to the Lehman creditors. He could say it had all been an accident and pitch the pair of transactions—the original sale and the later relief— as a matched set of rational decisions, one sale approved under great duress and in the midst of an international crisis, and the second made under the cold light of day, reasonably correcting past wrongs. That would be a perfectly appropriate and understandable way to approach the case.

It didn't happen. On February 22, 2011, Judge Peck sent down his ruling on the Barclays-Lehman case. The 103-page ruling is, to put it kindly, a hilarious cop-out from a legal standpoint. Peck flatly denied all relief to the Lehman creditors. His reasoning was based entirely on the idea that nothing would have been different if all these ugly facts had been disclosed. He wrote:

> Having dwelled at some length on this question, the Court concludes that nothing in the current record, if presented at the Sale Hearing, would have changed the outcome of that hearing. The Court still would have entered the very same Sale Order because there was no better alternative and, perhaps most importantly, because the sale to Barclays was the means both to avoid a potentially disastrous piecemeal liquidation and to save thousands of jobs in the troubled financial services industry.

This was the civil litigation version of Collateral Consequences. Let's not focus on what happened, let's focus on the larger picture, on the jobs that would have been lost!

Peck's point was that since Barclays was the only known buyer at the time, if in September 2008 it needed to make $13 billion on the deal to pull the trigger and buy the Lehman assets, it would always need $13 billion to do the deal—therefore its method of securing that $13 billion should not be reinvestigated.

But this is wrong on its face. What might or might not have happened if all that information had come out is completely unknowable, even to someone as close to God as a federal judge. Nobody else was willing to buy Lehman at the "official" sale price, but are we really to believe that no other company would have been willing to do the deal with a $12 billion discount? That no other firm would have been willing to take on a first-day $5 billion gain?

True, Peck admitted in his opinion that there was "a glaring problem of flawed disclosure." He conceded that "movants have proven that some very significant information was left out of the record," and he seemed particularly miffed about being duped with regard to the clarification letter.

He railed against the characterization of the letter as something less than it was, as a document that merely "purports to change and 'clarify' some fundamental terms," when it was in fact a "vital side letter," one that "makes major changes to the structure of the acquisition and that affects property rights of entities that quite obviously are subject to the Court's jurisdiction."

Even after admitting this, however, he decided to bless the validity of the clarification letter. "Despite the lack of explicit bankruptcy court approval and in recognition of the conduct of the parties in relying on the Clarification Letter as a controlling document," he wrote, "the Court has decided to treat the document as having been approved by virtue of the combination of references made to the Clarification Letter in the Sale Order and the conduct of the parties demonstrating unequivocal reliance on the document."

You will never see a starker example of legal buck-passing. Peck elected here not to rule on whether the clarification letter, with its insidious paragraph 13, should have been approved. Instead, he pirouetted away from the whole issue, saying that he would decide to "treat the document as having been approved" essentially because it had been in use since 2008. In AA, people say, "Fake it till you make it." In this case, Barclays faked having court approval for the vital side letter, and in the end Judge Peck decided to help Barclays make it, agreeing to "act as if" (to use another popular self-help catchphrase) the letter had been approved.

As for the problems with the sale, the details of the secret side deals and massive discounts that came out at the trial, those didn't bother Peck. None of it, he said, represented "fraud, misrepresentation or misconduct." Moreover, if anything was missed, it was nobody's fault—certainly not his. After all, there was a simple explanation:

> The Court has coined the term the "fog" of Lehman to characterize the confusion, ambiguity and uncertainty that prevailed during Lehman Week, something akin to the classic expression the "fog of war." . . . The disclosure problems are real, but they are due to the "fog" of Lehman and an emergency of a magnitude unlike any that has ever occurred in any sale hearing.

Thus the Lehman robbery was disappeared from public view, obscured by the "fog of war." As in real wars, Peck ruled, things happen. And it's not our job to judge those things.

So in the end, after hundreds of thousands of pages of motions and depositions, after all that harried effort scouring emails and documents in search of evidence, and after the long hearing in which it was all formally presented, this was the final excuse that all those expensive minds collectively used to wash away the Lehman case:

Shit happens!

Years after the collapse of Lehman Brothers, many of the company's creditors were still feeling the sting. The city of Long Beach, for instance, has been enacting sweeping budget cuts ever since the crash. In the first year after Lehman's collapse, the Long Beach school system cut summer school classes and bus routes for one thousand students. The city announced plans to lay off thirty-four policemen and close at least one fire station. The mayor asked the city council to cut all funding for the Long Beach Museum of Art. And the city continues to be way behind the financial eight ball. In fact, its projected deficit for 2013 almost exactly matches the Lehman shortfall—$20.3 million.

"It's impossible to quantify, but in this tight economy, that kind of money is very significant," says Robert Shannon, the Long Beach city attorney, of the loss. "And it certainly contributed to the problems we're having."

There are 76,000 stories like Shannon's. Not all of them involve towns or orphanages. Some involve other banks or other rich individuals. But in more than a few cases, you can draw a straight line from a cop being laid off or a union worker having his or her pension slashed back to the week of 2008 when a handful of Lehman executives took a payoff to mark down their own inventory.

A few years after that deal, investigators in four different

countries—the United States, Canada, Great Britain, and Japan—
began investigating a series of banks, including Barclays, for manipulating the London Interbank Offered Rate, also known as
LIBOR. As the benchmark rate that measures how much banks
charge to lend to one another, LIBOR is the basis for almost every
adjustable-rate investment vehicle on earth.

Investigators later found emails from Barclays traders who discussed manipulating LIBOR so that they could make more money
on a trade. In one particularly enlightening exchange, the Barclays
LIBOR reporter, in cheerily bromantic language, tells the trader
that he's happy to oblige.

> For you . . . anything. . . . Always happy to help, leave it
> with me, Sir.

Later, he added:

> Done . . . for you big boy.

The trader wrote back, offering to party with some fine champagne.

> Dude. I owe you big time! Come over one day after work
> and I'm opening a bottle of Bollinger.

When it came out that Barclays had been engaged in LIBOR manipulations since at least 2005, and that Bob Diamond himself had
at times okayed these manipulations, a major scandal erupted in the
U.K. The Bank of England fined Barclays $453 million and essen-
tially demanded that Diamond resign, which he did, in the spring of
2012. On his way out, Diamond released emails and other documents suggesting that the Bank of England not only knew about
these manipulations but had actually encouraged them during the
fall of 2008, right around the time of the Lehman bankruptcy. The
ostensible justification for the BOE wanting banks to suppress
LIBOR at that time is that it made banks look healthier and pre-

vented a worldwide panic. But there was no excuse at all for the manipulations that Barclays had engaged in prior to 2008, the "bottle of Bollinger" manipulations, which were done purely to make more money for Barclays and its traders.

It also came out during this investigation that Timothy Geithner himself knew about some of the LIBOR shenanigans, as far back as 2008. But he did nothing about it other than send a letter to the Bank of England with some recommendations for how to prevent future manipulations. When asked why he didn't contact the Department of Justice to help it begin a criminal investigation, Geithner essentially said that the DOJ had access to the information from media reports and didn't need his help. The primary banking regulator in America didn't contact the Justice Department because he said it could read about the case in the newspapers!

Forced to answer questions about the LIBOR incident in Congress, Geithner was presented with a transcript of conversations between a Barclays employee and a Fed official in which the Barclays employee admitted to fixing LIBOR rates.

"Is there any element of criminal fraud that isn't admitted to in this transcript?" North Carolina Democrat Brad Miller asked Geithner, wondering aloud how someone could openly admit a crime to a government official, a regulator no less, and not face charges for it.

Geithner avoided the question, saying that lawyers were working on the issue. By then, four years had elapsed since the scandal.

Many of the private lawsuits filed in search of payback for LIBOR manipulation have stalled, or wound up in dead ends and purgatories like the Lehman bankruptcy case. As of this writing, the chief LIBOR "relief" efforts stem from publicity stunts like the one dreamed up by Santa Clara County, California, which claimed it lost as much as $54 million thanks to LIBOR manipulation. The county was reduced to trying to sell muffins for a million dollars a pop at a "Big Bank Bake Sale," making the last note in this monster aristocrat conspiracy a macabre joke, as inspired as Judge Peck's "shit happens" ruling.

You can examine the Lehman collapse and the LIBOR scandal and see the same glaring enforcement problems in both narratives. Major regulators like the Fed and the SEC knew of frightening problems within both companies and elected (a) not to launch criminal investigations and (b) not to tell the investing public. You see the state making moves like warning other banks of problems within a firm like Lehman, or using public funds to help protect other banks from damage caused by Lehman's collapse. But the public, in the end, gets nothing. No justice, and not even a bake sale.

CHAPTER 5

BORDER TROUBLE, PART 1

Just after dawn in Gainesville, Georgia. I'm in the front seat of a big green-and-white taxicab, cruising toward a factory that packages frozen chicken parts. The cabbie is a moon-faced young Mexican named Jose Rico, the passenger an anxious-looking woman in her late twenties who gives a first name of Alma but doesn't offer a last name.

Jose is a resident, and that's why he's driving. He's got a license. Alma is undocumented, and that's why she's the passenger. Three years ago, she says, she got picked up by the police for driving without a license. As she tells the story, Jose peers at her querulously in his rearview mirror, clearly surprised that she's still around to tell the tale.

"You didn't get deported?" he asks.

"No," she says. "They just gave me a ticket."

Jose shrugs, as if to say, *Whatever.* We turn a corner. A patrol car, occupants hidden behind darkened windows, is parked on a median strip. Jose eases past it with deliberate calm, like a man trying not to startle a watchdog by running away.

Gainesville has 34,000 people and eight taxi companies, all of them Latino owned, despite the fact that the majority of the town is white. The company Jose drives for, Fiesta Taxi, owned by a local resident named Jose Diaz, is a functioning, profitable business. But this Latino cab company is a political act in its way, too, an echo of the private taxi services Martin Luther King Jr. and the Montgomery Improvement Association set up back in 1955, during the famed bus boycott.

Back in King's day, black men and women rode black-owned taxis to escape a segregated white bus system. In Gainesville, Latinos ride Latino-owned taxis to escape brutally punitive immigration laws that have created a disturbingly similar apartheidlike system. This small Georgia city is ground zero for enforcement of a ferocious federal immigration rule called 287(g) that essentially deputizes any and all state and local law enforcement officials to arrest undocumented aliens on behalf of the U.S. Immigration and Customs Enforcement agency (ICE). Today every local official with a badge—every cop, sheriff, ranger, or even game warden—has the power to instantly separate children from mothers, husbands from wives. All America, from the smallest town on up, has become a dragnet.

Initially there was some confusion about whether 287(g) and a related Obama-era initiative bearing the Bush-Orwellian catchphrase "Secure Communities" were mandatory, or whether states could opt out. Under Secure Communities, law enforcement officials are required to fingerprint all detainees in custody for criminal offenses and run checks on their immigration status. After the plan was announced, two states, Massachusetts and New York, decided in the spring of 2011 to opt out of the program, which was thought to be voluntary.

A year later Obama administration officials sent an icy email to police officials in both states, informing them that they'd been opted back into the program. Secure Communities, they were told, was to be activated in "all remaining jurisdictions."

So the draconian policies were now law everywhere, meaning all police forces in all states were essentially deputies of ICE. Under 287(g), for instance, if you're behind the wheel in Boss Hogg country, and you get stopped for the infamous broken taillight, you can be under federal detainment, in leg chains, and on a bus to Mexico within a few days. You fail to maintain your lane while driving: arrest, deportation. The Gainesville area in 2010 even had a man deported for fishing without a license. (The man, a Honduran named Josue Castro, was actually married to an American citizen.) The local police here have a particular fetish for the twin little lights that in most cars illuminate the rear license plate.

"If you're missing one of them, they pick you up," says Arturo Corso, the attorney who represented the deported fisherman. "And you get deported."

And more than anything, if you drive without a license, watch out. Rule 287(g) gives local police in every state in the Union a giant hammer to swing at immigrant communities. In recent years, the residents of the ballooning Latino neighborhoods growing up somewhere on the other side of the tracks of your town—the places where factory workers and housecleaners and similar manual laborers live—awake in the mornings to find police checkpoints strategically placed on the major thoroughfares to and from the white-people sides of town. These are the main roads to the immigrants' places of work, their schools, supermarkets, bus stops.

The squad cars perch on the sides of the road like ticks on a vein, hauling in alien after undocumented alien and tossing them into the criminal justice/deportation hopper. From there, in a complex, arbitrary, and mindlessly cruel legal process that puts people literally in chains for the crime of going to work or taking their kids to school, the detainees get ground up into a rich financial and political meal, shared in nearly equal parts by state and federal authorities on the one hand and private prison companies on the other.

On the local level, the police and the courts get to hit detainees with big tickets before they get chucked out of the country. In Georgia, the fees can be as high as a thousand dollars for driving without a license. The money is so good, police will show up anywhere where they're likely to find an undocumented Mexican near a car.

"They even used to camp out outside Hispanic churches on Sundays," says Corso.

"They're easy prey," concurs Victor Nieblas, a Los Angeles attorney who handles immigration cases. "For some police departments, these immigrants, they're walking ATM machines."

Gainesville was the first stop on a tour I took of a vast archipelago of roadblocks, convoys, and detention centers built and maintained specifically for a certain kind of alien—the poor, non-European kind. The archipelago, which has grown at breakneck speed over the last two decades, is like a giant legal purgatory in which detainees don't have any real rights or enjoy any real due process.

People disappear into it, hundreds of thousands a year, and become less like prisoners with rights than like objects or packages to be crated and shipped out like cargo. ICE even has a UPS-style tracking system that allows immigrant families to punch in a number and see where their deported relative is in his or her serpentine journey through the detention system. In the real justice system, you get habeas corpus; in the shadow system, you get a tracking number to see where your familial "package" is.

Many parts of the dragnet are like this, things that seem like shadows or echoes of real rights or real due process. You don't have an absolute right to counsel the same way you do if you're arrested in a regular criminal case. You have the right to *hire* an attorney, but one won't be provided for you.

In practice, the government will tend to tell you what the charges are and what the evidence is, but you don't have an absolute right to discovery as you would in a regular criminal case. You get to buy phone cards in immigrant detention centers (for very high prices— more on that later), but "you don't have a right to that 'one phone call,' the way we normally think of it," says Melissa Keaney, an attorney for the National Immigration Law Center.

The laws governing the rights of immigrants are overtly diluted, in a manner that would strike the average American as simply strange, if not outrageous. A natural-born citizen enjoys Fourth Amendment protections against unreasonable searches and seizures. Police can't come busting into your home without a warrant, can't wiretap your phone for no reason. Any evidence seized in an improper search is invalid. This basic principle, that evidence improperly obtained gets excluded, is called the exclusionary rule.

But according to a recent federal court decision called *INS v. Lopez-Mendoza,* in cases involving immigrants, a Fourth Amendment violation must be "egregious" for evidence to be thrown out. Moreover, thanks to a more recent case called *Gutierrez-Berdin v. Eric Holder,* even "very minor physical abuse coupled with aggressive questioning" does not rise to the level of an egregious Fourth Amendment violation.

The government's rationale here is beautiful in its simplicity. American criminals have constitutional rights not because they are natural-born Americans but precisely because they are criminals. Deportations, however, are not part of the criminal justice system. "Removal proceedings," wrote the circuit judge in the *Gutierrez-Berdin* case, "are civil, not criminal, and the exclusionary rule does not generally apply to them."

So the undocumented alien who kills a room full of Rotarians with an ax has a right to counsel, a phone call, and protection against improper searches. The alien caught crossing the street on his way to work has no rights at all.

Strangest of all, immigration proceedings are run by immigration judges, who are not "Article III" judges—not members of the judicial branch, as described in the U.S. Constitution. Immigration judges are actually employees of the Department of Homeland Security. In other words, they work for the same branch of government that prosecutes the cases.

"They're all executive branch employees," says Keaney. "The same people investigating the case are judging the case."

It all adds up to a system that has many of the features of a police state, right down to the nagging omnipresence of the police in the daily lives of the target community. Immigrants have to be thinking about the police every minute of every day. In towns like Gainesville, Hispanic immigrants hug and kiss one another every morning as they leave their homes, knowing that any of them can be snatched up at any moment and disappear down the rabbit hole, perhaps for good.

One woman I met, whom I'll call Ella, had been a doctor in Mexico but fled to the United States after she and her husband were victims of a violent crime there. Here in America two years ago, she found herself in jail after being rear-ended on the way home from a Gainesville grocery store.

"I was just buying milk," Ella says now. "I begged the woman in the other car, please, don't call the police, I'll be taken away from my children, please."

But the other driver (an Indian immigrant, incidentally) was a stickler for the rules and insisted, over a torrent of pleas, on calling the cops. The young doctor was quickly arrested. From the back of a squad car, she managed to call her local church, which sent some American members of the congregation to the accident scene. The churchgoers were able to take the woman's American-born daughter home for her and alert her husband, but they couldn't prevent an arrest.

Ella is a soft-spoken, frail woman with rail-thin arms who wears thick glasses with fine wire frames. She came to America after a pair of masked men broke into her home in a rural Mexican town, savagely beat her and her husband, took everything they had (including all the pharmaceuticals for their medical practice), and threatened to kill her entire family if she went to the police.

When she went to the police anyway, the authorities did nothing. They didn't even visit the crime scene. She quickly realized that the police and the criminals, if not actively in cahoots, were not exactly adversaries. Frightened, she and her husband moved to Mexico City, but that turned out not to be far enough. "Because they wore masks, I could never be sure," she says now. "I was looking at every man on the street and wondering. I stopped going outside."

Ella's husband had a brother who had long before moved to America and was living in Gainesville, working construction. So Ella and her husband decided to come to see him. They came on a tourist visa but stayed, hoping to make a better life. Her husband, also a doctor in Mexico, began to work construction. She began cleaning houses. They were getting by. The brother-in-law moved to another city an hour away, then soon disappeared.

It turned out later he had been caught in a car stop and deported. It was over a year before they heard from him again. That was on her mind as she sat in the squad car on the way to the Hall County Jail.

She ended up spending two days in jail. While there, she was visited over and over by an ICE official, who repeatedly waved a paper at her to sign. The paper was a sort of rights waiver that, once signed, leads to extradited deportation. This is a favored ICE tool called a stipulated order of removal. The usual pitch of an ICE official waving a stip order in front of an immigrant is that the result, deportation, will be the same as it will be if you contest the case, only you'll spend less time in ICE detention and get to your home country faster.

This waiver of rights was used to deport 160,000 people between 2000 and 2010. Its use exploded after Obama's election, moving from fewer than 5,000 orders a year in 2004 to more than 40,000 in 2008. Studies have shown that ICE officials routinely overestimate the amount of time detainees will spend in jail contesting their cases and that stips are mostly presented to people who have been detained on minor violations and don't have lawyers.

Documents released through FOIA requests show that ICE officials have been pushing stip orders as a way to get immigrants, even legal immigrants, out of the country before they somehow find a way to a lawyer.

"Please, please, please . . . encourage the agents to work harder on the stipulated orders of removal," wrote one ICE official in a circulated email. "Most of the [lawful permanent residents] who get out of jail are willing to take an order just to get out of jail sooner (that is until the judge encourages them to get a lawyer)."

"Encourage to stip away!" wrote another ICE official. A third, an attorney in the ICE counsel's office in San Francisco, commented on the amount of time agents should spend reviewing stip orders before presenting them to judges for final approval. He wanted the deportations to involve more speed and less thought. "Fifteen minutes is way too long," he wrote. "Cut that in half!"

Ella, however, wouldn't sign the stip. "I'm an educated person," she told me. "I know not to sign a document that I don't understand. He became very angry with me and kept coming back, acting like he was frustrated by my decision."

The decision turned out to be the right one, allowing her to stay in America pending a deportation hearing. Ella was fortunate after two days to find a clever lawyer, who scored for her the Holy Grail of immigration rulings, a deportation bond ("probably because she's a doctor," another lawyer told me), securing her release pending her immigration hearing.

But the truth is, she's likely to lose her case and will almost certainly be deported soon. Her seven children and her husband will almost certainly stay here in America. So she has a year left with her family. All because she got her fender nicked on the way to pick up some milk.

The number of stories like this boggles the mind. Three hundred ninety-six thousand, nine hundred and six people were deported from the United States in 2011.

Of those, just over a thousand (1,119) had records for homicide, and just under six thousand (5,848) had convictions for sexual offenses. Roughly 80,000 more had other, lesser convictions for offenses like DUIs.

The overwhelming remainder were like Ella, people guilty of little civil infractions, what immigration authorities term Level 3 offenses: traffic violations, immigration violations, and so on. In some communities, like Georgia's Cobb County, 60 percent of all detainees were caught for traffic violations. Many of those people were deported through rule 287(g), which is only supposed to target immigrants who are a "threat to public safety" and a "danger to the community." The rule was supposed to make it easier to deport Mexican murderers, but the distinction got lost in the wash. Instead, the people we're deporting are the ones who fled from Mexican murderers.

"Obama has broken all the deportation records," says Nieblas. "One million people in just a few years. Incredible."

Meanwhile, not one single employee of any foreign bank—not one banker from Barclays, Deutsche Bank, RBS, Dexia, Société Générale, or any of the other numerous foreign banks that have been caught up in the many serious fraud and manipulation scandals in recent years—has yet been deported or jailed for any crime connected to the 2008 financial crisis.

So we've built a massive and ruthless police apparatus for the ordinary immigrant population, complete with a sprawling, essentially extralegal detention complex, to catch and detain people who have not committed any actual crimes.

This gigantic, menacing complex of bars, chains, buses, and airplanes built to deal with the immigrant poor stands in stark contrast to the tiny, disorganized confederation of perhaps a few hundred lawyers policing transnational financial companies. We don't have special jails for foreigners or executives from foreign firms who steal by the million or billion.

So hundreds of thousands of people go to jail without committing crimes. Thousands or tens of thousands more commit extremely serious crimes, and no jail even exists to detain them.

There's a profound story here about what's happening to the very idea of citizenship, be it individual or corporate, in the new global economy. It used to be that citizenship in a strong and healthy state was universally prized, because citizenship confers rights. But with citizenship also comes responsibilities, and it turns out that not everybody wants those. In the minds of some, if you can get the rights without the responsibilities, you're really onto something.

In other words, there's a new class of people whose goal is to become above citizenship. Live in America, conduct your trades in the weaker regulatory arena in London, pay your taxes in Antigua or the Isle of Man. Keep the rights but offshore the responsibilities.

The flip side is that there is a growing subset of people, like undocumented immigrants, who live below the level of full citizenship. If the first group is stateless by choice, these people are involuntarily stateless and have virtually no rights at all.

For a country founded on the idea that rights are inalienable and inherent from birth, we've developed a high tolerance for conditional rights and conditional citizenship. And the one condition, it turns out, is money. If you have a lot of it, the legal road you get to travel is well lit and beautifully maintained. If you don't, it's a dark alley and most Americans would be shocked to find out what's at the end of it.

Gainesville isn't quite Mayberry. It's a bigger southern town that plausibly calls itself the Poultry Capital of the World. The economy here ebbs and flows with the fortunes of big chicken companies like Coleman Natural Foods, Prime Pak, Victory, Koch Foods, and Fieldale Farms. On one side of town, you can't miss the smell, even with the windows rolled up.

Once upon a time, most of the hardest labor in the chicken plants was done by black workers, and back then the area the workers lived in was called Niggertown. Then, after the Vietnam War, the town ghetto gained a Southeast Asian flavor with an influx of refugees, and the plants were suddenly manned by Vietnamese.

Arturo Corso, who in the 1990s worked as an assistant district attorney here, recalls a famous tale about white Gainesville's relationship to the Vietnamese community. In 1985 the town brought murder charges against Nguyen Ngoc Tieu, a twenty-seven-year-old Vietnamese man who had allegedly stabbed a white woman named Debbie Rollins.

"This was way before my time," says Corso. "The trial starts, and one witness after the other gets up on the stand and points at the defendant. They're saying, 'Yes, that's him, he did this, he did that.' And every time they testify that he did something, the guy just sits there and says, 'Not me, not me!'"

Corso pauses and shakes his head.

"A whole day of the trial goes by like this," he says. "The second day begins and it's the same thing—every time the witness points at the defendant, he keeps saying, 'Not me, not me!' And everyone thinks what he means is 'I didn't do it.'

"They were almost done with the second day of the trial before they figured out that what he really meant was, he wasn't Nguyen Ngoc Tieu! They had the wrong guy!"

It turned out the court had screwed up and dragged another Vietnamese man, a thief named Hen Van Nguyen, up from the jails to sit at trial for the Rollins murder. The real killer's own lawyer didn't even notice. It was a landmark moment in the history of "they all look alike to me." The judge declared a mistrial, but a month later the actual defendant, Tieu, was still sentenced to life in prison, despite the fact that most of the key witnesses had fingered a completely different person for the crime under oath.

That incident might have been part of the reason the Vietnamese community packed up and left Gainesville en masse in the late 1980s and early 1990s.

In their place came the Latinos, mostly from Mexico. Two decades ago Latinos made up 8 percent of the population here. By 2010 that number was 42 percent.

But now the Latinos, too, are starting to leave, which may be part of a larger trend of Latino immigrants returning home as the American economy worsens, making the country's less appealing sides less worth putting up with. In this small Georgia community, for instance, the endless roadblocks and car stops mean that most local

Latino residents get around using an exhausting regime of taxis, buses, and bicycles, and the constant harassment wears on them. "People are leaving," says Aaron Rico, Jose's brother and another Fiesta cabdriver. "Go to a city or something. It is getting to be too much."

The war on immigrants in Georgia took an extraordinary turn in the middle of the last decade when the state passed a series of harsh laws outlining punishments for driving without a license. Passed in 2008, Georgia codes 40-5-20 and 40-5-120 created two completely different sets of punishments for the same crime.

They dictated that a natural-born Georgia citizen who is caught driving without a license is innocent of the crime, provided he gets a license before trial. In other words, even if he is technically guilty of the crime at the time of arrest, he can be declared retroactively innocent, so long as he takes a trip down to the DMV and gets himself a license. He doesn't even have to pay a fine.

Meanwhile, an undocumented resident, who is not entitled to get a license before or after arrest, pays significant new penalties under the laws. He's jailed for a minimum of two days (and a maximum of twelve), pays a fine of five hundred to a thousand dollars, and is convicted of a misdemeanor—or a felony if there are four offenses in five years.

There are no other laws like this in America that provide retroactive amnesty to some while others face significant punishment for the same crime. Some immigration lawyers claim the Georgia statutes would seem to violate the U.S. Constitution in at least two ways, first by creating an ex post facto law (banned in Article 1) and second by violating the "privileges and immunities" clause.

None of that matters: the laws are on the books, and since 2008 there's been a sharp increase in the number of arrests of undocumented aliens for violating the no-license statute. The immigrants know this, which is why the daily effort to get to and from work has turned into something like an ongoing military campaign, with immigrants employing guerrilla strategies—cab networks, shared bicycles, carpooling, etc.—to try to avoid capture.

The problem is, some immigrants have no choice but to stay and take their chances, working in businesses where a bicycle won't cut it. Alvaro Fernandez* is one of those people.

A native of Colombia, Alvaro has been in America for more than ten years and runs a successful construction business in the Hall County area, around Gainesville. He has good relationships all over the county, especially with former clients, but his problem is that he has to drive a truck to and from work to carry tools and equipment. "No cabs for me," he says, shrugging and smiling.

"I was driving home one night at about ten p.m.," he says now. "And that's when the odyssey started."

The giant dragnet created by 287(g) is inspiring a whole new generation of epic survival tales. The stories you hear from people who've disappeared at checkpoints and roadblocks sound eerily like the literature of the Soviet gulag, with the same themes of repeat interrogations, marches, chains, total alienation from family, and clashes with harsh nature, lunatic bureaucracies, and petty human predators of every imaginable species, some wearing uniforms and some not.

Alvaro came to America in 1999 with his wife on legal tourist visas. Like many of the Latino immigrants I interviewed for this book, he at one time had a legal driver's license in America. "When I first came, I was able to get a license on my visa," he says. "But when my visa expired, so did my license."

For a while, things were cool. Alvaro built up his business, doing so well, in fact, that he's been able to buy farmland back in his native country, setting himself or his children up for a future life as Colombian rural gentry. But the document problem nagged. He needed a driver's license. At one point, as a stopgap measure, he made what would prove to be a fateful decision and bought himself a fake Mexican driver's license. "They were easier to get," he says. And when he

---

* Name changed to conceal identity.

got in a car accident in the early part of the last decade, he showed police his Mexican ID, which left him with a definite footprint in the system, as a Mexican.

All that past history came into play on the night in October 2010 when Alvaro was arrested at the checkpoint. He surrendered his truck and sat mute in the back of a squad car while two young white patrolmen took him to the local jail. He knew he would pop up in the system as a Mexican and, thinking it over in the car, silently made a command decision. If they sent him to Colombia, he realized, he might not see his wife and family again for a very long time, if ever.

"I would never be able to come back," he says. "Not from Colombia." Logistically, it's harder to make it to the United States from the other side of South America, as opposed to a bordering state like Mexico.

So he decided to keep his mouth shut. Then when offered a stip order—the same deal offered to Ella and nearly every other detainee caught under 287(g)—he would take it. Instead of spending months in jail in America pending an immigration hearing, it might only be weeks. He'd be sent to Mexico, though he didn't know *where* in Mexico, or how. And from Mexico, if he could find a way to connect with his family, he had a chance to have some money wired to him so he could buy a way back.

Alvaro had no idea what to expect. A fit, leather-skinned man of about fifty, with a shock of jet black hair, jovial eyes, a pronounced nose, and high cheekbones, he comes across as a worldly fellow and a man of experience but not necessarily a tough guy. He had never been in jail before.

"There were hard things, they were all hard," he says now. "But the hardest thing was county jail. I was mixed in with really dangerous people."

When he got to the jail, Alvaro's immediate concern was to call a relative, specifically his nephew, to let him know what had happened and to start planning a way out. There was a phone in the jail, and inmates were allowed a half hour a day to talk. When the jailers rounded him up in the morning for breakfast and a shower, Alvaro thought he could make a call, too, and walked to the phone.

"What I didn't know is that some of the black criminals in the jail 'ran' the phone," he says. "We weren't allowed to use it without their permission. I didn't know and just walked up to the phone, started dialing. Before I knew it, someone jumped on me, started hitting me. I took a blow on the side of the head."

Other Hispanic inmates rushed to his aid. The fight subsided, but Alvaro still didn't get to make the call. He tried a second time later on, and again he was attacked, only this time he fought back. "I hit the guy and knocked him down," he says, with a bit of pride. "But the jailers came, and because I was fighting, they put me in the hole."

The hole, he says, was a special cell three feet by four feet, with a solid iron door, an opening to shove food through, and no toilet. There was just a hole in the ground.

"It was really disgusting," he says. "Actually everything about the jail was disgusting. Even the orange jumpsuit they gave us, it stank of sweat. The blankets also stank. And the hole, there was no air in there.

"But I was lucky. I was out of there in four hours, transferred to the immigration detention center."

Alvaro's trip wasn't a long one. He moved to the North Georgia Detention Center, run by a private company called CCA, the Corrections Corporation of America. The CCA facility in Gainesville is basically a retooled version of an old city jail. In fact, it shares a building with the Gainesville Police Department. The facility, surrounded by giant coils of razor wire, is inopportunely located in a new enterprise-zone area of Gainesville, darkening the mood for the would-be yuppie-friendly coffee shop and poetry/arts center across the street.

Still, the facility's presence in the zone isn't inappropriate; CCA represents one of the great enterprise models in this new phase of the American economy, which is rich in such public-private profit schemes.

Alvaro's experience hints at why. He moved from smelly jump-suits and grimy blankets in the public jail to a Holiday Inn–like experience at CCA.

"Oh, yeah, *muy bonito*," he says. "Clean T-shirts. Clean underwear. *Tres pares*," he says, flashing a thumbs-up and laughing. "You get a sandwich, a good sandwich, a box lunch. You get a bath. Seriously, you get little shampoos, toothbrushes, toothpaste, a brush for your hair, you name it. It's all high class."

It should be. Depending on whom you believe, CCA receives upward of $166 per day from the federal government to care for immigrants like Alvaro, which is about four times what it used to cost the INS back in the days when the government took care of its own detainees.

The big influx of cash impressed investors on Wall Street. Back in 2000, when the federal government began housing immigrant detainees in mostly privately run prisons, CCA's share price hovered around a dollar. Today, as I write this in the summer of 2013, CCA's share price is $34.34. It was at $23 just two years ago. The company's revenues went from just around $300 million in 2000 to an astonishing $1.7 billion in 2011. Overall, the corrections industry is one of the soundest stock/equity bets in the world, with soaring revenues—the industry as a whole pulled in more than $5 billion in America in 2011.

The jailing-Hispanics business is the perfect mix of politics and profit. Companies like CCA donate generously to politicians everywhere, particularly at the state level. The firm has spent as much as $3.4 million lobbying in a single year and on average spends between $1 million and $2 million a year. Its lobbyists are everywhere, and in every major anti-immigrant bill, you can usually find a current or former CCA lobbyist lurking in the weeds somewhere. Arizona governor Jan Brewer, for instance, had two ex–CCA lobbyists on her staff helping write the legislation when she pushed through her notorious 1070 law, which essentially legalized racial profiling in the cause of catching illegal immigrants.

In Alvaro's Georgia, Governor Nathan Deal, Lieutenant Governor Casey Cagle, and State Senate Majority Leader Chip Rogers had all been longtime recipients of CCA contributions when they worked to pass HB 87, a profiling law very similar to Brewer's 1070 bill.

The result is a huge win-win for industry and the politicians they work with. A governor like Jan Brewer publicly knocks on hated immigrants and wins votes, while CCA takes home $166 a day for every immigrant caught in the law enforcement net.

Local police forces go along because the federal government compensates them for their detention of immigrants. A program called the State Criminal Alien Assistance Program (SCAAP) pays local police forces out of the federal kitty for any detained immigrants who meet certain criteria (they're undocumented, they stayed for at least four days, and they've been convicted of at least two misdemeanors). According to the GAO, states received about $1.6 billion annually in SCAAP payments through the end of the 2000s, and the numbers are likely to rise in this decade.

Meanwhile, local politicians go along with the arrests because they can pitch the construction of new detention facilities by firms like CCA, the GEO Group, and MTC as moves that create new jobs—just look at glowing press reports like this one, from a CBS affiliate along the Alabama-Georgia border, WRBL, in late 2011:

CCA BEGINS HIRING FOR NEW JENKINS FACILITY
New Georgia institution brings job prospects, economic boost to local community

There are only two losers in this daisy chain of political moves. First of course are the Hispanic immigrants, who don't vote and are essentially without a real political lobby. The second group is their employers, and they do have a lobby, but there's a compromise in the works for them (more on that later). Everyone else—the politicians, the company itself, the towns that see new jobs for white folks—they all win.

And someone else wins, too: Wall Street. Some of the biggest investors in private prison companies are, you guessed it, the too-big-to-fail banks. Wells Fargo, for instance, has nearly $100 million invested in the GEO Group, plus about $6 million in CCA. Bank of America, General Electric, Fidelity, and Vanguard are all major investors in at least one of the three big prison companies.

And why not? Like too-big-to-fail banking itself, private prisons are an industry that depends not on the unpredictable economy but upon political connections. It's the perfect kind of business in the oligarchical capitalism age, with guaranteed profits to provide a low-cost public insurance against the vagaries of the market. Stock analysts, naturally, are not blind to the brilliance of the business formula.

"One of the best presentations I heard discussed," wrote an analyst from Zacks, the stock research firm, "was the corrections industry and how it was a smart and uncommon place to put your money." CCA, the analyst went on, was

> one of the top selections for its steady growth and defensive nature of its business. Economies may ebb and flow, but the number of incarcerated Americans is steadily growing according to the U.S. Department of Justice.

And then the analyst in his report gleefully showed this graph:

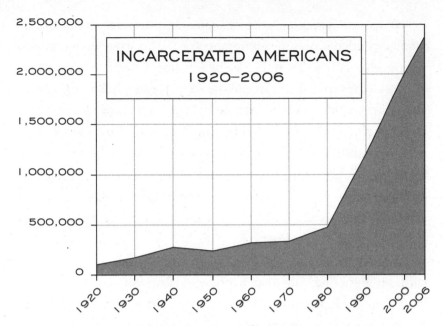

Sources: *"The Punishing Decade," Justice Policy Institute report;*
"Prisoners in 2006," Bureau of Justice Statistics Bulletin NCJ 219416.

Who wouldn't invest in that?

Theoretically, the political winds might have blown the same way without the profit motive. But there's no way to look at the financial picture and not conclude that the explosive combination of anti-immigrant politics and easy profits turbocharged the construction of the Big Dragnet. Ironically, the very brokest people in America, Hispanic immigrants, are one of America's last great cash crops.

One last reason immigrants are great business: as any good defense lawyer knows, the cost of freedom is always everything you have. To put it another way, people who have no documents and no rights are desperate, and desperation is a great natural price multiplier. For immigrants caught in the dragnet, the price of everything skyrockets, beginning, usually, with the traffic ticket, and the five-hundred-dollar or thousand-dollar no-license fines are extraordinarily high for what is essentially an administrative offense. In fact, a DUI, a far more serious crime, carries the same fine in the state of Georgia.

"It's a moneymaking scheme, pure and simple," sighs Corso, who's defended scores of immigrants for no-license violations.

For Alvaro, his first hint that he'd entered a new pricing paradigm as a captured alien came in the CCA facility. In virtually every CCA-run facility across America, detainees are allowed access to a commissary, where they can buy random items: Popsicles, ramen noodles, candy bars. "But everything costs three or four times the real price," he says. One item most every detainee buys is a prepaid phone card. In most CCA facilities, the prices for these cards are also extortionate, as much as nine dollars for a card that inmates can use to make three brief calls.

"You don't have a choice," says Alvaro. "You've got to buy the card. I bought one, called my nephew, explained what was happening to me. I told him to get some money ready. I didn't know what was coming, but I wanted to prepare."

Once they move from the local lockup to the CCA prison, detainees enter a weird legal gray area. Like disappeared persons from the gulag era, they're told nothing about their captivity and often have no idea how long it will be before their case is decided. The uncertainly becomes part of the interrogation process. "In my case, I didn't get to talk to an ICE caseworker for a week and a half," says Alvaro. "For some guys, it's two days. Others wait for two, three weeks. You have no idea."

When he did finally meet with his interrogator, he got the same pitch that Ella received: he had a piece of paper pushed at him, and he was asked to sign a waiver and accept voluntary deportation.

Most immigrants at least hesitate. Alvaro surprised his interrogator, a clean-shaven white ICE agent with a crew cut and heavily muscled forearms, by quickly accepting the voluntary deportation order. "I played dumb," he says. The ICE agent eyed him suspiciously, shrugged, and took the paper away.

Days went by. Alvaro passed the time in the comically cozy CCA facility playing checkers, soccer, a little basketball. It was a relief, he says now, to be in the immigration center. "I hate to say this," he says, "but it's so much more dangerous to be in the county jail with the other Americans. In the CCA center it was mostly all people who'd been caught on their way to work, people with jobs. It was not a dangerous place.

"I made some friends in there, especially some younger men from Mexico who were very scared. I think they looked up to me a little. I promised to look after them until we got to the border. It was in the back of my mind that they might be able to help me once we got there."

Nobody knew when that would be. But one morning Alvaro and all the other men were roused at five a.m. They were all put in leg chains, waist chains, and handcuffs and marched out of the CCA facility into a bus. "We were all chained," he says. "From five in the morning until we boarded an airplane later that night, we were in chains and couldn't go to the bathroom."

The journey Alvaro describes from Gainesville onward is surreal. "Like a movie," he says. They traveled from place to place, the caravan picking up more buses with more people caught in car stops and checkpoints at each place. "We went to Atlanta first, and there we met up with more people. More buses, buses, buses. I had to rub my eyes to make sure I was really seeing so many people.

"In my bus there were two men who had been in jail for drugs. The rest were people like me who'd been caught on the way to work. None of us knew exactly where we were going, but we knew we were headed for the border."

From Atlanta, the caravan made its way westward and eventually reached an airport in Columbus, Georgia, where it was understood that the group would be flown to the border. "It was hard because the plane wasn't ready," Alvaro explains. "We sat there in the heat in chains waiting, waiting. Some people were getting unwell.* From the windows we were all watching; we saw strange things.

---

* There were more than one hundred deaths of immigrants in ICE custody between 2003 and 2010, and the government has refused to release information about most of the cases. Many of the deaths were suspicious. In one case, a Salvadoran man named Nery Romero who suffered from severe pain was left untreated and committed suicide. It was later discovered that ICE officials faked documents to show they had, in

"The men and the women were segregated, of course, but we saw a bus full of women. One of them apparently had to go to the bathroom, so she was led out of the bus. She was in full chains—legs, hands, and hands chained to the waist. It seemed so unnecessary. Except for a few, none of us were criminals. We couldn't escape anywhere. Anyway this woman, they led her to one of those—what do you call them?"

A Porta-Potty?

"Yes, exactly," he says. "The guards, and there were several of them, they led her to the toilet and just pushed her in, still in chains. All of us on the bus watching this were in amazement. It would be hard even for a man to find a way to go to the bathroom with all those restraints on.

"You could see her asking the guard to undo her cuffs, but he wouldn't. She went inside the toilet, stayed in for a while, and came out. I don't know how she managed."

Finally the plane arrived. For the men it was a relief, because they were allowed to urinate before boarding. "But they kept the chains on," Alvaro says.*

The airplane he was boarding was bigger than anything he had ever seen. "There must have been four hundred fifty of us. It was a gigantic aircraft." The crowd of men and women got on board, still in chains, and sat through a short flight south, to Texas.

Once there, they were quickly loaded onto buses again and driven straight to an international bridge that would lead them across the border. Here, finally, the chains were removed, and Alvaro learned where he would be released, the Mexican city of Nuevo Laredo. From his seat on the bus, he peered through the window toward the border and started to think through his options, when suddenly there was a disturbance at the front of the vehicle.

---

fact, given him Motrin. The only problem was, they screwed up the documents, which showed that he got the drugs only after he was already dead.

* I asked several lawyers about the chains. Some of them didn't know what to say. "There are a lot of things in this world that . . . it's not just that they don't fit our idea of what the normal laws should be," says Melissa Keaney. "It's just not our values. We don't imagine this kind of thing."

"One of the men, I think, made some kind of sarcastic comment to one of the guards," he says. "I'm not sure what it was. Something about the chains, maybe. I remember the guard suddenly turning red. In English, he said something like, 'You want to get tough? You want to get smart?' And the guy, he didn't back down, and next thing you know there are four more guards in the bus. He's leaning back in his seat, pointing his chin out at them.

"I'm thinking, uh-oh. Within a few moments they dragged that guy out of the bus. Took him away somewhere, no idea where."

Not even certain why, Alvaro made a mental note of the man's face.

Soon the bus door was opened, and the men inside were motioned to get out. Each of the detainees was handed a box with his property, which was the clothes he had been wearing at the time of arrest, mainly. They all changed clothes and began walking. A line of guards on either side of the detainees created a makeshift corridor. The line of people was so long, Alvaro could not see the end of it.

As he walked over the Rio Grande into Mexico, he considered the absurdity of his situation. He was being repatriated to a country he had never been to, where he knew no one and had no connections. He thought everything he had been through to that point had been difficult. "In truth, that was just the warm-up," he says now. "The hard part was just starting."

Once over the bridge, the group took on the feeling of a gang of prison escapees, each man unsure of whether the survival odds were better alone or in a group. Some gathered in big crowds, others went off alone. Alvaro stayed with the two young Mexican men he'd taken under his wing in Gainesville.

An undocumented immigrant is like a bleeding fish. Every predator for miles around will swim at top speed to take a bite. For Alvaro, the process had begun back in America, with the police who stopped him at night and slapped him with a seven-hundred-dollar ticket. It continued with the overpriced soups and phone cards in the CCA facility. It was now about to continue in Mexico.

He had $60 in his pocket, and going off toward downtown Nuevo Laredo with the two young men, his first thought was to change his money. There was an exchange window right near the bridge. The exchange rate at the time was 12 pesos to a dollar. He pushed his $60 across. The woman handed him back 600 pesos, seemingly expecting he wouldn't notice she was shorting him 120 pesos.

"Apparently a lot of the men who come across the bridge do not count so well," he says. "It took some arguing, but I got my dollars back. We moved on."

From there Alvaro decided to get a hotel room with the two men, until they could find relatives to come and get them. He was on his way to doing that when he decided to call his nephew back in Gainesville at a phone booth. The instant he dialed the States, he felt a pair of arms grabbing him from behind. "I turned around, and it was a policeman," he says. "A bicycle policeman, as it happened— his bike was leaning up against a wall."

The two other young men Alvaro was with scattered when the policeman arrived. Meanwhile, the bike cop demanded that Alvaro identify himself and then told him he was under arrest.

"For what?" Alvaro asked.

"For making an illegal phone call," the policeman said. The ticket, he said, was going to be three hundred pesos.

Alvaro stood his ground, arguing with the bicycle policeman, who eventually gave up and went away. He shook his head and laughed. An illegal phone call?

Watching this scene the whole time was an elderly man who was sitting at a shoeshine stand, waiting for customers. When Alvaro was finally done with the policeman, the old man waved him over.

"He introduced himself, asked me where I was from," Alvaro says. "I told him, 'I've just come from up north.' He says to me, 'You come with me, you will be my guest for the night, forget about the hotel.'"

Alvaro headed toward the old man's house, stopping along the way to buy some groceries, some hot dogs, eggs, something to eat.

They walked for a long time, entering neighborhoods that were progressively more and more beaten down, until finally they reached a section of the city that was completely devastated. Alvaro again remarked to himself the strangeness of his situation. "The houses were burned down, or else in complete disrepair. They were empty and boarded up," he says. "This gave me pause. I asked the old man, 'What happened here?' He says, 'Don't ask.'"

Finally they made it to the old man's house. Alvaro immediately sensed that something was odd about the home. The old man was in his late sixties and almost in rags, but he had a wife who was young and pretty. "She was twenty-five at most," Alvaro says, "and pregnant with his child. She was very nice and didn't seem surprised that I was there. And there were two other children in the house who were not his, and might not have been hers, either. I didn't ask questions."

After the long journey, Alvaro slept well; the next morning the shoe shiner took him to a downtown plaza, where he was introduced to someone described to him as "the man. The *main* man." The *jefe* was some sort of local mafioso to whom the shoe shiner and everyone else in the area was paying tribute. "It was wild," Alvaro says. "The guy didn't have a telephone, but when he wanted to make a call, someone would bring him a telephone and say something like, 'Here's your telephone, boss.' It was like meeting Jabba the Hutt."

But the *jefe*, who went by the odd name Fitus, was good to Alvaro. Fitus told him that he could arrange a coyote, for a price. Alvaro, without getting into too many details about his life, explained that he could have some money wired, but it might take a day. Fitus seemed fine with that. He even lent Alvaro a few hundred dollars in the meantime and told him to come back the next day, or as soon as he could, with the deposit.

"While in town, I made some calls and arranged for money to be wired," Alvaro says. "Also it was Halloween night that night, so before I went back to the old man's house again, I bought candy for the children and some toys with the money I'd borrowed. But this second night, things went very wrong at the old man's house. He bought some very strong beer and he got very drunk.

"Almost right away, he quarreled with that pretty young wife of his. Then he began to really give it to her. He was hitting her. I tried to tell him, 'I know I'm a guest, but I can't let you hurt your wife.' So he threw me out of the house."

It was Halloween night. Alvaro found himself alone in the pitch-black, burned-out neighborhood. He looked for a cab. Passing a junkie on the street, he asked where he could get a taxi.

"He laughed and said, 'You must not be from around here. No taxis will come here,'" Alvaro says. "So I walked farther. Finally I found a cab after some time. They took me to a hotel, and I checked in. And then I made a very serious mistake. I called Colombia."

This call was the portal into the mirror image of the American deportation machine. It turns out there's a dragnet on the other side of the border, too.

In Mexico, there is crime, and then there's organized crime, and then there are the Zetas, a group of gangsters known for their extreme cruelty and technical sophistication. The group was originally formed in the 1990s by Special Forces commandos, had a brief alliance with a drug organization known as the Gulf Cartel, and then broke off on its own to create a powerful crime syndicate that not only traffics in drugs but makes money through extortion and kidnapping. The Zeta trademark includes beheadings and a preference for torture over bribery. And one of the Zeta businesses involves people like Alvaro.

When he made the call out of the country, he came to the attention of these gangsters, who monitor the calls of hotel residents. An hour after he made the call, men arrived at his hotel room, dragged him outside, and threw him into a car. Alvaro was terrified but said nothing. He was driven in total silence to a big house on the outskirts of town. When he was pushed inside, he was shocked to discover familiar faces.

"There must have been twenty-five or thirty of the people who'd walked over the bridge from Laredo with me," he says. "They'd all been kidnapped by the Zetas. They went straight from ICE custody to Zeta custody."

Among the men in custody was the unfortunate character who had argued with the ICE officials in Alvaro's bus on the other side of the border. Alvaro asked him what happened when the guards took him away. The man laughed. "Oh, they slapped me around a little," he said. "But nothing serious. Not like this."

The Zetas, Alvaro learned, operate on a simple business model. They know that most of the immigrants deported out of the United States have left relatives behind in America. Many of the deportees' relatives have saved money to bring more loved ones to the States from Mexico. That makes the deportees natural kidnapping targets.

Alvaro asked some of the men there what their situation was. Depending on the immigrant, the Zetas were demanding to be wired five thousand to seven thousand dollars before they would be released. Alvaro asked if there was any guarantee that they would even be released after the Zetas got the money. The men shrugged.

Soon, however, his captors took him aside. "So the Zetas start asking me questions about who I am and what I'm doing," he says. "I tell them, 'I'm no Mexican. I'm not like these men. I'm a Colombian, and I'm heading north.' They ask me, 'Who's helping you through? Who's arranging the coyote?'

"And that's when I got lucky. I told them Fitus was helping me. That changed everything."

Once he dropped Fitus's name, the Zetas disappeared and had a discussion. Soon they came back and told him, "Hang tight. We're going to check this out with Fitus."

So Alvaro spent a whole day in captivity, in the house outside Laredo, with the twenty-five other deportees. But Fitus vouched for Alvaro, and he was released from the haunted house. He has no idea what happened to the other men.

From there, Alvaro began the long journey back to America. He got money wired to Fitus's friends and was taken to a place in Nuevo Laredo called the Spot. It was like a safe house.

There were twenty to thirty people in a filthy room. "No ventilation, no bathrooms, these were people who wouldn't know what toilet paper is," Alvaro explains. "I spent three days there. I had to sleep on a terrace outside, because the mosquitoes on the first floor were unbearable."

Finally he and the others got on a bus, headed west, to the neighboring Mexican state of Coahuila. There, by the side of a road, they met up with two coyotes. One of them, Alvaro remembers, was extremely drunk.

Then, in a strange echo of the journey from Gainesville to Laredo, the group moved toward the Rio Grande, stopping from time to time to accumulate more members of the convoy. "At first there were three groups of twenty or so," he says. "Then we disappeared behind some trees and met up with some more. Finally, when we got to the banks of the river, there were about two hundred of us."

The two hundred huddled people were given minimal food and water while they waited for a boat to arrive. Night came and everyone slept in the open air. Then morning, then afternoon. The food and water vanished. There was nothing left. Alvaro began to get worried.

But finally men arrived with an inflatable raft and began moving people across the river a few at a time. "We got to the United States side," he says. "And we started walking. And walking. And walking."

The vegetation near the river disappeared into the background. Soon it was all desert. "After an hour we made it to the first fence," he says. "It was ten or twelve feet high. What could we do? We climbed over."

An hour or so later they made it to a second fence. But there was a problem. One of the travelers, a young man, was too weak to go on. "He couldn't walk anymore," Alvaro says. "So it was decided that he would walk toward the road and give himself up. We sent him one way, and the rest of us broke up into groups. The hope was that we would get some kind of head start. But within an hour, we saw the helicopter overhead."

Alvaro's group by that point consisted of twenty-three people.

When the helicopter came, they split into two groups and ran. When they found each other again, the two groups numbered seventeen and four.

"Two children were missing," Alvaro says, pausing. "The coyotes were communicating with each other by cell phone, and they were scrambling to find the missing kids. But they couldn't. They were gone."

Alvaro pauses while telling this part of the story, reliving this dilemma. It's clear he still hasn't quite sorted it all out in his head.

"We had no choice," he says finally. "We had to keep walking."

Alvaro and the group ended up walking for two more days. Eventually they met up with more coyotes and were driven by pickup truck to a mobile home outside San Antonio. The interior of the mobile home had recently been set on fire, so while it looked fine from the outside and drove well enough, the inside was almost completely charred. There were two men, a woman, and two grown children living inside this charred mobile home. All twenty-one of the remaining travelers piled into the blackened vehicle with them.

Once there, they were given an ultimatum. "The deal on the Mexico side had been one thousand dollars to get us to Houston," says Alvaro. "But we got in the RV, and suddenly the price was twelve hundred dollars. I refused to pay and so did the others. So now we were kidnapped again. They took our shoes at night and gave us only minimal food and water."

Alvaro says the situation got so desperate inside the RV that the group started going through the burned cabinets in the kitchen. The charred cabinet doors literally fell apart as they opened them up.

"Amazingly," Alvaro says, "we found some bread in there. It was a little black on the outside, but it was edible. We all split it and ate it. I couldn't believe I had been reduced to this."

Finally, Alvaro's family wired enough money to satisfy the coyotes. He hitched a ride with one of the other captives to Mississippi, and from there his nephew drove and picked him up to bring him back to Gainesville.

The whole adventure had taken about a month.

I ask Alvaro if he still drives to work.

He shrugs. "I have to," he says.

Not long after Alvaro returned to Gainesville, the city's local business leaders gathered together to discuss a problem. Nobody particularly minded that we were express-mailing human beings into the hands of kidnappers on the other side of the border, but the deportations were bad for business. Turnover at the local chicken plants was at an all-time high. Good, dependable cleaning ladies were being disappeared. The instability of the workforce was becoming a problem for the local white folks.

So in February 2011 some of those leaders marched on down to Atlanta to complain. Speaking before the state senate's Special Committee on Immigration and Georgia's Economy, Tom Hensley, president of a chicken processing firm called Fieldale Farms that is a big presence in the Gainesville area, stood up and complained about 287(g).

"We were 67 percent Hispanic in 2004. Our turnover was 25 percent. Our workers [compensation] cost was $50,000 a month. Our health care cost for the whole year was $8 million. It was about that time that the federal, state and local governments let it be known that these folks are not welcome," Hensley told the committee.

"Fast forward to 2010, we're about 33 percent Hispanic now. Our turnover is 75 percent. Workers comp costs are $150,000 a month. Our health care last year was $20 million. Those are staggering numbers, but that's the economic reality."

Hensley closed by begging the committee to ease back on the profiling and no-license statutes. "I implore you," he said. "Don't pass any more laws."

The plea by local business leaders, not just in Georgia but all over America, had a result. Instead of automatically snatching up every undocumented immigrant in sight and tossing them into the 287(g) grinder, local police were now allowed a little leeway to be merciful.

The leeway was in part provided by John Morton, chief of ICE and Barack Obama's top immigration official. Responding to a hail of criticism from around the country over the sharp increase in deportations and 287(g) actions, and perhaps thinking ahead to a 2012 election where the Hispanic vote might prove important, the Obama administration decided, through Morton, to offer America's 12 million undocumented aliens an olive branch.

On June 17, 2011, Morton issued a letter outlining a kinder, gentler immigration policy. The notorious "Morton Memo," as it would come to be known, essentially said that ICE officials and their partners in local law enforcement did not necessarily have to deport every last undocumented alien who came within eyeshot of a police officer.

"Agency employees," Morton wrote, "may exercise prosecutorial discretion and what factors should be considered." It went on to say that certain mitigating circumstances may be considered in immigration cases, like the individual's pursuit of education, his or her service in the U.S. Armed Forces, and so on.

Furthermore, special enforcement emphasis was to be placed on people who posed a "clear risk to national security," like for instance "serious felons" and "known gang members."

These, of course, were exactly the people whom 287(g) was originally supposed to target. The Morton Memo was essentially an admission that ICE had gone beyond its stated objectives and had unfairly swept up hardworking noncriminals like Ella and Alvaro. Now, however, the administration's new promise was to focus more on real criminals.

So what did that mean? Did it mean the dragnet would be relaxed? Fewer patrols and roadblocks?

Nope. In Gainesville, at least, what it meant was just as many arrests and just as many no-license tickets, if not more. Only the number of deportations relaxed. In the first five months of 2012, deportations dropped nationwide by about 10 percent. But in places like Gainesville, immigrants remained a constant target for those five-hundred-dollar and thousand-dollar tickets. This seemed to represent the ultimate white-folks win-win: local chicken-plant owners got to keep their cheap labor, while local police still got to milk the immigrant community for any money they made working at those plants.

"They need us here to work," one of the Fiesta passengers explained to me. "But they also want our money. We're between the rock and the hard place."

In 2012 and 2013, local officials began a new policy: they were still catching, ticketing, and deporting as many undocumented aliens as they could, but in many cases they were allowed to avoid incarceration in the meantime. "The people are still getting deported, but now they get to wait at home for their departure date," says Corso. "It's not that families aren't still being destroyed by bad immigration policy. Just that the cost for local detention is going down."

The lessened detention regime caused a blip in CCA's business. The new facility in Gainesville began to empty. Finally, in late 2013, the company announced that it was closing the facility. The city, which had issued bonds to pay for the construction of the facility, was left hanging. Employees of the facility would be laid off and there would be that much less revenue to pay off the bonds. "It's a blow," said Gainesville mayor pro tem Bob Hamrick. He was asked by local media how the city would pay off the bonds. "Obviously," Hamrick answered, "that will be a hot topic for us to discuss in the next several days."

This series of maneuvers demonstrates the evolution of the anti-immigrant police state. Even after the Morton Memo, it is bigger than ever. In fact, ICE in early 2012 shifted into emergency mode, pulling workers off desk jobs to go out into the field hunting more undocumented aliens. The stated purpose was to catch more of those elusive "real" criminals, but in practice the increased manpower has mostly led to ordinary, noncriminal immigrants having to negotiate an ever-heavier blanket of constant legal scrutiny.

It turns out that it's a waste of absolute political power to simply throw undocumented aliens over the border. When you have a group of people who have no rights at all, the more inspired corporate solution is to extract as much value from them as possible. That can be money, that can be property, and if they don't have either of those things left, you take their time and labor.

On the other side of the country, in California, I saw the squeeze in action.

I reached the Boyle Heights address early, parked my car, and took a long look around. The East L.A. neighborhood looks like a lot of American public housing projects, which is to say you can mistake it for a prison or a concentration camp if you're not looking too closely. There are crisscrossed blocks of long concrete buildings painted drab yellow, bars covering literally every single window in sight, addresses sprayed on the apartments in an institutional font.

Since I don't speak Spanish, I had brought a translator, who happened to be from this neighborhood. "The gang situation around here used to be really bad," the young woman, Zacil Pech, explained. "Really bad."

We knocked on the door of a first-floor apartment in one of the yellow cell-block-type buildings. A short, stout Latina in a yellow T-shirt, with a tired but friendly expression, answered and asked us inside. This was Natividad Felix, a native of Sinaloa, Mexico, who had a story to tell. Her front room had no rugs, nothing on the walls, and in fact was bare of anything but a plain brown couch on a plain wooden floor. Natividad signaled for us to sit down on the couch, and we sat. Faces peered in and out of doors and stairways at the visitors. Natividad has six children, two of them twins, the oldest being a seventeen-year-old son, a tall, lithe young man who stared in at us from time to time. I would learn later that Jairo is a musical talent like his father and that his mother has nicknamed him "the Musician."

I was here to talk to Natividad about her experiences as a three-time veteran of one of the craziest and most draconian law enforcement practices in America. But we agreed that she would start at the beginning.

"I came to America when I was fifteen," she says. "I had just gotten married."

That's young to be married, I commented.

"Not in Mexico," she says. "I was really young and naïve. I didn't really know how to make decisions on my own. He told me to come over here with him in search of a better life, and I agreed because I was in love with him."

In Sinaloa, she lived with her extended family on a farm and worked in the fields, even as a little girl. Today she remembers those days fondly. "Life when I was a girl was beautiful," she says. "Living out in the country, surrounded by all my family, mother and father, sisters and brothers, cousins, aunts and uncles, all of whom I took for granted. It wasn't until I came here that I realized how important family truly is in a person's life."

She shakes her head. "I remember wishing I was back there with all of them, worry free and happy. The sense of freedom I got being out in the fields with my brothers and sisters is still, to this day, incomparable to any sense of 'freedom' I've felt living here."

Nonetheless her husband, Gabriel, convinced his young wife to come to America. She was in love with the soft-spoken man, a teenager like her who played guitar in the evenings. "He serenaded me," she recalls, laughing. He convinced her that there was more opportunity in the north, and they left Sinaloa.

Neither of them was prepared for how hard the trip would be. "We crossed through a border town called San Isidro," she says. "We walked for a whole night through the desert. I could hear the coyotes howl, and all these thoughts raced through my head—I was terrified.

"It was the first time I was actually away from my family. I was overwhelmed with sadness and loneliness. I was only fifteen years old, without my mother or father, or the option of going to visit them."

The couple made their way to Los Angeles, where they found a tiny apartment on San Pedro and Forty-Third Street. Nati was in that apartment for less than a year when Jairo was born. Gabriel, who was handy and a skilled gardener, began to get work mainly by hanging around outside Home Depot. "He did everything, carpentry, gardening, construction," she says. When I ask her what the hardest job was, she laughs.

"Which one was the hardest? All of them," she says. "When you have no papers, they take advantage of you. You work long hours. You get low pay. He came home at night very late, always."

As the years went on, the couple had more children. A year after Jairo there was Maria, funny but also the mature child in the family—"we got the best of both worlds with her." Two years later came Jose, whom they called "the Prankster." Henry, now eleven, came three years later. An aspiring dancer, he was called "Mr. Hollywood" by the couple. Lastly there were the twins, Angel and Adan, two boys. They had just turned eight when I first met Natividad.

They had a big family and were getting by, but things were not all perfect. The neighborhood had a serious problem with gangs, in particular a group called the Hazards. The gang was named after a street in East L.A. where it used to run before it moved to the Ramona Gardens area near Nati's house. They were mostly young kids who wore tats and had shaved heads.

"None of the children were allowed to sleep on the first floor," explains Nati. "There were too many shootings. It wasn't safe."

The couple developed a problem. Gabriel, who by then had been doing mostly gardening work, had taken to shaving his head. "It was cleaner and cooler," Nati explains. "It was to keep the bugs and dirt out of his hair."

But their next-door neighbor was in the Hazards and took Gabriel's shaved head as a provocation. "This gang member—he thought Gabriel, despite the fact that he was much older and a working man, was in some kind of rival gang," says Nati. "Every day, when he came home, this gang member would yell and shout at Gabriel. Sometimes he would threaten him. Sometimes he would threaten us. It was becoming a problem."

Then one day Gabriel came home, got harassed as usual, and blew up. He attacked the gang member and hit him with a hammer. The police arrived. Nati was away with the kids at the time and came home to find that her husband had been taken away. She couldn't go to the police station because she had no papers and couldn't risk arrest. She didn't know it, but she had already spoken to her husband face to face for the last time.

In jail, Gabriel was presented with the same stip order that both Ella and Alvaro had seen. Not understanding the paper at all, he signed it. It wouldn't have mattered, because he was convicted of the assault anyway.

The courtroom was the last place Natividad saw Gabriel. They could not speak to each other there. Neither before conviction nor afterward would the authorities allow him a moment to say good-bye. He was taken away and deported.

This was 2006. When I ask Natividad if she thought she'd ever see her husband again, she shook her head.

"Probably not," she said impassively.

Later she would add: "We don't keep in touch much anymore. The distance proved to be too much for us. I can't go to visit him, and he can't come here."

Gabriel's arrest left Natividad in a serious bind. She had no money coming in, no way to pay the rent, and six children. The landlord looked the other way for a month and a half or so, and then he finally told her she was going to have to move out.

Also, the gang member was still living on her street, which made her feel unsafe. Either way, she had to leave. But how?

As the days wound down toward the moment she would lose the apartment, she felt terror building. She had no options. She had no family in the area. She tried to get the family into a shelter, but there was a waiting list. The most optimistic guess was that she and her kids could get shelter beds within three months. Finally the day of her eviction came, and the only solution she'd come up with was not even a solution; it was a half solution.

With the landlord standing in the outside corridor with his arms folded, the family filed out of the apartment with their belongings and jumped into a used Aerostar van that had been given to her by a little old man in her neighborhood. ("A good Samaritan," she recalls. "He had no idea he was giving me a future home.")

As she got behind the wheel, Natividad was conscious of how desperate the situation was. She had never before gotten into a car for any reason other than to go somewhere. Now the realization that she was in the driver's seat with nowhere to go was overwhelming. She was homeless.

She drove off to . . . where? This was the first of many times she would have to answer this question.

"I would search for a good location to park the van so we could spend the night there," she says now. "All seven of us would be crammed into that Aerostar. We didn't have a bathroom, didn't have a kitchen to cook in, didn't have enough money for food."

Her entire life suddenly boiled down to two huge daily challenges. Finding a safe parking space was the first, but the second was keeping the children fed. The family ate once a day through a meal services cafeteria in downtown L.A.

"For a whole month I went to the Los Angeles Department of Children and Family Services and fought with them," she says. "But they didn't want to give us food stamps or any kind of help."

She pauses, anticipating the next question. "Obviously they didn't have to help me. I just wanted them to help my children, who were citizens of this country, yet they were hungry because we couldn't get any help. I couldn't find a job, and even if I had, I wouldn't have had anyone to watch them.

"Watching my children suffer broke my heart every day."

Natividad remembers one particularly awful night from this period of her life. She had parked the van in a tough section of Boyle Heights. She and the kids were all sleeping when suddenly the

Aerostar started to shake. The neighborhood gangsters had discovered the sleeping family and decided to have a laugh.

"The *cholos* were shaking the car over and over again," she says. "We could hear them outside the van laughing at us. I didn't say anything, I told the kids to stay quiet." She shakes her head. "Those were some of the worst times."

After months of this, Natividad finally got the kids into a shelter. They were allowed to come in at seven every night, then had to leave at seven the next morning. The older kids could go to school, but Natividad had to keep the younger ones busy all day, which made it nearly impossible for her to find work.

This went on for about a month, until she found room in a halfway house at Fifth and San Pedro. Obviously this was better than the van, and she was grateful, but it wasn't an ideal solution either. "We were living among drug addicts and mentally ill people," she says. "I tried to shield my kids from all this as much as I could, but this was the environment we were living in."

She had a place to stay now, but the van remained the crucial possession in her life. She used it to drive the kids back and forth from school and to look for work, which she occasionally found, mainly odd jobs cooking and cleaning. She drove slowly and with exceeding caution, always on the lookout for car stops. Without papers or a license, the stakes were extremely high.

Then one morning in the winter of 2007, as she was dropping her children off at school, she spotted a police car in her rearview mirror.

"I was just coming out of Third Street," she says, pointing to an intersection down the block from where we're sitting now. "I saw him following me. I wasn't doing anything wrong, but he was just following behind. Finally they pulled me over."

There were two policemen, one white, one black. The white one leaned into the van and asked for her license and registration.

"I need the car to get my kids to school," she pleaded.

Nati's real problem wasn't what she'd done, but when she'd done it. It had actually been legal for an undocumented immigrant to obtain a driver's license until 1993. That was when then-governor Pete Wilson signed into law SB 976, which granted licenses to those who had Social Security numbers and were "authorized under federal law" to be in the state of California.

Natividad herself, just like Alvaro, had once had a legal driver's license; in 2003, then-governor Gray Davis had signed into law a measure briefly repealing Wilson's ban on immigrant licenses. But the window of legality was shut by Arnold Schwarzenegger very shortly after Davis was ousted from office, and Natividad was again left without a legal license. Years later, Governor Jerry Brown would again sign a law permitting undocumented residents to have driver's licenses.

So at the time of her first car stop in 2007, this single mother of six was driving in a van with four of her children, and suddenly the lives of seven people were hanging in the balance, not because she'd done something inherently wrong but because her state had recently changed governors.

Anyway, the policeman peered into her car. He threw up his hands.

"Look," he said, "you know you're wrong here. You can't drive without a license and a registration."

She and her family pleaded with the patrolman. "But the man wasn't interested," she says. "He took the car, gave us a ticket, and told us to get all our stuff out of the van. We took all our things, our laundry, everything, and we were just sitting on the side of the road there. I had to take them to school on the bus."

Soon afterward Natividad was stunned to find out that California had a special rule for cars seized from undocumented drivers.

All such cars were to be impounded for a minimum of thirty days, and in order to get the car back, you had to pay an enormous fee. In 2007 the fee was a thousand dollars, well more than the car itself was worth.

"There was no question of even thinking about paying the fee," Nati explains. "I knew I would never see the car again. By then I was way more worried about the ticket. The ticket was five hundred dollars. I didn't have the money to pay that one, either. So I opted for community service."

She ended up doing fifty hours of work.

"I cleaned up cans and garbage in various parks, like Hollenbeck Park," she says, indicating with a thumb the park not far from her Boyle Heights neighborhood.

Nati remembers being embarrassed on her first day of community service, but some of the other people she was carrying out her sentence with cheered her up. "They told me not to be ashamed," she says. "It wasn't for something I'd done wrong, really. It's not like I didn't *want* a license. I would have gotten one if I could have, but I wasn't allowed."

She picked up cans and papers in the park. Joggers and walkers passed by without noticing she was there. It wasn't so bad, in retrospect, but there were negatives. The worst part was that she couldn't do paying work while she was fulfilling her sentence. That, and having to use the buses all the time.

"Sometimes the buses would run late, and it was even worse when it would rain," she says. "I'd have to stand there with all my kids waiting for a bus in the rain."

In late 2007, shortly after she lost her first car, Natividad awoke with a start. Adan, one of her young twin boys, had awoken with a very high fever. It was one o'clock in the morning. She had to get the boy to a doctor, but she couldn't figure out how. When she called the taxi companies, they all refused to come to her neighborhood that late.

"The problem was, the gangsters had a system," she says. "When an unfamiliar car came into the neighborhood, they would use trash bins to block in cars and rob them. There was no escaping once the gangsters corralled them."

So when she called the taxi service, they told her they couldn't come to her neighborhood at night. "I had to get out of the neighborhood and meet the cab in a safe place," she says.

She gathered up all her children—five healthy ones and one sick one, whom she carried—and walked out of the Boyle Heights projects, where she'd moved a few years after her husband's deportation. She walked a mile through the neighborhood and over a footbridge to the intersection of Evergreen and Marengo, where a taxi was waiting for her. Then she piled the whole family into the cab and went to the clinic. Her son, it turned out, had bronchitis and a high fever. The doctors treated him, and by morning he was well enough to return home. Things had turned out as well as possible, but the incident rattled Natividad.

In 2009 she took a chance and got another car. It was another beater, a little brown Toyota Corolla. She was driving by herself at around five p.m. when she got caught up at a checkpoint at the intersection of Soto and Slauson Avenue, again not far from her home.

These checkpoints themselves were controversial. In fact, the LAPD itself ultimately rebelled against them. Ostensibly designed to weed out drunk drivers, the checkpoints attracted the attention of local politicians, activists, and others, who started to notice that police were choosing odd times and locations to set up their drunk-driver sweeps. Instead of at two in the morning outside strip clubs, the roadblocks were stationed at the start and close of workdays at the main traffic points connecting downtown L.A. with Latino neighborhoods.

"You'd have them late in the afternoon, even in the morning," says Zachary Hoover, director of LA Voice, an advocacy group for immigrants. "And they'd be in places like Boyle Heights."

Anyway, Natividad saw the checkpoint too late and got nabbed. This time she knew the drill. And at least this time she was by herself; no kids to worry about. She hopped out of the car, grabbed a few things out of the backseat, and walked back down the highway toward the nearest bus stop.

The impound arrangement was the same. It was a minimum thirty-day hold, plus a recovery fee, which had been raised since her last car stop and was now nearly $1,200.

So she forgot about that car. About a year later she had saved up enough for a third car, another Toyota, this one a red Celica. In early 2010 she took that Celica and picked up her kids from school.

It was late afternoon and she was heading home, when she got nailed for a third time. This time the mistake was trying to enter a highway via an on-ramp.

A police car was crouched at the highway entrance, the driver peering into cars as they came up the ramp. "It was pretty obvious, they were just looking to see what the drivers looked like," she says. "If the cars were beat up enough, they stopped them. That's all it was."

When she got stopped for the third time in what to her was an obvious profiling campaign, she lost it.

"Suddenly I wasn't afraid," she says. "I was really furious. I said to them, 'This is the third time you've done this to me. You're not fighting crime. You're just taking my car for your own benefit. I'm not dealing drugs. I'm driving because I *have* to, do you understand?'"

The officers just shrugged and handed her the ticket. She stood there and looked at the piece of paper in her hand. She knew what the implications of that ticket were. Closing her eyes for a moment, she gathered herself, put the ticket away, collected her children, and walked down the highway on-ramp to the nearest bus stop. She was already thinking of the hole she was in.

The impound fee, which by now had reached nearly $1,400, meant this third car was gone for good. But the bigger problem, again, was the ticket. She still hadn't paid her previous ticket. She would eventually find herself owing a total of $1,700 in fines for driving without a license. There was no possibility of paying that money. Her only hope was leniency from the judge.

Finally her day in court arrived. The L.A. County Superior Court was a hall packed with more than a hundred people, most of them poor immigrants like herself. Just as Alvaro was stunned to see the quantity of buses in his deportation caravan, she was amazed by the crowd of people like her in court. She came first thing in the morning and waited most of the day through one painfully slow case after another.

Natividad talked with other people in the gallery as she waited her turn. "About a quarter of the people there were in court for hav-ing no driver's license," she says. "It was like they had created this courtroom just for us."

Finally, she stood before the judge, a middle-aged white woman, whom Natividad describes as "not that hard on me. At least she thought she was not being hard on me—that was the impression I got."

The judge told Natividad she had to pay five hundred dollars in fines. The rest would be made up in community service, which had to be completed within three months. How much community ser-vice?

"A hundred and seventy hours," Natividad recalls. "I couldn't be-lieve it. I almost collapsed when she told me the number."

She tried to figure out how to complete the sentence. She spoke to the priest at her church, who helped her arrange to do her time through a local organization called Homeboy Industries, which sent her to clean offices and bathrooms and the like.

But finishing those 170 hours of community service would prove to be a challenge even greater than being homeless.

"I would get up at five in the morning," she recalls. "I'd get the kids ready, then take them to school by bus. Then I would come home to eat breakfast. From there, I would go to Homeboy and clean bath-rooms and vacuum until about two p.m. or so.

"Then I would leave, pick my kids up by bus, and go to a local homeless shelter, where I had a job as a cook. I didn't have day care or any relatives in town, so I had to bring my children to work with me. So my children would be sitting there at the shelter with the homeless all afternoon and evening. I was cooking for about sev-enty or eighty people a day and trying to watch them at the same time.

"I would get home every night at about eleven p.m. The kids were angry and exhausted, every night. They were suffering; it was awful to see. Also the senselessness of it was a very difficult thing to accept. I thought, 'Whom does this help? What's the reason for all this?'"

She shrugs, recalling the very recent past. "Actually, I was crying almost constantly that whole time," she says.

The Felix family takes the bus now, mostly. As of this writing, Natividad pays twenty-four dollars for a bus pass for each of her children every month, plus seventy-five dollars for one of her own. Since she has to leave for work at three a.m., before the buses run, she takes a taxi to work most days. The new law permitting drivers' licenses for undocumented immigrants may help, but her children, American citizens, tell her they're uninterested in getting licenses. Their experiences growing up have turned them off to driving.

In many states across the country still, immigrants from south of the border have to take taxis and bicycles everywhere they go, because the law enforcement presence is so massive that traveling any other way is a huge risk. Capture can mean the loss of everything, from never seeing a spouse again to being kidnapped, in addition to being thrust into debt for years. And this is for crimes that are essentially administrative in nature, immigrating in a proscribed way, trying to live without the right papers.

But on the flip side, there are certain kinds of crimes a native-born American can commit without any risk of arrest at all. It turns out that we prosecute administrative/political violations like serious crimes, and serious crimes like administrative violations. A completely different group of visitors found this out the hard way.

CHAPTER 6

BORDER TROUBLE, PART 2

On a warm summer afternoon nearly a decade ago, on August 3, 2005, to be exact, a man named Spyro Contogouris sat down at a computer in the office of a New York City hedge fund and began to type out an email. Short, fit, and handsome ("like a retired middle-weight or lightweight boxer" is how one acquaintance described him), the colorful Contogouris was just over a year away from being arrested for felony embezzlement in a real estate scam he'd been involved with years before. But he had no way of knowing about that that afternoon. Now he was thinking only about how to pro-vide reassurances to his current employer, a noted hedge fund hot-shot who happened to be one of the world's leading patrons of modern art.

Along with a number of other Wall Street billionaires and mil-lionaires, the art patron had hired Contogouris to do a little side job. His task was to destroy a Canadian insurance company called Fairfax Financial Holdings. The hedge fund wanted the company bankrupted, and they wanted its Indian-born CEO, a diminutive, soft-spoken Canadian immigrant named Prem Watsa, publicly disgraced. Despite nearly two years of constant trying, the job hadn't been done yet, and this particular hedge fund employer was becoming impatient.

Sensing this, Contogouris sent a message, assuring his employer that Fairfax was indeed doomed.

IT IS GOING TO GIVE IF IT IS THE LAST THING I
DO

"It" being Fairfax. Contogouris then added an attachment, a news story about a corporate executive going to jail. To the attachment, Contogouris added another comment:

PREM NEXT

Meaning that Prem Watsa, the CEO of Fairfax, would be the next CEO to go to jail.

Contogouris sent the email to his billionaire employer, then waited. Soon a series of replies came. The hedge fund manager was clearly pleased by Contogouris's email. Inspired by the thought that Watsa might soon be publicly shamed, he sent back a joyous fantasy "headline" about the future that awaited the little-known Canadian insurance executive:

PREM BREAKS RECORD FOR CUM SWALLOWED
AT SING SING

The hedge fund wizard who wrote that line is to this day a darling of high society, a man who owns more than one thousand works of art, patronizes the likes of Keith Haring and Cindy Sherman, and has been celebrated by journalists for both his "devotion to Ashtanga Yoga" and his nose for finding "the very best work." You can find news of him attending all sorts of cheery cultural events, like the time he invited society scribes into his five-thousand-square-foot

Miami home, which had been refashioned into a kind of museum—with Matthew Barney's take on Johnny Cash giving the finger perched atop his staircase and "Richard Prince's treatment of a Gary Gross photograph showing a naked, 10-year-old Brooke Shields" hanging on a wall in a child's bathroom.

Even now, the hedgie is considered one of the beautiful people by almost everyone who matters in the financial community. But he's apparently not always smiles and Miami sunshine. On that August day in 2005, he wrote this, continuing his thoughts about Fairfax and Prem Watsa:

I HEAR THAT FUKS VOICE IN MY HEAD AT NITE
MAKES ME SICK.
    I WANT HIS HEAD IN A BOX

The lines were written by Adam Sender, the CEO of Exis Capital. Why did Adam Sender want Prem Watsa's head in a box? Because nearly two years before, Sender had, along with half a dozen of some of the richest and most influential men in America, men with names like Loeb, Cohen, and Chanos, billionaires who were often collectively known as the "Masters of the Universe," placed a massive short bet against the company. If Fairfax went bust, they all stood to gain tens or hundreds of millions.

So beginning in late 2002 and early 2003, they tried to kill the firm the good old-fashioned way, with a simple insider trading scheme, massively shorting the company ahead of a fake negative research report that they knew was coming long before the public did. But when the company didn't die, they were forced to resort to extraordinary measures.

It's here that the Fairfax story became one of the more sordid and disturbing tales in the annals of Wall Street. The handful of hyper-aggressive billionaires who targeted this relatively small Canadian insurance company resorted to tactics that at first blush will seem unreal. Indeed, the targets of the scheme, the Canadians themselves, were initially paralyzed for a critical period of time by their utter

inability to believe what was happening to them. In fact, many journalists, myself included, stayed away from this story for a long time,
because even the baldest recitation of the facts sounds too much
like bad conspiracy theory.* "It was the kind of thing you'd only
expect to see in inelegantly written fiction," says Roddy Boyd, for-
merly of the *New York Post,* who became a character in the story in
the mid-2000s.

The Fairfax fiasco is a tale of harassment on a grand scale, in
which the cream of America's corporate culture followed executives, burgled information from private bank accounts, researched
the Canadians' sexual preferences for blackmail purposes, broke
into hotel rooms and left threatening messages, prank-called a
cancer-stricken woman in the middle of the night, and even harassed the pastor of the staid Anglican church where the Canadian
CEO worshipped on Sundays. They worked tirelessly to instigate
phony criminal investigations in multiple countries, tried relentlessly to scare away investors and convince ratings agencies to de-
nounce the firm, and in general spread so many lies and false
rumors to so many people using so many different false names that
they needed a spreadsheet to keep track of their aliases.

Sender, by the way, wasn't the only millionaire to commit his
bloodlust to paper. DIE PREM DIE, wrote the to-this-day well-
respected hedge fund manager Dan Loeb, adding:

---

* The Fairfax story is often included in with other legendary bear-raid stories involving companies like Overstock.com, Dendreon, Afinsa (a Spanish collectibles company), and Biovail, another Canadian firm, all of which were targeted by some of the
same hedge funds described in this story, many of which ended up out of business and/
or mired in scandal. Many of those tales revolve around the issue of naked short selling, a type of financial counterfeiting that allows short investors to artificially depress
the stock prices of target companies. Whether naked short selling is a serious social
contagion or meaningless conspiracy theory is a passionately debated topic on Wall
Street, and to even broach the subject inspires strong emotions: right or wrong (and I
believe wrong), in some quarters, if you bring it up at all, eyes roll automatically. One
of the reasons I originally shied away from the Fairfax story was that it has a naked
short-selling angle that makes some serious observers dismiss it out of hand as nutty
conspiracy. So even though naked short selling was actually a factor in the Fairfax case,
I've left it out of this narrative, because it's the *other* craziness that went on in this case
that's really interesting.

PREM WATSA BEND OVER THE HEDGE FUNDS HAVE SOMETHING SPECIAL FOR YOU.

The campaign to destroy the Canadian insurance company was protracted and complex and ingenious and involved a lot of behavior that was almost certainly illegal, in some cases obviously so. And as in almost all these cases, the nasty/antisocial behavior of Wall Street crooks went almost completely unpunished; the system failed due to a combination of corruption, regulatory capture, pusillanimity of government officials, structural biases in the civil courts, and other factors. But for all that, the issue of legality is of secondary importance in the Fairfax case.

"Almost everyone has the same reaction when they're first exposed to this story," says Michael Bowe, the lawyer who ended up representing Fairfax in its lawsuit. "They're like, 'I don't know if this is illegal, but it's definitely fucked up.'"

What happened with this Canadian company goes far beyond the merely cynical mechanisms of insider trading and market manipulation and takes us down into an even darker place in the national psyche, into the netherworld of pure violence and aggression that rules modern Wall Street. This is where the drive for money and conquest is so intense that it crosses over into a kind of hatred and bloodlust, where the payoff stops being about money at all and becomes a search for something more desperate and seminal. It's about winning, in the ultimate sense of the word.

Not many people in America have the stomach to really explore what that term means. But it's all here in the Fairfax case. Thanks to the miracle of legal discovery, which turned this into the most extensively documented bear raid in history, we now know the secrets of some of America's biggest winners. Like that they're crazy.

Before January 2003, Prem Watsa was known in Canada as an immigrant success story of mild renown, a twenty-first-century-

Toronto version of a Horatio Alger tale. He had come to his adopted country as an almost literally penniless Indian back in 1972. According to firm legend, he had just eight dollars in his pocket and six hundred dollars in the bank to cover tuition when he arrived as a business student that year in London, Ontario, at the University of Western Ontario. His South Asian education had left him with a chemical engineering degree, but in Ontario in the early 1970s, he made ends meet by selling air conditioners and furnaces, even selling greeting cards door to door.

Then, when he graduated from business school in 1974, a professor helped Watsa get a job with Confederation Life, an insurance company in Toronto. Over the course of the next ten years, managing funds in the insurance business, Watsa learned about investing and became obsessed with the buy-and-hold long-term investment strategies that would eventually come to be associated with the likes of John Templeton and Warren Buffett.

But it was exposure to popular economics writer Ben Graham's book *Security Analysis* that Watsa calls his "road to Damascus" moment—he was so enthralled with Graham's ideas that he eventually named his first son Ben.

A small, carefully dressed man with a distantly beatific manner and deep cocoa-brown skin covering his almost perfectly round bald head, Watsa seems almost religiously devoted to the ideas of Graham and other value investors. When I flew to Toronto and met him in person, he came across as a True Believer of the first order. The CEO was actually rattled momentarily when I confessed I'd never read Ben Graham, and as if concerned for my welfare, he urged me to read his books as soon as possible.

Graham's ideas stress the simple practice of finding the right price for a company, waiting for that price to fall a little to the point of being undervalued, and then buying and holding that stock with the attitude that you are now part owner of a business, one in whose success you should be invested for the long haul.

By 1985, Watsa was a proponent of these stock-picking methods and was sure he could do something with them on a grand scale.

But he still had almost no money of his own. He did, however, have a reputation in the Canadian insurance business and a few influential friends, including executives at the first firm he worked for, Confederation. That year those friends and former employers helped him put together a $5 million stake to buy out a small trucking insurance company called Markel Insurance, which proved a big success.

In the late 1980s they changed the company name from Markel to Fairfax—short for "Fair and Friendly Acquisitions." This seemingly trite homage to the firm's self-professed Canadian niceness had me groaning, until I actually met the company leaders and realized the earnestness wasn't an act. Under the surface, Fairfax may be all business, and ethically speaking, it's certainly had its problems, but on the surface, the firm has an ostentatious corporate culture that stresses piety, politeness, and old-fashioned rectitude.

Which would be meaningless, except that the Fairfax name and company culture would later stand in stark, humorous contrast to the ethos of the expletive-tossing pirates who tried to attack and seize Watsa's company. Attacking "Fair and Friendly" Fairfax would be corporate killers whose firm names would recall death metal bands, one of whose company culture would be symbolized by the giant, rotting shark that its owner purchased for tens of millions of dollars.

All that was still yet to be revealed. By the mid-1990s, Fairfax was becoming a major umbrella company in the North American insurance business. It was acquiring interests in everything from casualty to professional liability to trucking to home insurance.

Its stock soared on the Toronto Stock Exchange, moving from under 70 Canadian dollars a share, when it first listed in 1995, to highs of above $605 in 1999. The rocketing share price was due in large part to Fairfax's decision to pursue two major investments in U.S.-based insurance companies in the late 1990s, the American subsidiary of a Swedish firm called Skandia Re (later renamed OdysseyRe), and a Morristown, New Jersey–based company called Crum & Forster.

Watsa, who just a dozen or so years before had had no money of his own and had to court rich friends and former bosses to buy a tiny trucking insurance company, bought Crum & Forster in 1998 for the sizable sum of $680 million.

But both OdysseyRe and Crum & Forster turned out to be more problematic than many of Fairfax's other operations. For several years the company struggled to reorganize both firms successfully, leading to a dramatic fall in Fairfax's Canadian share price. Old asbestos claims and a string of disasters (including storms in Europe and 9/11) led to massive payouts that for a time made both American acquisitions seem like potentially crippling albatrosses. The company in 2001 lost money for the first time, and Watsa was forced to explain an 11.9 percent drop in shareholder equity to his investors in a year-end letter.

But by the middle of 2002, the company claims, things began to stabilize a bit in both operations. "We were just starting to turn things around," says Paul Rivett, Fairfax's president, "when all this craziness began."

That was when Fairfax made the fateful decision to list the company on the New York Stock Exchange for the first time. It was going to be a major new source of funds and also a major step up in international status. When the firm was finally listed on the NYSE on December 18, 2002, the event was celebrated with cheers and champagne in the company's Toronto offices. The troubles began a month later.

For a few weeks after the firm listed on the NYSE, during the Christmas holiday, things were quiet. Then, shortly after the New Year, Watsa became aware that something was, well, if not wrong exactly, a little bit odd.

"It was in the second week in January," Watsa says now. "On the Toronto Stock Exchange, Fairfax usually would trade, I don't know, maybe ten thousand shares a day, twenty thousand shares a day. But suddenly, on the New York exchange, we're trading two hundred thousand shares a day. Half a million shares a day." He shrugs. "I thought to myself, 'Well, this must be the great New York Stock Exchange.'"

In what looked at the time like an incredible coincidence, the massive run-up in the trading of Fairfax stock (listed on the NYSE as FFH) immediately preceded a string of sharply negative published reports.

The first report to come out, on January 15, was by *The Street*'s Peter Eavis, who today writes for the *New York Times* business news service, DealBook. Although he didn't throw out specific numbers, Eavis, in a piece called "Unsure Times for Insurer Fairfax Financial," wrote that Fairfax's American acquisitions "look deeply underreserved."

The substance of the Eavis article was that Fairfax, despite its claims of Buffett-style investing conservatism, was engaging in wide-scale smoke-and-mirrors accounting, using its offshore acquisitions, particularly its reinsurance subsidiaries, to make the bottom line of the parent company look better. Reinsurance is essentially insurance bought by insurance companies, as a hedge against cripplingly large numbers of claims. Insurance companies must have a certain amount of capital in reserve to cover claims. If an insurer has bought reinsurance, however, more of the insurer's capital is freed up, and the insurer's reserves look better.

Eavis reported that Fairfax was paying the reinsurance premiums for struggling subsidiary insurers like TIG, which were buying their reinsurance not from independent firms but from other Fairfax subsidiaries like Swiss Re and the Dublin-based ORC Re. To put it in less headache-inducing language, Fairfax was allegedly paying one group of subsidiaries to reinsure its other subsidiary insurers.

All this looked from the outside like global shell-game stuff, hiding liabilities by ginning up cloudy transactions between subsidiary companies. Furthermore, it was all going on not long after the world's largest insurer, AIG, had faced similar questions about its reserves and about some suspicious transactions that it had entered into with a Warren Buffett–owned reinsurance company called Gen Re. It looked bad.

Still, there was no proof of impropriety, just a lot of questions. "Of course, the sniping on the Swiss Re deal may turn out to be groundless," Eavis wrote, "but investors still need to focus hard on Fairfax's habit of using its own offshore entities to reinsure its on-shore business."

Two days after Eavis's article, on Friday, January 17, a report by the Memphis-based investment bank Morgan Keegan came out. It was similar to the Eavis article, only far more aggressive. Written by analyst John Gwynn, it echoed the Eavis claim that Fairfax was "under-reserved" but put a concrete number on its assertion, saying the company was undercapitalized by as much as $5 billion. That meant that it had $5 billion less than it would need, in a worst-case scenario, to pay its insurance claims and other liabilities.

The report floored the Canadians. Fairfax wasn't that big a com-pany. If it was really underreserved by $5 billion, that would mean it was insolvent. Gwynn was asserting that Fairfax was the next Enron, a massive accounting fraud posing as a thriving publicly traded company.

Watsa—in retrospect, naïvely—paid no attention to the report. "We laughed," he says. "We thought, 'It must be a joke. Nobody will take it seriously.'"

Watsa was wrong. On the following Monday, the New York Stock Exchange was closed, due to Martin Luther King Day, but trading was open in the Canadian exchange. That day the firm's Canadian stock began plummeting.

"It went down like twenty-five percent in one day," Watsa recalls. "Like a stone it went."

By 10:30 that Monday morning, January 20, the Canadian au-thorities were calling Watsa in a panic. Both the Ontario Securities Commission (the province's version of the SEC) and the Toronto Stock Exchange called Fairfax, demanding to know if there was some sort of "event" going on at the company that justified the mass sell-off of the firm's stock. When Watsa insisted that there wasn't, the TSX told him that he had to issue a statement to try to address investors' concerns.

So they did. Later that afternoon Fairfax issued a press release essentially saying that the analyst reports were false, that the company was not underreserved, and that there was no reason for alarm.

Hardly isolated in the investment community, Watsa called some influential friends on Wall Street, who told him his company was under attack by short sellers. But the credulous and devout Watsa was characteristically slow to digest the meaning of this news.

In fact, early in 2003, when first told he was under attack by short sellers, Watsa thought the only reason anyone would be shorting his company was that investors for some reason genuinely believed his company was a loser and that its stock was overvalued, in which case Watsa says he was convinced the firm was not in serious danger. If anything, he thought, the short attacks and the resultant plummeting stock price would provide opportunity for smart investors to buy low.

"I thought, in a way, this was good news for them," he says now. According to the classical economic theory he believed in, it was those smart investors who would ultimately win out.

"I kept insisting that all we had to do was do well, and we'd be fine," he says now. "I kept telling everyone at the firm, 'Results will out.'"

So the company moved aggressively to improve its "results," engaging in a series of maneuvers designed to reassure investors about the strength of the company's reserves. Some of those transactions would later come under scrutiny (more on that later), but the key here is that the firm did not yet know that it was in an alley fight with an organized group of aggressors who had moved outside the usual realm of quarterly results and analyst reports and SEC disclosures.

Watsa would deny the existence of such attacks and cling tenaciously to his "results will out" mantra for years, having no clue that he was playing right into the hands of his antagonists. Until it was almost too late, he had absolutely no idea what was really happening to his company.

Wall Street in 2003 was a very different place from the world Ben Graham had written about in his 1934 *Security Analysis.* A more definitive portrait of modern finance would probably be the movie *Wall Street,* which had a profound effect on the city's business culture, although probably not the effect its heavy-handed lefty director Oliver Stone expected. While the rest of America understood Michael Douglas's iconic Gordon Gekko character as a villain, and saw his famed "greed is good" speech as incisive satire, many aspiring Wall Street traders sincerely thought—and still think—that Gekko was the movie's hero.

In the early 1990s, Wall Street saw a massive influx of young Gekko wannabes who thought waiting any amount of time to get fabulously wealthy was for losers, or at the very least for people who had never read Sun Tzu. Many of these new world-beaters eschewed the old Wall Street career path of being a broker at a major investment bank and climbing the ladder to a partnership. Instead, they reached for a more direct path to the top.

They started hedge funds.

Hedge funds, basically big pools of money managed by professional traders, are almost totally unregulated. A fund often begins as a one-man operation, run by a smooth-talking Wall Street front man who trolls the very rich, hustling for seed money. There are no real regulatory audits of hedge funds, and no government body checks hedge funds' trades or verifies their claims. It even came out, in the famous Bernie Madoff case, that despite numerous complaints to the SEC over the years from reputable sources, nobody in the government even checked to make sure Madoff's hedge fund even *made* trades at all. Madoff actually went more than thirteen years without making a single stock purchase and yet somehow survived several SEC investigations—that's how flimsy government regulation of hedge funds has been and still is.

Thus the right kind of fast-talking operator can quickly find himself managing hundreds of millions of dollars just by having the right rap and boasting high enough returns. Many, like Madoff, or the similar but less-well-known character Sam Israel of the infamous Bayou Fund, secured gigantic investments by promising that they had a secret system to outperform the market. In Israel's case, the "system" he had actually learned, as a trading apprentice to early hedge fund pioneer Fred Graber, mainly revolved around a series of high-speed insider trading schemes. From the book *Octopus*, about Israel:

> As a velocity trader, Graber constantly bought and sold the same stocks. . . . He talked about the stock he traded with intense passion, passing around made-up gossip, false speculation, and occasionally real news—anything to stir up action. One of Graber's abilities was to "paint the tape," the illegal practice of trading with the sole purpose of moving the price of a stock. The agribusiness giant Archer Daniels Midland was one of the stocks Graber fooled with relentlessly. To paint the tape on ADM, Graber and Israel would call eight different brokers and put in buy orders simultaneously to run up the price—at a time when Graber was holding lots of the stock ready to sell into a rising market. It was a racket the Securities and Exchange Commission was hopelessly ill-equipped to stop.
>
> "The SEC questioned Freddy all the time," Phil Ratner recalled. "But they couldn't catch him. He traded so much that it was impossible to say he'd traded on inside information."

Israel ended up abandoning that velocity trading method and actually got in real trouble only when he tried to earn his money honestly, with a half-baked computer investing program that tried to automate a *Moneyball* approach to stock picking. When the losses mounted from his failed attempts at an honest system, Israel resorted to outright accounting fraud to hide his financial condition from investors.

Just as Sam Israel once had, many of the other big shots in the hedge fund revolution that gripped the Street in the early 1990s operated using some form of high-velocity trading system—not necessarily an illegal system, like the one Fred Graber taught Israel, but one based on speed and volume nonetheless. The result was a generation of traders who exemplified an ethos completely opposite that preached by Buffett, Graham, and, well, Prem Watsa: people who didn't invest in companies for the long haul but instead invested in stock positions and sometimes held those positions for just a few seconds.

These people did not think of themselves as part owners of companies. They boarded this or that ship only for a few minutes, raped and robbed as much as possible from the hold, and then took off back out into the open ocean.

If there's any one person in the global business community who represents the total polar opposite of Warren Buffett–style value investing, it's Stevie Cohen.* (Well, it might also be Warren Buffett, but that's another story for another day.) In the late 1970s, Cohen was a young arbitrage trader working for a middling firm called Gruntal & Co., where he quickly rose to a job most young men would be happy with, managing six traders and a $75 million fund.

But in 1992 Cohen broke off and founded SAC Capital, a secretive hedge fund whose awesomely rapid rise in that decade roughly paralleled the rapid growth of Watsa's Fairfax up north. But it wasn't long before the compensation numbers Cohen was putting up made Watsa look like a McDonald's franchisee by comparison.

Within ten years of branching off on his own, Cohen was person-

---

* Buffett himself, it should be said, has seemed to go against his own principles. The legendary investor has been heavily criticized in the postcrash era for his investments in companies that seemed to violate his business principles, most notably a large share of the ratings agency Moody's; Buffett had previously criticized the industry.

ally earning $350 million a year. A few years after that, Cohen had nearly tripled his compensation and was earning a billion a year. Less than a dozen years after founding SAC, Cohen was one of the top forty richest people in America, and he made a major statement to the rest of America's elite by building an obscene 35,000-square-foot mansion in the capital of Rich America, Greenwich, Connecticut.

The mansion shocked even the Greenwich crowd with its sprawling grounds and its Versailles-like architecture, complete with an often-visible Zamboni machine tending to a 6,000-square-foot skating rink. A *Vanity Fair* writer said Cohen's home "resembles Buckingham Palace.... One billionaire, whose name I've promised not to reveal here, said his jaw dropped the first time he visited." A physical transformation followed, as the no-longer-young fund manager adopted a severe, shaven-headed Lex Luthor look that perfectly fit his garishly enormous financial empire and supervillainish estate.

Where did the money come from? SAC had quickly become one of the world's largest hedge funds through its mysterious, impossible-sounding performance record. In the first fifteen years of its existence, SAC claimed an incredible 43 percent annual return for its clients. Somehow Cohen was beating the average growth of the stock market by four, five, or six times over, every single year for more than a decade.

For such incredible performance, Cohen's clients paid a premium that went beyond enviable into being outright suspicious. The standard fee for a hedge fund manager is a formula known on Wall Street as "two and twenty." If you give a hedge fund manager $10 million, he gets a 2 percent management fee for the ten mil, plus 20 percent of any profits he makes for you.

But Cohen, incredibly, charged his clients 50 percent for the profits he earned them, which is a little like paying five thousand dollars to get a one-hour massage from a Swedish coed. If you're paying that much, you're probably getting more than a massage. And with Cohen, what you paid for was guaranteed impossible profits.

"Some people in this business are dirty, definitely," says one hedge fund manager, who incidentally would end up being short Fairfax for a time. "Look at Cohen. It's a little like juicers in baseball—when a guy hits that many home runs every single year, and never has a down year, you just know."

That no one can post 40 percent returns for fifteen years without cheating is blatantly obvious to everyone on Wall Street, but instead of sounding the general alarm, the almost universal reaction of the world financial media has been to celebrate the genius of such miracle investors with worshipful profiles. (At least until Cohen was finally nailed by regulators many years after the Fairfax episode.) Early in his career, Cohen got to explain his "system" over and over again to starry-eyed reporters, and what they heard was the exact opposite of the Buffett/Graham value investing concept.

Cohen claimed to be making money based on minute-to-minute calculations made as he was monitoring trading flow, or "watching the tape." This was eerily similar to the "painting the tape" process that Fred Graber taught Sam Israel.

When he felt stock prices were wrong, as *The Wall Street Journal* explained, "Mr. Cohen would pounce, and then he would bail as soon as they ticked in the right direction." His huge profits, he said, were derived from the fact that his bets were so enormous and the volume of his trading so obscene. By the mid-2000s, SAC's trading all by itself accounted for as much as 2 percent of all trading activity on any given day on the New York Stock Exchange.

SAC grew so big so fast that, like a Bill Parcells or a Bill Belichick, Cohen quickly saw his coaching tree start to bloom. A number of former SAC traders branched off and created their own funds. Adam Sender was a sort of mini-Cohen who split off from his mentor in 1998 to form his own fund, Exis Capital Management. Like Cohen, Sender quickly began turning in impossible-sounding results. (He claimed a 53 percent return after fees in 2006.) And like Cohen, Sender couldn't wait to show the world how rich he was. Within a decade or so after founding Exis, he had a personal collection of more than one thousand works of modern art that were collectively valued at over $100 million.

Cohen and Sender were part of a new class of hedge fund conquerors who used their instant millions and billions to buy places in the pop-culture limelight, usually by patronizing modern artists. Cohen shocked the art world in 2005 when he gave $12 million—the highest sum ever paid to a living artist for a single piece of work—to the awesomely pretentious Englishman Damien Hirst for his *The Physical Impossibility of Death in the Mind of Someone Living*. This preposterous sculpture was a fourteen-foot pickled shark suspended in a formaldehydelike solution. The notion that Cohen had paid $12 million for a kind of schlock monument to his own self-image as a financial killing machine is a long-standing joke on Wall Street, right down to the fact that the dead animal started to rot almost immediately: shortly after purchase, Cohen had to hire the artist to refurbish the creature.

Another in the curator club was Dan Loeb, the billionaire head of a fund called Third Point, who by the early 2000s had become famous not just for being a dick but for being a very particular *kind* of dick. Loeb's favorite activity was to invest heavily in a big company (he at one point owned more than 5 percent of Yahoo!) and then write blisteringly insulting public letters to management, berating them for not making him enough money. When he spotted the CEO of one company courtside at the U.S. Open, he publicly attacked him for "hobnobbing and snacking on shrimp cocktail" when he should have been out making Loeb money. He launched a similar assault on the head of Star Gas Partners, Irik Sevin, urging him to step aside and "do what you do best: retreat to your waterfront mansion in the Hamptons where you can play tennis and hobnob with your fellow socialites." Loeb *loves* the word "hobnob."

That Loeb himself had been at the U.S. Open final, and also has a $15 million estate in East Hampton far bigger than Sevin's, is beside the point. Loeb's letters set him up as an inspiration to day traders and "outside investors" everywhere, a self-proclaimed populist hero who made his living publicly beating the hell out of America's decadent CEO class.* His act is a kind of living tribute to the legendary scene in *Wall Street* when Gekko-Douglas undresses the executives from Teldar Paper at a shareholder meeting, urging investors to defy the fat-cat "bureaucrats with their steak lunches, their hunting and fishing trips" who paid themselves big salaries but lacked the balls to buy stock in their own firms. Like Gekko, Loeb pitches himself as the guy who *does* have the balls, who puts his money where his mouth is. Known as the "Angry Investor," he's made a public career as a kind of investors' ombudsman.

Lastly, there's Jim Chanos, another billionaire who was Buffett's (or the mythical Buffett's) opposite for another reason: he almost exclusively bet against companies, not on them. Known as "the Catastrophe Capitalist" and elevated to fame on Wall Street for having helped uncover the Enron disaster (he had a huge short on against Enron, and his research is said to have essentially exposed the fraud), Chanos could move markets just by signaling that he was betting against this or that company.

Humorously, and appropriately, Chanos named his hedge fund Kynikos, which is Greek for "cynic." He described his campaigns against target companies as "jihads" and became well known for his withering, devastating criticisms of just about anybody who fell within his field of view. He sneered, for instance, at traders who blindly rode the tech boom while he was doing real work, seeking out bad companies like Enron. "The marginal people on the trading desks, there's no skill set," he chirped. "The next stop [for them] is driving a cab."

On one hand, Chanos represented everything that was good about short sellers. In an investment community policed by weakling regulators and a mostly blind press, it's often left to short sellers

---

* I myself experienced Loeb's legendary epistemological style in the fall of 2013, after I wrote a *Rolling Stone* article about hedge funds like his that received indefensibly high fees from state pension funds. The piece had been out only about three minutes when I started receiving angry emails from the "Angry Investor" about my literary irrelevance.

to spot and correct even the most blatant corruption, which Chanos apparently did in the Enron case.

But the high-roller shorts like Chanos almost by necessity have to be psychologically a little unhinged. An investor who bets on companies to succeed, a so-called long investor, always at the very least knows the worst-case scenario when he invests in a company. If you buy a share of IBM for $10, the most you can lose is that ten bucks. But a short's losses can be infinite. Every time you put a big short on, you risk your entire neck.

"You have to have titanium balls" is how one trader explains it. The reason has to do with the mechanics of the profession. When you short a stock, you first borrow shares in the company, then sell them off immediately for cash. Then, after the stock's value has dropped, you go out and buy the same amount of shares in the open market and return them to the original source.

So say you borrow a share of IBM at 10. You sell it immediately for that ten bucks, then wait for something bad to happen (IBM forced to announce a product recall, say). The stock drops to 9. You can then go out and buy a share of IBM on the open market, return that share to your original source, and pocket a one-dollar profit.

But what if IBM goes up? What if there is no product recall, and the next product IBM comes out with puts the iPad out of business? What if the stock goes past 10—to 15, 20, 40, 50 dollars? You still eventually have to return the stock. The higher the stock climbs, the more money you owe. And there's no zero down there to stop the bleeding. You could pick wrong, bet against Google or Microsoft in its infancy, and end up beyond broke, hurtling down a bottomless financial pit.

Another factor is that short sellers have to pay fees to borrow stocks before they can short them, which means that if you're shorting IBM at 10, you probably need it to drop below 9, maybe to 8 or even 7, to actually make a profit. It depends on how hard the stock is to borrow, how high those borrowing fees are. (This issue would come into play in a big way in the Fairfax case.) So if you're putting a big short on, you usually need to see a serious drop to make a buck, not just a tick or two in the right direction.

This is why the big short sellers tend to be wired differently from other Wall Street players. These men (and they're mostly men) live for the thrill of the chase and the high of conquest when the target of their short finally rolls over and dies.

Chanos perfectly embodies that spirit. "I'll always understand the Schadenfreude aspect to short-selling," he said early in his career. "I get that no one will always like it."

By the early 2000s, just those four men—Loeb, Chanos, Cohen, and Sender—collectively managed tens of billions of dollars and exerted enormous influence on the daily trading flow of the New York Stock Exchange.

And here's what we know. Sometime in 2002 this collection of high-profile, belligerent, letter-writing, art-collecting millionaires and billionaires, along with hotshots from a few other prominent hedge funds, began talking to one another about a new stock they might want to target: Fairfax Financial Holdings.

An important thing to understand about short sellers is that they can play not just a legitimate role in finance but an urgently necessary one, being as they are the world's best-funded researchers of corruption and inefficiency in the markets, far surpassing the press and federal regulators. When they're right, and they often are, they provide a valuable service.

Jim Chanos was famous for being right. His biggest claim to fame, of course, is Enron. But the short that actually made his career involved an insurance company. The firm was called Baldwin-United, and back in the Reagan years, it looked like one of the hottest companies in the world. The Ohio-based company used to make pianos but had switched to insurance and was making a killing selling a product called single premium deferred annuities, or SPDAs. By 1981, the firm had $24 billion in assets and was being lauded in *Fortune* magazine.

Within a year, though, the company went into bankruptcy—the largest bankruptcy of all time at that point. The firm went bust largely because a little-known trader at a Chicago-based firm called Gilford Securities, Jim Chanos, had exposed the company's financials as a sham. In an eerie preview of Enron, Baldwin had been using accounting tricks to book five and six years of income at a time, and Chanos, who was less than a year removed from graduating from Yale, didn't like the way the financials looked. "I've never seen financials that looked so cloudy," he said. When the company went bust, Chanos became a star, and the model for his victory was interesting: while places like *The Washington Post* and *The Wall Street Journal* were skeptical of his analysis, *Forbes* magazine believed Chanos's analysis and published an aggressive story against the firm. It was enough to bring the company down. The media were an essential weapon in the short campaign.

Years later Chanos would repeat this same technique, again to apparent social good, by attacking Enron's financials with the aid of Bethany McLean of *Fortune* magazine.

Now it was a few years after the Enron story, and Chanos, as he had in 1982 with Baldwin, got a tip about another insurance company with supposedly dicey financials.

Fairfax in many ways was similar to Baldwin. It was roughly the same size, in the $20-billion-to-$30-billion-in-assets range. When Chanos first heard of Baldwin in the early 1980s, it had just swallowed another huge company called MGIC. In 2002 Fairfax was still digesting its Crum & Forster and OdysseyRe acquisitions. And Chanos didn't like the look of the relationships among Fairfax's many subsidiaries. He was sure self-dealing was going on, just as there had been with Enron.

Chanos was the first of the really big hedge fund magnates to make a big short bet against Fairfax, in mid-2002. And the fact that it was Chanos targeting another insurance company swayed some other funds. "Jim knew about insurance," says Marc Cohodes, the former head of Copper River Partners, a hedge fund that would eventually short Fairfax. "He had made his name with the Baldwin thing. It carried a lot of weight."

The billionaire that summer evangelized his decision to short Fairfax all over town. Many were more than willing to bet down the stock. For all its positive press in Canada, Fairfax didn't have the greatest reputation in New York. "A third-rate insurer with crappy underwriting standards" is how one analyst put it. "Plus they were Canadian, and run by an Indian. In retrospect, that probably played into it, too. There were a lot of reasons to pile on."

By the end of 2002, nearly a dozen major hedge funds—including SAC, Kynikos, and Loeb's Third Point—had taken short positions against Fairfax and were trading information with one another about the stock. That's when the analysts came in.

The key player was Gwynn, the Morgan Keegan analyst. Fairfax was the first company he would ever cover as an analyst for Morgan Keegan. This was his first task after coming to the bank from the Trinity hedge fund, which, in an amazing coincidence, was one of the funds that would put a huge short on against Fairfax.

So the former hedge fund employee Gwynn joined a major investment bank and immediately began preparing a research report on a Canadian company that operated in a business he knew very little about. The report wouldn't be published until January 17, 2003, but well over a month before that, it mysteriously began circulating among the traders at many of these big hedge funds.

We know this because traders for Chanos and Cohen and others sent one another reams of emails and texts blithely bragging about their access to this nonpublic information. For instance, on December 21, 2002, an analyst for Chanos sent a note to a trader at another hedge fund about a new report on FFH, Fairfax Holdings:

> Last night John Gwynn at Morgan Keegan faxed over to me an outline detailing the issues at FFH, basically those he will be publishing on. He has been a huge help and

even offered to talk to me from his home today. We can look at these and talk to him next week. . . . On the major issue of reserve deficiencies . . . the entire company deficiency is shown to be $2.6 BN without tail, and $5.0 BN with tail.

Nearly a month before the analyst report came out, then, someone at the Kynikos fund knew the entire substance of the Morgan Keegan research and was sharing it with another hedge fund.

As it happens, this sort of behavior—bank analysts sharing their research with hedge fund clients—was so common at the time that it ultimately became the centerpiece of the so-called Global Settlement arranged by Eliot Spitzer and the SEC with big Wall Street banks like Goldman Sachs, Lehman Brothers, Bear Stearns, and Piper Jaffray.

There's nothing unethical about a private company doing research, and there's nothing unethical about a bank researching a firm and selling that research to clients. But a major bank releasing a major report on a publicly listed company can have a material impact on the movement of a stock, and here's where we get into unethical and/or illegal territory. Tipping off a hedge fund that your analyst is going to give a "buy" rating to a stock weeks before that research is made public can be enormously valuable to the hedge fund, for the obvious reason that the fund now has a pretty good idea of a concrete date and time when the stock is going to tick upward. If the release of the research will have a material impact on the value of the stock, it becomes illegal and improper to trade on knowledge of such a report ahead of time.

What Spitzer's investigation uncovered was that banks in the 1990s and early 2000s were routinely trading such valuable inside information in return for promises that the funds would choose their companies to do their investment banking work. It was straight quid pro quo: information for business. For instance, when asked in a questionnaire what his three most important goals were for the year 2000, a Goldman analyst replied, "1. Get more investment banking revenue. 2. Get more investment banking revenue. 3. Get more investment banking revenue."

The way the game evolved, big hedge fund clients had access to investment banking research far ahead of everyone else, creating a two-tiered investment environment. There was one market for insiders, and one for everyone else. As the former hedge fund manager Marc Cohodes explains, "Joe Sixpack has zero chance to succeed here."

Morgan Keegan in this case tried blatantly to secure the investment banking business of funds like Kynikos by handing out Gwynn's research report like Halloween candy to anyone and everyone capable of throwing it banking business.

Ten days before Gwynn's report came out, for instance, a Morgan Keegan salesman named Bill Hinckley berated an SAC Capital trader for not putting a bigger bet down against Fairfax. "Did you short that FFH on the listing?" he asked. When the SAC trader hemmed and hawed, Hinckley got impatient:

DAMN IT. DRINK FROM THE WATER, YOU HORSE.

The day before the report came out, Chanos himself was informed about Gwynn's research. One of his analysts briefed him:

Just got off the phone with Gwynn at Morgan Keegan—
his piece that rips FFH is supposed to be published to-
morrow.

By mid-January 2003, employees at nearly a dozen major hedge funds, many of which were already trading Fairfax stock or were about to, had either directly seen the unpublished Morgan Keegan report or had learned the substance of it. The email record detailing these communications between the hedge funds and the bank analysts during this time is surreal.

In the email record, both bankers and traders talked openly about the info-for-biz quid pro quo.

For instance, one of Dan Loeb's traders at Third Point, a certain Jeff Hires, sent an email to a Morgan Keegan rep named John Fox congratulating him on Gwynn's "damn good report."

"Kudos to your analyst," Hires told Fox in a cheery email.

Fox, in response, cravenly asked Hires for a handout:

> Thank you, Jeff. Please try to keep Morgan Keegan in mind for commission payments to our analyst. A small 50,000 share trade goes a long way. We go out of our way to hire individuals of the caliber of our John Gwynn. Looking forward to working with you. Thank you.

In any case, virtually all the hedge funds that saw the Gwynn report acted on it, deciding to place short bets against Fairfax. Chanos's fund, Kynikos, had actually started to pull its bets against Fairfax, but when it saw the Gwynn report, it doubled down and put about $5 million down on a short against the Canadians, about half of that on the day before the report came out.

And it wasn't just Heiman or some other minor Kynikos operative doing an end run. The billionaire Chanos himself was intimately involved in these trades. In fact, on January 16, 2003, the day before the Gwynn report came out, "Catastrophe Capitalist" Chanos and "Angry Investor" Loeb—two of the great icons of the hedge fund era—had an instant-message text conversation about Fairfax, in which Loeb asked Chanos if he should short the firm. Temporarily at least, the pair showed a little discretion:

LOEB: should short one more?
CHANOS: CAN'T COMMENT.
LOEB: understood.

Days later, after the report came out and Chanos had made a bundle on the damage done to Fairfax's stock, he and Loeb had another exchange:

LOEB: Just read the Morgan Keegan report which is one of the best and most extraordinarily good pieces of work I've ever read.
CHANOS: I KNOW. THAT'S WHY I COULDN'T TALK TO YOU LAST WEEK.

Again, this is one of the richest men in America, and one of the most respected figures on Wall Street, blithely admitting, in writing, that he'd read a crucial piece of insider information about a stock he was trading before its publication. Neither Chanos nor Loeb responded to requests for comment about any of this.

All these communications seem to account for the remarkable surge in trading activity that Watsa noticed in the days preceding the publication of the Morgan Keegan report. Subsequent analysis revealed that trading in the stock was at levels fourteen times higher than usual. When the Morgan Keegan report finally came out, the impact was predictably devastating: Fairfax's stock plummeted 25 percent in a single day.

Within a short period of time, in fact, the Canadian listing plummeted 32 percent, to an eight-year low. At Morgan Keegan, the news that Fairfax was in a death spiral was met with celebration. An internal bank memorandum circulated at the end of January said it all: "Gwynn—tremendous call on FFH sent the stock down 18 points!"

To recap quickly: in the summer of 2002, Jim Chanos, an investing legend who had made his bones disentangling bad accounting at an insurance holding company in the 1980s, decided there was something wrong at Fairfax and decided to wager against the firm. Chanos evangelized his belief in Fairfax's shortcomings, and other hedge funds also bet against Fairfax at the end of 2002. One of those funds, Trinity, seems to have played a role in getting an analyst hired at an investment bank. That analyst then came up with a negative research report on Fairfax that was passed around to other hedge funds and to journalists before it became public. The report came out, and like clockwork, the stock price of Fairfax plummeted.

The hedge funds may have genuinely believed that Fairfax was a corrupt and/or incompetently run company, and some of the hedge fund employees and their supporters will insist to this day that the initial bet against Fairfax was righteous. But the record suggests that their collective belief that enough bad press and negative market momentum would crater the firm was even stronger than their belief in Fairfax's actual problems.

And indeed, Fairfax's fate seemed to have been sealed when the Morgan Keegan report sent the stock down 32 percent. Under normal circumstances, this might have been enough to kill a company, particularly a financial company like Fairfax, whose business is entirely dependent upon public confidence. As Fairfax's lawyers would later repeatedly point out, Chanos himself once openly explained this dynamic. "With a financial services company like Fairfax, it can all be self-fulfilling," he said in a 2005 interview. "If the market finally decides the glass isn't half full any more, the trouble starts . . . you can see the stock go into a waterfall."

That was probably what was supposed to happen with Gwynn's report, but it didn't, because Gwynn screwed up and overplayed his hand. Almost immediately after issuing his report, questions began to surface about the accuracy of his $5 billion calculation. Moreover, in early February 2003, Fairfax issued a positive financial report, causing the market to start to doubt the rumors of Fairfax being the next Enron. As a result, the stock price began to tick menacingly upward: in one day, it went up ten dollars a share.

The hedge funds pressured Gwynn and Morgan Keegan to continue dumping on the Canadians.

For instance, on February 10, 2003, a day after Fairfax released its positive financial report and the stock ticked upward, Jeff Hires, Dan Loeb's trader at Third Point, reached out to John Fox at Morgan Keegan:

Where's the new report on FFH????

Fox stalled, telling Hires a full day later that the report was in the "editor's process" and wouldn't be out until the next day, February 12. At that, Hires sharply shot back:

Just make sure it's really negative.

On that same day, February 11, Morgan Keegan salesman Bill Hinckley urged a hedge fund manager named Eduardo Tomacelli to place another bet against Fairfax, telling him that the second report was coming out the following day and would be devastating.

WE SAY FFH RESULTS WERE WORSE THAN EXPECTED. . . . PUT THE SHORT BACK ON. . . . YOU NEED TO TALK TO JOHN GWYNN AND SLAP THAT DOG.

And slap the dog they did. Ultimately, over the course of three years John Gwynn would issue an incredible sixty-four reports about Fairfax, every single one negative to one degree or another. It's unclear exactly what his motivation was. Though some of the discovery shows the bank cravenly trying to extract business from hedge funds that seemed to relish Gwynn's conclusions, the bank also would eventually fire Gwynn (years later, it is true) for leaking information to those same funds. "Gwynn was discharged from Morgan Keegan for violation of a firm policy relating to his apparent advance disclosure of his pending research coverage of Fairfax Financial Holdings," a Morgan Keegan spokeswoman would say a full five years later, amid the chaos of September 2008.

Although negative press and analyst reports and high volumes of carefully timed short selling can definitely exert downward pressure on a stock, and can even "waterfall" a company into collapse, a firm with a solid enough foundation can stick it out for a good long time.

But the shorts didn't have time. The game these major hedge

funds were playing was a high-stakes, high-risk *totaler Krieg* where there's no room for patience, compromise, or pyrrhic victories. When you bet $50 million, $100 million, $200 million against a certain type of company, inflicting minor damage—like moving its stock down a few percentage points here and there—is not sufficient. You have to sink the boat, or else you yourself will be drowned.

Why? Because shorting a stock becomes more and more expensive the longer the short bet is on. Remember, in order to bet against a company, you have to borrow shares of that stock. But so many people may be clamoring to short a certain stock that the number of shares available for borrowing may not be sufficient to meet the demand. In that case (and it can happen for other reasons as well), a stock becomes "hard to borrow," and the cost to borrow a single share for any length of time can become exorbitant.

Short sellers talk about the price of "the borrow" when they figure their costs. And in the case of Fairfax, the borrow was through the roof. Between 2003 and 2006, the cost to borrow Fairfax stock skyrocketed, to the point where a short seller had to pay a surcharge of 30 percent or more just to borrow a share. Years later, when all this got aired out in court, Andy Heller—the chief operating officer of Adam Sender's Exis Capital—explained in a deposition why hedge funds like his needed Fairfax not just to wobble but to fall over completely. "Fairfax had an enormously expensive borrow," he said:

HELLER: If Fairfax didn't go out of business in three years, the trade was a loser.
Q: Automatically?
HELLER: Automatically. If I'm paying 35 percent a year to borrow the security, just do the math.

The short sellers had done a pretty fair job of battering Fairfax with the crude, old-school trade-ahead-of-negative-research scheme.

But when Fairfax didn't collapse after the first Morgan Keegan reports and the accompanying negative press from journalists like Peter Eavis, the shorts flipped out. In a text conversation, Loeb and a then–SAC trader named Jeff Perry reacted to a positive financial report released by Fairfax. In Loeb's mind, the good news coming from Fairfax meant they were both going to take it up the ass—literally.

LOEB: This is surreal
PERRY: WHAT?
LOEB: bend over and get your bungus grease. FFH

Moments later Loeb had a text conversation with Jeff Hires, one of his own cohorts at Third Point. At this crucial moment, Loeb realizes that the first blow wasn't enough and suggests that the shorts might need to look elsewhere for ways to drive Fairfax's stock downward.

LOEB: Holy shit . . . look at the FFH indication.
HIRES: Indeed
LOEB: This is insane.
HIRES: ugh
LOEB: We need to speak to the ratings agencies today . . . they could provide the downside catalyst.

Thus began the second stage of the attack on Fairfax, the search for an elusive "downside catalyst"—some outside force that would drive the stock down.

The usual weaponry wasn't working. They needed to think outside the box. They had to find some other way to bring Fairfax Financial Holdings all the way down.

A quick aside. Stories like this at first blush seem to have little relevance outside Lower Manhattan. Had Fairfax gone out of business, sure, thousands of jobs would have been lost, many in the metro New York area. (Morristown, New Jersey, alone would have lost thousands.) But for the most part, insider trading is a crime of fractional violence.

You steal from uninformed investors all over the world, a few pennies or dollars at a time. The damage fans out evenly across a vast geography, and it's hard to see. It's because of this that lots of Wall Street people genuinely think of insider trading and naked short selling as victimless crimes. People get hurt, sure, but the victims are mostly sophisticated investors who should know better, and it's not like you're hitting them in the head with a brick or anything. It's not a real crime. At least it doesn't look like one.

That may once have been true. But in the Fairfax case, the principals in this "victimless" scheme started to mimic the gangster aesthetic.

Like most privileged, overeducated Americans who try it, they would suck at being real tough guys. They tried, however, and here's the crazy thing: in a city where police in some neighborhoods define crime as standing on the sidewalk the wrong way, these idiots took their stock-trading act-like-a-thug life, screwed it up a hundred different ways, and not only couldn't get arrested, they couldn't even get police of any kind to notice.

On November 9, 2005, Barry Parker, pastor at St. Paul's Anglican church in Toronto, received a curious FedEx package at his office. Having for over a decade headed this, one of the largest Anglican churches in North America, he knew a thing or two about famous churches, and he immediately sensed something odd about the return address, 460 Madison Avenue in New York.

"I remember thinking the address looked familiar," he recalls today. "When I looked it up later, I realized the package was 'sent' from St. Patrick's Catholic Cathedral."

Parker opened the package. Inside, there was a letter addressed to him. It read:

Dear Father,

The attached documents are being sent to you out of my concern for the Church's finances. I am extremely sensitive to this as a result of losing a dear friend, Father Richard Bourgeois, an enlightened Benedictine Priest formally of the Collegio D'Anselmo, which as you may know is the Cardinal College of the Vatican.

On September 4, 1999 the fugitive Marty Frankel, who perpetrated a massive fraud on the Catholic Church, was arrested at the Hotel Prem in Germany. Interestingly, a review of your most recent "Talk in the Pews" shows Mr. Watsa as the Chairman of the investment committee of the church. More interesting are the similarities in facial features between Mr. Marty Frankel and Mr. Prem Watsa. While these coincidences are surprising, they do not compare to the similarities between the massive money-laundering schemes perpetrated by Marty Frankel and the massively convoluted paper shuffle created by Mr. Watsa through his public vehicle Fairfax Financial Holdings Ltd. . . .

The pattern of activities of Mr. Prem are too similar to the course of conduct of Marty Frankel to be overlooked by a person such as yourself, who is responsible ultimately for the funds of the congregation. Be aware, Father, be skeptical and ask Mr. Watsa to make confession.

God Bless,
P. Fate

Along with the bizarre letter was a thirty-page article about the real-world insurance scam artist Marty Frankel, a corporate huckster who had bilked some $200 million out of a variety of marks, including the Catholic Church. The article was complete with lurid descriptions of Frankel's obsessions with sadomasochism and group sex, as well as descriptions of a brothel apparently being run out of Frankel's home.

The brazenness of sending such material to one of Canada's most high-profile religious figures, coupled with the breathless, faux-Nabokovian fictional flourishes in "P. Fate's" letter (in ham-fistedly telling of losing his "dear" friend, the Catholic priest "Father Richard Bourgeois," is the author not so subtly calling Parker a bourgeois dick?), suggested that whoever sent the package had taken fiendish pleasure in the entire enterprise, and that was unsettling in itself.

Parker read the letter in a daze. He had known Prem Watsa for a very long time. The Fairfax CEO had in a sense helped hire Parker, having been chairperson of the selection committee that endorsed Parker's candidacy to become pastor of St. Paul's sixteen years before. In those sixteen years, Parker had come to know Watsa well. "Very faithful" is how Parker describes him.

And yet now someone was telling him that the man was a swindler, literally out to abscond with the church funds. Parker never took the accusation seriously, but the fact that someone had bothered to send him this outrageous letter seriously unnerved him. Wherever this had come from, it wasn't a universe he spent a lot of time in. "All I knew was that something was happening that I knew nothing about," he says now.

At exactly the same time that the package sent by "P. Fate" was arriving at Parker's office, the same documents were being emailed to Watsa himself, this time under the alias "Monty Gardener." Watsa was understandably rattled. Church activities took up virtually all the space in his life not claimed by his family and his business, and now someone was trying to convince his congregation that he was an embezzler and perhaps a pervert, too.

Before Watsa could think of what to do, Parker was calling him on the phone, telling him about the letter. "I had to explain to my priest what was going on with the company," Watsa recalls now. "He's a good man, but it was hard to explain."

The letter to his priest would be merely one of dozens of attempts to intimidate and frighten Watsa's friends and coworkers, in an effort to isolate him psychologically. Just days after the "P. Fate" letter, for instance, Watsa's personal assistant, Joan Cheos, who had worked for him from his earliest days in the insurance business, received by email a pair of similar letters from the same "Monty Gardener," with the same Marty Frankel accusations, only this letter came with a twist: they implied that Watsa was about to be criminally indicted, and so would his assistant, if she didn't leave the firm quickly.

"The attached documents are being sent to you out of concern for your unwitting participation in possibly very serious federal crimes committed by Mr. Prem Watsa," the letter began. It went on to outline a theory that Fairfax was an Enronesque maze of accounting deceptions that would eventually be unraveled by avenging authorities.

"Please understand that this behavior will not stand," the letter continued. ". . . A person such as you has a lot to lose. No doubt you are aware that those that don't help Prem end up leaving after years of service with the severance afforded those that work at a Burger King drive thru."

Note the eerie resemblance between this Burger King comment and Jim Chanos's line about those who have "no skill set," for whom the "next stop is driving a cab." It's the same sneering, losers-suck sentiment, where the worst thing in the world is to be an ordinary schmuck with an ordinary job.

"Be aware," the letter went on, "[Watsa] will be held accountable."

Watsa's assistant soon began to get phone calls in the middle of the night, warning her that she was about to be implicated in Watsa's crimes. "Get out now," the voice would say. "Fairfax is a fraudulent company. Save yourself!"

Joan Cheos was actually sick with cancer during the time she was getting these calls. She would die about a year afterward. To hear Fairfax employees (whose eyes light up with anger at the mention of her name) tell it, the constant barrage of calls and letters frightened her to her core. She especially began to dread the end of the work-day, between five and six p.m., when inevitably unfamiliar phone numbers with 212 area codes would ring up and ask for Watsa. "I'm a friend of Prem's, it's okay," the caller would say. Every time she asked for a name, the callers would hang up. This happened repeat-edly, multiple times per week, by the end of 2005.

Strange and upsetting messages began to appear on the Internet. In December 2005 a site called premwatsa.com appeared, showing the familiar Enron logo, only with the "E" changed to an "F" and the word "Fairfax" substituted for "Enron." Showing an impressively thorough approach, the site designers created two additional mir-ror sites, a premwatsa.net and a premwatsa.co.uk, in case anyone in England missed the message.

Then, on a financial website, someone posted a comment about Watsa's son, who was living in New York at the time. "Anyone know the name of prem's son?" the message read. "I am 5'2", 110 lbs, red hair (the drapes match the blinds). I am interested in young indian boys, especially those with their own private jet. . . . I like dancing under palm trees while throwing macadamia nuts in the air."

Meanwhile other employees at Fairfax began to receive P. Fate–style letters and similar late-night phone calls, all from callers who were either anonymous or bearing ridiculous pseudonyms, warn-ing them to resign from Fairfax before the arrests began.

From there the behavior escalated to people showing up and knocking on the doors of houses belonging to Fairfax employees. Watsa's own wife, Nalini, was visited at their suburban Toronto home during the daytime by a stranger pounding on her door. The man didn't say anything, just knocked on the door and left. "My wife went through a very tough time," Watsa recalls.

While all this was going on, Fairfax was constantly being be-sieged with new and unexpected commercial difficulties. A wave of accusations had come from, well, somewhere, many of them having to do with fraud, many of them sent to ratings agencies, regulators, even Fairfax's own business partners. One particularly damaging set of accusations had to do with one of its American acquisitions, OdysseyRe.

Someone had sent letters to Fairfax's auditors at Pricewater-houseCoopers, claiming that there were serious irregularities in OdysseyRe's accounting dating back four years. The letters went all the way to the top. "They actually sent a letter to the chairman of PwC in New York," Watsa now recalls. Because of these letters, Fairfax had to take the extraordinary step of delaying the release of OdysseyRe's annual audited accounting statements.

To deal with the OdysseyRe mess, Watsa in the early months of 2006 traveled to Stamford, Connecticut, the location of the firm's headquarters, to help the company's executives handle the crisis. He was in Stamford for more than ten days dealing with this accounting nightmare.

On one of the last nights, he exited OdysseyRe's offices, crossed the street to his hotel, and upon entering his room, met with a surprise. "I came back at ten-thirty or eleven o'clock at night," he says. "And there was a book, a little package in a plastic bag. . . . It was on the shelf, you know, the thing next to the television. . . . The book was called *The Tipping Point*."

The CEO stood there, staring at the book and trying to digest what it meant. The immediate objective facts were that someone had entered Watsa's hotel room while he was gone and left a Malcolm Gladwell book next to his television. His first thought was to search for some innocent explanation. "I called down to reception and asked if anyone had been let into my room. They said no," he remembers.

He stared at the book again. The implication of the *Tipping Point* title seemed obvious enough, given what Fairfax was going through with OdysseyRe, but the deeper message was clearly that even Watsa's personal space was no longer safe. For the first time, he found himself genuinely freaked out on a personal safety level.

"I was a little worried, yes," he says now.

Soon the neighbors near the suburban Connecticut home of

OdysseyRe's chief financial officer, Charles Troiano, began to get knocks on their doors. Standing outside were real-life FBI agents, asking where Troiano was.

In truth, the executive had gone to the Caribbean on vacation. But the FBI had been told by sources it apparently considered reliable that the CFO had fled the country after committing massive financial fraud. When neighbors asked why the agents were asking, they were told bluntly, "We're investigating him for fraud."

The Troiano incident sent Paul Rivett, at the time Fairfax's general counsel, over the edge. "The FBI staked out Troiano's house for a week," he says. "That's when I knew this was really serious."

The young sandy-haired Canadian Rivett was a relative newcomer at Fairfax, a corporation where most of the inner circle had been with the firm, and with Watsa, for twenty years or longer. Rivett, on the other hand, had until recently been an outside counsel, hired by Fairfax for certain specific jobs. He'd helped the company when it wanted to list itself on the NYSE, for instance, and had assisted on some bond financing deals.

When the company started having troubles, however, Watsa asked Rivett to look into the matter. Almost from the outset, Rivett's attitude differed from that of the other Fairfax executives. While most in the Fairfax inner circle believed implicitly that the best way for the company to beat back its problems was to perform better, work harder, and not to dignify the attacks by fighting them, Rivett suspected early on that the situation was more serious than those executives knew, and that a response would be needed.

One of his first moves was to try to gather evidence for his supposition that all Fairfax's troubles had an organized origin. He began to keep a chronological record of every weird thing that happened to the firm—every late-night phone call, every oddball query from a ratings agency or a journalist, every home visit, everything. In late 2005, he sent out a general letter to everyone in the firm asking them to report to him immediately if anything out of the ordinary occurred.

"Right away, I started getting responses," he says now.

One of the first came from the London-based office of one of Fairfax's subsidiaries, RiverStone, which had had a curious visit from a person posing as a journalist. The individual managed to sweet-talk his way past security and get into the building, where he met with executives and pressed them for secrets about Watsa and Fairfax, using the ludicrous pretense that Watsa had secretly sold the subsidiary without cluing in the firm's leaders. When he was finally tossed from the building, the man left behind a card that read "Special Situations Research Consultant, MI4 Reconnaissance." The phone number on the card, oddly enough, belonged to a real New York hedge fund called Exis Capital.

Other employees told Rivett about other letters they'd gotten, other calls. On the same day that Parker got the "P. Fate" letter, for instance, someone called Fairfax and left a message: "Tell Watsa that when he goes to jail next year we will visit him and bring him some treats."

Rivett himself was the subject of constant prank calls, and here we must digress for an interesting detail: whoever was doing this was customizing the harassment for each of Fairfax's employees. Although many received calls, each executive got different types of calls. Whoever was responsible for Rivett, for instance, had decided to harass him by reading excerpts of Harry Potter books in each call. Why Harry Potter? Who knows, but that was Rivett's personal albatross.

The attorney put the chronology together and became convinced that everything—the analyst reports, the negative press stories, the harassing phone calls and letters, and, most ominously, the apparent new interest in the company by the Justice Department and other regulators—was all connected and part of some kind of organized campaign. "It was the only explanation," he says.

Rivett had already been convinced that action needed to be taken after the Troiano incident, but what really spooked the other leaders in the company was an incident that summer. Beginning on June 22, 2006, the firm became the subject of rumors all over the globe, the substance of which was that Prem Watsa had sold his home and fled the company and that officers from Canada's Royal Canadian Mounted Police were occupying Fairfax's offices.

"The call log from that day shows sixty-five different calls to our CFO," says Rivett. "Everyone from ratings agencies to shareholders to Goldman Sachs, and they were all basically asking the same thing." They wanted to know if the RCMP was indeed camped out in Fairfax, and if Watsa had indeed sold his house. "They were like, 'Uh, by the way, is Prem in the office?'"

Rivett, Watsa, and the rest of the Fairfax executives had no way of knowing it at the time, but *all* this activity had been orchestrated by millionaire and billionaire hedge fund managers with bets against Fairfax, men who had gotten together and hired the aforementioned shadowy fixer extraordinaire Spyro Contogouris to commence a wide-ranging campaign of harassment against the firm. A hundred different antagonists with a hundred different names seemed to be descending upon the firm from all over the globe, but they were almost always just Spyro Contogouris, and a pseudonym, pretending to attack in force. The "P. Fate" letter had been written by one of Contogouris's buddies, and Contogouris apparently had also dreamed up the late-night phone calls, specifically targeting Watsa's secretary. The London journalist was Contogouris. He was Monty Gardener. He was everybody.

Who was this man? The charismatic Contogouris was something like the Zelig of the market-manipulation era, a kind of backroom wet man who ran mysterious errands for powerful hedge fund investors. In a stock market that was increasingly based on movements in public confidence, Contogouris was the perfect operational figure, a man who had no fixed job but was living out a kind of inspired homage to the very idea of a "confidence man." He was supremely confident in every role he played, and he played a hell of a lot of them.

Michael Bowe, Fairfax's lawyer, talks with awe about Contogouris's ability to answer difficult questions. "You'd catch him in some lie and press him on it," says Bowe, who would eventually depose Contogouris, "and he'd just start talking more and more loudly,

LIKE THIS, LOOKING YOU RIGHT IN THE EYE, and whatever he said, HE WAS ABSOLUTELY SURE ABOUT." Bowe laughs, remembering. "You'd get so distracted listening to the way he talked," he says, "you wouldn't realize that nothing he said made any sense."

What little early record there is of Contogouris shows him to have been a kind of celebrity hanger-on in L.A. in the early 1990s, when his brother Chris owned a nightclub called the Mint. Spyro was involved with some charities then, including a camp for low-income kids called the Bony Pony Ranch, where he sat on the board and, according to Bloomberg, "rubbed elbows" with the likes of Lionel Richie and Renée Zellweger.

Then in the mid-1990s, a Greek shipping magnate named Dimitri Manios hired Spyro to renovate a brownstone property in Manhattan for him. This sent him down two different career paths, one in real estate development and one as the involuntary subject of litigation. He seemed to founder as a developer but proved highly adept at getting sued. The two paths converged in 2002, when his real estate career ended with Manios firing him and his career as a defendant began with the Manios family suing him for having embezzled millions from a series of real estate deals, including several big ones in Houston. In a detail that reveals Contogouris's mania for multiplicity, for being everywhere at once, the suit accuses Contogouris of boosting money from Manios through no fewer than 130 different bank accounts.

While Contogouris was in Houston, he seems to have gotten involved with a company called Hanover Compressor, which was based in that city. The company at the turn of the millennium was pushing a scheme to build a natural gas compression barge in Africa and was trawling the country for investors. Contogouris, the man whose last known job had been a glorified houseboy for a Greek shipping magnate, suddenly appeared as one of those "investors," claiming to have put $3.75 million into the African gas-barge project.

Where did he get that kind of money? Well, the retiree medical benefits trust of the Pirelli Armstrong Tire Corporation claimed he never had it. The retirees, who claimed they were fraudulently induced to invest in Hanover, sued Hanover and claimed that Contogouris was paid a secret sum of $1 million by the company to make what was actually a fully refundable $3.75 million investment in the barge deal, as a scheme to inflate the value of the project.

Are you confused yet? You should be. But what happened next begins to put all this background in perspective: Contogouris became acquainted with Jeff Perry, who at the time was working for SAC Capital, and began a new career, in high finance.

Perry, who out of all the characters in this story seems to be the most universally despised—"a bad guy, a constant compliance problem, incapable of staying on anywhere long" is how one hedge fund manager described him—is unique in that he actually worked for all three of the major funds in this case, SAC, Kynikos, and Third Point, at various times during the Fairfax campaign. According to Fairfax's lawyers, Contogouris approached Perry when Perry was at SAC and "sold" him inside information about Hanover's fraudulent barge scheme. He had this inside knowledge to sell, they claim, because he had participated in the fraud himself. SAC from there placed a short bet on the company, a bet that later turned out to be profitable. Contogouris here was playing the role of Bud Fox in *Wall Street,* selling the one piece of insider information he had—his own life—to get in with the big boys. And it worked.

Around the same time that Contogouris was making his first contact with Perry at SAC, he showed up in the press, in a news article in *The Street,* posing as an outraged investor determined to tell the world about the fraud that was Hanover Compressor.

In the piece, Contogouris claims that Hanover didn't have access to enough natural gas to make the deal work and knew as much all along. Boldly, he implies in the article that the entire deal was a scam to bilk Hanover's partners back home.

"[Hanover] had to know they couldn't perform and if they knew that, then they must have had other motives for proceeding with the sale of the barge and guaranteeing a 2001 startup date to the partnership," he told *The Street*. The same article noted that the SEC had begun to investigate the company, and it's not hard to read between the lines and see that the investigation might have been instigated by Contogouris.

Man accuses company of being secretly underreserved/undercapitalized, man nudges regulators into investigating, man leaks news of investigation to journalist. Contogouris was developing a literary method. He was becoming a professional reality creator. And he liked the job.

After the Hanover experience, in which he proved his ability to move the needle on a stock, Contogouris was aided by SAC employees in getting a series of unpaid internlike jobs at a number of hedge funds around New York. From there he created a number of "independent research" firms, including one company with the international-man-of-mystery-sounding title "MI4."

Then when Perry moved from SAC to Kynikos in the early 2000s, he decided to hire Contogouris again, paying him $25,000 per quarter to subscribe to his "research" service. In early 2005 Chanos asked Contogouris to focus on Fairfax, which Contogouris told others would be like "another Hanover situation." Shortly afterward, in the spring of 2005, Contogouris was also hired by Sender at Exis, who also gave him space inside the Exis offices, his own telephone, and so on. Within months, Perry moved his operation again, this time to Dan Loeb's Third Point Capital, and Perry convinced Loeb to become a "subscriber" to Contogouris's service as well.

This was the crucial turning point in the story. Chanos, Loeb, and Sender were now all invested in crazy-ass loose cannon Spyro Contogouris—more than investors, they were his patrons, his bosses. Their decision to unleash this man on Fairfax was the moment when the fund managers went from being merely bent to being antisocial maniacs.

To aid in his efforts to "research" companies like Fairfax, Contogouris hired a New Jersey storefront accountant named Raymond Rekuc. Until he became the mastermind of what Contogouris pitched to the world as some of the most important research in the global investment community, Rekuc had just been an ordinary joe who did business tax returns for walk-in customers. His profile seems very much like David Friehling, the strip-mall accountant whom Bernard Madoff used for years to sign off on his bogus non-trades, with the only major difference being that Rekuc was from suburban New Jersey instead of suburban New York.

It would later come out that Rekuc forgot to file his own federal tax returns for four consecutive years, and he would be convicted of that offense in 2010, but nobody knew about it at the time. Instead, for much of the mid-2000s Rekuc played the part of high-powered international forensic accountant, and it was he, in conjunction with Contogouris, who helped craft the specifics of Contogouris's central theory, that Fairfax was the next Enron.

In fact, Contogouris in the summer of 2005 managed to get an audience with the FBI and dragged Rekuc along with him, presenting him as an expert forensic accountant who had done a detailed analysis of Fairfax and discovered a sizable fraud. Years later Rekuc in a deposition would cheerfully admit that he wasn't a forensic accountant, hadn't done a forensic examination of Fairfax, and in fact had discovered no evidence of fraud at Fairfax or at Crum & Forster when he met with the FBI. But he helped Contogouris argue to the FBI for the need to issue subpoenas anyway.

These oddball characters—Contogouris, Rekuc, another "MI4" operative named Max Bernstein, and a few others—were apparently responsible for virtually the entire covert campaign against Fairfax. The letters, the phone calls, the FBI surveillance, the problems with PricewaterhouseCoopers, the spate of negative press stories, the weird visit by the phony reporter in London—virtually all of it had come from one of these specimens.

They had promised Chanos, Sender, Loeb, and others to bring down Fairfax. "Where Spyro crossed the line is that he actually promised these guys he would bring down the company," says Roddy Boyd, the former *New York Post* reporter. "It's like a reporter promising to win the Pulitzer prize. You can't promise results." Contogouris's strategy would be to sink Fairfax by "closing access to the capital markets"—cutting off its access to funding by undermining its reputation. This was old-school Sun Tzu stuff, isolate-and-destroy tactics, "attacking by stratagem": General Contogouris would cut off his enemy's supply lines by, among other things, sullying the firm's standing with ratings agencies and shareholders and others in a group he termed "FoF," for "Friends of Fairfax." He wanted to "get them where they eat," cutting off their credit lines, particularly going after their ratings by agencies like A. M. Best.

All this Contogouris promised to Chanos, Loeb, Sender, and others from the start. He pledged to "get the message of what I think is a massive fraud to these long term value holders" by creating a "crisis of confidence" that would frighten investors and "shake them out of the stock."

In time, Contogouris would deliver regulatory attention, negative press scrutiny, and lots of doubt and hesitation among the "FoF." But the middleman offered more than that to the hedge funds. He also offered the purely sadistic service of just plain old wreaking havoc on Fairfax's employees, among other things with the late-night calls, for which Contogouris had a colorful descriptive term.

"We have to make this a rattle-his-cage ritual every night before we go to bed," Contogouris explained to Sender, who out of all the hedgies seemed the most interested in this particular part of the operation.

According to Fairfax's lawyers, Sender loved the cage-rattling phone calls so much, he asked Contogouris to conference him in, so he could listen while "Monty" or "P. Fate" made his after-midnight calls to Watsa's cancer-stricken personal secretary. Contogouris, apparently moved by some obscure con man's code of honor, refused, instead sending Sender the phone numbers so that he could make his own prank calls to Watsa's inner circle.

The email records between Sender and Contogouris are twisted and disturbing. During the key period of the case, the spring of 2006, the two corresponded either by email or Bloomberg message service or by telephone five times a day, on average. The pair loved speculating about bad things that might happen to Watsa, whom neither had ever met. At one point, for instance, Contogouris asked Sender if he wanted Watsa's marriage to fall apart:

Is it good if Prem Watsa's wife divorced him?

To which Sender, the art patron, replied:

She probably can't stand his nasty Paky smell.

But Sender wasn't the only hedge fund titan to be enthralled by Contogouris. Chanos, too, spent an inordinate amount of time personally communicating with the man.

In fact, Chanos actually helped disseminate Contogouris's work. Chanos personally sent the business school at the University of Toronto a Contogouris-penned "report" on Fairfax and, as Contogouris had done with Watsa's priest, warned the university to be wary of interacting with the Fairfax CEO. "I am sending you this note on Fairfax because the author, who is doing the best work on this company (and believes it to be an Enron-like fraud) is Greek," Chanos wrote. "I would just like to make two observations: First, if we are right, it would be wise to get Mr. Watsa's future pledges or future gifts in cash. Also, keep in mind that no amount of support is worth besmirching a university's reputation."

That a New York billionaire would take time out to harass a Canadian business school with threats about its reputation would be surprising, except that the hedge funds seemingly had left no stone unturned in their efforts to intimidate anyone connected with Fairfax. At their direction, Contogouris stole confidential information from Fairfax executives and delivered dossiers to the Wall Street gamblers showing private bank account info, credit card information, cell phone records, brokerage account information, any private material you can possibly steal. They researched sexual habits and preferences and religious beliefs and even investigated a woman one executive met for dinner.

The hedge funds hired a former FBI agent, Gregory Suhajda, to conduct these "investigations." The clear objective of researching things like sexual orientation was to try to smooth the way for blackmail. Suhajda explicitly outlined this idea in an email to Exis Capital's Andy Heller in May 2006 that contained a background report on a Fairfax executive, explaining that possessing compromising information might lead to "an informal interview which would allow for the highest probability of success."

And indeed, Suhajda and Contogouris tried repeatedly to "informally interview" current and former Fairfax executives. In one incredible episode that demonstrates the lunatic, fourth-rate *Spy vs. Spy* stupidities that Contogouris and his hedge fund buddies stooped to in an attempt to wrest inside information out of Fairfax employees, they targeted a Fairfax executive named Trevor Ambridge, who at the time was working for a Fairfax subsidiary in London.

Before approaching Ambridge, Contogouris and Suhajda had managed to get themselves registered as FBI informants. Again, they used real questions about Fairfax's accounting and a paucity of public information about the relationships among the many subsidiaries of the umbrella company to pique the interest of authorities. Particularly in the wake of the superficially similar Gen Re/AIG case—which by the mid-2000s had developed into a full-blown Justice Department investigation (with another prominent insurance CEO, AIG's Maurice "Hank" Greenberg, as the central prosecutorial target)—the government had a genuine interest in Fairfax. Nobody on either side of this story disputes that Contogouris for a time was genuinely working with the FBI in some capacity.

And Contogouris used that status to entice Fairfax employees like Ambridge to come forward and spill secrets to the authorities. Showing off his familiarity with intelligence/cop lingo, or at least with cop movies, Contogouris boasted to Ambridge that while he couldn't guarantee Ambridge immunity, he might be able to have a word with someone about getting him a "queen for a day" deal with the Justice Department—a one-day off-the-record agreement where nothing he said could be held against him. Contogouris urged Ambridge to come to a secret meeting at a hotel room in London, where he would meet with authorities.

Impressively, he managed to convince real FBI agents to come to the would-be meeting with the would-be inside whistle-blower, upon whom Contogouris constantly impressed the need to cooperate. "Believe me when I tell you that it is my best interest to try to insulate you from prosecution," Contogouris told Ambridge. "The person who is first to cooperate usually gets the best deal and gets it put behind him."

Contogouris had no idea of this at the time, but Ambridge was working with Fairfax security personnel. Fairfax by then had hired a New York law firm, Kasowitz Benson Torres & Friedman, to investigate its situation. One of the firm's lawyers, the aforementioned Michael Bowe, traveled to London along with a former NYPD investigator to observe the would-be meeting with the strange character who was approaching one of Fairfax's executives. "We wanted to see who this guy was," Bowe says, laughing as he recalls the story. In the end, Ambridge, at their instruction, canceled the secret meeting when Contogouris refused to accede to a demand that it be conducted in a public place.

But the episode wasn't a total loss for the Fairfax lawyers, who later discovered extraordinary exchanges between Sender and Contogouris about this would-be London spy meeting. As registered informants with the FBI, Contogouris and Suhajda had both had to sign confidentiality agreements with the government, promising not to disclose anything about their activities or, particularly, make any trades based upon their knowledge of the investigation.

But Contogouris was so constitutionally incapable of containing his excitement at all the hubbub that he blew off the confidentiality issue and continued emailing and texting Sender throughout the entire episode. On the very day Contogouris was supposed to meet with Ambridge, he sent Sender a preposterous coded message in which he described an upcoming government action against Fairfax using the metaphor of a hurricane about to hit the Gulf of Mexico. In the message, he describes Ambridge as the "Gulf of Mexico guy," and while expressing disappointment that "GOM guy" isn't showing up for the meeting, he still bubbles over with excitement about a coming "storm" being predicted by "U.S. meteorologists"— in other words, a raid by the FBI:

CONTOGOURIS: GOM guy acting finicky, can't reach him. I got three peolpe [*sic*] trying its bad news. The good news is though the U.S. meteorologists confirm a hurricane coming. you get me . . . ?*

SENDER: When the hurricane comes its going 2 be nasty regardless.†

CONTOGOURIS: Fuccckkk Ya. Its going to make Katrina look like a sneeze‡

Sender and Contogouris at one point in the middle of this dialogue realize that they can't understand each other's half-baked codes, and they have to email each other asking to clarify what the hell they're both talking about. Sender sheepishly admits he's not sure what Contogouris means by his message about the "GOM guy"—is it good news or bad news? After all, he's got a ton of money shorted against Fairfax . . . er, his drilling in the Gulf was very large:

SENDER: Im a bit confused. Is the GOM Guy talking 2 u or not. Our position in Energy, driling [*sic*] is very large as u know. Not worried about this one, one second just curious?§

CONTOGOURIS: He' is very talkative but is very worried about some current hurricanes. executives from all over the world have flown

---

* A279 [Jul. 17, 2006, email from SpymI4 to Sender, EXIS-0001312].
† A282 [Jul. 17, 2006, email from Sender to Contogouris, EXIS-0001316].
‡ A283 [Jul. 17, 2006, email from Contogouris to Sender, EXIS-0001317].
§ A520 [Jul. 18, 2006, email from Sender to Contogouris, EXIS-0095883].

in for emergency meetings and he can't get out to talk to me. My meteorological crew can't be in the field and in the open indefinitely waiting. Scheduling is the problem, but the gom guy appears to want to come in and tell my guys what he knows about these hurricanes that are due in August*

SENDER: I wish it was Aug.†

CONTOGOURIS: me too.‡

After this exchange, Contogouris exploded with a series of threats against Ambridge for not showing, promising to spill secrets about his communications with him. "Just think what I could do with your emails," he hissed, adding that he, Spyro, was going to "consider all my options as maintaining our confidentiality," and that if the executive didn't cooperate, he could "no longer rely on my discretion."

Contogouris seemed to be playing a triple game. First, he was genuinely trying to deliver an informant to the FBI and set himself up as an FBI informant. Second, he was trying to deliver confidential information to the hedge funds, to whom he had set himself up as an expert at information retrieval. And third, he was playing secret source to "reputable" journalists, to whom he had promised to deliver stunning exposés. Contogouris even referenced one of those contacts in his adolescent coded emails to Sender sent from London that day:

CONTOGOURIS: We have been rapping here about the postman. He's going to deliver mail. The senders want a message delivered§

"The postman" here was Boyd of the *New York Post,* with whom Contogouris had been working to prepare a major "exposé" on Fair-

---

* A284 [Jul. 18, 2006, email from Contogouris to Sender, EXIS-0001320].
† A3763 [Jul. 18, 2006, email from Sender to Contogouris, EXIS-0063838].
‡ A3764 [Jul. 18, 2006, email from Contogouris to Sender, EXIS-0063839].
§ A281 [Jul. 17, 2006, email from Contogouris to Sender, EXIS-0001315].

fax. Boyd in the late spring of 2006 had spoken to Chanos himself, who introduced him to Contogouris, who in turn began working with the journalist on a series of exposés about Fairfax's supposed Enron-like machinations in offshore accounts.

Like others who met Contogouris, Boyd says he was initially impressed by the man's energy and magnetism. "He's a different kind of guy," Boyd says now. "Unbelievably obsessive and driven. A very hard worker." Boyd says he met with him four or five times, and although he denies that Contogouris was an important source for the stories he would ultimately write about Fairfax (Boyd claims he had already begun pursuing a different theory about Fairfax, a tax-evasion angle, than the one Contogouris was pushing), he was initially receptive to Contogouris's information. At the very least, the two were in contact before Boyd ran a story about Fairfax that summer, and Contogouris could plausibly tell his bosses that a devastating exposé from a prominent journalist was coming.

Thus throughout July 2006, Sender, Chanos, Loeb, and others were joyously writing to one another about the imminent demise of Fairfax, among other things because they knew that Boyd was planning an exposé on Fairfax that would accuse the company of self-dealing. Contogouris would even tell them the publication date of the first piece: July 22.

And in the days before that piece ran, the hedge funds gnashed their collective teeth in orgiastic expectation. As always, the men wrote to one another in ghastly pidgin English, full of bad sex jokes and comic misspellings. Contogouris wrote to Chanos:

> Oh ya . . . FFH just about rapped up like a skandanavian mistress love slave

The billionaire wrote back:

> I bet Prem is a nervous as a goat in a Greek monastery . . . lol

Nothing like a little goat-fucking humor between Greek stock scammers. While that conversation was going on, Sender was joking to Loeb:

SOUNDS LIKE WHAT'S GOING TO HAPPEN TO
PREM IN SING SING

The next day, however, Fairfax's stock disappointingly went up, prompting Sender to write:

MAKES ME SICK, BUT . . . PREM DOESN'T HAVE
MUCH MORE TIME 2 FUK AROUND SO I HOPE HE
IS HAVING FUN WITH HIMSELF

The *Post* story came out as planned on July 22, but the stock didn't crater. Contogouris blamed Boyd, among other things for not getting the story up on the Web fast enough. "Stocks up a dollar," he whined to Boyd. "Your guys really fuk you with this not on the internet BS."

It was around this time that Boyd started to have a change of heart about Contogouris. He says the Fairfax story came out while he was on a vacation, and when he came back, he found certified letters from Spyro jamming up his mailbox, and his answering machine lit up with messages. "There were like nineteen messages. It was crazy. He was getting increasingly more difficult," says Boyd, who decided to freeze out Contogouris for a while.

The day after the story ran, July 23, Sender's nerves were so raw that he exploded at Contogouris. Spyro had texted him that he was working on another project that day, because his "brain is fairfax fried."

"NOOOOOOOOOOOOOOO," Sender moaned in an instant message. "FAIRFAX #1 UNTIL WE C THE CORPSE."

By that third week of July 2006, the war between the hedge funds and Fairfax had already been going on for three and a half agonizingly long years. Over that extended period of time, the argument against the company being put forward by its short investors and its allies in the investment banking world and in the press had evolved dramatically.

The original complaint made in early 2003 by analyst John Gwynn, remember, had been that Fairfax was undercapitalized by $5 billion. By the spring of 2006, the new story being put out by Contogouris to reporters like Boyd was a brilliantly involved tale of conspiracy and international intrigue. In his sales pitch about Fairfax's problems, Contogouris would bring with him a gigantic, conference-table-size poster purporting to show the structure of Fairfax's accounting.

The scam depicted in the chart was an Enronesque maze of phantom revenues and hidden budget holes, an ingenious robbing-Peter-to-pay-Paul scheme in which Fairfax was essentially borrowing billions against its European assets and capitalizing its subsidiaries with shares in other subsidiaries, a complex and indecipherable bookkeeping merry-go-round. Far different and more complex from the original charge of simply being undercapitalized, the new charges were a lurid and compelling suspense tale, complete with all the bells and whistles of great storytelling that had been absent from the original dry Gwynn report.

It was a story that seemed too complex and idiosyncratic to be made up, and that was Fairfax's problem. There were just too many amazing details out there for it not to be a little bit true. At the very least, the markets seemed to feel that way. By that critical period in late July, Fairfax really was on the verge of collapse. Its stock price was declining, long-loyal shareholders were slowly departing, it was being besieged by questions from ratings agencies, its executives were under surveillance by the FBI, and it was receiving subpoenas from the SEC.

Beginning in late 2005, Rivett tried to get every regulator he could find to listen to his story of being mass-fragged by mysterious hedge fund gamblers. He got no help at all.

"I went to the New York Stock Exchange first," he says. "I went to the Ontario Securities Commission [the province's version of the SEC], I went to the Royal Canadian Mounted Police. . . . They all look at you like you're crazy." The Canadian regulators, like everyone else, had seen the news stories and heard the rumors, which of course had mainly been generated by the hedge funds. "Their attitude was, where there's smoke, there's fire."

Rivett traveled to Washington and New York. He met with members of Congress and the Senate. He tried the FBI, tried the SEC, but had no luck, particularly with the latter crew. "They were hostile because they were investigating us," Rivett explains. As for the congressmen and the other regulators, they weren't interested. "I was like, 'Jobs will be lost, everything will be lost, will you help us?' But there was nothing."

By late spring of 2006, Fairfax's situation was desperate. There was a great internal debate in the company over what to do. Many Fairfax executives were fearful of taking any kind of action against the likes of Chanos and Cohen. "These guys were the Masters of the Universe," says Rivett. "People were like, 'They'll crush us.'"

But Watsa by then had come to a conclusion. "We had no choice," he said. He believed that if the company didn't act, it was going to be destroyed anyway. Rivett was worried that unless the firm fought back, the story would end in some kind of Justice Department action, an arrest, something, and that would destroy the company and its eight thousand jobs.

Moreover, the law firm it had retained to investigate its problems, Kasowitz Benson Torres & Friedman, had told the Canadians that they were in deep trouble—so deep that the funds were already planning a blowout victory party on the occasion of Fairfax's bankruptcy. Like any financial firm, an insurance company can quickly implode in a run-on-the-bank-like crisis of confidence, and Fairfax was not only facing real regulatory inquiries but the possibility of mass defections by investors. If it didn't answer its detractors soon, the law firm explained, the company's share price might crater, and the firm might go out of business.

So Fairfax ultimately made the only move it had left to make: it sued. It hired Kasowitz to draw up an extensive complaint that answered in detail all the accusations of fraud leveled by the hedge funds. Both sides in this war were racing to put their version out before the public in bold type at more or less exactly the same moment, at the end of July 2006.

Boyd's exposé came out on July 22, 2006; Fairfax filed its suit against the hedge funds four days later, on July 26.

The filing of the lawsuit—not *winning* a lawsuit, but merely filing it—was what saved the firm. The detailed response spooked some short investors who had jumped on the bandwagon with Chanos and Sender and the rest. Jonathan Kalikow of the hedge fund Stanfield Capital, for instance, responded angrily when the Fairfax suit was filed. According to the discovery materials, Kalikow had been all but assured by people like Andy Heller at Exis Capital that Fairfax was about to be busted by authorities at any moment and was sure to go out of business. He had also been briefed about Boyd's *New York Post* story ahead of time.

So when he saw Fairfax file its suit, he was shocked that the Canadians had gone into such detail about all the allegations and was also displeased that the company appeared to be gearing up for a long battle instead of simply rolling over and/or surrendering to the authorities. It wasn't the behavior of a guilty company.

"It's all out in the open," Kalikow emailed Heller. "[The suit] mentions the Luxembourg sub, the Gibralter [*sic*] sub . . . why would they disclose their own fraud in such a way? Ans: they wouldn't."

"No one can explain to me the fraud," Kalikow continued. "Is money actually missing or not? Not even your experts know," he barked at Heller. "Now this trade is a disaster. All the news that was supposed to take this lower hasn't."

In depositions later on, Kalikow explained that the lawsuit was "the final straw . . . in believing that there wasn't going to be any fraud disclosure, the way I assumed it was going to occur." He explained in the deposition how he subsequently pulled out of his bet:

Q: Did you exit the positions sometime after the lawsuit started?
KALIKOW: Absolutely.
Q: And did you take a loss?
KALIKOW: Yes.
Q: Do you remember how much?
KALIKOW: Probably $60–70 million.

Kalikow, relatively speaking, was only a minor player in the team of short sellers, yet he lost $70 million. In the deposition, Kalikow shrugged off the loss of such a sum, as if it were no big deal.

Simultaneous to the filing of the suit against Cohen, Loeb, and the others, Fairfax issued a restatement, admitting to accounting errors in the 2001–2005 period. Under normal circumstances, admitting to a serious accounting problem in the middle of a swarming short attack would be disastrous, but the Fairfax restatement had the opposite effect. Instead of disclosing billions of hidden losses and off-balance-sheet transactions of the Enron type—the rumored problems—the restatement disclosed a serious but straightforward error in its accounting treatment of an old reinsurance contract with its subsidiary Swiss Re. The total impact of the error was around $240 million, less than the rumors guessed at.

The combined impact of the lawsuit and the restatement convinced some investors like Kalikow to bail on their short bets. The simple decision to fight back proved to be a key to the company's survival; other short targets were often vaporized and bankrupted before they could even get into court. "The anomaly is that Fairfax was one of the only companies that went out and defended itself," says Bowe.

Unquestionably, the filing of the suit stabilized the company's share price in the summer of 2006, but what really turned the tide for Fairfax was a second event that year. In September 2006, in a story entitled "FBI's Secret Source," the *Post*'s Boyd reported that Contogouris,. whom he described only as someone who "analyzes companies' balance sheets"—not as someone who had been introduced to him by one of the world's biggest short sellers—had been "deputized by the FBI" to approach a Fairfax executive as part of an investigation.

As one government source explained it, "The FBI went ape-shit" when they saw the Boyd piece. The sheer embarrassment of having a prank-calling *Matchstick Men* wannabe like Contogouris claiming in public to be a deputized FBI operative was a terrible black eye for the Bureau, which was eventually forced to answer questions about the incident in a Senate Judiciary Committee hearing. Asked about the *Post* story, and Contogouris specifically, FBI director Robert Mueller answered icily, "The FBI does not deputize members of the general public."

The writing was on the wall. About a month after the Boyd piece, Contogouris was fired by the hedge funds, which seemed anxious to leave a written record of their displeasure. "Not kicking a dog while he's down, but I have to say how disappointed I am personally in the research," Exis Capital's Andy Heller wrote to Contogouris. "I just don't think you're qualified to be making the assumptions you make."* He added, referring to Contogouris's *Dumb and Dumber* "MI4" compadre Max Bernstein, "You should not be taking opinions from Max. U cant explain it. Don't have Max try and make things up."

Contogouris, quite sensibly it would seem, exploded in response—*now* they tell him not to make things up? "Now you're saying I'm not qualified?" he wrote back. He added (with his usual tortured spelling), "I didn't have Max make up anything, are you accusing me of having MAX MAKE THINGS UP? Are you fukking kidding?"

Within six weeks after the *Post* piece, on November 14, 2006, Contogouris was arrested in federal court on unrelated charges, apparently for defrauding his old Greek employer Manios out of

---

* A4128–A4143 [Nov. 6, 2006, email from Heller to Contogouris, EXIS-0064564]; A4138–A4143 [Nov. 6, 2006, email from Heller to Sender: ("[Contogouris] tells me he told us FFH would lose 22 a share. Like he has any clue about their #s. but ep fcx and mmr he wiffed"), EXIS-0093214–EXIS-0093219].

$5 million. It was a curiously ancient offense, and people familiar with the case almost universally believe that Contogouris's real crime was running his mouth in the *New York Post* in the Fairfax matter. "The Feds wanted to send a message to any idiot who goes around blabbing about being an FBI informant," says Marc Cohodes.

The complaint in that case was humorous:

> Even after CONTOGOURIS was fired in April 2002 due to CW's concerns over the management of the Companies' funds, CONTOGOURIS collected three tax refund checks, totaling over $770,000, that were issued to the Companies. Shortly after he received each check, CONTOGOURIS opened bank accounts into which he deposited the money. Then, CONTOGOURIS completed the fraud by wiring the funds to other accounts that he or his associates controlled.

It had nothing to do with the company at all, but Spyro Contogouris getting busted for boosting tax refund checks from his old boss was the single most important thing that happened to Fairfax in the entire decade of the 2000s. Overnight the company's stock jumped about 10 percent.

In all, in the eight months after July 26, 2006, Fairfax regained about $2 billion in stock value. The two critical events, the filing of the lawsuit and the arrest of Contogouris, said absolutely nothing about the company's performance as an insurer. The only thing that changed in that time was the attitude of the global investing community toward the company. It had nothing to do with justice, the regulatory system, or the wisdom of the good old-fashioned Adam Smith capitalist marketplace. Instead, what began as a confidence game ended as a confidence game. The entire thing was a battle of public relations. It had nothing to do with real economics.

———

Morristown, New Jersey, early on a Friday afternoon in January 2012. There is complete silence in the small, well-kept, windowless courtroom. The place is teeming with lawyers. Up in the front of the courtroom, I can see Bowe, the lead counsel for Fairfax. An Irishman from northern New Jersey, Bowe doesn't look like a white-shoe lawyer; he was probably a homicide detective or a bartender in an Irish saloon in another life. When he talks, he sounds more like an assemblyman from Monmouth or Cherry Hill than a corporate mouthpiece. He's got a couple of other lawyers with him, but otherwise the plaintiff's table is pretty spare.

On the other side, however, the defendants' table is crowded with what looks like dozens of lawyers. The lead dog is a Texan named Bruce Collins, a drawling, dark-haired hotshot corporate defense lawyer who made *The Best Lawyers in America* three years running, from 2011 to 2013. As it happened, I'd seen Collins in court before, back when he was Ken Lay's lead attorney in the Enron criminal trial. Surrounding Collins, who is here on behalf of Morgan Keegan, is a small army of associates and cocounsel. The gallery is filled with clipboard-carrying men and women in suits and ties, most of them lawyers for the many hedge funds that are, were, or potentially still could be part of the historic lawsuit filed by Fairfax against its short attackers.

In the entire courtroom I count two reporters—myself and a *Bloomberg* man—plus three plaintiff's attorneys and roughly three dozen defense lawyers. There are no civilian spectators. The court junkies who show up and hang out in the back rows of murder and rape trials do not come to high-powered civil trials about market manipulation by hedge funds. In big-time civil trials of this type, virtually all the participants are paid to attend, and it's obvious which side has more money to spend to pack the room.

It's been eight full years since Fairfax was first besieged, and nearly six years since Fairfax first filed suit. But the company is still miles away from gaining any relief. The Fairfax lawsuit would prove to be a textbook example of how hard it is to use America's civil court system to stave off market manipulation.

Although the key players in the case brazenly used emails and other written communications to discuss the various lowball moves against Fairfax, the Canadians found that it wasn't easy even to keep the actual perpetrators of the scheme in the lawsuit. The hedge funds' high-powered lawyers appealed to technicality after technicality to try to sever their clients from the case, and over and over again, judges accepted their arguments.

By the fall of 2012, Steve Cohen's SAC had been dismissed from the case by New Jersey Superior Court judge Stephan Hansbury, who accepted SAC's argument that it couldn't possibly have been part of a scheme to destroy Fairfax, since it was not short Fairfax for "most of 2004" and had no position at all in the company in 2005. In his ruling, Hansbury restricted his definition of "shorting Fairfax" to simple short bets against the parent company. Despite the fact that shorting subsidiaries like OdysseyRe had the identical effect, Hansbury dismissed evidence that SAC had done exactly that as irrelevant. The judge was also unmoved by the fact that SAC was a major investor in Exis Capital, which Hansbury himself ruled was indeed consistently short Fairfax during the time period in question.

Hansbury also accepted SAC's argument that much of SAC's trading was done in so-called quant funds, in which trades were executed not by day-to-day decisions of human beings but automatically, by computerized formulas. Thus while SAC might have had positions shorting Fairfax, its lawyers argued, those investments had not been birthed in the mind of Stevie Cohen or anyone else at SAC, but by computerized formulas. Therefore, the lawyers argued successfully, there could not have been manipulation.

A month or so after that decision, Hansbury bounced Chanos and Loeb from the case. Why? Mainly because they worked out of New York, not New Jersey.

"One must establish that the defendants purposely availed themselves of the State of New Jersey," he wrote, "and that the alleged improper conduct was expected or intended to be felt within the State of New Jersey." Hansbury was apparently not impressed by the fact that Fairfax's biggest American subsidiary, and its fifteen hundred or so jobs, was headquartered less than a few miles from where he sat in judgment, in the very city of Morristown, New Jersey.

Fairfax had chosen to sue in the state of New Jersey for two reasons. One was that it was where Crum & Forster was located. Second, a corporate citizen based in New Jersey like Crum & Forster had a perfect legal avenue to pursue—a private racketeering claim. Unlike the state of New York, which doesn't allow such lawsuits, New Jersey allows plaintiffs to file lawsuits under the Racketeer Influenced and Corrupt Organizations (RICO) statute. A RICO suit is a powerful tool for a company in Fairfax's position, because it theoretically prevents short sellers from dumping the whole of their legal responsibility on a low-level middleman like Contogouris.

Under RICO, the leaders of a criminal syndicate are responsible for the actions of the people they hire to do their dirty work. In criminal law, it covers a mobster who orders a hit but doesn't pull the trigger himself. In civil law, RICO is a perfectly appropriate net for use in catching a stock manipulator who hires a thug to depress a company's share price artificially.

The problem, however, is the one that confronts financial regulators everywhere. Since modern finance is an almost completely global enterprise, the major players can make a habit of regulator shopping. A large number of financial companies base their trading operations in London, for instance, because the regulatory framework there for certain kinds of trades (particularly derivative trades) is even weaker than in the United States. Other companies place subsidiaries in tax havens or other foreign locales and park profits there.

In one sense, the maneuverings by Contogouris and Morgan Keegan and the hedge funds occurred everywhere—in New York (where many key emails and phone calls originated), in Toronto (where executives were followed and prank-called), in Washington (where key figures attempted to involve the SEC in investigations), in New Jersey (where Crum & Forster was located and a number of defendants kept offices), in London (where Contogouris met with FBI agents), and really all over the world, where potential investors received false information and moved the value of Fairfax stock by buying and selling shares.

In another sense, though, the crime occurred nowhere in particular. If a hedge fund magnate in Westchester or Long Island sends an email to a bank analyst in Tennessee (where Morgan Keegan keeps its headquarters) to discuss the manipulation of the stock of a Canadian insurance company that's listed on the New York Stock Exchange but retains a major subsidiary in New Jersey, where did the offense take place? It depended, entirely, on how you looked at things.

Here again we have a major difference between the prosecution of ordinary street crime and the regulation of global finance. If you jump a fare on East 125th Street in Harlem, there's no question which police force and which city's set of laws apply to you. No lawyer is going to stand up in court and make the pseudometaphysical argument that the bus was actually built in Conway, Arkansas, or that the injured parties were actually the Chinese buyers of a transportation bond issued by the city of New York. No, you jump a fare in Manhattan, and it's Manhattan cops who will knock you on the head and throw you in jail. And no judge will excuse you from the New York City dock because your home address happens to be Paterson, New Jersey.

But this sort of thing happens all the time in global financial crime. Crimes happen everywhere and nowhere, and unless a major federal regulator asserts jurisdiction, defense lawyers can keep their clients from ever going near a courtroom simply by challenging the venue. This is exactly what happened in the Fairfax case.

After he stripped Chanos and Loeb from the case, Hansbury held his next hearing in January 2012. This was the one where I sat watching as Bowe faced off against Collins and the rest of the law-yering multitude defending Morgan Keegan and the remaining hedge funds (Sender's Exis Capital, for instance) still in the suit. This next hearing was to decide an even bigger metaphysical question—whether Fairfax was entitled to use New Jersey's RICO statute to make its case.

If Bowe and Fairfax could not use the RICO statute to sue, they had little chance of winning a case in which most of the bad acts had technically been committed by middlemen and stooges. Like mob cases in the days before racketeering laws, the big shots would get off without ever seeing the inside of a courtroom.

Hansbury showed up in court that January afternoon looking bored. His Honor is a frowning, thin-lipped, narrow-shouldered man with Bob Newhart's balding head and laconic delivery. He yawningly asked Collins to begin his presentation, and the hotshot Texan lawyer complied by entering into the legal version of a *Sesame Street* counting game. Collins proceeded to list each of the major players in the case, then note their addresses and locations at the time of their alleged involvement. After each entry, he would argue to the judge about whether that person's conduct could really be said to have occurred in New Jersey.

In some cases, he would mention a player like Contogouris's ridiculous accountant Rekuc, whose office was in New Jersey, and he would generously "give" that player to Bowe despite the fact that Rekuc only ever met with the other defendants in New York.

Using this generous math, Collins actually calculated, down to the percentage point, how much of the crime had taken place in New Jersey. Even if you conceded every possible New Jersey connection to Bowe and Fairfax's lawyers, Collins said, less than 8 percent of the crime had taken place there. "So giving them all that, what do you end up with?" Collins asked. "You get 7.6 percent, doing the right comparative analysis, using their statement of facts . . . 7.6 percent."

Collins went on, explaining that even some foreign countries could claim more ownership of the crime alleged in the lawsuit. "Your Honor, they're barely beating Australia, barely beating Australia here," he deadpanned.

Around the courtroom, all the lawyers in the gallery were frantically entering that 7.6 percent number into their notepads. Nobody laughed at the absurdity of calculating what percentage of a crime took place in what state. In my mind, the matter was much simpler: if a crime took place in New Jersey at all, be it 7 percent of the overall scheme or 1 percent of it, and the ostensible victims lived in New Jersey, then any law officer in that state should want to see the local laws applied. Why did it matter if the crime also took place in New York, and Toronto, and Australia, and wherever else?

Bowe tried frantically to make the same argument when Collins finally finished and Hansbury gave him a chance to respond. "We're talking about a New Jersey statute," Bowe said. "And if the intent of that New Jersey statute was to apply to the conduct in this case then the New Jersey Court should apply it without doing a balancing test to determine whether or not some other state has a bigger interest or not."

Hansbury shrugged, seeming unimpressed. When speaking to Bowe, he acted like a man taking a sales call from a telemarketer.

I'd seen the same phenomenon at more than one white-collar fraud case. If judges in regular criminal courts treat everything that comes out of the mouth of a defense lawyer like a ploy to get some definitely guilty scoundrel out of trouble, in civil trials involving financial companies, they treat plaintiff's counsel like parasites trying to use the courts to wrangle money out of hardworking, successful people.

Throughout the Fairfax case, this seemed to be the main preoccupation with the judges. Were the Fairfax lawyers engaged in some elaborate ambulance-chasing effort, trying to use the civil code of the state of New Jersey as a weapon to take down their target? The fact that the democratically elected state legislature of New Jersey had in fact passed a tough civil RICO law for, quite possibly, precisely this sort of case seemed secondary to the possibility that someone was trying to use a New Jersey judge to suck money out of a bunch of New York hedge funds.

It was obvious that the latter possibility greatly troubled Hansbury as he repeatedly interrogated Bowe. "Isn't that a significant policy difference," he asked, "that in New York you can't bring a private RICO claim, but in New Jersey you can?"

Bowe, caught off guard, hesitantly tried to argue that it wasn't a significant difference in the sense that both states have a RICO statute and bar the same conduct, but there was just a "procedural" difference in that while in New York the state has to file those charges, in New Jersey the people are explicitly allowed to "bring private rights of action."

"But if I accept your argument," the judge said, wincing, "is that not going to open the flood gates to New Jersey every time somebody is unhappy with an outcome in New York under a RICO claim? If they can touch New Jersey, they file it here? Isn't that what's going to happen?"

Bowe tried to argue. "The fact of the matter is, if the New Jersey statute so provides, it so provides," he sighed. "And the fact is the New Jersey statute provides."

It was a valiant effort, but everyone in the room could tell Bowe was toast. Every question the judge asked him was a laser blasted right into the heart of his case. When addressing Collins, meanwhile, the judge was more often asking, collegially as it were, what the Texan's opinion was on a matter of law. In fact, the judge didn't interrupt Collins at all during his entire argument and bothered to ask him a question or two only toward the end of the hearing, as though it wouldn't look good if he didn't challenge him at all.

As I was walking out of the courtroom, the other reporter covering the case chuckled. "Those guys are dead," he said, referring to Fairfax.

He was right. A year later, on September 12, the entire case was dismissed, this time by a different judge, Donald Coburn. This was despite the fact that Hansbury that spring had agreed that Fairfax had "suffered massive pecuniary/economic loss in this case" and that Coburn himself agreed that "it's clear here that there was evidence of intent to adversely affect the actual business dealings." Toward the end, Coburn even seemed to signal his belief in the underlying claim of the suit. "If someone says an insurance company doesn't pay its debts and doesn't settle its claims, that could certainly affect its ability to sell its product," he said. "There is sufficient evidence on which a jury could find there is an intention to harm their interests."

But Coburn disallowed the testimony of one of Fairfax's expert witnesses, whose main function was to calculate the amount of damage the attacks against Fairfax had caused. Among other things, the company had been forced to borrow money and liquidate assets at disadvantageous prices during the most desperate period of its war with the hedge funds, and the company claimed it suffered losses of up to $6 billion through these transactions. Coburn didn't buy Fairfax's arguments and allowed the company to proceed with a suit only for $19 million against the two remaining defendants, Morgan Keegan and Exis.

Rather than go to court over $19 million, Fairfax decided not to fight a motion to dismiss and elected to appeal the case later on and try to bring all the defendants back in. Who knew? Maybe there would be news of some kind that would change the landscape a little.

A few months later news broke that the federal government was pursuing what it called "the most lucrative insider trading scheme ever charged" against SAC Capital. The complaint asserted that an SAC employee, Mathew Martoma, had obtained inside information about a failed trial for an Alzheimer's drug that was being tested by a pair of companies SAC was invested in. According to the Feds, Martoma passed that information to "Portfolio Manager A," the "owner" of the hedge fund, who in turn liquidated the firm's $700 million position in the two companies and then turned around and shorted them. According to the complaint, the two moves saved the firm from $194 million in losses and then earned it about $83 million on the short trade. News reports confirmed the obvious, that the unnamed coconspirator was Cohen.

Another SAC vet, Noah Freeman, told the FBI that "you were expected to provide your trading ideas to Cohen" and that doing so meant providing insider information. "At SAC Capital you were paid a percentage of Cohen's trade if Cohen placed a trade based on your tip," Freeman said. Another SAC analyst, Jon Horvath, pleaded guilty to being part of a "criminal club" that swapped nonpublic information about technology companies.

For a while, it looked as if Cohen himself might get away. In March 2013 the SEC settled insider trading charges with Cohen for $616 million, and Cohen was so depressed by the paltry fine (which was only a fraction of his rumored $8 billion personal fortune) that he immediately went out and bought a $155 million Picasso (*Le Rêve*) and a $60 million, Gordon Gekko–style beach house in the Hamptons (right next to his existing $18 million house on the same beach). But later in the year, SAC itself was criminally indicted on insider trading charges, and Cohen was also charged civilly by the SEC for failure to supervise in the Martoma case. As of this writing, it appears that at the very least, SAC will be shut down. Meanwhile ten former SAC employees have been charged or implicated in illegal trading, and five have admitted guilt.

But none of the charges had anything to do with Fairfax, and no action has yet been taken against any of the others in the case. Anyone who took the extremely belated action against Cohen as proof that the state actually polices the stock markets in a meaningful way would be missing the point.

When Harlem residents Michael McMichael and Anthony Odom drove down 161st Street in a new-looking Range Rover, police immediately profiled the car as being bought with illegal income. But when Stevie Cohen claimed to be 400 percent more efficient than the entire investing world fifteen years running, talked publicly about his billion-bucks-a-year income, and bought a 6,000-square-foot, Zamboni-treated skating rink for his mansion just a few years after opening his own business, nobody blinked until decades had passed and multiple companies had been destroyed.

Put it this way: If someone is breaking into your home, you call 911 and the cops show up right away, sirens blaring. You don't have to put in any work convincing anyone you're really in trouble, no matter who you are.

But if someone tries to destroy your company with an insider trading scheme, getting regulatory help is a delicate political matter. Unlike street crime, where there are always enough officers to pound on a door, the resources devoted to policing financial markets are so meager that allocating any of them is a major political decision. And the issues are confusing enough that if one side hires enough lawyers and analysts and presses the case aggressively enough, the victim could end up being investigated before the aggressor, which is a serious problem in a business where the mere announcement of an inquiry can result in huge amounts of money being won or lost.

What happened with Fairfax was the opposite of Justice by Attrition. An offense takes place, the perpetrators are identified, but over a period of years the whole thing just goes away in a cloud of paperwork. Regulators used the fine print not to lean on a suspect or whittle away his right to a speedy trial but to avoid claiming jurisdiction; the courts used it to avoid imposing punishment, and defense lawyers used it to disappear the case altogether.

CHAPTER 7

LITTLE FRAUDS

Maria Espinosa didn't know what hit her. It was like waking up underwater and not knowing which way to swim to get to the surface. There'd been a loud banging noise, and now there was a man standing before her at her apartment door, in his forties and nearly twice her age, like her Spanish speaking and of Latin origin, but unlike her a full American citizen, American born.

He was gruff and powerful looking and he held up some kind of ID before reaching across the doorway, putting his hand on her shoulder, and moving her aside to let himself in.

"He pushed me," Maria would explain later. "He just walked right in. Went straight to the kitchen."

Maria thought maybe it was the police. The police had been to her tiny Los Angeles apartment many times in recent years because her boyfriend, Eduardo, the father of her three-year-old son, Carlos, beat and terrorized her regularly. It was worse when he drank, and he drank a lot. She'd been staying with the boyfriend for the sake of her son, but lately things had gotten so out of hand that she'd finally kicked him out. Now she was alone, jobless, taking care of a young child, with barely any English, and far from her family in Mexico.

And now there's a strange man in her apartment, American but Spanish speaking, and she has no idea what he's doing there. He's in the kitchen, opening her cabinets, looking in her refrigerator. She asks him what he's doing.

"You applied for help," he says. "You applied for food stamps, right?"

Now Maria remembers. She had indeed gone down to the local welfare office a few days before and applied for food stamps and temporary assistance. She had legal status, and as a victim of domestic violence, she qualified for benefits. They'd been very nice to her at the welfare office, and when the counselor approved her application he added, with a smile, that everything was fine, but they were just going to "send someone to check."

They didn't tell her they were sending someone to barge into her apartment and start conducting a bizarre search through her kitchen cabinets. He's looking at cans of beans, peering under bags of flour, like he's looking for something in particular. He turns to her.

"You have a problem with drugs, right?" he asks.

Maria is mortified.

"No," she says. "No, I don't have a problem with drugs. I never take drugs."

He shrugs. She starts to explain about Eduardo. At the mention of that name he raises a finger, like he's remembering something.

"Oh, *that's* right," he says. "We hear you've had a lot of problems with the police."

Maria shakes her head anxiously. He's got her confused with someone. "No, no, *I* didn't have problems with the police," she protests. "I called the police because I'm afraid of that man. I'm worried he's going to kill me, each time that's what I was worried about. I'm not in trouble with the police."

The man says nothing, moves into her bedroom. It only takes a few steps to get there because it's a one-room apartment. The apartment is so small, it's almost like a walk-in freezer.

The man starts going through her dresser drawers. He's looking for men's clothes. He thinks Eduardo still lives here, that the whole thing is a con. Maria explains: You're not going to find anything, he doesn't live here anymore. That's why I applied for help, because I finally got him to move out. "Why would I want him back, after going through all that trouble?"

The man shrugs again. "Well," he says, fixing his eyes on her, "maybe you like that kind of life."

Maria says nothing.

"I mean, maybe that's the kind of man you like," he says, grinning. "How should I know?"

Maria feels herself getting dizzy and reaches out to try to find a chair to support herself. If this man works for the welfare office, she thinks, he must have seen the police reports, he must know my situation. So why is he saying these things? She's so stunned that she barely notices that he's asking her another question.

"Huh, what?" she says. "I didn't hear you."

"I said," he repeats, "if he's so bad, if he's so mean, how come you haven't moved away? Why are you still in Los Angeles? Why don't you go back to Mexico?"

Maria shakes her head. "Because I don't have any money to move. That's why I applied for welfare!"

He shakes his head, chuckling. He's still sifting through her drawers. He checks the socks, the underwear. He holds up pairs of pants to see if they might be big enough for a man. No, those are women's clothes; he puts them back. As he goes about this benign-looking activity—he might be a bachelor folding clothes in a laundromat—he then mentions, offhandedly as it were, that she needs to pick up the phone if Eduardo ever comes back.

"You need to report it if you let him back in your life," he says. "Because I can take your kid from you. You understand?"

Maria freezes.

"Again, just so you're clear. If you continue that relationship, I can take the kid. I *will* take your kid."

Maria is crying by now. The social worker finishes his bedroom exam, takes a cursory look in the bathroom—these inspectors glean quite a bit from the contents of a bathroom—then walks out the door.

This all happened in 1989. Twenty-two years later Maria is telling me this story in her new home city of San Diego. We're meeting in a ramshackle office on the outskirts of town that's used by a local AA group. The lights are down, and just above us there are two huge dust-streaked posters in old calligraphy listing the twelve steps.

Midway through the story, I could see Maria's eyes wandering. She was reliving the experience. When she got to the part where the social worker says, "I mean, maybe that's the kind of man you like," she burst out crying. There was a stack of almost cardboardlike paper towels next to the coffee machine (all AA offices have an old, stained coffee machine) and by the end of the story she had gone through six or seven of those rough towels; she was falling apart.

"They make you feel like a piece of garbage," she says.

Maria Espinosa was a pioneer. The sifting-through-the-dresser-drawer search she experienced in the early years of the George H. W. Bush presidency was an informal precursor to a *Minority Report*-style program that, in the Bill Clinton years, would become formalized in her new home county of San Diego. In San Diego County, from the late 1990s on, through today, the state preemptively searches for evidence of fraud in the homes of the tens of thousands of people who have applied and are applying for cash assistance via CalWORKs, the California version of Temporary Assistance for Needy Families, or TANF—what we used to call welfare.

Today, every single person who applies for aid and is accepted has to be preemptively searched. These people are almost all non-white. And while in L.A. in the late 1980s, the person visiting the home of someone like Maria Espinosa was just a social worker from the local welfare office, the state has since upgraded. In San Diego now it's a law enforcement official, a representative of the district attorney's office, who comes in to look through your underwear drawer. The city has a team of investigators whose sole purpose is to conduct the searches for this program, which is called Project 100% or "P100" for short.

One hundred percent compliance, that's the idea. No outliers, no excuses. Fraud must not be tolerated, not even the smallest kind. So the program must be large, and appropriate resources must naturally be devoted to crime detection. In just one year, 2011, the county conducted an astonishing 26,000 home searches.

P100 generates, by the thousand, stories that sound like testimonials culled from refugees of some distant, low-rent, third-world despotate. The stories are terrible, humiliating, abusive.

"The first case I ever had was a Vietnamese woman who had lost one of her children in a refugee camp," says Joni Halpern, a San Diego lawyer who has spent the last decade defending people on public assistance. "She'd come to America after suffering all kinds of abuse; she was a rape victim.

"She applies for public assistance and a few days later there's a knock on the door. The investigator comes in and immediately starts yelling at her, telling her he can take her children or take her to jail if she's lying about not having a boyfriend.

"He starts going through her dresser drawer. He opens her underwear drawer, sticks a pencil in there, and uses the pencil eraser to pull out a pair of panties that he thinks are too sexy for a woman living alone. And still holding them up by the eraser, he waves them at her, accusing her of having a man in the house.

"That woman didn't open the door to *anyone* for any reason for over a year after that," Halpern says.

Karen Bjorland, a white woman, applied for welfare in her twenties, when she was jobless and trying to raise her two-year-old son by herself. She remembers the caseworker coming through her door and immediately telling her that he can arrest her on the spot if she lied on her application. She remembers him going through everything in her apartment, commenting that the fridge was too stocked with food, sifting through her drawers, her medicine cabinet, even examining the stuffed animals in her son's crib.

Then she remembers how he went into the bathroom and whipped around in an apparent *eureka!* moment after finding two toothbrushes in her toothbrush holder.

"What do you need two toothbrushes for?" he snapped.

"I use them!" she protested.

Years later, when Bjorland became one of a number of women who joined in a lawsuit against the county challenging the legality of the P100 program, she was again asked about the two toothbrushes by one of the county's lawyers.

"He asked me, 'Why did you need two toothbrushes?'" Bjorland recalls today. "And I turned it right back around at him. 'Let me ask you something, how many toothbrushes do *you* have?' I said. And he was like, 'Okay, forget about that question.'"

In those tens of thousands of searches over the years, P100 investigators have looked in every nook and cranny, finding sins everywhere. They rejected an applicant who shared an apartment with a roommate for failing to properly label her food in the refrigerator—how could the state be sure, after all, that the applicant wasn't illegally sharing food with her roommate? They rejected a woman for having a Victoria's Secret bra ("How can you afford this?" the investigator asked, again holding up the item with the favored pencil eraser end), for having too big a jacket in the closet (it must be a man's!), for having a teenage son whose pants were too ghetto (too baggy—again, it must be a man's clothes). Searchers looked in dresser drawers, in bathrooms, in freezers and refrigerators, under and behind couches, everywhere.

And eventually, of course, after twenty or thirty thousand of these searches, a few of these mostly black and Latina women on benefits who were in a job-counseling class together got together and decided, with the help of a few do-gooder local lawyers, to sue. After all, how could a preemptive search by a law enforcement officer possibly be constitutional? Didn't the state need a warrant, or probable cause, to conduct any kind of intrusive search, even of a car—much less someone's home?

That was the idea behind *Rocio Sanchez et al. v. County of San Diego,* a case filed with the aid of the local ACLU in 2004. Karen Bjorland, the woman who had too many toothbrushes, was one of six litigants in the class-action case. You would think this was a slam-dunk civil liberties case, but you'd be wrong. In fact, courts have been slowly chipping away at the Fourth Amendment protection against unreasonable searches and seizures for a long time, and the dominant theme in this gradual legal erosion has been an innovative new form of institutional racism, and a creepy inverse correlation between *rights* and *need.*

Over and over again, we hear that if you owe money in a certain way, or if you receive a certain kind of public assistance, you forfeit this or that line item in the Bill of Rights. If you're a person of means, you get full service for all ten amendments, and even a few that aren't listed. But if you owe, if you rent, you get a slightly thinner, more tubercular version of the Fourth Amendment, the First Amendment, the Fifth and Sixth Amendments, and so on.

It's not that it's written anywhere that if you're black and you live in the projects, you don't get protection against illegal searches—it just sort of works out that way. And if this makes any sense at all, it's not about skin color. This is a cultural kind of bias. White people who live the wrong way get caught in the net, too. And as the income gap gets bigger and bigger, more and more white people are being pushed behind the line.

The major precedent for the *Sanchez v. San Diego* suit was a Supreme Court case from the 1970s called *Wyman v. James.* In that one, a black single mother named Barbara James applied for and received welfare. After some time on public assistance, a caseworker called and asked to set up an appointment to see James in her home. James told the caseworker she was happy to meet on neutral territory, but that she didn't see any need to let the caseworker into the house. The caseworker disagreed and nixed her benefits. A lawsuit ensued, and it made it all the way to the Supreme Court in 1971, where the nation's top justices asked the question: Does the Fourth Amendment apply to people on welfare?

Justice Harry Blackmun, writing for the majority, explained that it didn't. The state, Blackmun wrote, "has appropriate and paramount interest and concern in seeing and assuring that the intended and proper objects of that tax-produced assistance are the ones who benefit from the aid it dispenses." He added that "surely it is not unreasonable . . . that the State have at its command a gentle means . . . of achieving that assurance."

Writing the dissent in *Wyman* was Justice William Douglas, ably playing the supporting-actor part of the concerned-but-habitually-ignored civil libertarian. (Most of the legal dramas resulting in lost rights over the years would feature the same mopey character.) Douglas argued that the *Wyman* ruling was nuts because not just poor black ladies from the Bronx, but almost everyone lives off the government teat to one degree or another:

> We are living in a society where one of the most important forms of property is government largesse which some call the "new property." . . . Defense contracts, highway contracts, and the other multifarious forms of contracts are another part. So are subsidies to air, rail, and other carriers. So are disbursements by government for scientific research. So are TV and radio licenses to use the air space which of course is part of the public domain. . . .
>
> In 1969 roughly 127 billion dollars were spent by the federal, state, and local governments on "social welfare." To farmers alone almost four billion dollars were paid. . . . Almost 129,000 farmers received $5,000 or more, their total benefits exceeding $1,450,000,000.

If we eliminate Fourth Amendment protection for everyone who receives public assistance, he implied, where does it end? Who wouldn't have to let a government worker into his house? Would all 129,000 farmers have to let government agents into their homes, to make sure the subsidies reached the right target?

"If you go by the logic in *Wyman,*" says Halpern, the San Diego lawyer, "anyone who claims a tax deduction could be searched."

But Douglas was overruled, of course, because the implicit intent of *Wyman*—not its explicit intent, but very much the implied meaning—didn't cover everyone, just black welfare moms like Barbara James. No one else had to trade the Bill of Rights for government aid. So the state got to keep its "gentle means" of checking to make sure tax dollars were reaching appropriate destinations.

Incidentally, the Court back then specifically noted that the "gentle means" was not made by "police or uniformed authority," and that the visiting agent was "not a sleuth but rather, we trust . . . a friend to one in need."

Thirty-five years later, in *Sanchez v. San Diego,* the visiting agent would be transformed into a law enforcement agent and professional sleuth, and the "friend in need" would be someone who roots around in underwear drawers with pencil ends. But the U.S. Ninth Circuit Court of Appeals, led by an internment camp survivor named A. Wallace Tashima, nonetheless decided P100 wasn't in any way unconstitutional. Tashima's bizarre reasoning was that the P100 visits were not searches under the Fourth Amendment—but even if they were searches, they were not unreasonable.

Why are they reasonable? Because, Tashima said, the public "has a strong interest in ensuring that aid provided from tax dollars reaches its proper and intended recipients."

So the standard is, anyone who receives aid from taxpayers forgoes his rights, because the state has a "strong interest" in rooting out fraud.

But of course not everyone who receives state aid forgoes his or her rights, not really. To whom does this legal principle apply?

Well, we know to whom, but we can't put it on paper. It's like pornography, you know it when you see it. As Americans, we're all beginning to develop a second sense about who gets to feel the business end of the criminal justice system, and when, and who doesn't, and why.

That second sense we all carry around in our minds is our true government. It's very different from the *Schoolhouse Rock!* official version, and different from the one we see celebrated every four years in our presidential campaign system. *Schoolhouse Rock!* teaches us that everyone is treated equally under the law, and that our government is one we've chosen in free elections, but at the same time we somehow know not to be surprised when that turns out not to be completely true. This has been hammered home to all of us in the recent years following the financial crash, when the dichotomy in the system has grown more and more visible, creeping higher and higher in our collective consciousness.

For instance, while the San Diego District Attorney's Office spent more than a decade sifting through thousands of dresser drawers and bringing felony cases all the way to court for frauds as small as four hundred dollars, executives in the same general area of Southern California, at companies like Countrywide and Long Beach Mortgage, were pioneering the brilliant mass fraud scheme that involved the sales of toxic mortgage-backed securities.

One of the favorite targets of that fraud scheme was government and the taxpayer. These companies, along with their bankers, loved more than anything to sell worthless mortgage bonds to Fannie Mae and Freddie Mac, the government-backed housing agencies.

Just one Southern Californian company, Countrywide, dumped as much as $26.6 billion on the taxpayer and the state when it sold overvalued bonds to Fannie and Freddie. Bank of America, its eventual parent company, sold another $6 billion to Fannie and Freddie. Fifteen other companies also targeted the federal government for hundreds of millions and billions more. The state of California's pension fund, CalPERS, was also the target of massive fraud schemes, as banks, mortgage lenders, and ratings agencies conspired to sell California workers billions more in worthless securities in exchange for their life savings.

By the time all these companies were finished first inflating and then crashing a huge global asset bubble based on overvalued mortgages, the world had lost trillions of dollars—one extremely conservative estimate by the IMF put the losses at $4 trillion. But despite having been warned about the possibility of widespread mortgage fraud by the FBI as early as 2004, financial cops in regulatory agencies like the SEC and the OCC didn't respond to the problem at all until well after the crash.

When they finally *did* respond, they did so by bringing civil suits against companies like Countrywide, JPMorgan Chase, Bank of America, Wachovia, TD Ameritrade, Goldman Sachs, Charles Schwab, and others.

In the twenty-one biggest federal settlements over mortgage fraud abuses—$300 million from State Street for lying to investors, $153 million from Chase in the Magnetar settlement, and so on—those companies and a few others paid a total of $26 billion in damages to the government. In every single one of those cases, the relevant companies were allowed to settle without admitting wrongdoing. Not a single individual was charged in any of those cases. Not a single individual had to pay so much as a dime of his own money in damages.

Not one home was searched. No banker ever had someone pick up his underwear by a pencil end and wave it in his face.

Twenty-six billion dollars of fraud: no felony cases. But when the stakes are in the hundreds of dollars, we kick in 26,000 doors a year, in just one county.

You can drive yourself crazy trying to figure out how this makes sense, financial or otherwise. But it does make sense. It's just not about money. It's about fucking with people. It's the logic of our new shadow government.

It turns out that we're too lazy to govern ourselves, so we've put society on bureaucratic autopilot—and autopilot turns out to be a steel trap for losers and a greased pipeline to money, power, and impunity for winners.

This goes far beyond the oft-quoted liberal cliché about how we now have "two Americas," one for the rich and one for the poor, with different sets of laws and different levels of punishment (or more to the point, nonpunishment) for each. The rich have always gotten breaks and the poor have always had to swim upstream. The new truth is infinitely darker and more twisted.

The new truth is a sci-fi movie, a dystopia. And in this sci-fi world the issues aren't justice and injustice, but biology and mortality. We have a giant, meat-grinding bureaucracy that literally alters the physical makeup of its citizens, systematically grinding down the losers into a smaller, meeker, lower race of animal while aggrandizing the winners, making them bigger than life, impervious, super-people.

Again, the poor have always faced the sharp end of the stick. And the rich have always fought ferociously to protect their privilege, not just in America but everywhere.

What's different now is that these quaint old inequities have become internalized in that "second government"—a vast system of increasingly unmanageable bureaucracies, spanning both the public and the private sectors. These inscrutable, irrational structures, crisscrossing back and forth between the worlds of debt and banking and law enforcement, are growing up organically around the pounding twin impulses that drive modern America: burning hatred of all losers and the poor, and breathless, abject worship of the rich, even the talentless and undeserving rich.

No one is managing these bureaucracies anymore. They are managing us. Just as corporations are brainless machines for making profits, this sweepingly complex system of public-private bureaucracies that constitutes our modern politics is just a giant, brainless machine for creating social inequity.

It mechanically, automatically keeps the poor poor, devours money from the middle class, and sends it upward. And because it's fueled by the irrepressibly rising vapor of our darkest hidden values, it attacks people without money, particularly nonwhite people, with a weirdly venomous kind of hatred, treating them like they're already guilty of something, which of course they are—namely, being that which we're all afraid of becoming.

In the Orwellian dystopia the original sin was thoughtcrime, but in our new corporate dystopia the secret inner crime is need, particularly financial need. People in America hide financial need like they hide sexual perversions.

Why? Because there's a direct correlation between need and rights. The more you need, the more you owe, the fewer rights you have.

Conversely, the less you need, the more you have, the more of a free citizen you get to be. On the extreme ends of this spectrum it is literally a crime to be poor, while a person with enough money literally cannot be prosecuted for certain kinds of crimes.

What keeps the poor poor and rushes the money upward is the complexity of the bureaucracy. If you're the wrong kind of person and you get caught up in the criminal justice system, or stuck in the welfare bureaucracy, or mired in debt, you can't get out without navigating a maze so complex and dispiriting and irrational that it can't possibly even be mapped. It's not brains that you need to get through it, but time, energy, strength. You have to stand on line after line, send letter after letter, make call after call.

And if you want to change even the smallest law, in your home state or in Washington, you need an army of thousands of lobbyists to get it done. And even in the rare case that you succeed, you then need to commit to ten years or more of furiously boring legal battles and inane bureaucratic rule-writing sessions and fend off tens or hundreds of thousands of pages of dissenting reports and comment letters and policy papers, all developed mechanically by an industry that responds not by human decision, but bureaucratic reflex.

On the other side of the coin, the secret to conquering the financial bureaucracy isn't savvy and business sense, or the ability to spot a good entrepreneurial idea. Instead, it's pure bureaucratic force, the ability to throw a hundred lawyers at every problem, to file a thousand motions and never get tired, to file ten thousand, a hundred thousand, a million lawsuits.

In other words, you need to *be* a bureaucracy in order to survive one. This is the overwhelming narrative of modern American economics, that the individual, particularly the individual without a lot of money, is inherently overmatched. He's a loser. And if he falls into any part of the machine, he goes straight to the bottom.

And then there's the most disturbing truth of all. People assume that a system that favors the rich likes rich *people*. This isn't true. Our bureaucracies respond to the money rich people have, and they bend to the legal might the rich can hire, but they don't give a damn about rich people. You can be rich and still fall into any one of a dozen financial/legal meat grinders, from an erroneously collapsed credit score to a robo-signed foreclosure to a stolen identity to a retirement account vaporized by institutional theft and fraud.

The system eats up rich people, too, because it's not concerned with protecting any individuals, even the rich ones. These bureaucracies accomplish just two things: they make small piles of money smaller and big piles of money bigger. It's a system that doesn't care whose hands end up holding the bag, or how long those hands get to hold the bag. It just relentlessly creates and punishes losers, who get to sit beneath an ever-narrowing group of winners, who may or may not stay on top for long.

What does get preserved, in all cases, is a small constellation of sprawling, interconnected financial companies, whose names and managements may change (Bear becomes Chase, Wachovia becomes Wells Fargo, etc.), but whose entrenched influence remains the same. In other words, this is a machine that loves and protects money but somehow hates all people.

Of course, this mechanism hates some people more than others. In particular, it hates black people. Again, this is not so much about skin color as it is about culture. There's a cultural spectrum these bureaucracies are attuned to that roughly ranges from black poverty to white wealth. Where you are on that spectrum determines how much of a citizen you get to be.

Things that are jailable crimes on one end of that spectrum become speeding tickets on the other. We find white people on the jail end and black people on the speeding ticket end, but for the most part . . . well, for the most part, you know what I mean. That winking understanding we all share about who gets the book thrown at him and who doesn't, that's where American racism has gone: unspoken and hidden, but bureaucratized and automated, and therefore more powerful than ever.

And nowhere do we see the outlines of that thing more clearly than in the prosecution of fraud. We generally define fraud as lying to trick someone out of money. At the top end of American society, we've found out in recent years that lying for profit is actually considered a virtue, and a certain sector of the population fiercely defends its right to earn a living that way.

When a former Goldman Sachs executive named Greg Smith publicly resigned in the pages of *The New York Times,* claiming that his company routinely screwed its own clients (derided within the firm as "muppets") and misled them into buying crappy deals, Smith was blasted by the financial community for being a "Kumbaya"-singing weenie who felt sorry for people who didn't deserve anyone's pity—people too stupid not to know when they're being screwed.

John Mack, the former head of Morgan Stanley, blasted the *Times* for even printing the Smith letter, saying, "Last time I checked, we were in business to be profitable." Mack, incidentally, had once been involved in an insider trading case—for a multimillion-dollar commission, he appeared to have tipped off a hedge fund trader that GE was acquiring a company called Heller Financial, allowing the hedge fund to buy Heller stock before the merger and thus steal from GE shareholders, who made significantly less than they would have without the tip. But Mack was never charged; high-ranking officials at the SEC, citing his "powerful political connections," intervened to prevent his investigation.

Mack in other words was the perfect symbol of the idea, generally accepted on Wall Street, that lying and cheating to make money is acceptable. The code word for this concept is "sophistication," meaning that it's okay to screw certain kinds of investors because, after all, anyone doing business with Goldman Sachs should be "sophisticated" enough to look out for that sort of thing.

When Goldman executive Fabrice Tourre testified before the Senate in the wake of the notorious Abacus scandal, he used the term "sophisticated" four times. In two letters to the SEC about the same case, in which Goldman helped a hedge fund swindler named John Paulson dump more than a billion dollars of worthless mortgage-based assets on a pair of European banks, Goldman's lawyers used the word a hilarious twenty-three times.

But poor people don't get to use the sophistication defense, and the definition of fraud in their corner of the world is vastly different than the one on Wall Street. A person on public assistance essentially has to make lengthy regular reports about his situation in life and include in those reports a wealth of personal information. He then spends his entire life being scanned by bankers, social workers, agents of the district attorney's office, even neighbors and traffic cops, for any evidence of inconsistency in his statements.

The entire world becomes a legal minefield. If you're poor and on public assistance, just about anything you do that defines you as a living human being can turn into the basis of a fraud case. Getting laid can be fraud. Getting sick can be fraud. Putting your kids in day care can be fraud. Not "sounding poor" can be fraud.

Well, so what? If you don't want to be charged with fraud, just don't lie, then. Right?

That would be true if our legal system made any sense. But our legal system does not make sense. Our legal system is insane.

When she was sixteen, just before she was about to deliver her first baby, Markisha Powell got high on meth. The baby's father, a sailor in the navy, was away at sea. She was freaking out, she was wild, and she was stupid. Getting high just before labor so upset her family and friends that she ended up facing a kind of all-out intervention. The father came home to San Diego from sea and there was a court proceeding even before the baby was born.

"I lost custody of the baby," she says now. "They let me hold him after he was born, then they took him away."

Markisha is thirty-two years old now, very thin, with her hair kept in an elaborate African-style cut, with tight braids wrapping around her head in concentric circles, from low on her forehead all the way up into a topknot. She has a pretty face, but she's been homeless and you can see the years. When I first met her she was wearing a long-sleeved black shirt on a very warm day, and she kept her hands all the way inside the sleeves, fidgeting and pushing the sleeves out straight with her thumbs from time to time as she talked.

There's no way to explain the lunacy of the criminal justice system/welfare state—call it the "poverty bureaucracy" for short—unless you see it from the point of view of the people in the system. I spent a year following a few people in different parts of the country and watched as they tried to receive their benefits on the one hand and avoid being prosecuted for fraud on the other. Both activities turn out to be essentially full-time jobs.

A quick aside about the point of this exercise. This was never about welfare. You can have almost any opinion about welfare, you can be bitterly opposed to its very existence, and you could and perhaps should still find what goes on with welfare fraud prosecution in America crazy, even shocking.

Because the issue here isn't the efficacy of the welfare state. This is about fairness. Do we treat people the same way everywhere? How does a poor person end up getting arrested for fraud, and does the state have the same playbook for rich people?

The obvious answer is no, but you have to see the difference up close, at a day-to-day level, to really grasp the breadth of the gap. When you see, up close, where the awesome power of the American criminal justice space station is directed, you will begin scratching your head, no matter what you think of people on welfare.

Back to Markisha: after the disaster of losing that first child, she went right out and did the same thing over and over again, having three more children with three more fathers and losing custody of them all because she was getting high, selling drugs, and perhaps worse. Then she told a story about something that happened to her in 2003.

She'd just met the father of her youngest son, and the way she tells it is that he pulled up in his red Honda as she was "walking to her mother's house" on the street. He asked if she wanted a ride, she says now, and she said yes, because, "I didn't want to walk, you know?"

So she hopped in the car with this forty-something man, an engineer named Eric who makes high-end fish tanks, and he gave the twenty-year-old Markisha the proverbial ride to her proverbial mother's house. One part of this story is certainly true, however: during all those years when Markisha was dealing and getting high, the one connection she kept with anything like family life was with her mother. She visited her mother constantly, even during her wildest periods. And so in 2003, just after Markisha had met this man, whom her mother actually liked, her mother laid down the law.

"She told me that I had to get clean, had to get off the streets, had to stop hanging out with the wrong people," Markisha says.

So she did. She entered a detox clinic called the House of Metamorphosis in the spring of 2003. She was in there with her aunt, her father's sister, who also had a problem. The first two weeks she was in the program were the longest she'd ever gone without being in touch with her mother, who grew frantic. Finally Markisha called after two weeks and told her mother where she was. A few days later Mom showed up at the clinic and told Markisha that she was glad she was getting clean, that she'd be back the following Saturday.

"She told me she'd bring me some things," Markisha says now. "So I waited."

But next Saturday came and went. The following morning, Markisha got a call from the head of the program, who was in an office across the street from the dorm. Reflexively, Markisha assumed she was in trouble or being tossed from the clinic. "I thought I'd done something wrong," she says. "I thought they were mad."

But then she got over there and the program chief, a young white woman, was sitting there with Markisha's aunt. They told Markisha that her mother had died, from a burst blood vessel in her leg.

"I about destroyed the office," she says now. "I was tearing stuff off the walls. . . . I couldn't stop crying."

When she finally got out of the program, she found herself in charge of her five younger siblings, with one as young as seven years old. Her mother's husband, her stepfather, was on dialysis and in no shape to take care of anyone. Markisha's boyfriend Eric, the forty-year-old with the Honda, set her up in an apartment, and the two of them lived together for a while with all Markisha's brothers and sisters. During this time Markisha was clean and even got a square job, working as a receptionist in a time-share real estate office.

In 2005 Markisha and Eric had another baby. She was having problems taking care of some of her older siblings, and even convinced some of her uncles and aunts to take on the older teenagers, but aside from that, life was more or less bearable. Then one day, when her new baby son was nine months old, she got a call at work from the state-run day care clinic that was taking care of him. Eric, they told her, had not come to pick him up.

"They start telling me they're going to call CPS on me if nobody comes," Markisha says. "Like they're going to take the baby away. Now, I didn't have the car, the boy's father had the car. I called him and got no answer. So I asked my bosses if I could leave early; they let me, and I took the bus and went and got him."

Markisha went home to the apartment. She liked that apartment. With the money she'd earned from the job, she'd recently bought a new bed and some other furniture. She turned the key, went inside, and on that new bed, she found Eric, naked, with another woman, also naked.

Markisha recounts matter-of-factly: "I threw the girl out on the street naked. Then I went back inside and started beating his ass up."

In stories like this you'd usually hear someone say "I tossed her out on the street," and in reality that would mean the woman is rudely asked to leave, or maybe has a door slammed in her face. But Markisha *literally* tosses this girl out on the street naked. When I ask how she managed it, she shrugs.

"I just drug her out by her legs, then I closed the door. Then I went back upstairs and dealt with Captain Save-a-Bitch, who was trying to get her her things. I wasn't about to give her her clothes back. And I was like, 'Dang, you couldn't even pick up your own son?'"

Markisha "beat his ass" for a good long while and then grabbed her son and walked outside in a daze. She was moving out, but she didn't know where to yet. She sat down on a stoop with her boy and zoned out. Within minutes, police came. They arrested her and hit her with a domestic violence charge. And that was how she lost custody of her fifth child.

After that incident, she ended up back on the streets and back on meth. She was homeless for four months in the spring and summer of 2011, and it would take me a while to find out where exactly she was during that time (more on that later). Finally, in the summer of 2011 she got arrested again. As part of her court settlement, she had to go into a program. And she got clean.

When she came out of detox, she and her youngest son's father made up, although they didn't get back together. "We sort of ping-ponged it around," she says. Her main goal was to get her youngest son back. Markisha doesn't talk about her other children much; the world pretty much begins and ends with her youngest. Getting him back became the entire focus of her life—and she has a hard time focusing.

Anyway, the boy's father made her a deal: if you can get your own home, and keep it, I'll let you have your son.

It was at that moment that Markisha decided to apply for Cal-WORKs. She'd rented a room in an apartment she shared with a barber in her neighborhood, and she needed some help paying for it. CalWORKs meant three hundred dollars a month, plus food stamps. So she went to the local welfare office—a "Family Resource Center," known as an FRC—and walked inside. She was barely sober, emotionally a wreck, literally penniless, and her entire ambition in life was to keep and maintain a room and a half in a run-down section of west San Diego without having to sell her body to pay the rent.

This is the kind of person at whom the weight of the state's financial fraud prosecution apparatus tends to be trained in America. Markisha entered the financial fraud patrol zone when she walked through those doors at the FRC. For three hundred dollars a month, she was about to become more heavily scrutinized by the state than any twelve Wall Street bankers put together.

The amounts of money spent in these kinds of welfare programs are very small, but the levels of political capital involved are mountainous. You can always score political points banging on black welfare moms on meth. And the bureaucracy she was about to enter reflects that intense, bitterly contemptuous interest. Markisha was walking into a vast, machinelike system that is not only more or less designed to produce felony fraud convictions, but is also amazingly effective at a second goal—letting her know exactly what voters out there think of her.

On the day she goes to sign up for CalWORKs, Markisha knows to show up early. Friends she knew who'd been in the system had warned her: get there early. Get there way before the doors open. You'll see why when you get there, they told her.

In the neighborhoods people talk. Some welfare offices are more notorious than others. In San Diego I heard over and over again that the Lemon Grove office was the best. Sometimes, people say, you can see a counselor at Lemon Grove in less than an hour—you might not even see people yelling and screaming. The Market Street office, on the other hand, has a bad rep. Same with the Seventy-Third Street office. The problem is, you can't choose which office to go to. It depends on your address. And Markisha's address puts her in the Seventy-Third Street group.

On the morning of October 15, 2011, she shows up at the Seventy-Third Street office at 8:30 a.m. It's a giant hall with linoleum floors and plastic chairs—exactly what you'd expect, like a DMV, only even more depressing. There's already a huge line of people.

"People were standing up against the walls, there was people everywhere, all over, it was crazy," she says. The drill is, you show up, take a number, and wait—and wait. Markisha takes her number and sits down.

An hour passes, two hours. She has no idea when anyone is going to see her, and all the people in the packed room are in the same boat.

Mothers with children are in the office, and by late morning the children are starting to get antsy because they haven't eaten, but you can't leave the place or you lose your spot in line. A chill goes through the room in the middle of the day when a woman steps outside the building to get a smoke and returns to find that her number has been called. She has to leave and come back another day.

More hours pass. Markisha is squirming in her seat. By the late afternoon the crowd, which not only hasn't subsided over the course of the day but has just gotten bigger, is turning hostile. At around three in the afternoon there's a screaming match somewhere in the recesses of the office. Markisha can hear a man yelling at a welfare worker because a glitch in the system has cost him his benefits; something about a wrong address, which they're telling him they can't fix. He storms out of the office to oohs and aahs. By then the place is a zoo. "The kids is running around, because they hungry," she says. "They're running around, snatching stuff off the walls, drinking water, screaming."

The scene gets so intense, Markisha ends up pulling out her cell phone and taking a video panorama of the chaos. Nobody even blinks when they see her standing up filming the nightmare. You see all kinds of stuff in here: Who cares about some girl filming something?

More hours pass. It's after five now. A young Latin man just ahead of Markisha goes in and just as quickly is dragged out by security when he explodes at a worker after finding out he can't get his food stamp card—Markisha doesn't know why. "I've been here since eight o'clock in the morning and I'm still here after five o'clock!" he shouts. "I'm just coming for my EBT card! I need my EBT card!"

Security drags him past Markisha, chucks him out the door. "I was like, dang," she says. "I didn't know what to think." Finally, at 5:30, after nine hours, Markisha is shown into an office where a bored-looking older black woman stares blankly at her from behind a mass of papers.

"Let me tell you something right away, honey," the woman says. "We got two whole rooms of papers right behind us here. Two rooms of applications to go through. So it's going to be forty-five days before you get your benefits."

By law, forty-five days is the maximum period of time the state can take before processing benefits. Markisha needs the money yesterday, but whatever; she knows enough not to say anything. She answers the woman's questions. How many people live in your household? What's your income? How come you can't get a job?

Then the whopper. "How much," the woman asks, "is your baby daddy giving you a month?"

"My what?" Markisha says.

"Your baby daddy," the woman repeats. "He giving you money or not?"

Markisha answers: he is not. By the time the woman finishes with her, Markisha is in a panic, but she's been approved for benefits. Go home, they tell her, and wait for someone from the DA's office to search your home.

Wait when?

Just wait, they tell her.

Trying to get on welfare is like trying to get Rolling Stones tickets in the 1970s—you have to camp out in front of the entrance long before the ticket window opens. You go there, you take a number, then you sit all day long while people scream and yell all around you. If you have kids, you have to bring their lunches and you have to be careful about when you take them to the bathroom, because you might miss your call. "It's worst in the afternoon," says Anna

Alvarez, a twenty-one-year-old with a newborn baby who applied for benefits with her husband, Diego. "The kids get hungry and they start screaming and acting out."

Some people I interviewed went to the FRC and went through this all-day-in-a-DMV-from-hell process three and four times before they even got their initial meeting.

But the kicker is, if you get all the way through the process, and actually get your meeting, and you get approved, they then tell you to go home and sit tight for your P100 search. And they don't tell you when that will be, except to say that it's generally within a week and a half. You then have to be at home at all times until they show up—it's like sitting shivah, except you have to do it for more than a week.

"If the investigator shows up and no one's there," says Halpern, "they shove a card under your door that says, 'We could not verify your eligibility,' and you don't get your benefits."

The couple Diego and Anna handled their vigil in shifts, with one staying at home at all times, and the other, usually Diego, going out to work (he works at a Little Caesars) or to buy groceries. In their case, the investigator showed up six days later. In Markisha's case, it was only a few days, but she had a problem: she was attending a court-ordered recovery program at eleven a.m. every Wednesday. It was literally illegal for her to miss the class; she could face charges. She explained this to the people at the FRC, but they weren't interested. Right on cue, the investigator then showed up at 10:30 a.m. on that following Wednesday. He's an older white guy, about fifty years old. He knocks, steps just barely inside the apartment, and takes a quick look around.

"You sure you don't live here with the baby's father?" he says.

Eric had just come by to take their son to school. The boy wasn't home. The investigator doesn't like this.

"I don't think you're really living here with your son," he says.

Again, this is a constant feature of the welfare application process. Literally every single person I interviewed in San Diego at some point had a caseworker or someone from the DA's office accuse them of lying within minutes. One woman named Selena, a quiet twenty-eight-year-old from Mexico who cleans houses and lives with her elderly mother, met the investigator by chance, coming home from work cleaning apartments just as he was leaving— Selena's mother had let him in. The investigator asked Selena where she had been.

Cleaning houses, she said.

Yeah? the investigator asked. How much did you make?

Selena opened her wallet and showed him: $120. That money was for four apartments, she tried to explain, but he wouldn't hear it. The investigator chirped that the going rate for an apartment cleaning was sixty bucks. Apparently he was speaking from experience haggling with maids.

"You're lying to me about that money," he said. "You didn't earn that much cleaning apartments."

Selena is meek, quiet, a little stout, and looks very much like someone who cleans houses for a living. The investigator, within minutes of meeting her, was accusing her of . . . what? Hooking? Selling crack?

Back to Markisha's home search: the investigator didn't like the absence of the child, despite the fact that it was 10:30 a.m. on a school day. She was sharing the apartment with another tenant, a local barber, but the investigator didn't want to see his room. In fact, he didn't want to see Markisha's room, which had two beds in it, one for her and one for her son. He just stood in the doorway, looking around.

"I asked him if he wanted to see my room," Markisha says. "But he said no. He just stood there."

After a few minutes, the investigator jotted a few notes down, clicked his pen, and turned to walk out the door. "Okay," he said. "That's my investigation."

Just like they don't tell you when they're coming, they don't tell you what their investigatory conclusions are. Markisha had to wait. A few weeks later she found out she was rejected—because the investigator didn't believe she was living with her son.

Now she's appealing the decision. In the meantime, she lost her apartment and is living with her aunt. Technically speaking, however, she's temporarily in a safer place than applicants who immediately pass the search process. She dodged a bullet in the sense that the state decided she was lying before she started getting her checks. Once you start actually collecting benefits, you get put on the clock for a fraud case.

The couple Diego and Anna, for instance, were doing everything right. They are both bright, fit young kids; Anna is petite and cherubic, and Diego is on the shorter side but clean-cut, engaging, and good-looking. They met at the gym in the first months of 2011 and quickly fell in love. In the summer, they discovered Anna was pregnant, but they were not panicking then. Both were working, at the only sorts of jobs really available to young people in America— Anna at a Carl's Jr., and Diego at a Panda Express. Diego actually had gotten a raise at Panda Express and was doing well.

"I was making pretty decent money there," he says. "We were doing okay." And though Anna had to ride on the bus for two hours in each direction to go to her job at Carl's Jr., she was managing.

"We were able to pay our rent," she says.

But then Panda Express downsized and Diego lost his job. And Anna, growing more and more visibly pregnant, was not going to be able to keep working the night shift at Carl's Jr., with two-hour bus rides each way. So late in 2011, they made a fateful decision, to go on benefits, to help them at the very least through the birth of the baby.

Diego had immigration status because his mother had been the victim of extensive domestic violence. The Violence Against Women Act of 1994, signed into law by Bill Clinton, gave temporary immigration status to the victims of domestic violence, for the simple reason that in many immigrant households, abusive husbands prevent their wives and children from going through the naturalization process as a way of keeping power over them. (Selena, the housecleaner, fell into that category.) So when the husband is removed from the home, his wife and children are given temporary status and immediately qualify for benefits.

Diego had had his U visa since 2006 and had qualified to receive his own benefits as an adult for two years, but he was only now applying, and he was only applying for food stamps. Anna, meanwhile, applied for the full CalWORKs package, which included cash aid and food stamps. They went into the Market Street FRC in December 2011, and initially everything seemed fine. "The woman was really nice," Anna says. "We had no problems at all. She told us we qualified."

You have to be so poor as to have nothing at all to qualify for welfare. In California, to qualify for benefits, you can't have more than $2,000 in assets to your name. If you have a car, the car can't be worth more than $3,000. The actual equation for income level in California is complicated, but put it this way: a hypothetical family of three, like Diego and Anna would soon be, cannot have a gross income of more than $714 a month and still qualify for CalWORKs. The math is too involved to list here, but if you're getting benefits, you have to know those formulas like the back of your hand.

Why? Because when you apply for CalWORKs, they hand you a very involved application form, and this form becomes the legal bible by which you must live, on pain of prosecution. The CalWORKs cover sheet/application comes with a snappy little Orwellian logo at the top of the first page, a cutesy drawing of a small pile of dollar bills surrounded by the words:

WORK PAYS
In so many ways

The form goes on to give a summary of the benefits process (you receive a more detailed package of all the rules separately) and contains a lengthy passage about the consequences of lying to the state. You are reminded that you must attest to the veracity of everything you write and that you can be jailed for up to three years for lying about getting cash aid and up to twenty years for lying about food stamps (we will find, as we look at the frauds committed at banks and other such companies, that the penalties for fraud seem to increase as the amounts lost get smaller).

You're also told, ominously, that if there is an overpayment, "you will have to pay it back even if the County made an error."

You're then asked to answer nineteen questions, which include things like "How much income does everyone, including children, get or will get this month?" (You find out at another part of the form that the words "You, anyone, everyone" in welfare applications *all* mean "any and all persons who live in your home.") You're asked if "your food will run out in three days"; you're asked if you have an eviction notice "or notice to pay or quit."

You fill out this form, and then at the bottom you sign your name to the following statement:

> I declare under penalty of perjury under the laws of the
> United States of America and the State of California that
> the information I have given on this form is true, correct,
> and complete.

And you keep signing those forms for as long as you have benefits. If you're on any kind of public assistance, you have to fill out, every quarter, a form called a QR 7, or "Eligibility/Status Report." In that form you have to attest to all the basic facts of your life—whom you live with, whether you have a car, where you work and how much you earn, and so on. And if any of that information doesn't jibe with what the state knows or thinks it knows, you get started down the road to a fraud case.

In any case, Anna and Diego signed the form, went home, waited and waited for the P100 search ("A drag because you can't go out and look for a job," says Diego), made it through that, and appeared from there to be fine, receiving benefits at the end of the month, as expected.

The sum total of the benefits was $246 in cash for Anna, plus food stamps for both of them. As the New Year rolled around, they began to think they were going to be okay. Diego got another job at another fast food place, this time at Little Caesars ("No delivering—I'm making pizzas," he says cheerfully), and they were already thinking about the time when they might be able to get off the benefits.

Then they got a letter in the mail.

Welfare applicants all talk in hushed tones about the dread of the mail system. Everyone in the California system has a monster collection of ominous little green forms, and to the last they all tell stories about getting a letter with good news one day that is contradicted by a new letter the next day accusing them of fraud.

This is what happened to Diego and Anna. Almost immediately after receiving their first month's benefits, Anna got a letter saying that upon further review, the state had ruled that Diego had not been eligible to receive benefits. Therefore, the notice said, Anna—not Diego, but Anna—now owed the state $148 to compensate for the month of food stamps he had "improperly" received.

The state was wrong—Diego did qualify for the food stamps—but that didn't matter. Recouping "erroneous" overpayments to welfare recipients has become a craze for states all over the country. In 2010 Barack Obama's Department of Agriculture lifted a ten-year ban on collecting food stamp overpayments, and states all over the country went hog wild trying to recover lost monies.

For instance, in 2011, the state of Ohio—the same state that lost tens of millions in the early 2000s when its pension fund bought severely overpriced mortgage-backed securities from a Lehman Brothers banker named John Kasich, who would later become governor—tried to recoup some of its losses by sending out 22,000 notices to Ohioans seeking "overpayments" in either welfare or food stamps.

Many if not most of these "overpayments" were actually the state's own errors, but they went as far back as 1986 anyway, seeking checks as small as $78. A sixty-four-year-old retired construction worker named Dave Jenkinson got a notice asking him to repay $248 for cash assistance he got in the 1980s; if he didn't pay, it would be with-held from his paycheck.

"They blame me like it's my fault," says Jenkinson, who doesn't even remember getting cash aid.

This, roughly, is the situation Anna and Diego found themselves in. They were told to pony up the cash or else the money would be withheld from their paychecks. More notices piled up that month. One, curiously, informed them that according to their calculations, Diego had earned more than seven hundred dollars in January.

Diego and Anna were flabbergasted. Diego had gotten just one paycheck from Little Caesars in January, and it was for only two days' work. "I made thirty-six dollars," he laughs now.

In late January they went into the FRC to plead their case, one of ten different trips they would make to the office between December 2011 and March 2012. In the course of that meeting a bizarre inci-dent took place. Diego saw that the caseworker had his photo ID on file; he asked for a copy of that document. The caseworker exploded.

"He got up and threw a pair of scissors down on the desk," says Anna. "We had no idea what was going on."

"He's like, 'How do I know that's even you?'" says Diego. "Then he stormed out."

Not surprisingly, nothing at that meeting got resolved. Oh, well; they at least still had Anna's benefits. The couple dug in and tried to enjoy the last month before their first child was born. Meanwhile the notices kept coming in the mail, most still harping about that food stamp money. By March there would be more than twenty of them.

Then, two weeks before their first son, Jonah, was born, they got a bombshell in the mail. "I got a new notice," says Anna. "It said I had received an overpayment. They said I had received five hun-dred sixteen dollars in cash aid. But I'd actually only received two hundred forty-six dollars. I had the stubs to prove it and every-thing."

As a result of this "overpayment," Anna was now permanently denied benefits. Both young people were pushed off the rolls because of errors made by the state. The total amount of "overpayment" was now perilously close to the four-hundred-dollar number that is generally considered the minimum threshold for the state to press a fraud case. As it was, the Alvarezes were going to be out at least that much money in taxes, which would be taken out of any future paychecks earned by Diego or (if and when she goes back to Carl's Jr. or some other, closer workplace) Anna.

But according to the state, they'd also committed fraud at least three times: when Diego received benefits without qualifying for them, when Diego "lied" about his January income, and when Anna overcollected in cash aid without paying the money back.

The young couple are now in a permanent state of dread, never knowing when they might be dragged into another mess or charged with a crime. "I think about it a lot," says Anna. "It's on my mind all the time." In addition to having an uphill climb just to keep food on the table every month, she and her husband are in a zone where one wrong number, one slip of the tongue, one computer error, can put you in legal jeopardy forever. "It's literally dangerous to be poor," says Halpern.

The couple's only shot to fix things is to get a volunteer lawyer to help them sort it all out before it turns into a criminal case. And you have to sort it out now, because once prosecutors file in cases like this, it's over.

"Welfare recipients are so unsympathetic that public defenders don't even bother trying to fight the cases," says Hilda Chan, a young lawyer who works with the poor in San Diego.

I found this out myself when I contacted the public defender's office in one California county (not San Diego) and asked to speak to an attorney who handles welfare fraud cases. I was initially told there was no such person. When I countered that there had to be someone, given that I'd just been told by that county's district attorney's office that they processed thirty felony fraud cases a month, I was put on hold. When the receptionist came back, I was told that "we do of course handle welfare fraud cases, but that attorney is not in at the moment."

While the country's best and highest-paying legal jobs are the province of superstar corporate defense firms like Davis Polk and WilmerHale that routinely handle financial fraud cases—if you want to find a lawyer who's defended a bank against an SEC fraud charge, you won't have to go very far—it's very difficult to find a lawyer, any lawyer, who has actually put up a defense in a welfare fraud case. They beg off them, find excuses to avoid them, and if they do get stuck with them, they plead them out. "Public defenders don't want to take these cases," says Kaaryn Gustafson, a professor at the University of Connecticut.

Meanwhile, one of the curious, and curiously stupid, features of the way welfare is administered in many states is that no single caseworker stays with any applicant's case; each time the recipient interacts with the state, he deals with a new person. And each new person who looks at the file may interpret the facts differently. Thus Diego may qualify in the first caseworker's eyes, but not in the second. A person can be in the CalWORKs program for years and never get to know any caseworker.

That virtually guarantees a few things. One is that no sympathetic relationship ever develops between client and caseworker, which politically is probably considered a good thing.

Two is that there's an explosion of errors that are infinitely more difficult and more expensive to sort out than they would be if someone with personal knowledge of the case was involved from the jump. Now there's an endless parade of Annas and Diegos and Markishas filing formal appeals with the state, explaining their whole life stories from the start in each meeting, instead of just calling a caseworker on the phone, reminding them of a fact or two, and having them change a number on a screen.

The system therefore clearly doesn't really work for the state, either. It's like opening a hospital where no doctor could ever see the same patient twice—the bureaucratic version of *Memento*, where the characters have to go back in time to re-create a whole universe of facts from the beginning in each new scene.

Lastly, minus the possibility for human interaction (or the satisfaction of seeing a client get back on his feet), the welfare casework-er's job inevitably becomes a blistering hell of constant, irrational paperwork and seemingly inane requests from needy people. It's no wonder that so many of them throw scissors and explode at their clients. You would, too, if that was your life every day.

In fact, the only creative component to the caseworker's job in the current system is the investigative angle, which is not an acci-dent. Since the great welfare reforms of the mid-1990s, when Bill Clinton broke up the traditional welfare state and introduced re-forms like workfare and the end to permanent cash aid, the entire welfare apparatus has gone through a transformation, wherein thousands of people who were caseworkers previously became fraud investigators under the new system. "Sometimes, they even kept the same offices," says Gustafson. "They would take a welfare caseworker, retrain him or her to be a fraud investigator, and put him or her back in the same desk."

In many places (and San Diego is one such place), the welfare caseworkers and fraud investigators working for the DA's office ac-tually work out of the same building, wing, or office. "San Diego has satellite DA's offices in the welfare offices," says Gustafson. "People come in to talk to a caseworker, they have no idea they're talking to a fraud investigator."

To give an example of how many welfare workers have migrated to law enforcement in the post-Clinton era: in 2002, in just one Cal-ifornia county (Santa Clara), the Board of Supervisors reassigned thirty-seven welfare caseworkers to new jobs as investigators. There are so many welfare fraud investigators now, they're actually union-izing and bargaining collectively. They even have their own lobbyist organizations; in California, for instance, we now have the Califor-nia Welfare Fraud Investigators Association, and similar organiza-tions now exist in Nevada, New York, Ohio, Colorado, and numerous other states.

These associations have effectively lobbied for increased welfare fraud prosecution and investigation and have helped create a new cottage industry within government. Some states have actually increased funding for fraud investigation because the programs are paid for by federal funds they would lose if they weren't spent—in other words, rather than lose funding because of reduced welfare rolls, states simply increase the amount of staff for welfare fraud investigation.

This results in mountains of fraud cases. At the end of 2007, for instance, there were more than 52,000 welfare fraud investigations pending in the state of California alone. That number is actually lower than it was in the late Clinton years, when the state of California paid counties a cash incentive to make welfare fraud cases— they were given 25 percent of any cash recovered. Between 2001 and 2007, the number of cases that actually went to court dropped by about half.

But the caseload is still huge. California counties like San Diego, Alameda, Riverside, Bayview, and others all file upward of forty or fifty cases a month, and in some cases as many as a hundred cases a month. These cases are often felony fraud cases, and DAs are hot for them because (a) they never, ever lose them and (b) it boosts their records. Fans of *The Wire* will connect to this dynamic: nothing quite jukes the stats like forty unopposed felony convictions a month. "DAs love these cases," says Gustafson. "It raises their profiles before elections."

So how does a numerical glitch like any of the ones in Diego and Anna's case turn into a criminal charge? It happens in dozens of ways. A caseworker at an FRC sees an applicant leaving in a nice car, a P100 investigator sees those Victoria's Secret panties, or, very often, a neighbor calls in with a tip, sometimes for a cash reward. Beyond that, the state has computers scanning countless different databases—phone and utility bills, school registration, birth certificates, leases, voter registration, the DMV, tax data, unemployment compensation, and on and on—that can uncover discrepancies. The recipient is then sent a notice and asked to come in to speak to a fraud investigator.

In some parts of California, welfare recipients when they first walk into that initial meeting are asked to sign what is called a disqualification consent agreement. The form reads as follows:

> (1) [T]he accused understands the consequences of the signed consent agreement; (2) consenting to the disqualification will result in a reduction in benefits for the disqualification period; (3) the actual disqualification penalty to be imposed; and (4) any remaining members of the [family] may be held liable for any overpayments that the accused has not already repaid.

Many people who sign this form do so thinking that they will simply be asked to pay money back, and they have no idea that it could be used as the basis of a criminal prosecution. They walk into these offices and not only sign away their benefits, they talk themselves right into jail.

And that's the last thing that people need to understand about these cases: people really go to real jail behind this madness. It happens casually and effortlessly. And quickly. If you follow white-collar fraud cases like the federal government's halfhearted investigation of Goldman Sachs executive Fabrice Tourre, accused of helping a hedge fund billionaire named John Paulson defraud a pair of European banks out of over a billion dollars, you see that these cases move at the speed of a molasses spill. Motions and countermotions drag cases out for years and years.

While writing this book, I covered a trial, *USA v. Carollo, Goldberg and Grimm*, that involved the rigging of municipal bond auctions by a trio of GE Capital executives. The government had the crimes of all the defendants on tape (the companies taped themselves), and none of the defendants had anything like a credible defense for crimes that collectively cost states many millions of dollars. Yet not one of the accused saw the inside of a jail cell for nearly fifteen years (the offenses dated back as far as 1999), and even after all three were convicted and handed down multiyear sentences, they were eventually freed by a judge who essentially punished prosecu-tors for missing the statute of limitations for filing charges.

High-finance fraud cases are drawn out for dozens of reasons, including the obfuscatory efforts of superior defense lawyers and the overwhelming complexity of the crimes.

But welfare fraud? These cases can be generated in the blink of an eye, often because a family member or a neighbor simply decided to pick up the telephone. "No one can snitch you off like your ex or your ex's girlfriend or your neighbor or your landlord," says one former California district attorney whose county in the late 1990s processed more than a hundred fraud cases a month.

Gustafson, the professor, recalls interviewing a single father named Jerome for a study she was doing on how well welfare re-cipients understand the rules. Jerome was raising his toddler son by himself. Why? Because back when he was living with the child's mother and her sister, the sister didn't like him and called the wel-fare office to snitch him out, hoping that authorities would kick him out of the house. But the consequence of that decision was that the authorities busted not Jerome, but the mother, for not registering Jerome as a resident in the home. The mother ended up doing a *year* in jail. Jerome and his son now rent out a room in a converted ga-rage.

The ad in the Riverside, California, *Press-Enterprise* is of the big banner variety, nicely placed in the Sunday edition—at four col-umns square, it's a nice size, too, costing a thousand bucks to pub-lish. The message is simple: the government of Riverside County, California—a politically conservative, mostly affluent region east of Los Angeles that extends to the Arizona border and includes the resort town of Palm Springs—is looking for whistle-blowers to aid the state in making fraud cases.

What kinds of fraud cases? Big cases? Well, not exactly. The ad reads:

$ I OO REWARD OFFERED BY

RIVERSIDE COUNTY DEPT. OF PUBLIC SOCIAL SERVICES

Dockets of the Riverside County Court System show the following persons were convicted of welfare fraud on the dates specified:

And then the ad goes on to list the names and conviction dates of six persons convicted of improperly receiving benefits. The government of Riverside County, California, essentially puts the heads of six welfare cheats on pikes and plants them in the public square once a month, to send a message to the community. "Yeah, shaming is definitely part of the motivation," sighs Philip Robb, a former prosecutor from neighboring San Bernardino County, now engaged in a (to date unsuccessful) campaign against the ads.

Month after month, Riverside County runs the same ad and picks six new names each month to advertise. Like welfare recipients in general, the guilty are overwhelmingly female, and usually nonwhite. "They don't do this to rapists or murderers," says Robb. "Not even to pedophiles. It's incredible."

No, the only offenders the local burghers will spend money to embarrass publicly are young, single, nonwhite mothers guilty of the crime of improperly receiving benefits. And as we've seen, it's a stretch to assume that they're all really guilty. The one thing we do know is that the people on this list every month are all flat broke and incapable of hiring a decent lawyer—and who knows, the fancy folk in Palm Springs might have an interest in shaming these people for that crime, as well.

All of this goes back to Bill Clinton. It's not a coincidence that radical welfare reform took place on the same watch that also saw a radical deregulation of the financial services industry. Clinton was a man born with a keen nose for two things: women with low self-esteem and political opportunity. When he was in the middle of a tough primary fight in 1992 and came out with a speech promising to "end welfare as we know it," he could immediately smell the political possibilities, and it wasn't long before this was a major plank in his convention speech (and soon in his first State of the Union address).

Clinton understood that putting the Democrats back in the business of banging on black dependency would allow his party to re-seize the political middle that Democrats had lost when Lyndon Johnson threw the weight of the White House behind the civil rights effort and the War on Poverty.

If you dig deeply enough in America, the big political swings always have something to do with race. And Clinton's vacillating but cleverly packaged campaign to "end welfare as we know it" was a brilliant ploy by the man Toni Morrison called the "first black president" to take back the southern white voters the Democrats had seemingly lost forever when they sent the FBI into Alabama and Mississippi in the 1960s. That, and a little rolled-up-newspaper training session with rapper Sister Souljah, allowed Clinton to take four of the eleven Confederate states, seizing ground no Democrat had won for more than two decades.

But Clinton didn't just go after Republican votes. He went after the Republicans' money, too. He brought in a team of economic advisers who offered what was, for the Democrats, a bold new approach on the economy, an approach based upon balancing the budget on the one hand and deregulating Wall Street on the other.

In the wake of the 2008 crisis, Clinton is most frequently criticized for overseeing two radical changes to our regulatory structure: the repeal of the Glass-Steagall Act to allow the mergers of investment banks, commercial banks, and insurance companies, and the Commodity Futures Modernization Act of 2000, which deregulated the burgeoning derivatives market. Less commonly understood is that Clinton, Greenspan, Rubin, and Summers also oversaw the collapse of what are known as "selective credit controls," the tools used to rein in irresponsible lending.

Rules like the Federal Reserve's Regulations X and W, which mandated minimum down payments for things like home and automobile loans, were watered down if not eliminated completely

during the Clinton years, and regulators under Clinton likewise refused to insist that banks and financial companies at least jack up
their reserve capital to match all the crazy lending they were doing.
At a critical juncture in 1993, for instance, Clinton's SEC considered
a proposal to raise capital requirements in the (then little known)
derivatives market, but ultimately decided against it.

The cumulative effect of all this was an explosion of easy credit
for the financial services sector, wedded to an across-the-board re-
laxation of economic regulations. Staffs were cut at all the major
regulatory agencies, and banking watchdogs like the Office of the
Comptroller of the Currency and the Office of Thrift Supervision
simply stopped pursuing criminal investigations; groups that had
referred thousands of cases a year to the Justice Department for
prosecution during the S&L crisis completely stopped that activity
by the turn of the millennium. In 2009 the OCC referred zero cases
for prosecution.

On the other hand, welfare fraud was prosecuted like never before, and welfare fraud investigators multiplied like rats in every
state of the country, forming unions and lobbying agencies.

Bill Clinton's political formula for seizing the presidency was
simple. He made money tight in the ghettos and let it flow free on
Wall Street. He showered the projects with cops and bean counters
and pulled the cops off the beat in the financial services sector. And
in one place he created vast new mountain ranges of paperwork,
while in another, paperwork simply vanished.

After Clinton, just to get food stamps to buy potatoes and flour,
you suddenly had to hand in a detailed financial history dating back
years, submit to wholesale invasions of privacy, and give in to a
range of humiliating conditions. Meanwhile banks in the 1990s
were increasingly encouraged to lend and speculate without filling
out any paperwork at all, and eventually borrowers were freed of
the burden of even having to show proof of income when they took
out mortgages or car loans.

Clinton's "third way" political strategy, in which Democrats laid
down their arms of business regulation, allowed his party to com-

pete with the Republicans for the campaign contributions of the big banks on Wall Street. By 1996, Bill Clinton's single biggest private campaign contributor would be Goldman Sachs, a distinction he would share with the next Democratic president, Barack Obama. The other side of the new strategy also stole the Republicans' political thunder by preemptively bashing black dependency through the welfare issue, allowing Democrats to sink their fangs into a big chunk of Richard Nixon's "Southern strategy" based on white voters in the South.

This was canny politics for the Democratic Party, but it had an obvious consequence—a consensus. Now the political momentum in both parties traveled in the same direction. Both parties wanted to merge the social welfare system with law enforcement, creating a world that for the poor would be peopled everywhere by cops and bureaucrats and inane, humiliating rules. They wanted to put all the sharp edges of American life in that one arena, and they succeeded.

And on the other hand, both parties wanted the financial services sector to become an endless naked pillow fight, fueled by increasingly limitless amounts of cheap cash from the Federal Reserve (literally free cash, eventually). If they turned life in the projects into a police state, they turned life on Wall Street into its opposite. One lie in San Diego is a crime. But a million lies? That's just good business.

LINDA ALMONTE

CHAPTER 8

BIG FRAUDS

She has long sandy hair, a big smile, and a booming voice, and when I first met her, Linda Almonte distantly reminded me of a somewhat louder, more manic version of Kate Hudson. We met in a tiny, foreclosure-ravaged Florida town called Satellite Beach, where she was living in her father's ramshackle beach house, on a strip of weather-battered one-story pastel homes with sun-roasted brown or tan lawns. Walking in, I sat on a pleasant but worn couch in the house's one main room; Linda's three-legged rescue dog jumped on my lap, and two of her three children listened in as she began to tell her story.

Linda was once very well-to-do, a champion shopper who splurged at malls and drove nice cars. She'd traveled all over the world as an executive for GE. She'd never thought much about politics or big-picture financial issues.

A single mother, she was now living, temporarily anyway, with her retired Marine father, and her family was basically surviving off his Social Security checks. It was a long fall down, but it had actually been worse. Not long before I met her, she and her kids had been living in Kissimmee, Florida, and had been forced to go on public assistance.

In Riverside, California, you get a hundred bucks and a thank-you for bringing a fraud case to light. When you scratch the same civic itch at JPMorgan Chase, you lose everything you own and end up living the life of a financial fugitive. Linda and her kids, when I met them, seemed like a family on the run. Her experience was an early precursor to the Edward Snowden story, and I was meeting her in the Sheremetyevo airport stage of her odyssey.

She told me to whip out a notebook and get ready for a long story.

"I first got to Chase," she began, "by way of Washington Mutual."

She'd worked at WaMu as the vice president of enterprise operations, from 2004 till Washington Mutual was sold to JPMorgan Chase during the banking crisis of 2008. Hers was a sort of roving-fixer job, in which she and a team of executives would deal with potentially embarrassing messes as they popped up across the bank's different administrative systems. In this capacity, she had traveled all across the country, moving her family from Melbourne, Florida, to Jacksonville to San Antonio to Seattle, then back to San Antonio, then back to Seattle—all in less than four years. Chasing banking crises made for a very peripatetic home life.

"I was fixing defects," she says now. "I was going everywhere."

At WaMu, at any given time, she worked on between one hundred and three hundred different projects, reengineering administrative systems to clean up messes and keep the bank from getting into trouble, legal or otherwise.

This experience is part of the reason why, initially anyway, Linda was not terribly shocked by what she would end up seeing at Chase. All giant banks have major bureaucratic screw-ups from time to time, and it was her job to be aware of that, and to deal with these problems in a nonjudgmental way. She was a little like the financial version of a proctologist: if you think that bug you picked up in Tijuana is going to shock her, guess what, she's seen it all before.

Once the sixth-biggest bank in America, Washington Mutual in September 2008 collapsed in what was at the time the largest bank failure in our nation's history. The bank had gone out of business thanks in large part to its mania for trading in fraudulent, designed-to-fail subprime mortgages. In fact, in 2003, in one of the most unintentionally prophetic statements in the recent history of high finance, then-CEO of WaMu Kerry Killinger had announced an audacious plan to turn his bank into a kind of Walmart of debt.

"We hope to do to this industry what Walmart did to theirs, Starbucks did to theirs, Costco did to theirs and Lowe's–Home Depot did to their industry," he said. "And I think if we've done our job, five years from now you're not going to call us a bank."

Killinger was exactly right. In exactly five years, people stopped calling Washington Mutual a bank. But it wasn't because it revolutionized the industry, it was because it so completely gorged itself on phony loans that it went out of business.

In his craven desperation to become the country's great volume distributor of debt, Killinger, among other things, acquired one of the most corrupt companies on earth, a California-based subprime mortgage lender called Long Beach. In an era where companies like Countrywide and New Century set new standards for underwriting negligence, Long Beach was the worst of the bunch. It was completely indiscriminate, lending to anything that moved, falsifying income statements, faking credit scores, doing anything to get people approved.

Over a four-year period, Washington Mutual and Long Beach teamed up to become a veritable factory of subprime mortgages, going from spinning $4.5 billion of subprime securitizations in 2003 to $29 billion in 2006. They would ultimately securitize more than $77 billion in subprime loans.

WaMu knew that the loans it was getting from Long Beach were fraudulent. A Senate investigation later revealed that the bank had, among other things, done internal audits of two of Long Beach's most productive loan officers. They found fraud in 58 percent of the loans coming from one of those officers' operations and in 83 percent of the other's. Instead of firing the two men, they were given prizes for loan production.

Another internal bank review, in 2008, found that loan officers were literally manufacturing information for loan applications in order to speed things up—yet they weren't fired.

Why? Because they were doing their jobs. They weren't in the business of making good loans. They were in the business of creating "assets," and almost nobody created more assets than WaMu. The two problem officers were like toy factories that were caught using edible lead paint on the products but also produced lots of toys at low cost. The wrong kind of parent company wouldn't care, and WaMu was the wrong kind of parent.

The Senate report also found that the bank intentionally chose failing loans to sell off and systematically hid negative information from the investors who bought these mortgage-backed securities. From the report:

> Documents obtained [show] . . . Washington Mutual selected loans for its securities because they were likely to default, and failed to disclose that fact to investors. It also included loans that had been identified as containing fraudulent borrower information, again without alerting investors when the fraud was discovered. An internal 2008 report found that lax controls had allowed loans that had been identified as fraudulent to be sold to investors.

WaMu's efficiency in creating bad loans was not what killed it. What killed it was its failure to efficiently get rid of its own defective product. The bank was dumb enough to get caught holding, or "warehousing," too much of its own born-to-lose mortgage paper. So in 2008, when home prices declined and home defaults started to pile up, the bank suddenly split open like a ship hitting an iceberg.

Seeing this, depositors and investors began to flee. In a ten-day period from September 15 to 25, customers pulled $16.7 billion in deposits out of the firm. A classic run on the bank had begun. In order to prevent a catastrophe in which the government and the FDIC would have to compensate thousands of wiped-out customers, the state, in the persons of such luminaries as Hank Paulson and Timothy Geithner, first seized the bank and then hastily arranged for it to be shotgun-wedded to JPMorgan Chase in an eleventh-hour backroom deal.

In that highly sordid and mostly overlooked chapter in the history of the bailout period, WaMu and its $307 billion in assets were delivered by the state into the hands of Chase and its CEO, Jamie Dimon, for the preposterously low price of $1.9 billion, a bargain deal that was struck just a few weeks before Chase was given $25 billion in cash by the government as part of the TARP bailouts.

This was Chase's second sweetheart deal in less than a year. Six months before, in March 2008, Chase had "rescued" the imploding investment banking giant Bear Stearns, buying the venerable firm with the aid of $29 billion in guarantees extended by the New York branch of the Federal Reserve—whose chairman of the board of directors at the time was, get this, JPMorgan Chase CEO *Jamie Dimon.*

That means that six months after Jamie Dimon was the lucky recipient of his own Federal Reserve bailout in order to acquire Bear Stearns, his bank was given another $25 billion in cash by the state to go on another shopping spree, cash he used, among other things, to buy Washington Mutual.

Why would the state agree to give two of the jewel assets of the commercial banking world to Chase for almost nothing? What service was Chase providing? The official story was that it helped stabilize the markets, but another answer seems to be that Chase was swallowing up a potentially disastrous public scandal at a time when the markets couldn't survive too many more of those.

Both of these cozy deals, for Bear and for WaMu, allowed the state to conceal massive criminal conspiracies from the public and the markets by burying the toxic, fraudulently generated assets of these corrupt companies in the billowing skirts of a stable, "reputable," too-big-to-fail company. In exchange, all Chase really had to do was cover up the mess by keeping the extent of the fraud and toxicity under wraps.

All this is important background to Linda Almonte's story. Because when Linda discovered that Chase itself was jumping head-first into the business of knowingly unloading fraudulent assets onto the market, she would run to the government to blow the whistle, as any good citizen would.

But Almonte had arrived at Chase in the first place only by means of a government-approved scheme to conceal toxic assets from the public. The company's state-sanctioned job was to hide fraud from the public. So when she found more fraud at Chase, where was she supposed to go? To the same government that used Chase to cover up two earlier scandals?

I first met Linda in the summer of 2011, about a year after she'd been fired from Chase, seven months after the low point of living off food stamps in the Kissimmee motel, and just a few weeks after her marriage had broken up. A pariah in her profession, she had been unable to get any kind of job, not even one waiting tables. She was still in a manic state. Her experience with Chase still clearly stung, and the story fairly spilled out of her mouth in a series of urgent monologues. She explained that when Washington Mutual went out of business at the peak of the crash in 2008, the new parent company, Chase, sent her to work at another one of its subsidiaries, a debt-buying and collections firm called NCO that Chase had acquired in 2006 for $950 million.

The easiest way to explain the debt-buying business is to think in mafia terms. If you owe money to a bookie and he gets tired of trying to collect from you, he might sell your debt to some leg-breaking ex-boxer for twenty-five cents on the dollar. The boxer then shows up at your house and slams your hand in a car door until you pay.

Everybody makes out. The bookie gets at least 25 percent of money that he thought was lost forever, a sunk cost. The boxer gets a 400 percent profit on a small investment. A win-win business.

It's the same with banking and, in particular, credit cards. You might open a credit card account with Chase, but if you go delinquent and Chase can't get you to pay by normal means, it can sell your account for pennies on the dollar to a debt buyer like NCO—which is basically just a giant clearinghouse for lawyers (legal leg breakers) who earn their living filing lawsuits against delinquent borrowers.

NCO is one of the biggest lawsuit factories in America, filing thousands of suits a year against delinquent holders of consumer credit accounts. "When you see someone has been sued by a bank, a lot of the time, it's actually NCO," says Almonte. She worked for NCO for that four-month period in 2009, helping the company coordinate communications among the vast network of collections lawyers to whom it farmed out its accounts. "I was the liaison between NCO and their attorney network of one hundred fifty-four firms," she says.

That experience of working for its major debt-buying subsidiary and liaising with attorneys is part of the reason Chase decided to bring Linda to San Antonio on May 16, 2009. Its plan was to put her in Chase's credit card litigation department, a kind of bureaucratic way station for processing the accounts of Chase cardholders who had gone past a certain point of no return.

A sprawling consumer operation with millions of customers, Chase maintains a giant centralized database called the System of Record.

In the System of Record—think of it as a kind of all-knowing HAL from *2001: A Space Odyssey*—the bank enters all kinds of account information, everything from the name and address of, say, a credit card holder, to his or her payment history, the current balance, the customer's specific spending limit, and so on. Anytime anyone has contact with the customer, anywhere, the result of that contact gets entered into HAL's memory.

However, once Chase decides that a certain credit card customer is too delinquent in his payments and must be sued, HAL turns that person's account over to the credit card litigation department. From that point forward, the department is responsible for maintaining everything to do with that account, from reading correspondence from the cardholder or the cardholder's lawyer, to gathering information from the cardholder's file to help Chase's pit-bull lawyers sue the delinquent customer, to checking and rechecking the documents in those files if and when Chase decides it wants to sell the account to a leg-breaking debt buyer like NCO.

Linda expected that her job at Chase credit card litigation would be roughly similar to the jobs she'd had at WaMu and NCO, liaising among multiple departments, troubleshooting administrative system problems, and in particular handling communications between Chase executives and company attorneys.

But there were many things Linda didn't know about the job she was taking. In her first months she claims she witnessed fellow employees shredding correspondence from delinquent credit card holders, a practice she says sent many customers—some of whom may even have been agreeing to settlement offers—straight into litigation. She also claims that some of the shredded documents belonged to active-duty servicemembers in places like Iraq, who under federal law (the Servicemembers Civil Relief Act) cannot be sued for, among other things, credit card debt.

"Guys . . . who were over in Iraq, we got default judgments against them and wiped out their bank accounts." But she became even more concerned when, at a regular meeting of audit and compliance executives, she learned about the bank's robo-signing practices.

When a bank like Chase goes into court to sue a credit card holder, it must formally list the facts of the case: who owes what, how long the amount has been owed, when the account was opened, and so on. The procedures in every state are different, but at some point in the process, all states require an affidavit from the bank asserting these facts. The same process holds true, incidentally, for foreclosure filings. The files for all these court actions, be they credit card default suits or home foreclosures, include affidavits in which an ostensibly authoritative bank executive attests to the facts of the case.

At Chase, those authoritative bank executives were low-ranking employees who also doubled as roving auditors of Chase's out-of-house lawyers. In Linda's office, there was a small cubicle island of these employees stationed about twenty feet from her. They were "late twenty-something and early thirty-something" workers and Linda gave me a list of their names. I would eventually see the same names with regularity on random visits to courthouses to look through public records of credit card lawsuits.

Linda didn't know much about what these people did for a living initially, but she took notice of who they were. Despite their exalted titles, they were not high-powered, serious business executives, but rather entry-level employees who until recently had been hourly wage workers. She remembers particularly that one of the robo-signers had a cubicle decorated with "pink, foofy things" and a sign that read, "The Princess is IN."

These entry-level types would be sent around the country to visit Chase's partner law firms and "audit" their operations. Linda thought that was odd enough, but what really caught her attention was when, in one of her first audit and compliance meetings, one of these employees talked about how much work he got done on the road. "He was like, 'It was a six-hour flight and I signed like two thousand affidavits,'" Linda says.

Soon Linda was walking by the desks of these robo-signers and noticing that on any given day, they would be furiously attaching signatures to monstrous stacks of documents. She eventually learned that the whole system operated like a factory. At one end of the office, a paid-by-the-hour temp worker would generate an affidavit on a computer screen, using an automated program that created the legal document and automatically filled in data from the customer account. Once the document was generated, the temp worker would print it out and then stick all the unsigned affidavits in a drawer.

The robo-signers would then open the drawer, pick up hundreds of affidavits at a time, head back to their cubicles, and sign their names to them, one after another. Technically speaking, the signatories were supposed to verify the numbers in the affidavits and make sure the balance number was the same in all the various databases—in the HAL-like System of Record, in the prelitigation database, and perhaps even in the databases of the law firms doing the suing.

But the robo-signers checked none of these figures. They simply signed their names one after the other.

Then, once they were finished, they would stick the stacks of documents *back* into the same drawer, where they would be retrieved (maybe that day, maybe later) by a notary, who would stamp the affidavits. The notaries, according to Linda, were almost never in the room when the documents were signed.

Here we should digress for a moment to talk about a legend that's been circulating about the financial crisis, a legend our leaders like to tell over and over. It goes something like this: Yes, bad things happened, but none of those bad things were crimes. Greed isn't illegal. Making too much money isn't illegal. Nothing to see here, move along.

In October 2011, just a few weeks into the Occupy Wall Street protests, that fairy tale gained new life. It came directly from the top this time. President Barack Obama, the great progressive hope, explained in a series of televised interviews why there hadn't been more criminal prosecutions of bankers on his watch. Obama gave a simple explanation.

"Banks are in the business of making money," he said. "And they find loopholes."

So what kind of "loophole finding" went on in Chase's credit card litigation office? Not only did the bank apparently have full-time employees assigned to the job of committing mass perjury, it even went so far as to rope the entire department into the cause when the normal robo-signing staff couldn't handle the workload. According to another employee in Linda's department, who has since left the bank, it was routine for the bosses to come trolling through the San Antonio office with stacks of documents and pull people out of their desks for robo-signing duty. "They [the bosses] were going into an empty room and sitting with stacks and stacks at a table in front of them," the former employee says. Then "everybody that wasn't doing something was given a stack and told to sign. . . . They were all in one room, signing crap."

The employee, who had been with Chase for years, eventually had to resign because "jail is not where I wanted to spend my retirement. . . . It just got flat ignorant crazy there."

In any case, the bank in its affidavits would often attach preposterous titles to these robo-signer employees who had attested to personal knowledge of the case without even looking at the files.

Long after my first interview with Linda in Satellite Beach, I would bring her up to a courthouse in Newark, New Jersey, for an experiment. We randomly selected a series of credit card judgments that had been filed in that court building and examined the affidavits. Sure enough, the very first case we picked out—*Chase Bank, NA, v. Louis Pascale*—contained an affidavit from one of Linda's former officemates.

"Kevin Fletcher, by way of certification," the affidavit reads, "says, I am Assistant Treasurer of Chase Bankcard . . . and I am familiar with the plaintiff's file in the matter."

The actual title of most of the robo-signers, including Fletcher, was and is "attorney liaison." But when it came time to attach their names to affidavits, they were, according to Linda and others, explicitly instructed to use much grander titles.

"Chase made me robo-sign over two thousand documents without verifying the balances and using an incorrect/false title," one of Linda's coworkers would later explain. "We were strictly forbidden to use 'assistant vice president' as a title, but when it came time to robo-sign and sue, they forced us to use that title."

But these problems were all very quickly pushed to the side by a mushrooming crisis that would result in Linda's firing. Just a few months after she was hired, in October 2009, she found out from her immediate supervisor, Jason Lazinbat, that she was going to be asked to oversee a Herculean administrative job, gathering the documentation for what she was told would be "the biggest judgment sale in Chase's history."

To back up for a moment, the most valuable kind of credit card account that any bank can sell to a debt buyer is a court judgment. If you have a delinquent account with a bank like Chase but haven't been taken to court yet, well, that's one thing. Maybe the bank made a mistake. Maybe you don't really owe money, or you don't owe as much money as they say. If Chase goes and sells your account to a third party, that third party will have an uphill climb getting its money, especially if you dispute its claims.

But if Chase has already taken you to court, and a judge has already rapped his gavel over a judgment against you for that thousand dollars, well, that account is worth a lot more. The legal leg breaker/buyer of that account needs only to find you and take his money, by any means necessary (and the means now available to these collectors are extraordinary; more on that later), and you won't have the right to argue the matter.

So whenever a bank like Chase needs to raise quick cash, selling judgments is a quick-and-dirty way to go. You scrounge your entire client list to see who among your credit card borrowers has already been litigated against, you gather up all those court documents, and then you sell five hundred or a thousand or two thousand judgments at a time to a third party like NCO.

There were more than 23,000 accounts in the proposed sale. Linda had two weeks, and a full-time staff of three, to complete a job that would, if done correctly, require thousands of man-hours.

She would ultimately get to bring in more staff to help go through all the accounts, but at the time, it seemed like an impossible task.

Linda went to work to gather the documentation. The sale of the judgment accounts had been brokered by a company called National Loan Exchange, a sort of middleman firm that put together debt buyers and companies like Chase that had judgments to sell. These middleman firms typically have to tell the buyers that they've done due diligence on the sale, so when a big sale like this is brokered, they'll work with a company like Chase to make sure the bank is selling what it claims it's selling. This is what happened here, and NLE employees, along with Linda, started to go through the 23,000 judgments Chase had promised to sell.

They started with California, where a large chunk of the credit card holders who'd lost these court judgments lived. Linda asked for, and began to receive, documentation for 11,472 judgment accounts involving borrowers who lived in California.

"There were thousands of boxes," Linda says. "There were rooms filled with this stuff."

She started going through the accounts. On the very first day of the review, October 10, she noticed a big problem. In each of the boxes coming in from California, there were about forty-five customer files. "On average, about ten files in each box didn't contain judgments, and there were another ten that had judgments that weren't signed and stamped," she says. This early review suggested to her that up to 44 percent of the "judgments" that Chase planned on selling were not in fact valid judgments.

Worried, she conducted a more thorough review. Five days later she had the disturbing results, which she emailed to Lazinbat, the Chase sales executives, and Chase's lead counsel, Gail Siegel:

> Upon completion of the California PAN files we have 11,472 accounts (including MRA's) with a total balance of $110,138,641.18. Between 50–60% of the files are missing judgments, or the judgment does not contain a date and signature.

Linda's bosses told her not to worry, that if the judgment wasn't in there, the debt buyers would just have to go get it themselves. Chase, they said, didn't have the resources to scare up all those documents.

Linda plowed on as ordered and started to go through the documents from Illinois judgments. This time she was told by the Illinois office that Cook County had gone digital, and that as a result, most of the account files wouldn't contain a paper judgment. Again, she was told, Chase didn't have the resources to print out all those judgments to confirm that they actually existed.

Now, there were many problems with the accounts Linda was seeing flowing in from places like California and Illinois. Some were not even judgments. In some files, the cardholders were not even delinquent. In still others, *Chase* actually owed the cardholders money. In still more, there were judgments, but the judgments weren't against the borrower—they were against Chase itself.

And there was one last category of screw-up: in large numbers of these files, the judgments were not final. Some of them had been rescinded by later court actions. So the files might have two legal notices in them: the original judgment, and the later court reversal.

When Linda explained this situation, her bosses essentially ignored her and told her to plow ahead with the sale (she says she was even asked to edit the files, sending only the judgments, not orders rescinding the judgments). She was mortified by Chase's seeming indifference to the fact that they were about to sell what seemed to her a huge quantity of defective accounts.

For Linda, this was the major, sobering difference between even a firm like Washington Mutual and Chase. At WaMu, there had been rampant system problems, too, but in Linda's experience anyway, the company had tried to fix them. "I thought it was the same at Chase, until they were like, 'Hide it. Bury it.' "

Finally, as the date of the sale approached, Linda was sent a kind of query document by National Loan Exchange. "It had this whole long list of questions that I was supposed to email back, saying they were all true," she says. "Like for instance, that the accounts being sold were free of any liens and garnishments—or that there's a judg-ment against each one."

Linda was now being asked to put her own signature on a docu-ment that said that Chase was selling $200 million in valid judg-ments, when she believed that this wasn't remotely close to being true.

Linda was frightened, but at the same time she was also naïve enough to think that the moment might be an opportunity for her. As she later explained to her lawyers, she thought that by stopping the sale, and preventing this gigantic fraud from going through, she would be noticed upstairs and become a superstar at Chase. She even tried to end-run her immediate bosses and stop the sale her-self, believing that she was taking dramatic action to save the com-pany from future trouble. Instead, she was fired.

Once Linda was out the door, Chase put the sale back on, errors or no errors. They quickly found a buyer, and 23,000 "judgments" went out into the world—a teeming school of little mutant fish, swimming blindly into courthouses from one coast to the other, each in search of a human being to collect from.

In March 2010, just a few short months after Linda was fired, a stack of papers arrived via post at a tiny redbrick courthouse on the north shore of Staten Island, New York. The clerk of the court, a young woman named Deborah Tortorice, took a look at the papers and raised an eyebrow. This was a stack of 133 "assignments," legal fil-ings sent from a Louisiana-based debt-buying company called DebtOne, in which the firm asserted its rights of ownership over a series of credit card accounts originally held by Chase Bank.

It wasn't unusual for Tortorice to receive such assignments. As clerk of Richmond County Civil Court, serving under a colorful judge named Philip Straniere, who among other things ran a small claims court on Tuesdays and Wednesdays, she often saw notices from debt buyers announcing their intention to collect on past-due accounts they'd purchased from companies like Chase and American Express. Any company that intended to collect on a debt purchased from another creditor had to notify the local courthouse officially of its intent to conduct such business in that county.

What was unusual about this batch was the volume. Tortorice generally saw four or five of these assignments at once, at most. Here DebtOne had sent well over a hundred. Either a historically enormous sale of credit card accounts had gone through somewhere in the world (remember, this was 133 accounts landing just in Staten Island) or some kind of mistake had been made. "If they had just sent a few of these at a time," Tortorice recalls now, "we might never have noticed anything."

Tortorice notified Judge Straniere of the unusual occurrence. The sixty-four-year-old judge is an anomaly in many respects, not the least of which being the fact that he is, as he claims, the "only conservative Republican civil court judge in New York City." But along with his conservative politics, Judge Straniere—a trim, cheerful-looking man with a bushy white mustache—conducts his business with a populist flair.

The walls of his chambers teem with baseball memorabilia and posters from musicals, and in his decisions, the judge eschews complex legal language and makes his arguments using images the everyday person can understand. His favored technique is to use references to movies, comic books, and other pop culture sources, and his decisions contain allusions to everything from *Superman* to *Seinfeld* to *Miss Saigon*.

In fact, less than a year after the DebtOne assignments appeared at his courthouse, Judge Straniere would enjoy a brief run of urban-folk-hero status after *The New York Times* ran a feature about his unique decisions, calling him the "bard of the Staten Island courts."

The story, entitled "A Judge's Biggest Decision—Which Movie to Quote," described a judge with a quick trigger finger who liked to toss off a pointed joke when confronted. In one case, after a lawyer argued that the judge's rulings weren't adequately supported, Judge Straniere sarcastically responded by footnoting every single word of the first paragraph of his ruling. Every single word, according to the *Times:*

> including "a," "the" and "two" ("the cardinal number between one and three in the Arabic number system probably derived from Old English," according to Footnote 4).

The judge is definitely a funny guy, but the humor has a serious reasoning behind it that has direct relevance to the world of consumer debt law that he administers. Comparing the consumer debt business to "the Land of Oz, run by a Wizard who no one has ever seen," his densely colored rulings are in part designed to make the business's dizzying behind-the-curtain machinations more accessible to ordinary people. "If you use references to movies and sports and so on," he says, "ordinary people have a better chance to understand it."

Anyway, it took an out-of-the-box judge like Straniere to take a second look at the 133 assignments from DebtOne that arrived in his courthouse in March 2010. Incredibly, this courthouse in Staten Island was the only one in the entire country that paused before letting DebtOne proceed with the collections on the 23,000 mutant accounts Chase just months before had pushed out into the world, costing Linda Almonte her job. The fact that Straniere sits in such a small courthouse was probably a factor. "The bigger courts probably wouldn't have time to take another look," concedes Tortorice.

The law is, of course, supposed to be precise, and civil lawsuits are designed to be careful, evidence-based determinations of right and wrong, liability and no liability. But the business of credit card litigation by its very nature has to be half-assed, brutal, reckless, and stupid. The business model just doesn't work otherwise. The giant consumer credit merchants like Chase who file lawsuits against cardholders by the tens of thousands couldn't even begin to make real money, real margins, if they had to do anything like real legal work or meet anything like a real evidentiary standard.

Why? First of all, because the services of even the worst civil litigator cost hundreds of dollars an hour. If a bank like Chase had to hire a real lawyer to collect on each and every past-due $780 credit card balance, it would almost certainly go into the red long before the complaint was even written up. In fact, just getting a live human being to look at each and every file for more than a few seconds, or to individually prepare the evidence for every lawsuit, would make the cost of litigation prohibitive for these massive companies.

Therefore the only way to make this thing work to scale is to fully automate the litigation process. You must reduce the entire business to a series of dumb mechanical maneuvers that ruthlessly eliminate even the mere possibility of subjective judgment.

And that's exactly how it is. The system is really a game of mathematical probabilities that the companies have built around the high likelihood of obtaining uncontested legal judgments.

The game begins when the bank serves a summons to the cardholder. In this key first step lies a huge share of the industry's dependable profits. In most states, companies have no real obligation to make sure that the cardholder actually sees and understands his summons.

Thanks to intense state-by-state lobbying by companies like Chase and MBNA, it's usually enough to send a notice by mail to some old address, often the original mailing address when the account was opened, which might have been ten years earlier. In some states, banks and debt buyers can even make use of an automated online summons system, in which a few lines of customer data are entered (perhaps or perhaps not by an actual human being), and, get this, a *postcard* is then sent in the mail to whatever ancient address the company has on file. Visitors to online high-speed litigation sites like the deliciously named www.turbocourt.com can get a window into the world of up-tempo collections. Its website, complete with cutesy illustrations, promises friction-free collection:

> We'll **GUIDE** you through a customized interview, **PRE-PARE** the exact documents you need, **HELP** you file and prepare the next steps! It's as easy as that—a do-it-yourself service that's fast and stress-free!

Even in those instances where a flesh-and-blood process server is supposed to be employed, the system is full of cracks. The command structure here typically goes from the bank, which wants to sue the customer, to the law firm hired by the bank to press the suit, to the process servers hired by the law firm to find and serve the cardholder.

On paper, it's a simple and logical system, but here again the question of margin creeps in. Most of these process servers are paid bulk rates by the lawyers and make as little as four dollars per customer to serve notice.

Four dollars per customer.

How does anyone make money driving thirty or forty miles to personally deliver a summons to one defendant, just to make four bucks? Your local pizza maker has a higher rate of return on a delivery, and even he knows that that job stops being economically viable beyond ten or fifteen miles.

So what happens? Many process servers and law firms engage in a wink-wink-nudge-nudge business called gutter service or sewer service, in which the law firm hands the list of summonses to the server, and the server simply dumps them (in the "gutter," hence the name).

In return, the process server hands the law firm an "affidavit of service," swearing that he properly served the customer. Process service once required a signature of the defendant to prove proper service; now all that's needed is the server's own word that he did the job.

Around the time that Chase was obtaining judgments against those 23,000 account holders, dozens of law firms and process servers in New York State alone were being accused of gutter service practices. William Singler, the head of a Long Island firm called

American Legal Process, was arrested for gutter service in the spring of 2009; soon afterward lawsuits in other parts of the state asked thirty-six different law firms, including national firms like Zwicker & Associates often used by Chase, to disclose how often they used American Legal Process to issue summonses.

Later on, several states would sue Chase, based in part upon information given by Linda, and some would mention the practice. A suit filed and signed by California attorney general Kamala Harris in the spring of 2013 would make particular note of it. "Defendants, through their agents for service of process," the state's complaint read, "falsely state in proofs of service that the consumer was personally served, when in fact he or she was not served at all—a practice known as 'sewer service.'"

Thus not only may a credit card customer legally be served at some ancient address without her knowledge, it's highly possible that the server won't even bother to extend her that courtesy.

This is why, in a huge percentage of credit card cases, the cardholder never even sees the summons and consequently never appears in court to defend himself. For instance, in the year many of these cases were pursued, 2009, there were 240,000 filings of credit card suits in New York City alone. In an astonishing 158,000 of those cases, the creditor won a default judgment. "In two-thirds of the cases," says Straniere, "no one even shows up."

Once a bank like Chase "serves" its delinquent customer, there are just three paths on the flowchart of outcomes. They are:

> The customer doesn't show up in court and loses by default judgment.
> The customer answers the summons and settles with the bank.
> The customer answers the summons and contests the case.

In the first two cases—and this is a crucial part of this entire scheme, and the key reason that Linda's bosses were so unconcerned about the absence of good paperwork in the debt sale—the collector typically does not come into court with any supporting documentary evidence. "They almost never have [evidence] on the first appearance," says Straniere. All the collectors have, typically, is a complaint and the assertion of an owed balance.

But in the vast majority of cases, that's enough. Two-thirds of the time, the defendant doesn't show and loses automatically. Others get the summons, assume they really do owe the balance stated, and either agree to pay or settle, never forcing the bank to prove its claims.

In the third path, however, when the customer contests the case, the bank is forced to go back and dig up supporting documents. If the entity doing the suing is the actual bank that issued the card, that's less of a problem. Say Chase's credit card litigation department is filing the suit. In that case, all it needs to do is make a few calls to its regional offices to dig up the card balances and other documents. It's a time-consuming process and puts some strain on the bottom line cost-wise, but it's feasible.

But if the collector on the account is a debt buyer like DebtOne that has bought the account from the bank like Chase, now there's a problem, because the big banks often intentionally keep the files thin when they sell their credit card accounts to companies like these.

Why? Because very often, the contract between a company like Chase and a company like DebtOne specifies that if the buyer needs any additional documents to collect on the debt, he has to come back to Chase and *buy* them. "Each time you need more paperwork to press your case, the bank charges you for more paperwork," explains Straniere.

"It's another way for them to make money," explains Linda.

For this reason, when credit card holders actually contest the lawsuits filed against them, the plaintiff in the vast majority of cases (particularly if it's a debt buyer) simply drops the case.

So to recap: Two-thirds of the defendants who get served with summonses don't show up, and they lose. A large portion of the remaining cardholders settle or pay voluntarily. In the rare case where the defendant contests, the plaintiff most often simply vanishes and drops the case. In only the rarest of instances does a credit card lawsuit ever stay contested by both sides long enough to actually proceed to trial. "I haven't tried a credit card case since, I don't know, 1997 or 1998," says Straniere.

What all this means is that the bulk of the credit card collection business is conducted without any supporting documentation showing up or being seen by human eyes at any part of the process. The meat of the business is collecting unopposed default judgments from defendants who either never receive a summons or receive one and never appear in court.

For debt buyers like DebtOne, the whole game is a bluff. If they buy a pile of open accounts or already-won judgments, what they're banking on is collecting from delinquent customers who don't fight back. If the collection is contested at all, the firm simply disappears and moves on. At no time in the process do most collectors ever actually need to produce evidence of a legitimate debt or a legitimate judgment. This is why executives like the ones who fired Linda, perversely enough, have an accurate read on the situation.

In the big picture, it doesn't matter what documents you send when you sell a bunch of credit card accounts. All you need is a list of names and addresses.

So how do you collect money from a cardholder who doesn't answer his or her summons? That's easy: you take it! The laws are different from state to state, but in most places in America, once the bank or debt buyer has that default judgment in hand, it can legally do just about anything to the cardholder. It can put a lien on his property, it can attach her salary, it can even take his car or her office furniture. A bank or debt buyer's collection powers aren't as elaborate as, say, the federal government's powers to reseize money owed by student borrowers. But they're a lot broader than you would think.

In the state of New Jersey, for instance, the bank or debt buyer can basically take anything the cardholder owns, so long as it leaves him with the clothes he's wearing and maybe a little pocket change—technically, a thousand dollars' worth of personal property. The state charges only a five-dollar fee to green-light the attachment of a bank account or the repossession of an automobile. From the Superior Court's brochure "Collecting a Money Judgment":

> If you ask that the court officer seize the debtor's motor vehicle, you must be able to show that the vehicle is registered in the name of the debtor. This is done by getting a certified copy of the title. . . . The fee for this procedure is $5.

Collectors can also request a "statement of docketing" from the court, which essentially puts a freeze on the cardholder's property:

> Once your judgment is recorded in the Superior Court, the debtor cannot sell with clear title any real estate owned in New Jersey until your debt is paid.

"There are people out there who never even knew they were served and taken to court," says Linda. "Then five years later they go to sell their house, and they find they can't do it because of a missed payment at Circuit City years ago."

All this extraordinary behavior never took place a few decades ago. Credit card companies almost never sued delinquent cardholders, particularly those with small balances. It simply wasn't economical for companies to devote any resources at all to chasing after a thousand dollars here and there.

But as time passed, and the machinery of collections became more streamlined and brutal, we reached the current state of affairs. Now a Chase bank executive can sit in an office in San Antonio and with a few brief keystrokes transfer the right to seize the salary and automobile of a stranger in Chicago or Newark to some random company in Louisiana.

At one point in time that process also required significant legal due diligence and the transfer of documentation, but executives soon realized that in the overwhelmed modern court system, simply attesting to having the right documentation works just as well as really having it. This is the same realization that struck Bank of America when it found that saying it had foreclosure documents was almost as good as having them—and the same one that touched process servers at American Legal Process, who found that claiming to have delivered a summons was almost as good as (and certainly cheaper than) actually doing it.

In this case, Straniere's office took one look at DebtOne's assignments and immediately saw a host of problems. For one thing, the assignments were signed, not by a lawyer for either Chase or DebtOne, but by Chase robo-signers. Moreover, DebtOne, a Louisiana company, was not registered to do business in the state of New York.

Also, Chase never informed any of its customers that their debt had been assigned to a new company, which according to the judge's ruling was a red flag in light of recent experience. "On a regular basis this court encounters defendants being sued on the same debt by more than one creditor alleging it is the assignee of the original credit card obligation," he wrote. ". . . Without receiving such notice of the assignment, a debtor seeking to make any application to the court would not have any idea as to which alleged creditor is to be served."

Straniere in his decision also expressed concern about whether the defendants had been served properly, noting that "the recent experience of the Civil Court show[s] large numbers of default judgments being obtained in credit card cases against consumers far in excess of the default rate in regard to all other litigation."

For that and other reasons, Straniere vacated all 133 assignments. His decision had absolutely nothing to do with the abuses Linda Almonte had witnessed. In fact, until I told him, he had never heard of her and had no idea those problems even existed.

All Straniere saw was the broad sloppiness and inattention to procedure that attended the entire deal in general. The DebtOne deal was simply a typical transaction in a consumer credit industry that depends upon robo-signing, mass fraud, and intentionally thin paperwork as essential elements of its profit model.

Straniere didn't nix the DebtOne judgments because he knew, as Almonte knew, that a large percentage of them were rife with errors and might not even have been valid judgments. He did it because the accounts had been so sloppily transferred that it was impossible to tell the difference.

Months later, perhaps because of the Straniere decision (which caused judges in other jurisdictions to review their own batches of assignments from this debt sale), Chase issued a series of curious decisions. In June 2011 it announced that it had dropped one thousand collection suits related to the Almonte allegations. The suits were from five of the biggest states in the debt sale: New Jersey, California, Florida, New York, and Illinois. In May the bank had already announced the firing of its lead counsel in four of those five states, along with the bank's senior counsel overall, Gail Siegel, who was one of the lawyers present in San Antonio on the day Linda was fired.

The decision by Chase to give up on collections from one thousand accounts was hailed by the few reporters who covered it as a big deal. *Forbes* reporter Stephanie Eidelman, who had previously interviewed Linda, called it "A Whistleblower Triumph," while CNN reporter Colin Barr wondered, "Do we have a credit-card robosigning scandal on our hands?" But Barr pointed out that even this embarrassing episode, which apparently resulted in a purge of the bank's top lawyers, was not likely to hurt the company's bottom line much:

> Assuming the bank has dropped 1,000 cases against debtors with an average balance of, say, $30,000—twice the national average balance—the amount JPMorgan is forgoing is on the order of $30 million. That's about 12 hours' worth of profits at the first-quarter rate.

In point of fact, the average balance in the thousand cases was about a thousand dollars—meaning that Chase was really only forgoing about a million dollars in collections. In other words, Linda Almonte's whistle-blowing odyssey—a journey that had cost her all her savings, nearly wrecked her marriage, and reduced her kids to dependence on food stamps—had ultimately cost JPMorgan just a few minutes in profits. From the bank's point of view, Linda's defection was very nearly a worst-case scenario. And even the worst case, it turns out, isn't all that bad.

Months after Chase made those decisions, in September 2011, which by then was nearly two years after her firing, I would stand with Linda in the lobby of One World Financial Center in Lower Manhattan, listening vaguely as she shouted into a cell phone. Nearby, a group of tourists were looking out an east-facing window, gazing down at the first floors of the new World Trade Center. Some of them peered back at us with quizzical expressions.

"ALMONTE," she repeated. "A-L-M-O-N-T-E. I filed my complaint over a year ago."

Linda had come up from Florida to take me on a tour through the court system in nearby Newark, showing me how to search for credit card judgments pertaining to her case. At the end of her trip, she decided to drop in on the local SEC office to check on the status of her whistle-blower complaint.

Linda had formally filed her claim in November 2010, nearly a full year earlier. But now she was showing up at the SEC office in New York, asking for a status update, and here's what they were asking her: *What complaint?* They were saying they had no record of her claim whatsoever.

Linda eventually got permission to go upstairs to the SEC's New York office, where she was essentially fed the same line she'd heard over and over again in the last year: "We're looking into it."

In May 2012, Mary Schapiro testified before the House Appropriations Committee about the SEC whistle-blower program. She told the House that the program was "already providing high-quality information," but when asked how many awards had actually been paid out, she admitted—none. The program was just under two years old, and not a single whistle-blower case had been made.

The final irony in all this? At the same time that Chase was pumping out tens of thousands of bogus collection notices into the economy, the company was being supported, financially, by the federal government in a dozen different ways.

Most people, when they hear the term "bailouts," think of the Troubled Asset Relief Program, called TARP. And when people think of TARP, they reflexively remember hearing that the banks that borrowed billions from that program have all paid their money back. So—no harm, no foul. It's not like we gave them the money. Thus while it is true, for instance, that Linda Almonte's employer, JPMorgan Chase, accepted $25 billion through the TARP program and used that money to buy not only Washington Mutual (for a state-struck pennies-on-the-dollar price) but a pair of $60 million Gulfstream jets and an $18 million hangar facility in Westchester County, that's all okay because, well, Chase paid the money back a year later. So it's not like it came out of our pockets.

Less well known is that Chase was extended billions more in guarantees to help buy the corpse of Bear Stearns. It was allowed to borrow $33 billion more against the state's credit card—if it defaulted on those loans, we'd have picked up the bill—through an even more obscure Federal Reserve program called the Temporary Liquidity Guarantee Program. A whole alphabet soup of other Fed bailout programs, like the Commercial Paper Funding Facility, the Term Auction Facility, and the Primary Dealer Credit Facility, allow banks like Chase to borrow billions of dollars at near-zero or zero interest.

But all of it—TARP, the more obscure bailout facilities like TAF, even the fact that the Federal Reserve and the SEC allow banks like Chase to overestimate the value of their portfolios systematically in their annual accounting statements—it all pales in importance to the fact that, as a commercial bank holding company, Chase gets to borrow virtually unlimited sums of money from the Fed for free. In

2010 we found out through an audit of the Federal Reserve that America's biggest banks had borrowed $16 trillion from the Fed at far below market interest rates, through the Fed's emergency lending program. Chase itself, according to one calculation, had borrowed $390 billion in these cheap loans from the Fed.

What this means is that the entire business model for something like Chase's credit card business is not much more than a gigantic welfare fraud scheme. These companies borrow hundreds of billions of dollars from the Fed at rock-bottom rates, then turn around and lend it out to the world at 5, 10, 15, 20 percent, as credit cards and mortgages, boat loans and aircraft loans, and so on. If you pay it back, great, it's a 500 percent or 1,000 percent or 4,000 percent profit for the bank. If you don't pay it back, the company can put your name in the hopper to be sued. A $5,000 debt on a credit card for the now-defunct Circuit City, which was actually a Chase card, became a $13,000 or $14,000 debt by the time the bank finished applying fees and penalties. Just like a welfare application, you have to read the fine print. "They make more on lawsuits than they make on credit interest," says Linda.

Along the way, the bank gets to grease its accomplices with the fruits of that cheap government cash. You might wonder how it is that banks manage to get overworked sheriff's departments in high-crime areas to actually detail deputies to evacuate foreclosed-upon houses. The answer is that every single one of those hundreds of thousands of credit judgments—be they foreclosures or credit card accounts—contains a line item with a court-mandated collection fee or other such payout to local law enforcement. When I went prospecting for robo-signed affidavits in the New Jersey court system, I found sheriff's fees of five hundred, eight hundred, a thousand dollars in each and every judgment. In this way, the banks pay a kind of kickback to local police.

In recent years, Chase has been caught in numerous wide-ranging systematic frauds, the Almonte incident being just one. In 2011 it paid a $211 million fine for rigging the bids for municipal bond offerings (yet another variety of fraud against the state). It agreed to a $722 million settlement (much of this "fine" was actually forgiveness of Chase-imposed fees) for its part in the Jefferson County, Alabama, disaster, in which officials in the city of Birmingham were literally bribed (with watches and new suits, among other things) into signing off on a deadly financing deal with the bank. Remember those letters involving service members that Linda said went into the shredder? Well, Chase ended up having to pay $27 million for defrauding active-duty military men and women by systematically overcharging them for their mortgages.

Yet despite all this, Chase in 2011 surged to the top spot in the list of American banks winning government bond business, managing $35 billion in bond sales that year. It's not just that there's no criminal penalty for fraud on such a grand scale; your business doesn't even have to suffer. You can defraud the state over and over again, and the state will still be happy to do business with you. You can still issue municipal bonds, and you can still be one of twenty-one banks given the privilege of being primary dealers of government debt.

The crucial thing to understand is that if businesses like consumer credit cards are going to give cards away in the mail to everyone with a pulse, then the process almost by definition has to involve fraud. In a mass society where obtaining credit is as easy as it is, there's probably no way to efficiently collect on delinquent accounts by writing real affidavits, filing legitimate, error-free lawsuits, and serving legitimate summonses in each and every individual case. Without the shortcuts, it doesn't work. So techniques like robo-signing and sewer service are essential to the profitability of the business. Plenty of people—consumers and merchants both—are probably glad that so much credit is available, but they don't realize that systematic fraud is part of what makes it available.

Legally, there's absolutely no difference between a woman on welfare who falsely declares that her boyfriend no longer lives in the home and a bank that uses a robo-signer to cook up a document swearing that he has kept regular records of your credit card account. But morally and politically, they're worlds apart. When the state brings a fraud case against a welfare mom, it brings it with disgust, with rage, because in addition to committing the legal crime, she's committed the political crime of being needy and an eyesore.

Banks commit the legal crime of fraud wholesale; they do so out in the open, have entire departments committed to it, and have employees who've spent years literally doing nothing but commit, over and over again, the same legal crime that some welfare mothers go to jail for doing once. But they're not charged, because there's no political crime. The system is not disgusted by the organized, mechanized search for profit. It's more like it's impressed by it. And even when circumstances force the government to take notice, they act like Marcia Clark or Chris Darden in summation, apologizing for having the temerity to point a finger at lovable ol' O.J.

CHAPTER 9

COLLATERAL CONSEQUENCES

On the morning of March 23, 2011, a young white saxophonist and music teacher named Patrick Jewell woke up in Brooklyn in a good mood.

Everything in his life was moving in the right direction. A few months earlier, he'd met a girl and fallen in love. Just that morning, as per their brand-new routine, he'd made her breakfast and walked her from her Brooklyn apartment to the subway stop on Marcy Avenue, where she left every morning to go to work in Manhattan. He watched her walk up the stairs to the elevated subway platform, leaned up against the stairs on street level, carefully rolled a cigarette of American Spirit pouch tobacco (in New York, where cigarette taxes are through the roof, rolling your own saves about four dollars a pack), and smiled. Life was good.

Patrick was born in the heart of Bible-belt Kentucky—two hours south of Lexington. "In a dry county surrounded by eight other dry counties," he says. He'd come to New York a few years before from

Los Angeles, where he'd gotten a master's degree in jazz studies at the California Institute of the Arts.

Slightly built, bearded, likely to be dressed in a porkpie hat and clothes that are mellow and vintage, Patrick looks like what he is, a musical ascetic and a gentle soul. He's a vegetarian who once went on a five-day seminar with the Dalai Lama to study compassionate living, a person who does cancer walks and studies tai chi and meditation. He volunteers at a homeless shelter. He describes his outlook on life as "Buddhish." Staying in Southern California probably would have suited him just fine.

But after finishing school in L.A. and beginning a career taking on students to put food on the table, things quickly got tight. The 2008 financial crash forced the move. "People there don't stop driving BMWs and living in big houses when they lose money," he says, laughing. "What they do is stop sending their kids to music lessons."

So in the summer of 2009, when he started to become even more broke than usual, he and about twenty of his musician friends packed up and made an exodus to New York, the city of Birdland and the Blue Note, to try to make it there.

They didn't have a lot of money, so they found a house in the one place they could afford: Bedford-Stuyvesant, living just a few avenues away from the war zone where Andrew Brown had lived his whole life. A racially mixed mobile commune of California musicians wasn't the usual resident profile for Bed-Stuy, but they made it work. He would eventually move south to the less-imposing Lefferts Gardens area of Brooklyn, but some of his friends stayed in and around the old house in Bed-Stuy. One night he was back in that neighborhood when he met a girl who had moved in with some of his old friends.

Her name was Lauren, and she was about ten years younger than he was (Patrick was thirty-two by then), but they took to each other immediately. They started making plans to live together. All that was missing was a steady job, and by March 2011, even that was coming around. He had just gotten a gig teaching nine- and ten-year-olds at after-school band practices for the Brooklyn Conservatory of Music.

Patrick had no formal background in teaching so many different instruments. He'd spent his whole college and postgrad career studying to be a sax performer. But he'd learned how to do it in California the hard way. "Basically, I had to take an old trumpet home and kind of had to learn 'Mary Had a Little Lamb,' man," he says.

He was performing occasionally at some clubs in Manhattan, he was working on an album, he had a new job, and he didn't know it yet, but he'd just met the girl he was going to marry someday. Life was good. He had no reason not to stop and take it all in on the steps of the Marcy Avenue subway station over a rolled cigarette, early on the morning of March 23, 2011.

Suddenly, someone grabbed him by the arm.

"He was a short, stocky Hispanic guy, dressed in a black leather jacket, boots, and jeans," Patrick says. "And I think he had a black fleece pullover."

The man grabbed him and dragged him toward a brick wall.

"He said, 'Come here, I want to talk to you,'" he recalls. Patrick shakes his head as he retells the story. "And I'm like a meek guy, and he's a big, football-player-type guy."

The man was looking back and forth as he pushed Patrick up against a wall. He leaned up close to Patrick's face and yelled at him: "What the fuck do you think you're doing here?"

Patrick is not a New Yorker. He had no experience here. He'd obviously been warned that he was hanging out in a dangerous neighborhood, but this was broad daylight, the morning, next to a subway station entrance.

"What?" Patrick said in response. "What do you mean?"

"What the fuck do you think you're doing here?" the man repeated.

Then, "out of nowhere," Patrick recounts, two more men arrived. They were both stocky guys, wearing the same kind of getup: boots, jeans, leather jackets. They surrounded Patrick.

By this time, Patrick was convinced he was being robbed. He reached to his pocket, to get out whatever money he had. "Look," he said, the panic in his voice rising, "I've got about ten dollars—"

The first man swatted Patrick's hand away. "Don't you put your fucking hand in your pocket!" he screamed, pushing Patrick up against the wall really hard.

Now Patrick's mind was racing. If they didn't want money, what did they want? "Was I just about to get beaten up, or what?" he says. "I didn't know." He quickly looked around and saw a couple of people on the street. Plus, across the street, there was a brand-new apartment building, and he could see through the glass of the first floor a bunch of Hasidic women and their children.

"Help me!" Patrick screamed. "Help! Help!"

Nobody helped.

He screamed toward the Hasidic women in particular: *Help me, call the cops!*

Nothing.

At this point, one of the three men pulled out a set of handcuffs. Patrick involuntarily flashed to a movie he had just seen days before, the absurd Liam Neeson B thriller *Taken,* and all he could think about was the strange plot about a young person being kidnapped and sold overseas into white slavery. He also suddenly remembered being on tour in Brazil and hearing stories about people being kidnapped for their organs.

"To me, something bad was going to happen," he says. "I thought a van would pull up, someone would throw me in it, and nobody would ever know what happened to me. My kidneys will be on eBay."

Patrick gamely tried to flee. The three men chased after him and knocked him to the ground. One of them reached under his shirt and pulled out a "badge," but the badge was turned around, so all Patrick could see was the clasp pin on the reverse side of a piece of metal, a flimsy thing that made the whole contraption look homemade.

"To me, it looked like a safety pin," Patrick says. "I thought, 'That shit's fake.' And I thought, 'If these guys have a fake badge, then they're some kind of professionals.' So I got up and tried to run away."

They tackled him again and began slamming his head against the sidewalk. They hit him repeatedly, and blood started spouting from his head.

Patrick managed to get up once or twice, preventing them from getting the second hand in cuffs. They had cuffed one hand by then. But finally he was tackled for the last time and put in a headlock by his first attacker. He heard the man say, "Don't resist, it'll be bad." Then Patrick blacked out, or semi-blacked out.

His next memory is sitting on the street, up against a wall, Indian style, his hands cuffed. And he saw a police car coming up. A uniformed cop popped out of the car, came up to him. Patrick had been crying, out of terror before, but now out of relief.

"Oh, my God," he said, almost in a begging tone. "Thank God you're here, thank God you're here. Help me! These guys, they were acting like cops—"

The uniform cop leaned down to Patrick.

"Shut the fuck up," he said.

Patrick nearly passed out in shock. It was the first time it had ever even occurred to him that his attackers might actually have been police. Now he realized, with a cold shiver, that he was in really serious trouble, though he didn't know why.

The uniformed officer looked at the three attackers—undercover officers, Patrick now realized—and said, "You guys got this?"

Yeah, we got this, they said.

The uniform walked down the street, leaving Patrick with his original attackers. From there, they started in on him. They picked him up, took his hat off, threw the hat on the ground, then started searching his pockets, tossing each item into the hat. They found the pouch of rolling tobacco. Then they looked on the ground and found the rolled cigarette Patrick had been smoking and pulled it apart—all tobacco.

Undercover #1: "This wasn't it, right?"

Undercover #2: "No, that wasn't it."

They threw the cigarette on the ground. Then the second man made a show of walking over toward the subway station entrance, reaching down to the space between the station entrance and the street, and "picking up" a third object. In fact, Patrick saw, he took the thing out of his pocket, rather than picking it up off the street.

He tossed it into the hat.

The uniform came back from down the street. Patrick shouted at him, "They're trying to frame me! Do something!"

The uniform looked back at him with expressionless eyes. "Why don't you try to be a fucking man?" he said.

Patrick squirmed over toward the hat close enough to see that there was a sort of pill bottle in it now, with something inside. It would later turn out that the object inside the bottle was an empty vial of what had once been crack.

Patrick would spend much of the next years turning over the absurdity of the situation in his head. Who carries around an *empty* crack vial? "Was I going to get free refills?" he asks now.

The next thing he knew, a marked police van showed up. They threw him in there, handcuffed tightly, and as the van pulled away, Patrick started to lose the feeling in his fingers.

A new sort of panic came over him. He was a professional saxophonist; neurological damage to his fingers could ruin his life permanently. He started kicking and screaming.

Finally the cop driving the van stopped, came around to the back, and opened the door. "I'm going to open these cuffs up a little bit," he said. "But if you yell one more time, I'm going to put you in the hospital."

In the van, the undercovers started going through Patrick's phone. They found texts from Lauren. They started asking questions. "What are you doing down here?" they asked.

Patrick's father, a country lawyer in Kentucky, would later admonish his son for opening his mouth at all during this sequence.

But Patrick answered, "My girl lives down here."

"Oh, yeah?" said one, almost accusatorily. "What, are you dating a sister?"

"No," Patrick said. "She just moved here from Michigan. . . ."

"Really?" said one of them. "What's her address? We'll go check on her sometime, if you like. We'll go check and see how she's doing."

Patrick froze. "No. That's okay, I'm fine."

They took him back to a precinct house and threw him into a cell, where he waited by himself. He yelled: *What's going on?*

Finally, the first undercover, the man who attacked him, came into the cell and started talking. "I know what you're doing," he said. "You're screaming so you can get out of this. But we got you."

Patrick, genuinely confused, looked back. "Man, what did you get me for? I have no idea what I've been arrested for. Please, just tell me what I've been arrested for."

"Buddy," he said, "we've got you for everything."

Everything?

"We got you for crack. We got you for weed. And you reached for my belt. That's a felony. You're going to jail for three to six."

He left Patrick to stew on that for a few more hours. Finally they transferred him to central booking.

"It was like a truck stop bathroom, with forty of your closest friends," he says. He stayed there for twenty-four hours, during which time he was fingerprinted and photographed. A million things went through his mind. He spoke to his father by phone, who got him a private lawyer, who in turn got him arraigned and out of there.

During the whole time he was in jail, everyone Patrick spoke to—police, other prisoners, even his own lawyer—said exactly the same thing to him. They told him not to worry, it'd be fine, but that they just "had to run him through the system."

Nobody so much as batted an eyelid about what had happened. This was just a thing that went on—he just had to go through the motions now and not get emotional about it. In fact, the number-one reaction he got from everyone he appealed to during this time was annoyance that he was making a big deal about it. Take your charge, take your medicine, and shut the hell up.

"The casualness of it was what got me," he says now. "Everybody was acting the same way, like it was no big deal."

When Patrick was being photographed, he saw that the original charges were possession of a controlled substance, possession of marijuana, and resisting. By the time he was arraigned, the marijuana charge had been dropped, replaced by a tampering-with-evidence charge.

A few weeks later Patrick went back to court, and the judge immediately gave him an ACD, meaning the whole thing would go away, provided he didn't get "in trouble" again in the next six months. Under the circumstances even an ACD was monstrous, but it was the best possible outcome in a system that's designed to arrest and detain first, then sort out the crime later.

Patrick was never the same after that incident.

Almost immediately after it happened, he started having nightmares. He'd wake up in the middle of the night, ready to defend himself against attack. He'd leap out of bed, physically jumping up.

Or he'd have panic attacks, long periods of near-total paralysis, heart racing, anxiety through the roof. And even when he was fine, the panic attacks would sometimes take so much out of him, he'd be too drained to be fully functional.

"A good friend would be telling me something really important to him," he says, "and I would just be like, 'Uh-huh.' I couldn't be the way I wanted to be with people. I stopped going out, which doesn't sound like much, but for a musician, networking is kind of important.

"I started going to therapy. And I found out that what I was experiencing was post-traumatic stress disorder."

Patrick in person seems strong, pleasant, and put together, a mature, responsible young man about to get married, his life still going on.

But he's had something taken from him. He seems like the kind of person who wants to be a peaceful, positive presence in everyone's life, but he can't be that to everyone anymore, not always any-way, and it obviously troubles him. "The weird thing is, it's not like I'm angry at the cops," he says. "It'll come out in an argument with my girlfriend, or at the guy who cut in line in front of me a little while ago."

He shakes his head. "It changed my life forever."

A collateral consequence, but this is the kind we've decided we can live with.

Of course this reads like a shocker story only because Patrick Jewell is a white, college-educated musician. Imagine the same story a few hundred thousand times over, and you're starting to plug into the ordinary urban nonwhite experience. And that, too, is a collateral consequence we've decided we can live with.

Patrick Jewell most likely was some plainclothes policeman's fleeting visual error—a rolled cigarette mistaken from a distance as a joint. But instead of simply walking up to him and asking him what he was smoking, law enforcement's first move was to assault him, then frame him, toss him in jail, and run him all the way through the system without apology, rather than admit the mistake.

Patrick's arrest was the essence of stop-and-frisk, which itself was the perfect symbol of the new stats-based approach to city policing. You throw a big net over a whole city region, bounce some heads off sidewalks, then throw back the little fish. Almost as important (and this aspect of it is little discussed), you gather intelligence with each catch.

The thing is, this particular ocean, to push the metaphor a bit further, is getting overfished. So they're trawling more remote wa-ters, the nets being cast are wider. Which is a fancy way of saying that it's not just blacks from Bed-Stuy or Hispanic workers in rural Georgia or Mexican single moms living out of vans who are getting the treatment.

Being white and middle class never meant your kids breezed into Yale with a C average. That kind of privilege was always reserved for a special kind of wealth. But it did once mean that police would think twice before bouncing your head off a sidewalk. Not anymore.

And it's not just the streets. Financial regulators, too, are expanding their range of targets. Once HSBC and Barclays and UBS and Chase and Goldman and the rest of the Collateral Consequences All-Stars secured their status as unprosecutable, too-big-to-jail institutions, the margin of regulatory error suddenly became that much smaller for the giant subset of All Other Businesses. The SEC tells Congress it makes about 735 enforcement cases a year,* and it

---

* The SEC has been hilariously consistent in its numbers of enforcement actions. It gets there through a classic stat-padding technique that Congress for some inexplicable reason swallows year after year, without calling BS.

Every year hundreds or thousands of publicly traded companies either go out of business or come close to it, and many of those companies stop bothering with their regular SEC filings. You had an idea for a new kind of synthetic rubber tire, you got some investors together, you went public, your tires turned out to be no good, the business died, you went broke. And before closing up shop formally, you stopped bothering to file your quarterly disclosure forms.

This is called a 12(j) disclosure violation. And at the end of every year, when the SEC starts getting more and more desperate to show that it actually did work the previous year, it starts looking for dead companies with lapsed paperwork and files "enforcement actions" against these zombie firms.

At the end of 2011, the SEC bragged to Congress that it had completed 735 enforcement actions. It didn't mention that fully one-sixth—131 of them—were 12(j) deals, shooting the corpses of companies like Longtop Financial or American Capital Partners or Austral Pacific Energy. It issues fancy press releases for a lot of these actions, often tossing in something sexy in the headline if there's a Congress-friendly angle— "SEC Charges China-Based Longtop Financial Technologies for Deficient Filings" is an example.

If you search for these releases, you'll find that a surprisingly high number of these enforcement actions come in October and November—that is, just before the agency has to go to Congress with its hat in hand. One former SEC official compared it to how a meter maid on a quota operates. At the beginning of the shift, she's only giving tickets to cars that are two or three hours expired. "By the end of the shift, she's giving tickets for being five minutes over," he went on. "If you've got a quota, you've got a quota."

Again, the numbers are hilariously, ridiculously consistent. In 2011 the agency announced 735 enforcement actions. In 2012, it magically came out with almost exactly the same number—734, to be exact. Only this time, it had a slightly harder time making real cases. If 131 of the agency's 735 "actions" in 2011 were shooting unarmed companies, in 2012 the number was 134 out of 734.

At this writing, the third quarter of 2013 is wrapping up. The commission is right on schedule, blasting 44 companies this quarter. This year the dead Asian-firm flavors of the day have names like Duoyuan Printing and China Intelligent Lighting and Electronics, while in 2012 it was China Agritech and Paradise Tan.

Despite the absurdity of these "triumphs," the SEC nonetheless bragged about its

COLLATERAL CONSEQUENCES | *397*

needs to hit or surpass that number every year to expect its budget to keep flowing. But if the SEC has a powerful disinclination to make those cases against the Lloyd Blankfeins and Jamie Dimons of the world, it's going to start looking at everyone else's books far more closely. It's going after smaller businesses more aggressively than before.

It's profiling, except it's expanding the profile. And on the flip side, it's doing the same thing, only in reverse.

> "I can tell you, just from forty thousand feet, that some of the most damaging behavior on Wall Street, some of the least ethical behavior on Wall Street, wasn't illegal. That's exactly why we had to change the laws."
> BARACK OBAMA, DECEMBER 11, 2011, *60 Minutes*

Like most things spoken out loud by lawyers of Barack Obama's caliber, the president's now-infamous *60 Minutes* statement was parsed to mean nothing at all, if you examined it closely.

Some of the least ethical behavior wasn't illegal? Okay, that's probably true. But did that mean some of it was illegal? Or alternatively, did it mean all of it wasn't illegal? He didn't say either way. From a factual standpoint, the statement was meaningless.

But psychologically, it was meaningful. It showed us how they think up there, in the upper reaches of this giant cultural bureaucracy.

Obama was echoing the main mantra that continued to emanate from Wall Street after the crash, in which high-level executives involved in this or that scandal repeatedly insisted that what they had done was not actually against the law. The thing that's interesting about this claim isn't that it's factually wrong, which incidentally it

---

sheer numbers when its enforcement chief, the former Deutsche Bank general counsel Robert Khuzami, left office following Barack Obama's reelection leading into the winter of 2012. "In addition to the all-time record number of 735 SEC enforcement actions in FY 2011," the SEC noted in a press release, "Mr. Khuzami led the Division to record results in a number of specific enforcement areas."

almost always is, often to a humorously enormous degree. What's interesting is that the people who make this claim usually believe it to be true. Even Barack Obama, despite the fact that he's almost universally understood to be an outstanding lawyer and should know better, probably believes it to be true.

This weird psychological kink is where the Divide lives. Increasingly, the people who make decisions about justice and punishment in this country see a meaningful difference between crime and merely breaking the law. There's a community of maybe ten or twenty thousand lawyers and businesspeople, living mostly in New York and Washington, who are being asked to evaluate the behavior of their peers. And out of sheer, dumb sympathy and shared perspective, they just can't see certain behavior as criminal, in the sense that the rest of America thinks of crime.

Bizarrely, they don't understand the material. People like Eric Holder and Lanny Breuer in particular had the unique problem of having worked in a top corporate defense firm where they probably saw many capers in larval form, through the prism of their clients' long-term goals. These companies wanted to beef up their bottom lines, make more money. So maybe they cut a few corners along the way. The lawyers in retrospect must have thought: *That's a very different thing from beating up prostitutes or robbing liquor stores. People like that, they're criminals. We send those people to jail.*

This other thing, cutting corners on paper—they actually have a word for that: *aggressive.* That's the lawyers' euphemism for pushing the limits of the law. It's considered a good quality in a certain kind of lawyer, the ability to be "aggressive" and get away with it. Eric Holder, back in the Clinton days, was actually being "aggressive" when he came up with the enforcement idea that he later hated, forcing companies to waive privilege.

It's the grad-school version of reaching into a cookie jar: *Can I get away with this? Can I get this by my professors? Let's see just how ballsy I can be.*

The clarification letter cooked up by the Lehman/Barclays lawyers was the ultimate example of "aggressive," a high-stakes intellectual gambit that required a quadruple backflip and a perfect, reverse-spinning dismount to cover up a humongous theft with a fig leaf of argued legality that held firm for a fleeting second or two. To dream it up was ingenious; to not alert the judge to its contents was hubris and the ultimate example of "aggressive."

Lawyers admire the right kind of "aggressive" for the same reason we love heist movies: we sympathize with anyone clever enough to penetrate the impenetrable. But those same attorneys sometimes have a hard time seeing past the daring all the way to the consequences on the other end, which might very well be something like seventy thousand creditors losing thousands of dollars apiece, or a whole company's shareholders losing a total of $600 million. So when somebody gets caught doing it, the immediate thought is, *Sure, there are obviously sanctions, penalties, for being a little aggressive with your paperwork. Maybe a hearing of the Bar Association.*

But jail? Are you kidding? People get stabbed in jails! Those places are dangerous!

There are thousands of other things at work here, but the last straw in every great social tragedy is always something absurd like this, like the nation's top law enforcement officials unable to spot the greatest crime wave of a generation, because they can't see the victims from their offices.

The problem is, if the law is applied unequally enough over a long enough period of time, at some point, law enforcement becomes politically illegitimate. Whole classes of arrests become (circle one) illegal, improper, morally unenforceable.

We have to be really close to that point now. Too many of the same damning themes keep jumping out.

The first and most obvious is that two people caught committing the same crime rarely suffer the same punishments, if they aren't the same kinds of people. There are enough examples in this book. Abacus versus every other bank in the world, or Tory Marone in jail for a joint while HSBC executives walk for washing hundreds of millions for drug dealers. Some guy in backwoods Arkansas gets arrested for forging a check for $450 to bail his girlfriend out of jail, but nobody gets arrested for systematically forging thousands of signatures in foreclosure affidavits.

One of the most amazing examples of arrest/no-arrest lunacy in recent times was witnessed by former SEC investigator and famed whistle-blower Gary Aguirre.

Aguirre joined the SEC in 2004, less than a year before the Arthur Andersen case would be overturned. Upon joining the agency as an attorney/investigator, he famously was assigned to look into a series of suspicious trades involving a company called Heller Financial, which had been acquired by General Electric in 2001.

In a story that has since been extensively documented by Senate investigators, Aguirre found that the star trader of a hedge fund called Pequot Capital, Art Samberg, had made a series of suspiciously prescient trades ahead of the Heller merger, pocketing about $18 million in a period of weeks by buying up Heller shares before the merger, among other things.

But Samberg had never had a meeting about Heller and appeared never to have spent even a minute researching the stock. "It was as if Samberg woke up one morning and God told him to start buying Heller shares," Aguirre says. Aguirre did some digging and found that just before making those trades, Samberg had been in contact with his old friend John Mack. Mack had recently stepped down as president of Morgan Stanley and had just flown to Switzerland, where he'd interviewed for a top job at Credit Suisse First Boston, the company that happened to be the investment banker for . . . Heller Financial.

Now, Mack had been on Samberg's case to cut him in on a deal involving a spinoff of Lucent. "Mack is busting my chops" to let him in on the Lucent deal, Samberg told a coworker. So when Mack returned from Switzerland, he called Samberg. Samberg suddenly decided to buy every Heller share in sight. Then he cut Mack into the Lucent deal, a favor that was worth $10 million to Mack. Dot connects to dot: a seemingly open-and-shut case.

The SEC refused to investigate this highly suspicious-looking series of events, denying Aguirre the right even to talk to Mack about these trades. Again, this is well known and became the central focus of widely covered Senate hearings later in the decade. Aguirre was eventually ruled to have been wrongfully terminated and won a $755,000 settlement from the SEC.

What is less well known about the Aguirre case is that the SEC did actually pursue an insider trading case involving Heller Financial. It just wasn't against a powerful, well-defended figure like John Mack (who was represented at the time by former U.S. Attorney and future SEC chief Mary Jo White),* but instead against, well, a pair of schmucks.

The two hard-luck cases were a mid-level GE executive and, wait for it, his kung-fu instructor. The two had conspired to make a $157,000 trade ahead of the merger. You can look it up: *United States v. Anthony Chrysikos and Michael Martello,* filed in 2002.

These two idiots realized a total profit of $157,259.09. Chrysikos, the GE exec, ended up getting fifteen months in jail for the crime. Samberg, meanwhile, made $18 million on his Heller trade, and Mack made about $10 million through the seemingly linked Lucent deal. But Mack got off scot free and was not even interviewed until right after the statute of limitations expired.

Aguirre remembers being astonished to learn that the SEC had chased such small fry when such a big target was sitting right there in front of them. "Two cases, the same stock, but they went after the small guy," he says.

Then there are the myriad approaches to the same crime, fraud.

---

* White is like the Zelig of the white-collar nonprosecution era. Her name seems to pop up in case after important case involving big-time targets that the government ultimately decided not to prosecute. Most notably, White led a successful presentation to Justice Department officials about why it should not press a case against a trio of executives from AIG Financial Products, the unit whose exploding half-trillion-dollar portfolio of toxic credit default swaps led to the collapse of AIG and the federal bailout of same and, according to some, triggered the crash of 2008. White represented Tom Athan, deputy to Joe Cassano, the infamous head of AIGFP, who along with Angelo Mozilo is one of the most conspicuous nontargets of this era. After White's presentation, the DOJ dropped its investigation of AIGFP.

Viewed through the eyes of law enforcement, fraud comes in two types. When it's committed by some single mom in the projects on her welfare application, it has the stink of theft and desperation, and the response is by the book. When it's committed systematically, it's just some lawyers somewhere being "aggressive," and the government response is more idiosyncratic.

Here's a crazy example. About a decade ago, Washington Mutual gave a second mortgage to O. J. Simpson—yes, that O. J. Simpson—a loan that ended up being securitized and sold to investors all around the world. The bank at the time was pursuing a new policy of giving loans to anything that breathed. Loan officers were discouraged from gathering too much material on their borrowers. "A skinny file is a good file" is how a loan consultant named Nancy Erken later explained it. Erken was admonished for collecting too much paperwork on a WaMu loan applicant. "Nancy, why do you have all this stuff in here? We're just going to take this stuff and throw it out," she was told.

And in one such skinny file was the data for a second home loan to O.J. This was long after both the criminal and civil trials following the murder of Nicole Simpson had run their courses. So when WaMu's chief legal officer, Fay Chapman, saw the loan, she flipped out, knowing Simpson had a $33.5 million judgment against him and couldn't possibly afford to buy property. "When I asked how we could possibly foreclose on [the loan], they said there was a letter in the file from O. J. Simpson," she said. The letter read:

the judgment is no good, because I didn't do it

Now, someone at WaMu sold this preposterous loan into a pool of mortgages that was bought by investors all around the world. Among the buyers of such loans was Stichting Pensioenfonds ABP, a Dutch state pension fund, which ultimately sued JPMorgan Chase, which by then had acquired WaMu in a state-aided shotgun wedding. The Dutch plaintiffs described the Simpson loan in their suit.

That same year the fund was forced to cut pensions for some three million workers by 0.5 percent.

Selling that loan into a securitized pool that would be marketed everywhere wasn't just fraud, it was as bad as grinding horsemeat into hot dogs and sending them by the truckload to supermarkets around the world. There were tens of thousands of cases just as insidious as the Simpson case, and each one of them was a truly despicable criminal fraud. But no individuals were ever prosecuted for this kind of crime.

Meanwhile you can open up the newspaper virtually any day of the week—not just in Riverside County, California, but just about anywhere—and read about someone who's been criminally sentenced for welfare fraud. As I write this, the case of the day involves an immigrant named Graciela Antonio in Green Bay, Wisconsin, who in April 2013 was busted after she "illegally received $25,416 in taxpayer-funded public assistance for food and medical bills over three years."

The twenty-nine-year-old mother of three's crime was concealing the fact that while receiving benefits, she was working under another name, at American Foods, for $12.65 an hour. "Really the victims are the community at large," Kate Zuidmulder, assistant district attorney for Brown County, Wisconsin, righteously told a local TV station. Antonio got two years of probation and 180 hours of community service.

Nobody is saying people like this aren't guilty, or that there shouldn't be a punishment for deceiving the government and for making taxpayers pay the medical bills for her and her husband's three kids.

But if her crime gets punished, someone else committing the same crime has to receive the same punishment. This stuff isn't brain surgery. But there just aren't cases of bankers or mortgage lenders doing jail time or lengthy community service stints for dumping bad loans into mortgage pools. Nobody from a bank or a ratings agency is losing his or her kids or housing because he or she sold or helped sell bad loans to, say, King County, Washington, or the Iowa Student Loan Liquidity Corporation. It just doesn't happen. The method for dealing with that kind of offender increasingly involves fines and noncriminal sanctions. Responsibility for the fraud redounds to the institution, which takes the punishment.

The only thing that changes is that as the economy stagnates more and more, and the wealth divide gets bigger, it becomes less and less possible for law enforcement to imagine the jail-or-garbage option for the Collateral Consequences crowd, and more and more possible to imagine it for an ever-expanding population of Everyone Else. The significance of the new Holder-era cases was only that they formalized an already-evolving system of legal schizophrenia, a weird *Two Faces of Eve* approach to sentencing.

Take the HSBC case. In the rest of America, stiff money-laundering punishments are handed out to all sorts of people in the newspapers pretty much on a weekly basis. Very shortly after the HSBC fiasco, for instance, the federal government sentenced a Texas racetrack owner named Jose Trevino Morales, who had been busted for conspiracy to commit money laundering after he reportedly bought millions of dollars of racehorses from Mexican drug lords.

Tried alongside four others, Trevino was held up by federal prosecutors as a menace to decent American society. "The government was able to show how the corrupting influence of drug cartels has extended into the United States, with cartel bosses using an otherwise legitimate domestic industry to launder proceeds from drug trafficking and other crimes," said local U.S. attorney Robert Pittman. "They hang themselves by their actions," added federal prosecutor Douglas Gardner in his closing.

The total amount of money reportedly laundered in his case was somewhere in the area of $16 million. HSBC admitted to laundering more than $800 million. Trevino laundered for the Zetas; HSBC, for their rivals, the Sinaloa cartel. Trevino could get twenty years. At HSBC, again, nobody got even one day.

These are enormous discrepancies. There's a huge difference between twenty years and nothing—that is, a banker slapped with fines he doesn't even personally pay. So what justifies the difference? Is there any conceivable reasonable explanation?

I've heard the counterargument firsthand, for instance from the federal prosecutors who put together the settlements with companies like HSBC and UBS. In the course of the years I spent working on this book, I had numerous discussions with people from that side of the bar, usually on background. The people whose job it is to take on these big companies bristle at the notion that they're not working hard to lock up the bad guys.

They moreover violently reject the idea that the fact that local cops all over the country are breaking heads and tossing people into jails and prisons for smoking joints and stealing socks and road flares—while their own white-collar targets get off with negotiated settlements—has anything to do with them. These are two completely different things, they say. They take it all very personally and make what at first blush sounds like very compelling arguments in their own defense.

The arguments go something like this:

We *want* to lock up bad guys. If we could, we would. The problem is, it's very hard to gather evidence against single individuals in these massive corporate cases. "What you don't understand," I was told pointedly by one prosecutor, "is that you can't just throw these guys in jail just because you know they did it. You need witnesses. You need evidence."

And getting such evidence is definitely not easy in these huge commercial schemes, where oftentimes it's not even clear where the offense took place, who had guilty knowledge and who was just following orders, who thought their activities were sanctified by legal opinion and who didn't, and so on.

As a corollary, these people often ask about the public utility of throwing a few midlevel peons from a bank like HSBC in jail versus collecting 1.9 billion actual dollars. What's better, they ask, for the state? What's better for the people? With some regulatory agencies like the SEC, the settlements they collect go directly to victims. Within the walls of those agencies, the calculus starts to feel exactly like the math employed by any private civil law firm, where you're weighing the possibility of getting nothing at all versus the chance, today, at $100 million or $200 million.

So given these factors, prosecutors will tell you that these massive financial settlements, and the binding deferred prosecution agreements that theoretically give the government enormous leverage over these offender firms, are not only good deals, they're great deals.

This sounds like a good argument, it really does. Trapped in a room with a federal prosecutor who argues for a living, you would find yourself buying it.

But it's bullshit. It's belied by the entire history of these settlements.

Since the mid-2000s, and especially since 2008, we've seen one settlement after another with the same characteristics: very high fines, limited (or no) admission of responsibility, and no criminal charges against individuals.

It's an incredibly long list. Take just one company, Bank of America, which paid out some $29 billion in settlements between 2009 and September 2012.

There was the $150 million settlement it paid to the SEC for lying to shareholders about the Merrill Lynch acquisition. There was the $600 million settlement for concealing a lack of underwriting standards in the loans put in pools mostly sold, as usual, to the defenseless elderly. There was a $3 billion settlement for defrauding Fannie and Freddie. Then there was $410 million paid for charging phony overdraft fees, $20 million paid to the DOJ for illegally foreclosing on actively serving members of the military, $11.8 billion paid out in a foreclosure settlement, $1.6 billion paid to Assured Guaranty for coaxing the insurer to wrap toxic bonds . . . the list goes on and on.

You could make up similarly long lists for Chase, Goldman, Wells

Fargo, HSBC, UBS, Deutsche Bank, Barclays, and many others. All those firms have paid upward of a billion dollars in settlements, if not more, since 2008. (Again, for Chase, the number is more than $16 billion, or 12 percent of its net revenue from 2009 to 2012, and an even greater percentage of its net went to cover a $13 billion settlement in 2013.) And in all but a very few of these cases, the narrative is exactly the same. There is somehow just enough evidence to extract hundreds of millions or even billions of dollars in penalties, but somehow not quite enough evidence to force any individual to do so much as a day in jail. Every single time, the state lands itself right in that oddly enormous sweet spot between spectacular leverage (to extract fines) and no leverage at all (to hand down criminal penalties).

This makes the "not enough evidence" defense either a total lie or the most unbelievable coincidence in history. In one case, maybe. But across all these diverse settlements, in so many different types of cases, there's not one case against an individual?

Then there's the damning question of resources. How many bodies has the state even assigned to gather evidence for these difficult cases? How much money has it been willing to spend for that kind of justice? It never put together a task force to concentrate on this corruption, never had a coordinated strategy. In fact, it barely even studied the problem.

Fun fact: When the economy crashed in 2008, the federal government formed an investigatory group to look into the causes. That Financial Crisis Inquiry Committee was given a budget of $9.8 million. Committee chairman Phil Angelides acidly noted that this was "roughly one-seventh of the budget of Oliver Stone's *Wall Street: Money Never Sleeps.*"

Meanwhile, that same year the federal drug enforcement budget leaped from $13.275 billion to $15.278 billion. That meant that just the increase in the national drug enforcement budget for the year of the biggest financial crisis since the Depression was roughly two hundred times the size of the budget for the sole executive branch effort at formally investigating the causes of financial corruption.

This is an important distinction, that in this period of extreme crisis, we not only didn't allocate funds to investigate the crash, we actively did increase the budget to tackle street crime, incidentally at a time of declining street violence.

If you press prosecutors, sooner or later they'll forget about the evidence and resources questions and come back to the social utility argument. What is better for society, they ask, sending a few HSBC bankers to jail, or snagging $1.9 billion in fines from the bank? Why go after intangible rewards like political optics when you can have, bird-in-hand-style, $2 billion right now, without even risking the possibility of losing?

That's an argument one can have. It might even have, who knows, some merit. But to even have that argument, one has to admit what it concedes. And what it concedes is that there's a concrete difference between how we treat an individual who commits fraud within the structure of a giant multinational company with a lot of settlement money lying around, and how we treat, say, an ordinary broke person who commits welfare or unemployment fraud.

If you choose to take the money over and over again from the Wall Street crowd while the welfare moms keep getting jail and community service, now suddenly you've institutionalized the imbalance. From there, it's not long before the tail starts wagging the dog. A massive, unconscious tendency toward reverse profiling occurs. Because, thanks to all these various factors, executives from giant multinationals simply don't end up in the prison population, law enforcement soon starts to operate on the reverse principle, that those huge companies are not the places where jailable crimes take place. So even white-collar investigators start to look for targets elsewhere, like at smaller businesses.

A commissioner for the SEC, Daniel Gallagher, even talked about this out loud, in April 2012, when he gave a speech in Denver, Colorado. This was right in the middle of the Chase "London Whale" story and just before the LIBOR story, the HSBC story, and a half-dozen other financial scandals of various degrees of horribleness blew up. Despite all this, Gallagher came out with an interesting take on where to look for white-collar crime.

"It is critically important that our enforcement program be extremely efficient," Gallagher said. "Recognizing that it is unrealistic to imagine we will ever achieve a one-to-one correspondence between incidents of misfeasance and SEC Enforcement staff, we'd better plan to do everything we can to increase our hit-rate per investigation opened, and should commit our staff resources carefully, which is to say, consciously."

This passage would have required translation into human English, except that Gallagher went on to spell out exactly what he meant:

> Experience teaches us, for example, that **fraud tends to proliferate in smaller entities** that may lack highly developed compliance programs. It also means thinking carefully about what we might, borrowing again from the world of sports, call "shot selection." **It can be tempting to tangle with prominent institutions. But chasing headlines and solving problems are two different things.** The question is what will do most good—where our focus should be. And the record seems to suggest that we can do most to protect smaller, unsophisticated investors by focusing more attention on smaller entities.

In other words, we've got a limited budget, and there's a bigger degree of difficulty in going after big banks with powerful lawyers. Therefore the SEC shouldn't give in to the "temptation" of tangling with big banks because, rhetorically speaking, those shots are harder to make. Better to go for uncontested dunks and lay-ins than heave deep threes at the buzzer.

This is coward's language. No true cop would ever think like this. Real police will go after the bad guy no matter who he is or how well protected he might be. In fact, the best of them will take on a villain even when winning is a long shot. There's value even in trying and losing sometimes. It's not as tangible as a billion dollars, but it's real enough.

Sometimes you can even see it. In one great example, the Commodity Futures Trading Commission and the Justice Department joined forces in the mid-2000s to go after four traders for BP, who were gaming the market for a fuel called TET propane. Vaguely similar to the Goldman-aluminum-storage scandal that broke in the summer of 2013, the case involved traders buying up huge stores of propane in the Mont Belvieu storage fields in Texas, then hoarding it until the end of a given month, when businesses would be short of propane and in greater need. The BP swindlers would then jack up the price of the product and clean up. Classic market cornering. The traders were so dead to rights, they were even caught on tape talking about wanting to "control the market at will."

The government indicted four traders, even though there was an obvious problem with the case. The Commodity Futures Modernization Act of 2000, a crazy law deregulating much of the derivatives market that had been pushed through Congress in the waning days of the Clinton presidency thanks to the advocacy of Phil Gramm and a host of financial and energy industry lobbyists, contained a little-known exemption to laws against market manipulation. Cornering markets was okay, it turned out, so long as traders did their crooked deals with other sophisticated participants, outside regulated trading platforms.

This little loophole to the Commodity Exchange Act of 1936, known as the "2(g) exception," is one of many exemptions that have been written into law, thanks to industry lobbyists in the last twenty or thirty years, that say things like "Insider trading is against the law unless you're hopping on one leg and air-guitaring 'Smells Like Teen Spirit' at the time of the trade." The BP traders had clearly manipulated the price of TET propane, but they had done so hopping on one leg and humming the right song. As a result, in 2009 a federal judge named Gray Miller thought he had no choice but to throw out all four indictments. Not that he was happy about it. The decision, he said, "should not be taken as condoning the defendants' alleged actions in this case."

The BP lawyers clucked loudly after Miller's ruling, saying among other things, "We always knew it was a foolish indictment." But the case was such a fiasco that it got the attention of Congress. Less than two years later the 2(g) exemption was summarily removed during the Dodd-Frank negotiations. Congress would never have acted had the DOJ not brought the BP case forward in the mid-2000s, and had members of Congress not been forced to watch obviously guilty financial criminals end-zone-dancing in the newspapers over a silly technicality.

So prosecutors lost, but they won in the end.

"I'd rather do that case and lose, than not do it at all," says one former federal prosecutor.

As this book goes to press, the Justice Department is sending signals that it's beginning to realize its mistakes. Eric Holder is reportedly thinking of nominating a tough prosecutor, Leslie Caldwell, to permanently fill Lanny Breuer's vacated post. Holder also talked about raising the statute of limitations on Wall Street cases, to give themselves another shot at all the crimes they ignored in the last five years, warning that those who committed crimes are "not out of the woods yet." Hedge fund villain Stevie Cohen is being put out of business. As this book goes to press, criminal cases are reportedly coming against the megabank Chase for the "London Whale" episode and perhaps other misdeeds, including some related to its status as Bernie Madoff's banker.

At the very least, on the federal level, officials seem to recognize the political necessity of saying these things out loud, and this has to be in very large part due to the public outrage over the lack of Wall Street prosecutions. Decisions like the HSBC settlement were blunt bureaucratic calculations, where the risk of losing and/or disrupting the economy was weighed against the benefit of receiving $1.9 billion in settlement money. But these new moves by Holder & Co. show that public outrage sometimes can change the calculus.

At the same time that Eric Holder was experimenting with a public change of mind, a federal judge named Shira Scheindlin handed down a ruling against New York's stop-and-frisk policies. This was late in the summer of 2013. Scheindlin, among other things, cited a popular new book, *The New Jim Crow,* in her ruling and noted that since 2004 more blacks and Latinos have been accosted by police than actually live in the city. The ruling came at the end of a long and well-coordinated campaign by groups like the Center for Constitutional Rights and the NAACP.

Of course, a federal judge striking down stop-and-frisk as unconstitutional doesn't mean the practice will end anytime soon. "You're not going to see any change in tactics overnight," promised Mayor Mike Bloomberg. But the fact that Bloomberg was put in the position of having to fight back—and that his successor, Bill de Blasio, won in part by running *against* those tactics—shows that public pressure can work. Just trying to do the right thing legitimizes the entire system. We don't do it often enough.

ACKNOWLEDGMENTS

The Divide is a book I couldn't have written without the help of a great many people, many of whom I can't even name in this space. First and foremost I must thank my editor at Spiegel & Grau, Christopher Jackson, as well as publishers Cindy Spiegel and Julie Grau, who once again all took a leap of faith with an evolving book project. Molly Crabapple I want to thank for her intense interest in the subject—we always wanted to work together and I'm thrilled this could be the vehicle. The two of us also want to thank Lydia Wills, who represents us both, for helping make this possible.

Andrew Brown, the Man Who Couldn't Stand Up, is someone to whom I want to give heartfelt thanks, both for the patience he showed as he walked me through his life story and for the friendship he showed later on, counseling me as a fellow father through the birth of my son. Andrew, thank you, and you're right, this experience is everything you told me it would be.

A number of lawyers helped me through some very complex material. Leo Glickman was a great help in walking me through the

New York City court system, as were Josh Saunders, Kasia Donohue, Roy Wasserman, Jane Fox, and others. Joni Halpern was a huge help in helping me navigate the California welfare system, while Arturo Corso, down in Georgia, helped me throughout with the federal immigration laws. Michael Bowe of Kasowitz Benson met me at an Irish pub one day, and the next thing I knew I was spending years researching the Fairfax case, probably much to his chagrin—thank you, Michael, for taking so much time. Former Lehman lawyer and whistleblower Oliver Budde, who I hope is reincarnated as attorney general with unlimited powers, has been a great resource for me on a number of topics, Lehman-related and not. Finally, I owe great thanks to Neil Barofsky, the former TARP inspector, and to his former deputy, Kevin Puvalowski, who both helped me throughout my research on a variety of subjects.

Some of the people to whom I owe the most I can't name by name. Natividad Felix was able to speak in her own name, but many others were not, a reflection of how difficult the subject of fairness in law enforcement is to talk about, particularly for undocumented immigrants and people on public assistance. Ochion Jewell I want to thank for being brave enough to talk about a difficult experience, as were Michael McMichael and Anthony Odom.

There are many others I should mention whose names don't appear in the book. Old friend Joel Barkin nudged me in the direction of this subject over drinks and wings in Maplewood, New Jersey, years ago. And Eric Salzman, whose misfortune it is to have been the person who taught me what little I know about the financial services industry, helped me as he always has with some of the more complicated portions of this book.

Lastly, I want to thank my wife, Jeanne, for her patience and love throughout this time, and to my son, Max, who was born the day the manuscript was due. Because of you both, I'll always remember this time with special fondness.

ABOUT THE AUTHOR

MATT TAIBBI has been a contributing editor for *Rolling Stone* and is the author of five previous books, including the *New York Times* bestsellers *The Great Derangement* and *Griftopia*. He lives in New Jersey.

@mtaibbi

ABOUT THE TYPE

This book was set in Minion, a 1990 Adobe Originals typeface by Robert Slimbach (b. 1956). Minion is inspired by classical, old-style typefaces of the late Renaissance, a period of elegant, beautiful, and highly readable type designs. Created primarily for text setting, Minion combines the aesthetic and functional qualities that make text type highly readable with the versatility of digital technology.